Japan and the Shackles of the Past

Japan and the Shackles of the Past

R. TAGGART MURPHY

OXFORD
UNIVERSITY PRESS

OXFORD
UNIVERSITY PRESS

Oxford University Press is a department of the University of
Oxford. It furthers the University's objective of excellence in research,
scholarship, and education by publishing worldwide.

Oxford   New York
Auckland   Cape Town   Dar es Salaam   Hong Kong   Karachi
Kuala Lumpur   Madrid   Melbourne   Mexico City   Nairobi
New Delhi   Shanghai   Taipei   Toronto

With offices in
Argentina   Austria   Brazil   Chile   Czech Republic   France   Greece
Guatemala   Hungary   Italy   Japan   Poland   Portugal   Singapore
South Korea   Switzerland   Thailand   Turkey   Ukraine   Vietnam

Oxford is a registered trademark of Oxford University Press
in the UK and certain other countries.

Published in the United States of America by
Oxford University Press

198 Madison Avenue, New York, NY 10016

Library of Congress Cataloging-in-Publication Data
Murphy, R. Taggart.
Japan and the shackles of the past/R. Taggart Murphy.
  pages cm
Summary: "A penetrating overview of Japan, from a historical, social, political,
economic, and cultural perspective"—Provided by publisher.
Includes bibliographical references and index.
ISBN 978-0-19-984598-9 (hardback : alkaline paper)   1. Japan—History.
2. Japan—Economic conditions.   3. Japan—Social conditions.   4. Japan—
Politics and government.   5. Social change—Japan—History.   I. Title.
DS836.M885 2015
952—dc23
2014013756

9 8 7 6 5 4 3 2 1
Printed in the United States of America
on acid-free paper

For Osamu

I

Allegro con spirito

Contents

List of Illustrations   ix

Preface and Acknowledgments   xi

Introduction   xix

Part One: The Forging of the Shackles

1. Japan Before the Edo Period   3

2. The Incubation of the Modern Japanese State   33

3. "Restoration" to Occupation   63

4. The Miracle   95

5. The Institutions of High-Speed Growth   127

6. Consequences: Intended and Otherwise   149

Part Two: The Shackles Trap
Today's Japan

7. Economy and Finance   177

8. Business   203

9. Social and Cultural Change   233

10. **Politics**   265

11. **Japan and the World**   315

   Appendices   391

   Notes and Suggestions for Further Reading   409

   Index   421

List of Illustrations

1. Fourth-Century Tomb of Emperor Nintoku   2

2. Kitagawa Utamaro *"Lovers in the Upstairs
   Room of a Teahouse"*   32

3. Portrait of Iwasaki Yataro, the Founder
   of Mitsubishi and the Father of Modern
   Japanese Industrial Organization   62

4. The Assassination in 1960 of Hard-line
   Socialist Leader Asanuma Inejiro   94

5. Ikeda Hayato, Father of the Economic Miracle,
   Is Voted Prime Minister on the Floor of the Diet   126

6. The Kyoto Tower Hotel from the Grounds of
   the Toji Temple   148

7. The Red-Light District Kabukicho and the
   Skyscrapers of the Shinjuku in Tokyo in 1986,
   the First Year of the Bubble Economy   176

8. The Logo of Keyence, the Most Profitable
   Company in Japan During the First Decade of
   the Twenty-first Century   202

9. The New Female Archetype in Japanese
   Popular Culture: The *Gyaru* ("gal")   232

10. Tanaka Kakuei, the Most Formidable Politician of
    Postwar Japan   264

11. Prime Minister Kishi Nobusuke Signs the
    US–Japan Security Treaty while President Dwight
    D. Eisenhower Looks on   314

Preface and Acknowledgments

This book started out as an entry in the Oxford University Press series *What Everyone Needs to Know*. Japan merits the kind of treatment other subjects in this series have received, and I was flattered when David McBride asked me to provide it. But I was also uneasy. I feared that no one who knew anything about Japan would pick up a book with such a title, and everyone else would ignore it. For it seemed back in 2010 that the only thing about Japan that still interested the outside world was its culture: the cuisine, the traditional arts, contemporary fashion and design, Murakami's fiction, and all those bizarre videos and comics. If the country's politics, business, and economics still commanded any attention from anyone other than the Japanese themselves and a handful of oddballs like me whose lives had somehow become intertwined with the place, it was purely as lessons in what not to do. While I thought that notion mistaken—Japan offers lessons of all kinds and those lessons extend well beyond the "what not to do" type—all my previous published writing concerned itself precisely with those issues no one seemed to care about any longer (i.e., Japanese politics, business, and economics). One more book wasn't going to change this state of affairs, rekindling the kind of widespread fascination that the country once commanded.

But David's proposal offered me an opportunity to do what I'd never be able to get away with in any other kind of writing: integrate my thinking on Japan's politics and economics with precisely the historical and cultural issues that seem to continue to interest people. The more I have pondered such things as the way credit creation in Japan translates into economic activity or the central (if little understood) role Japan played in the construction of the current global financial framework—issues that dominate my other books—the more I have become convinced that it is not possible to understand these matters in isolation; that grasping any aspect of Japanese reality requires grappling with the totality of the Japanese experience. To put this in other words, the Bank of Japan's monetary aggregates, personnel practices in Japanese corporations, Tokyo's wacky street fashions, the endless musical chairs of Japanese politics, and Japan's centuries of seclusion are connected in all kinds of ways. David was offering me the opportunity to tease out some of these connections. If few ended up reading the result, well, writing the book would nonetheless allow me to put some order into a lifetime worth of reflections, to clarify my thinking on subjects that have obsessed me since I was 15 years old, got off the plane at a shabby, crowded Haneda airport, and took a long bus ride through a gray, throbbing, teeming urban landscape that didn't look like anything I had ever seen before. I decided the book was worth doing.

I had barely started work when events proved that I might have been wrong in assuming no one cared much about Japan anymore. The terrible earthquake-*cum*-tsunami of March 2011 thrust the country into the center of the world's attention. People everywhere were struck by the heroism and humanity of the tens of thousands of Japanese whose lives had been torn apart. Then, as news trickled in of what lay behind the wreckage of the nuclear power plant destroyed in the catastrophe, questions began to crop up. What kind of country was this that could call forth the social cohesion and sheer human decency on display while at the same time spawning a leadership class that had locked this seismically volatile land into such a deadly and implacably unforgiving power source? And then proceeded to ignore the risks with a negligence that bordered on the criminal?

As I continued my work on the manuscript, I began to see other questions surfacing in the usual places where such things are debated. How was it that an electorate that had thrown out a manifestly dysfunctional ruling party could restore that party to power not four years later? What made it possible for the developed world's most "right-wing" government to implement its most "left-wing" mix of monetary and fiscal policies? Did rising levels of verbal belligerence in East Asia presage a miscalculation that could lead to war? Would outsiders—most specifically, the United States—be drawn into the conflict? Maybe I wasn't just writing for myself after all.

Much of the credit for whatever success this book has in the way of raising these questions—not to mention answering them—goes to people who helped me along the way. Heading that list would be David McBride himself, who first saw the potential for this project and took the trouble to track me down and encourage me to do it. He has been patient both with the way the book grew and the time it took me to finish it. He saw that my ambitions had outstripped the *What Everyone Needs to Know* format and, rather than forcing me to cut back to meet the requirements of that series, helped in all kinds of crucial ways to reposition the book into what it has become. Mark Selden and Gavan McCormack at *Asia Pacific Journal: Japan Focus* (http://japanfocus.org) had given me the platform for some of my writing that first attracted David's attention; Mark read parts of the manuscript and offered his usual penetrating advice. I asked Robert Aliber, Kumiko Makihara, and Leo Phillips to read some of the individual chapters—they gave me more useful suggestions than I can count.

When I began writing, I knew I would need an ideal reader—someone who hadn't spent a lot of time in Japan or much energy thinking about the country but who was interested and curious—i.e., the kind of person I was trying to reach in the first place. I found him in George Williard, not only an ideal reader and dear friend but a wonderful editor and writer himself. I sent him every chapter and he responded with generous outpourings of time and effort, giving everything I had written the kind of close attention that is every writer's dream, calling me out when I was unclear or confusing or even just less good than he thought I ought to be. I owe him a lot.

I also owe a lot to Rodney Armstrong. His erudite posts at the *NBR Japan Forum* on the background of the disputes over the relocation of the US Marine base at Futenma in Okinawa attracted my attention. I sought him out, and he patiently spent hours educating me on the relevant issues and then giving what I had written on the subject a close and critical read. I am very grateful.

My debt to Karel van Wolferen will be obvious to any alert reader who is familiar with Karel's writing. This book would be inconceivable without his writing and personal example. Karel gave unstinting encouragement as I worked; his suggestions on the final two chapters were particularly important.

As I was finishing the first draft, I asked two good friends to read the entire manuscript—to tell me what I had gotten wrong and suggest how I might fix things. Fukuhara Toshio and Mike Verretto come as close as any people I know to being perfectly bicultural in the sense that they can see things both through Japanese and American eyes. We don't agree about everything—and they don't agree with everything I have written—but their close, line-by-line reading and their comments were enormously valuable. I thank them.

I need to thank someone who is almost surely unaware that I exist: Robert Caro, whose magnificent unfinished biography of Lyndon Johnson I finally got around to reading as I was working on the chapters about Japanese politics. Caro's writing helped me to bring into focus the central role of Tanaka Kakuei in Japan's political story as it has unfolded over the past half-century.

I asked my brother Alexander for advice on what to do about maps. Alec—a lifelong source of support and intellectual stimulation—recommended his graduate student, Nicholas A. Perdue. Nicholas did a great job and I thank them both.

I wrote considerable chunks of the book in the beautiful Singapore home of my dear friends Linda and Lance Roberts. I thank them for opening their home to me.

Seeing this book from inception through publication required several trips to New York. My "B-school" classmate Jun Makihara and former colleague Mimi Oka allowed me to use the guest wing of their lovely apartment in the East Village as a base of operations each time I was there and I thank them. Not only are they dear friends but they have for decades been important sources of insight for me on Japan and its place in the world. I also benefitted from two searching discussions about the career and significance of Ozawa Ichiro with Mimi's father, the eminent journalist Takashi Oka, who has written an important biography of Ozawa.

Most of the book I wrote in my office at the MBA Program in International Business at the Tokyo campus of the University of Tsukuba. Whenever I found myself feeling too pessimistic about Japan, the MBA program itself—not to mention my colleagues and students—acted as a wonderful corrective. The very existence of the program—its support from the University and ultimately from the Ministry of Education—is proof that there are people in Japan determined to loosen the shackles that seem to trap this country; to light candles rather than curse the darkness. My colleagues on the faculty are a formidable source of intellectual stimulation, companionship, and support, and as for our students—well, one need not fret too much about the future if they are the kinds of people in whose hands Japan's fate rests or, in the case of our students who come from somewhere other than Japan, one need not fret about the relationship Japan has with these other places if our foreign students are the kinds of people who will help determine that relationship.

As I was finishing up the manuscript, some letters my late father had written and mailed home during the Second World War came to light following the death of his younger sister, my beloved aunt, Ethel Goolsby. My father had seen action in the Pacific; he was one of the millions of young men sent to fight and possibly die in a war that he had done nothing to start. The letters were riveting—and not just because they showed a side of someone who had meant so much to me, a side I had only glimpsed growing up. He was scarcely more than a boy himself when he wrote the letters; thus many of his observations about the war—particularly in the letters meant for his mother to see—consist of conventional sentiments of the "why we fight" type and disparaging remarks about the "Japs" and the "Nips," interspersed with acute and amusing observations on the Filipino society in which his unit was embedded. But then in a letter intended only for his older sister Marjory's eyes, he admits he has been shading things to avoid upsetting their mother. He writes to Marjory of his aching homesickness, of the "innumerable hours (he has) felt the oppression of incredible dullness," interspersed with "sheer terror" when his unit is under attack. He describes how his "stomach would growl, and (he) would begin to tremble uncontrollably." He goes on to note that "this is a frequent reaction of many, but few mention it." His loathing of the way the Japanese conducted themselves in the Philippines is obvious, but then he writes of a morning after his unit had beaten back a Japanese attack during the previous night. He walked out of his unit's small camp to find that amid "the shattered bodies, newly slaughtered, unburied corpses, blackened and bloated and stinking, and wounds terrible to behold" was "a little card case in which was a pretty picture of a young Japanese girl" lying on top of the remains of one of the soldiers. I was mesmerized by the following paragraphs where he wrestles with this evidence of the dead man's humanity. The sentiments expressed were akin to those in Wilfred Owen's

"Strange Meeting," arguably the greatest antiwar poem ever written. My father may not have been quite in Owen's league as a poet (who was?), but since I knew him the way a son knows his father, able to picture with total vividness the way he would grapple in words and facial expressions and body language with any really serious issue, his account—and the palpable struggle it conveyed—struck me with the same force that Owen's poem once did. My father writes: "We are not young handsome men with great forearms and magnificent physiques, pitting our physical strength against that of the enemy. We are men behind machines. Many are not young. This is no gladiators' fight. The weakest man with a machine gun is more deadly than a super-man with his bare hands. We do not fight with the excitement and thrill of bodily combat. We fight with the most awful devices for destruction ever conceived by man's ingenuity, and human bodies seem as paper when they meet hot lead or cold steel."

So I need to thank my father not only in practical terms—I first came to Japan because Japanese scholars with whom he had been collaborating invited him to spend a year at their university—but because these letters brought home to me the stakes involved. You hear a lot of loose talk in East Asia today about national honor and glory complete with sagas of victimization and historical wrongs, all conveyed in language that smacks of xenophobia-*cum*-racism. Most of this talk comes from people who have never faced combat and never will; people for whom outrage at the *other*— whether posed or genuinely felt—invariably trumps self-examination; people for whom anything that goes wrong is always someone else's fault. The atmosphere has been poisoned. Leaders snub each other, while websites are clogged with nationalist breast-beating. In one country, a government pays its citizens to take to the streets to shout hatred for their country's neighbors, in another, subway cars are filled with advertisements for articles in scurrilous journals on the perfidy of those across the water while people from across the water find themselves jeered at in the places where they congregate. Americans may tut-tut at all this, but Washington is directly culpable, having kicked over an admittedly fragile, half-finished structure that had offered the region the hope of a *modus vivendi*—kicked it over because it meant relocating a Marine base back to the United States.

I tell the story of how this happened; it serves as one more example— if perhaps the most important in recent years—of how nothing in the Japanese context makes complete sense in isolation. Unless one has some feel for the long, fraught tale of Japan's relationship to the outside world, of the way in which the dependence of Japan on the United States has allowed political pathologies to go undiagnosed and untreated, the base issue and the way it destroyed Japan's best chance in two generations for real peace with its neighbors comes across the way it is usually portrayed: a disjointed tale of ingratitude, incompetence, and irrationality.

Any success I have in conveying the context in which this and other critical issues are unfolding is due in large measure to those I thanked above (needless to say, the errors are all mine) and to the many Japanese people I have worked with, played with, and loved over the decades I have spent in this country. Principal among them is my life partner, Kawada Osamu. Most acknowledgments like these end in thanking someone behind the scenes whose support and advice made the labor in writing a book like this possible. In this case, that person is Osamu and it is to him that I dedicate this book.

While working on this book, I had to remind myself from time to time what it would be like to explain American politics to someone who might have heard of Barack Obama and Ronald Reagan, but for whom Lyndon Johnson and Richard Nixon were just names and Barry Goldwater or George McGovern not even that. In an effort to help the reader cope with the occasional thicket of unfamiliar Japanese names, I have provided two appendices: a list of the principal figures of the Meiji period together with short descriptions of each of them, and, a comparable list of important political leaders of the postwar era.

Throughout this book, I have used standard Japanese practice in the treatment of names: family name followed by given name (e.g., Tanaka Kakuei; Abe Shinzo). Exceptions are Japanese people who have made their homes in the West and those who are household names in the West (e.g., Haruki Murakami; Hideo Nomo).

Tokyo, July 2014

MAP 1 Japan Today. Courtesy Nicholas A. Perdue. Redrawn from map at World Sites Atlas.com

Introduction

As I sit down to write this introduction, I confront a piece in the *New York Times* by Steven Rattner, the Wall Street banker whom the Obama administration recruited back in 2009 to lead the restructuring of the American automobile industry. Rattner has just made a brief trip here and he wants to tell us what he thinks we need to know about what is going on in Japan. He touches on the Japanese government's recent macroeconomic measures— gunning the money supply, fiscal stimulus—before moving on to the real message of his piece: that "insufficient attention" has been given to "smaller-bore policy challenges," that "Japan is certainly as shackled by its own rigidities as any other country," and that "the need for microeconomic reform is glaring."

Do we need to know these things? Mr. Rattner obviously thinks we do; even more obviously, he thinks we need to know them lest we land in some sort of trap akin to the one into which he believes Japan has fallen. He tells us the Japanese should lower taxes on income while boosting shareholder say-so in what goes on inside companies. He writes that the country requires more economic "efficiency," a smaller gap between "revenue" and "gaping budget deficits," a loosening of "exceptionally strict immigration laws" and "meaningful changes in rigid labor policies," by which he seems to mean making it easier to fire people. Otherwise, Japan's "failure to take on sacred cows" makes it "unlikely that the country will ever again rank as an economic juggernaut."

With apologies to Mr. Rattner, this is the sort of stuff that everyone already knows. It does not require a book or even an op-ed piece in the *Sunday New York Times* to tell us what upstanding investment bankers think we need to know about Japan and why we need to know it. It is not news to anyone that Japan is stuck with a "faltering" economy, that people like Mr. Rattner believe "other developed countries" should "worry" lest they fail to "absorb" the relevant "lessons" from Japan—and that Mr. Rattner knows what those lessons are.

Oscar Wilde wrote: "The whole of Japan is a pure invention. There is no such country; there are no such people." Well over a century after Wilde's gibe, the West, as Mr. Rattner's piece suggests, is still inventing Japans to suit its own purposes—the latest of these Japans serving as a kind of stick with which to beat the rest of us. Now Mr. Rattner has not quite gone and invented a Japan out of whole cloth—he is often right about many of those "smaller-bore policy challenges" the country faces. Rather what makes his Japan more of an invention than a real place facing real challenges is an unspoken assumption behind his writing: that Tokyo's decision makers do not see these challenges, or if they do, act like stubborn children in their willful refusal to deal with them. Understanding why this might be so requires knowing something about a place's history, geography, political institutions, cultural heritage, and, above all, the ability to identify who in that place has the power to require what of whom. To put this in other words, to tell everyone what they need to know about Japan, you have to start by figuring out who the real decision makers are and how they came to have the power to determine the way other people lead their lives. These decision makers do not consist exclusively or even primarily of Japan's elected leaders; some of them are not even Japanese—they live in Washington.

For Japan does indeed offer some lessons—some even of the sort Mr. Rattner might urge on us. But those lessons are a lot more interesting than exhortations on taxes, labor markets, and economic efficiency. For really important lessons lie not in statements of the obvious—a country's labor and compensation practices need to change when economics and demography change; a minority of zealots in a minority party should not have the ability to threaten financial Armageddon if they do not get their way—but rather in the teasing out of the cultural, historical, geographical, institutional, and political factors that stymie an overhaul of Japan's labor relations or, as the case may be, allowed crazed demagogues to amass sufficient power that they could make credible threats to force the American government to default on its obligations. (Anyone who believes it is a challenge to explain Japan to Americans should try explaining the Tea Party and US congressional rules to the Japanese.) It is unlikely that in the process we will uncover many lessons of the "see what happens if you don't do this!" type; the world is much too complex and, blessedly, too stubbornly particular for that. But we might learn a little about how to ask the right questions. We might discover something about the ways in which conceptual shackles in our own countries keep us from finding out what everyone needs to know by analyzing how shackles distort things in another place. We might even get some ideas on how to do what everyone knows needs to be done in our own countries by studying how and why another country—particularly one as distinctive as Japan—has or has not done what everyone knows needs to be done.

What do you do, for example, when women stop having babies? When millions of healthy, young straight men tell you they have no interest in marriage and family—or even in sex with real women? How do you care for your old people? Particularly when you are loathe to see large-scale immigration endanger the social solidarity that is still your country's prime asset? How do you fix an economic model that once worked so well it was called a miracle and has all kinds of people invested in its continuation even though it manifestly requires overhaul? How do you write off the trillions of yen sunk into a power source that could poison your country forever after you had tricked yourself into believing it offered limitless, clean, risk-free energy? How do you manage to divide up an economic pie that has essentially stopped growing without squabbles over who gets what ripping your society apart? How do you face the rise of a touchy, pugnacious new superpower just over the horizon that has nominated you as its principal villain in the nationalist narrative it feeds its citizens? Particularly when your erstwhile "ally" and protector treats you with a mixture of ignorance and contempt, and cavalierly destroys your best hope of a government that could cope with such things? How do you face up to a past that you really have to deal with—not only because no one else will trust you unless you do, but because you are in danger of making the same kinds of mistakes again that led to the greatest disaster in your country's history unless you figure out what those mistakes were? But how do you start the process when your country's sense of itself is totally wrapped up in the myths that led to those mistakes, and the people who now run things in your country are the direct heirs of the men who wove those myths to justify their seizure of power some 150 years ago? What is it about your country's culture that so fascinates the world, even though you did not invent that culture for outside consumption and you cannot figure out how to translate that fascination into geopolitical or even narrow commercial advantage?

In the unlikely event that this book—or any book—were to answer these questions definitively, then yes, it would contain what everyone needs to know about Japan. I do not kid myself that I have succeeded in this quest, but I hope I have at least managed to get some of the questions right. I first arrived in Japan as a 15-year-old schoolboy, and like many *gaijin*, I fell hopelessly in love with the place. I came back to Japan on my own as an adult and have spent most of the last four decades here; many of the most important people in my life are Japanese and my early infatuation has not gone away. Instead, like all genuine loves, it has become colored by an awareness of tragedy—the inevitable price of fixing one's love on imperfect, mortal human beings and what they (we) have made. For I now understand what I did not really grasp then—that much of modern Japanese history is a tragedy; a tragedy stemming not simply from the usual formula of external circumstance mixed with internal failings but from the very things about the place (the people) that make one love it (them) so.

Generations of foreign writers have attempted to put their fingers on just what it is they find so alluring about Japan. The most successful at this exercise—I would nominate Lafcadio Hearn, Kurt Singer, Ian Buruma, and, above all, the late Donald Richie—have pointed to an acceptance of things as they are. Japanese people do not bellyache; they take pleasure in little things that would be beneath the notice of grander peoples. They are hopeless romantics, clinging to dreams even when the dreams are demonstrably hollow. "Reality" may be ugly, cheap, tawdry—but so what? Why let that get in the way of sentiment, of pleasure? One encounters words like "particular" and "situational" in discussions of the Japanese, and maybe these cold, abstract terms are the best we can do to describe a people that has collectively decided simply not to notice contradictions.

I recently encountered a video broadcast on YouTube by yet one more enterprising *gaijin* attempting to explain the strange sexual byways of the Japanese. Amidst trips to a studio where one can pay to be bound and whipped by a dominatrix and visits to nightclubs where he interviews customers whom one might think are sufficiently good–looking and personable to attract boyfriends and girlfriends on their own but who prefer to

fork over wads of yen to drink and chat with working "hosts" of the opposite sex, the journalist finds himself in an establishment where for 7,000
yen (about $70) he can be cuddled for an hour by a young woman. She will
look into his eyes, "spoon" with him, and even clean his ears with his head
in her lap; there will not be anything physical beyond that.

One can imagine paying for sex—not to mention something more
kinky—but to pay to be *cuddled*? For most of us, any hint of the merce-
nary would destroy the whole point of cuddling—a temporary return to
the kind of blissful, all-enveloping, undemanding love one enjoyed as an
infant. I have lived here long enough to say with authority that even most
Japanese would find paying for a cuddle preposterous. Yet at the same time
I can see why someone has figured out how to make money by providing
this "service" in Japan. If you are used to compartmentalizing everything,
if you have been socialized not to make a fuss over even the most blatant
of contradictions, then maybe if you need a bit of mothering—and we all
do from time to time—you will be able to pay for it without noticing that a
cuddle hardly qualifies as such when it is being done for money.

This kind of thing is everywhere, even when it is less sensational than
paid cuddling.[1] It is perhaps the principal reason why life can be so pleasant
here: most everyone takes their responsibilities with total seriousness. In
the West we like to say that if a job is worth doing, it is worth doing well.
In Japan, even if a job is not worth doing—*and everyone knows it*—it is
worth doing well. The levels of politeness and service one encounters in
Japan, even when the most minor—or, truth be told, tawdry—of transactions are involved, are so far beyond what one is used to elsewhere that
at times one can fall into a kind of reverie that suggests the entire world
has been arranged for one's pleasure. The slightest effort on one's part will
be greeted with cries of *o-tsukaresama deshita!* (it means something like
"you must be exhausted" with overtones of gratitude for one's immense

---

1. A friend pointed out to me that "cuddle parties" can be found in the United States—and
sure enough, a web search turns up plenty of evidence. But they appear to be in the grand
American tradition of self-help and group therapy, national traits noted as far back as de
Tocqueville. They are not one-on-one events staged by those looking to turn a profit. That
Japanese and American responses to what amounts to the same phenomenon—the atomism
that modern society brings in its wake—could be so different points to a theme that will run
throughout this book: the unique and characteristic ways in which the Japanese have reacted
to phenomena universal in at least the developed world. It is just as hard to imagine Japanese
adults attending cuddle parties with groups of strangers as it is to imagine Americans paying
a specific person to cuddle them.

sacrifice). Serve someone a cup of tea with a sweet and one will be thanked for the feast (*gochisō sama deshita*). Alternatively, just before sitting down to a sumptuous repast, one will be told there is so little to eat that it is shameful. Of course, all this reaches the level of ritual, but even though it is a ritual and everyone knows it, one is expected to act as if the ritual were infused with genuine spontaneity and feeling. Since everyone acts in the expected way and is, in a manner of speaking, in on the secret, then somehow the most empty and ritualistic of occasions can become infused with meaning.

That aura of ritual extends to human relations. One starts out pretending to be someone's bosom buddy, enthusiastic colleague, or eager supplier even when one does not really like the other person or finds the job a bore while the customer is a demanding jerk who does not begin in financial terms to justify the effort one puts into satisfying his or her needs. Yet because one is expected to act as if one really cared for the well-being of the other, that one's colleagues are the world's greatest co-workers and nothing could be more important than filling the needs of whatever customer one is dealing with at the moment, one does end up actually internalizing feelings of affection, respect, and commitment to doing the job at hand as well as it can possibly be done. One ends up with a wide circle of people about whom one cares very deeply—and a sense that one is cared for by many others. And one comes quickly to understand the tremendous advantage to a society where practically everyone can be relied upon to do what they say they have promised to do, and to do it well.

But this resolute refusal to notice contradictions—to act as if everything were the way it should be even when everything isn't—has a key political dimension that is often overlooked. It may be the source of what makes Japan so alluring and successful; it also, as I noted above, explains much of the tragedy of modern Japanese history. For it creates almost ideal conditions for exploitation.

These conditions are not limited to the internalization of a mindset that identifies maturity with an acceptance of things as they are and that dictates that one derive purpose in life from pursuing aims that one knows at some level are unworthy. At elite levels, this situational perspective that is so ingrained in Japan fosters a kind of doublethink that allows power holders to deceive themselves both about what they are doing and about their motives for doing it.

The great Japanese political philosopher Maruyama Masao put his finger on this when he noted the contrast between the swaggering behavior of the Nazi war criminals at the Nuremberg Trials and that of their supposed Japanese counterparts at the Tokyo war crimes trials. Men like Himmler knew they were evil and reveled in it; their nominal Japanese counterparts acted like reluctant, passive victims, dragged into a catastrophe that had not been of their making—and this is the key point—they believed it; it was not a pose.

Despite all the bluster coming out of Beijing these days, Japan no longer seriously threatens to engulf itself and its neighbors in a sea of flames. But this sense of living in a world without agency where things happen for inexplicable reasons—that the most one can do is adapt as best one can while giving one's all—is still pervasive. The Japanese have a term for it: *higaisha ishiki* or "victim consciousness." In practical terms, among other things, it threatens to bring about a situation where Japan solves its admittedly frightening fiscal dilemma by tearing up the social contract that once provided something close to universal economic security, hiking taxes and prices, destroying the purchasing power of household savings, welshing on pension obligations, and substituting a world of poorly paid temporary work with no prospects and no security for the historic commitment by Japanese companies to see to the livelihood of their employees. The men who seek to carry out this program will not cackle with glee like Wall Street bankers gloating over the ruins of companies whose assets they have stripped and workers they have fired; they will instead bow low with long faces, convinced they are participating in a general sacrifice over which they have no choice even when they are personally benefiting from the results. And they are likely to get away with it because millions of ordinary Japanese will shrug their shoulders, sigh, and say to themselves *shikata ga nai* (it can't be helped). That there is another approach—an approach of strong unions, robust political parties that speak for working people, an explicit safety net, and other policies that spark the domestic demand needed to revive Japanese industry by putting money in people's pockets—will not be considered. And if it is, it will be dismissed as immature populism; if it begins nonetheless to show any sign of getting traction, it will be attacked as "un-Japanese" and discredited by the institutions that have been developed to silence—*mokusatsu* is the Japanese term—those who would threaten existing power relations.

We will look at some of those institutions in this book and in the last two chapters go into some detail into the ways in which the best hope Japan has had in recent decades of a different and better approach to escaping its current dilemmas was destroyed with the direct complicity and involvement of Washington. This a story everyone does need to know, particularly Americans. For it casts light on the broader challenge that all of us face—not just the Japanese.

That challenge begins with understanding how institutions—companies, banks, governments, armies, police—whose original purpose lay in providing a decent and secure living for everyone have been corrupted and captured by those who would use them to enrich themselves and to ward off phantoms through fantasies of total control and total awareness. Running these institutions in such ways requires the mental agility to understand what needs to be done while deceiving oneself about actual motive—a conceptual dance that George Orwell would famously label doublethink. Orwell was such a penetrating analyst of power because he understood and articulated the intellectual and psychological demands made on anyone who would seize and control for their own purposes the political and economic institutions that constitute modernity. Japan's power elite has been marinated in a political and cultural tradition in which tolerance of contradiction was not only accepted but essential—why Japan provides something close to a template for what we now see cropping up in so many other places.

This template forms perhaps the most important reason why anyone who is politically aware and cares about the fate of the world needs to know something about Japan. Japan is still the world's third largest economy. Japan still has the power to force human history onto new and unexpected trajectories, as it has done over and over again since Commodore Perry yanked it out of its seclusion (those trajectories include modern painting, architecture, and cinema, the Russian Revolution, the Chinese Revolution, the restructuring of the American economy, and the financial hegemony of a US dollar backed by nothing but the computers in the Federal Reserve). Japan has already had two decades to cope—or not to cope—with challenges that have now emerged everywhere in the developed world: an aging population, a ruined financial system, monetary policy that no longer works the way the textbooks say it should, falling profits, excess capacity.

All this would suggest that everyone needs to know something about Japan. But that need acquires a particular urgency once one begins to grasp how much of the world is beginning to resemble Japan. It has long been predicted that Japan's distinctiveness—and it is unquestionably the most distinctive of all modern industrial societies—would dissolve under the overwhelming force of Western culture. This has not happened. Industrialization and modernity have, to be sure, utterly transformed this country. But they have not turned it into a knock-off or some sort of Oriental copy of the West. Even Marx's haunting and prescient observation that the coming of capitalism would melt everything solid while profaning all holiness has not quite worked out that way in Japan—and that is not because Japan somehow got stuck in some sort of preindustrial phase of development; its economy is as modern and sophisticated as any.

Japan has remained Japan. But in the rest of the world, ruling elites have become more Japanese in at least this one crucial respect: learning to live with the constant presence of contradiction while perfecting the mental gymnastics necessary to deceive oneself about motive while still acting on that motive. "Political aims need not be conscious to be realized," wrote the most acute analyst of Japanese power relations in recent decades. Once one grasps the importance of this observation, events unfolding in London, in Berlin, in Beijing, in Brussels, in Frankfurt, in New York, in Jerusalem, in Cairo, in Riyadh, in Tehran, and above all in Washington end up providing the most crucial clues on what everyone needs to know about Japan and why we need to know it.

Part One

The Forging of the Shackles

FIGURE 1. Fourth-Century Tomb of Emperor Nintoku. © City of Sakae; Courtesy City of Sakae.

1

Japan Before the Edo Period

The Japanese archipelago stretches beyond the outer rim of Eurasia for nearly 2,000 miles in something of a geographic sweet spot—close enough to absorb developments on the continent, but not so close as to be overwhelmed, either culturally or militarily. One is tempted to draw parallels with the Gothic and Germanic tribes during the Roman Empire or, later, with Great Britain vis-à-vis continental Europe; certainly Japan could serve as a perfect example of what can happen to societies just over the fence from magnetic metropolitan civilizations. In recent centuries, Japan's impact on the continent may have been as great as the reverse, but during much of its history, the country existed at what was effectively the edge of the known world. Perhaps as a result, only once did it attract the attention of a would-be conqueror from outside: Kublai Khan in the thirteenth century. Fortuitous storms (*kamikaze* or divine wind) sank his fleets and with the passing of that danger, Japan avoided the fate of so much of Eurasia—succumbing to the Mongol hordes.

Japan grew up on the outer fringes of a Chinese civilization that was the world's most advanced in almost every technological and political respect during Japan's premodern history. Much of what Japan took from the continent (and it took a lot) came filtered through another, much smaller country: Korea. That shaped the ways Japan would absorb and internalize continental institutions, although pulling apart what is specifically Korean in these institutions, what is Chinese, and what comes from farther afield (e.g., the Mahayana Buddhism that arrived in Japan via China and Korea from the ancient Hellenized kingdom of Bactria in what is now northern Afghanistan) has become a largely hopeless exercise. The process has not been helped by the baggage of the last 150 years. Mutual resentment, contempt, and outright hatred between the Japanese and the Koreans not only blocks an agreed-upon narrative of modern history but also clouds analysis of the earlier relationship between the two countries. Any attempt to identify specifically Korean elements in Japan's cultural and institutional inheritance generates controversy in Japan equal in its intensity only to the controversy generated in Korea by crediting anything in the legacy of Japan's colonization for the success story of the modern South Korean economy. (For that matter, a visitor to Pyongyang would be advised to avoid pointing out to his or her North Korean hosts the roots in Japan's prewar emperor-worship of the cult that has been built around the country's ruling Kim dynasty.)

No such controversy dogs discussion of Japan's geographical endowment. Thanks to Japan's four-season, temperate climate, and rich volcanic soils, premodern—albeit intensive—farming techniques yielded enough calories to feed up to thirty million people, particularly when an exceptionally long coastline provided such easy access to the food resources of the ocean. The Japanese figured out how to exploit these resources in ways that surpassed anything else any other culture had ever attempted; it is no surprise that Japan became the home of the world's most exquisite seafood-based cuisine. The sea served as a barrier to would-be invaders while providing the Japanese themselves with a unifying thoroughfare for travel up and down the length of the archipelago. The country's mountainous topography may have limited the amount of land that could be devoted to farming, but it also provided a rich forest cover—and thus vast and renewable supplies of timber. Japan's magnificent wooden temples, shrines, and palaces formed a timber-based architectural counterpart to its ocean-based cuisine; no culture has ever built so magnificently out of wood. The mountains provided ample amounts of fresh, clean running water that could be used for irrigation and power as well as drinking.

These three factors explain a great deal that is distinctive in Japan's history. Japan took its writing, much of its religion and philosophy, its technology, and at least the outward form of many of its institutions from continental—primarily Chinese—models. But unlike countries such as

Korea and Vietnam, which also heavily borrowed from China, Japan never fell into China's political orbit. It was never seen by itself and very rarely by the Chinese as a tributary state or as part of the Chinese imperial system. (The one exception is discussed below.)

The Japanese have always had an acute sense of what has been borrowed from abroad and what is indigenous. This division between "Japanese" and "foreign" extends into the very language itself. Japan's first sustained encounter with continental civilization in the sixth century led inevitably to attempts to write Japanese. Having no other example, Chinese characters were imported for the purpose. Each character was assigned a minimum of two readings. The first, a "meaning" reading, was the Japanese word for the character's meaning. The other readings, the "sound" readings, were as close as the Japanese vocalization of the time could come to the original Chinese pronunciations.[1] Thus, the "sound" reading of the character for person, 人, is pronounced *jin* (the northern Chinese pronunciation) or *nin* (the southern), while the "meaning" reading is *hito*—the original Japanese word for person.[2] We have something like this in English: a fancy word—mansion/chair—derived from Norman French and a simple word meaning much the same thing—house/stool—coming from Anglo-Saxon. But while "mansion" and "chair" lost their French associations centuries ago for English speakers, every Japanese student knows that *jin* came from Chinese while *hito* is the original Japanese word.

Something similar took place with all the other borrowings. Continental models in everything from architecture to music, religion, painting, governing institutions, and metallurgy were imported and grafted onto native models. Sometimes the result was a considerable improvement on the original. Even the Chinese, who were loath to grant that outer barbarians could do anything better than they, acknowledged that the Japanese had perfected paper-making and dyeing beyond anything in China itself. Samurai swords were forged of the world's finest steel until the coming of modern steel-making.

1. The vocalizations in Japanese usually only vaguely evoked the original Chinese pronunciations because Chinese has a much more complex phonetic system than the Polynesian-like simplicity of Japanese pronunciation.
2. The limited character set meant that characters often were given more than one Japanese reading as well. An extreme example like 生 has some nine readings—*shō, sei, ha(eru), i(kasu), na(ru), u(mu), nama, -fu, ki-*, while four or five readings for a given character are common. 生 means "live, living"—it is, for example, stamped on bottles of unpasteurized beer. A draft beer is a 生—*nama*—beer.

Thus, from the earliest recorded contact with continental civilization, Japan always understood itself to be distinct from China—separate, with its own history and traditions. While the premodern peasant might not have had much political consciousness beyond his village affiliation, members of the Japanese ruling elite placed their most important political identity at the national level (i.e., Japanese) rather than the regional or local. And they knew of other nationalities—Chinese, of course, but also Korean, Indian, Mongol. Thus, when Japan was forced open by the Western powers in the mid-nineteenth century, elites had no conceptual difficulty in adapting themselves to the sovereign territorial ideal of the Westphalian system, the notion that "the land surface of the earth should be divided up into discrete territorial units, each with a government that exercises substantial authority within its own territory" and that the key territorial unit was the nation: "a group of people who saw themselves as a cultural-historical unit."

THE IMPERIAL INSTITUTION

Japan's Imperial Institution is the oldest hereditary monarchy in the world; among political institutions that survive to this day, only the papacy is demonstrably older. Yet paradoxically, Japanese emperors rarely exercised direct political power. This may have been the key to the Institution's longevity. While Japan's founding myths accord divine lineage to the Imperial Household and date the Institution to 660 B.C., the first actual emperors probably emerged closer to the third or fourth century A.D. No written records predate the early sixth century, but the Imperial Household seems to have its roots as *primus inter pares* among the clans that formed the Japanese polity of the time.

Before the coming to Japan in the late sixth century of Buddhism and its practice of cremation, deceased emperors were buried in large tombs shaped like giant keyholes surrounded by moats. (An example can be found in the frontispiece to this chapter.) The Imperial Household Agency, which controls these tombs, rarely allows archaeologists to excavate them, maintaining that their ceremonial, sacred nature should be preserved against desecration. But there are also concerns that excavation might reveal matters that would be problematical for the notion of an unbroken succession said to characterize the Imperial House.

Emperors seem originally to have been shamans of a sort, and the institution has since earliest times been defined by its religious role. The emperor was effectively the *Pontifex Maximus* of Shinto. Shinto literally means "way of the gods"—the name given after the introduction of Buddhism from Korea to distinguish indigenous beliefs from the "way of the Buddha."

There was little conflict between Buddhism and Shinto until the late nineteenth century when the Meiji government deliberately inculcated a militarized cult of State Shinto theoretically purged of all "imported" elements. Until that time, Shinto and Buddhist practices coexisted with each other. Small Shinto shrines still cluster on the edges of major Buddhist temples, much like the side chapels devoted to saints one sees in medieval European cathedrals. Indeed, Shinto gods were often regarded as incarnations of Buddhist guardian angels or bodhisattvas. Even today, it would be entirely unremarkable for a Japanese to start his or her religious life with a baptismal type of ceremony conducted in a Shinto shrine and finish it with a Buddhist funeral—and to have a nominally Christian wedding at some point along the way. Until a generation ago, his or her ancestors would not have had the Christian wedding, but they would have been even less conscious of any contradiction between Shinto rites for certain purposes and Buddhist for others.

The Imperial Institution embodied this religious eclecticism. At the same time that major Buddhist temples operated under direct Imperial protection—often with abbots of Imperial blood—the emperor himself, who remains the high priest of Shinto, conducted the most important of Shinto rituals: the rites held at the Ise Shrine in honor of the Sun Goddess, herself held to be the direct ancestor of the Imperial Household.

A sixteenth-century European visitor trying to make sense of Japan's political setup reported that Japan had both a pope and an emperor. He got things backwards; he called the actual emperor Japan's pope and mislabeled the shogun as the emperor. We will have more to say about the shoguns later, but the visitor's description may actually have gotten closer to the reality of Japan's ruling institutions than did the unfortunate designation in English of Japan's nominally supreme ruler as "His Majesty the Emperor"—the English translation the Japanese provided for the Japanese title, *Tennō Heika,* which literally means "heavenly sovereign." By calling the *Tennō Heika* Emperor, the Japanese were trying to suggest that he was somehow more than a king. But the choice of the European word "emperor" was misplaced, derived as the word is from *Imperator* the military designation given to Roman supreme commanders (i.e., military rulers of groups of nations that form an empire). The *Tennō Heika* was the religious leader of one nation—the Japanese nation—the fountainhead of its religion and the source of its political legitimacy. *Sei-i Tai Shō Gun*—literally, "barbarian-subduing generalissimo"—has a meaning much closer to the original connotation of *Imperator* than does *Tennō*.

But the term "emperor" is now in such wide use worldwide for the Japanese monarch that it is unlikely to change. It is helpful to keep in mind, however, that for most of Japan's history, the emperor served as the country's spiritual leader and did not actively rule. Thus, when power changed hands, emperors were not overthrown and replaced by new rulers forming new dynasties as their nominal counterparts were in China, Korea, and Vietnam. Instead, the Imperial Household served as a crucial token of political legitimacy—of the right to rule.

THE FUJIWARA FAMILY AND THE FOUNDING OF HEIAN-KYŌ

From the end of the eighth century through the end of the twelfth, actual power was concentrated in the hands of the Fujiwara clan, a family of aristocrats that controlled the Imperial Household through what came to be known as "marriage politics." The Fujiwara usually managed to ensure that a Fujiwara daughter married the Heir Apparent. Often these marriages occurred when both bride and groom were still children. The Fujiwara understood the latent threat to their power from anyone who could wrest from them their control of the Imperial succession. They typically arranged for emperors to ascend the Throne as boys—able to perform religious rituals, but not yet up to participation in political intrigue—and then to abdicate shortly after reaching adulthood. Meanwhile, a Fujiwara regent usually exercised real power.

The Fujiwara emerged out of a decades-long struggle among powerful clans beginning late in the sixth century that accompanied the first waves of continental civilization to pour into Japan. These culminated in what was known as the Taika Reform of the year 645, instigated by the progenitors of the Fujiwara who had shoved aside another clan in their bid to control state organs. (They changed their name to Fujiwara in 685.) The Taika Reform amounted to a wholesale import of the sophisticated bureaucratized political institutions of China. Clan leaders grouped around the Imperial Household intended to consolidate their power over the nascent Japanese state by modeling Japan's institutional setup on that of the most advanced polity known to them.

Japan's first permanent capital was established at Nara in 710—before that time, a new capital had been declared whenever an emperor died. Nara was preeminently a political city like St. Petersburg or Washington, founded by fiat to make palpable the political reality of the Japanese state.[3] Modeled on Chang'An (now Xi'an), the capital of Tang dynasty China and then the largest city in the world, Nara had a similar rectangular/grid layout with the Imperial Palace at its apex. Nara formed Japan's first real city, boasting a population of some 200,000 within a few decades of its founding. Studded with important temples built along Tang lines that acted as founts of continental art and learning, Nara's greatest edifice was the *Tōdai-ji* (literally, Eastern Great Temple). Consecrated in 728, it housed the world's largest bronze statue inside the world's largest wooden building. Its construction facilitated the consolidation of power in and around Nara since resources had to be raised from far and wide to finance it. The *Tōdai-ji* itself served as a sort of Vatican of Japanese Buddhism, standing at the apex of an organized nationwide hierarchy of temples.

The eighth century was a golden age for Japanese Buddhism.[4] The Buddhist clergy grew so powerful, however, that it threatened both to bankrupt the country with endless temple construction and to interfere with Imperial succession. The Empress Koken came under such strong influence from a Rasputin-type Buddhist priest that she tried to place him directly on the Throne while ordering the execution of a high-ranking Fujiwara official who stood in her way.

She managed to frighten Japan's ruling aristocracy so badly that they stipulated that no more women would be allowed to ascend the Throne.

---

3. The first Japanese city that arose organically for economic/trading reasons as distinct from political was Osaka.

4. Even today, enough remains from that era to give a visitor to Nara a sense of what it must have been like. Nothing is left of the original *Tōdai-ji*—what you see now is an eighteenth-century structure, 30 percent smaller than the original, albeit still the world's largest wooden building housing a huge, if artistically undistinguished, Buddha statue also of fairly recently forging. But a number of other temples have survived in and around Nara in much the form they were.

(There were a few subsequent reigning empresses centuries later, but they served only as stop-gaps until a designated Imperial prince came of age.) They also divested the Buddhist clergy of much of its political authority. And to ensure that the great Nara temples would never again threaten to capture state organs, the capital was moved away from Nara.

After a couple of false starts, the ruling clans settled in 794 on a well-watered valley surrounded on three sides by mountains for their new capital city. They named it *Heian-kyō*—Capital of Heavenly Peace— although in later years it came to be known simply as *Kyōto*, literally, Capital City. Again modeled on Chang'an with its grid of great boulevards and the grounds of the Imperial Palace at its apex, Kyoto had all the right attributes dictated by Chinese geomancy: a river flowing through the city, and to the northeast—the "unlucky" direction—Mt. Hiei, the highest of the mountains that ringed Kyoto on three sides. There, the great network of temples known as *Enryaku-ji* was established, supplanting *Tōdai-ji*'s role at the apex of Japanese Buddhism. The temples would perform their spiritual function of protecting the city from bad influences but at suffi- cient remove so the abbots could not directly interfere in politics. In later times, warrior monks from Mt. Hiei would, despite these precautions, pe- riodically sweep into Kyoto to intervene in factional disputes of one sort of another, until the warlord Oda Nobunaga finally and irrevocably broke the political power of the Buddhist clergy for good by burning *Enryaku-ji* to the ground in 1571.

But that was all centuries later. In the meantime, the Fujiwara estab- lished in Kyoto one of the world's most aesthetically and artistically so- phisticated centers of civilization. The ruling aristocrats would digest and refine what they had learned over the preceding centuries. Freed of serious external pressure, they had the leisure to devote themselves to art. One would have to look to such distant comparisons as Versailles or the Mughal courts to find a civilization where the refinement of taste was developed to such an extraordinary degree—and with such long-lasting effects.

THE LEGACY OF THE HEIAN PERIOD

During the centuries labeled "Heian" a genuinely distinctive civilization developed in Japan. Japan had, of course, existed as a nation conscious of itself for several centuries before Heian. But Nara, for all its brilliance, was clearly derivative of Tang culture, and until a few decades before Nara, "Japan" had been little more than a group of tribes or clans. Heian, however, would see Japan's trajectory—political, artistic, and social—diverge very far from the continental model, reverting to a distinct and separate culture after having assimilated and absorbed the Chinese cultural and institutional imports. This pattern—the digestion and reshaping of foreign institutions in ways that render them wholly Japanese—would be repeated again and again throughout Japanese history, right down into our own time.

While its economic and political foundations may have been eaten away during the centuries after its founding, Heian drove its cultural roots deep and hard—and they survived. The rituals of the Imperial Court and the hierarchy of the Heian aristocracy continued to serve as the ultimate locus of political legitimacy into the twentieth century. The aristocracy was finally abolished with the adoption of the present constitution in 1949, but Imperial ceremonies—coronations, weddings, funerals—continue to this day to be conducted by people wearing Heian court dress along lines first laid out in the Heian period to the accompaniment of Heian music which, together with that of the Coptic Church, forms the world's oldest continuously performed music.

The exquisite taste and refinement that still pervades much of Japanese life has its origins in the rarified aesthetics of the Heian court. Whenever the visitor to a Japanese inn finds a perfectly placed sprig of flowers in her room, receives an exquisitely wrapped gift delivered from a Japanese department store complete with a seasonal allusion in the flowing script that describes the product, or, for that matter, opens the door to a Japanese automobile with its clean lines and manic attention to the surface finish, she is catching a faint echo from that tiny cluster of beauty- and form-obsessed aristocrats of a millennium ago.

And that, of course, is perhaps the ultimate reason why Heian matters: its artistic legacy. Not much of the architecture survives—the breathtaking *Byōdō-in*, the temple depicted on the back of the 10 yen coin that first served as the pleasure pavilion of a great Fujiwara regent, is about the only fully intact building left from the period. That plus some statues and scrolls are pretty much all that remains to hint at the visual splendor of the Heian court.

The literature, however, is another matter. It has come down to us mostly complete. It consists of a vast body of poetry, a number of novels, and two of the greatest masterpieces of world literature—*The Pillow Book* and *The Tale of Genji*, both written by court ladies who were contemporaries. Indeed, as a body of writing, Heian's is unique in world history in that virtually all of it that matters was composed by women.

A LITERATURE WRITTEN BY WOMEN

The reason why women (or men writing under female pseudonyms) wrote all the Heian literature that matters to us goes back to that dichotomy between the continental import and the original Japanese—perhaps the oldest and most important central theme of Japanese history and culture. When Japan first encountered continental culture some three hundred years before the founding of *Heian-kyō*, Japan embarked on one of the world's most arduous exercises in forging a written language by forcing the round peg of Japanese into the square hole of written Chinese.

Fifth-century Chinese was already an entirely distributive language (i.e., a language in which the position of the word in the sentence determines its meaning). (English is also largely distributive, although we retain a few inflections—the "s" added to the third person singular—I walk, you walk, he walks.) It makes sense to write Chinese using intricate—and beautiful—ideograms or characters with each character standing for a single word.

But Japanese has a lot of inflections or "grammar"—different verb endings depending on who is saying what to whom and when they are saying it; "particles" that are vaguely similar to the case endings of Latin nouns. Even adjectives in Japanese get conjugated. Ideograph-based writing systems do not handle inflections well, which is why early ideographs in the Mediterranean were modified into the Phoenician and—later—the Greek and Roman alphabets. Something similar happened in India with the development of the Brahmi and Sanskrit scripts.

Representing the inflections of Japanese with Chinese characters was a horribly unwieldy matter. Eventually not one, but two alphabets would be developed, possibly under the example of Buddhism's Pali canon scriptures written with the Sanskrit alphabet. Technically, Japan's *kana*—*hiragana* and *katakana*—are syllabaries rather than alphabets since each letter represents a syllable rather than a sound. According to legend, the *kana* were invented by Kobo Daishi (774–835), a Buddhist monk who had been the abbot of the *Tōdai-ji*.[5]

While the *kana* were derived from the Chinese characters, they did not supplant them. In modern written Japanese, the *hiragana* is generally used for the inflections while most root words are written in Chinese characters. Meanwhile, words imported from Western languages such as English and French are written in *katakana*. Thus, modern written Japanese is a unique hybrid of ideograms and two syllabaries.

The *kana* were already in use in Heian times, but they had not yet been integrated with Chinese characters. Writing was either done in a terribly awkward and difficult modified Chinese known as *kambun* (literally, "Chinese sentences") or else entirely in *kana*. The former was used for formal documents and other "important" writing; the latter for more casual functions, including imaginative and intimate communication. Thus, *kambun* became "men's writing" in a manner of speaking and *kana* "women's writing." Since writing *kambun* essentially meant using a language one really couldn't speak, most of the *kambun* as literature is about as memorable as its medieval European counterpart written in ossified Latin—that is to say, not very. *Kana*, however, served as the written medium for the language in which people actually talked and thought; thus it is the *kana* literature that still speaks to us today. Its greatest examples were the two works written, respectively, by Sei Shōnagon and Murasaki Shikibu.

THE PILLOW BOOK AND THE TALE OF GENJI

Like all great literature, these two masterpieces manage to transcend their time and place and speak to certain universals in the human condition. *The Pillow Book* comes across at times as a startlingly contemporary take on human foibles while *The Tale of Genji*, in its concerns with the inner life and development of its principal characters counts, as the world's first genuine novel.

The two works depict a society in which aesthetics and "breeding" are essentially the only standards of value—and are intertwined; someone

---

5. Kobo Daishi is said, in the fashion of St. Patrick, to have travelled all over Japan leaving scores of new temples in his wake. He reportedly founded the great temple complex at Mt. Koya south of Osaka where some believe his spirit still resides.

with "good taste" is almost certainly high born (and the reverse). Lapses in taste—failing to coordinate properly the colors of one's various robes, poor handwriting or imagery in one's poetry, choosing an inappropriate type of paper for the season—are treated as major moral failings, indicative of inferior breeding.

Meanwhile, sexual promiscuity is not only tolerated, but expected. Sexual fidelity—not to mention chastity—are the exception and thought eccentric (at least until middle age when both men and women express a longing to "retire from the world" and "take the tonsure"). Lower-ranked people—women in particular—are entirely dependent on the benevolence of higher-ranked people (i.e., there was no way of "earning a living" save being in the service of a superior). Theirs is an economy essentially without money, and those who fall out of favor will end up not only lonely but probably destitute. The Pillow Book is a brilliant, sparkling series of jottings/ impressions, but in the Tale of Genji, Murasaki succeeds in getting inside the minds of her characters to describe what the social standards of the time do to them. In particular, as Ivan Morris pointed out in The World of the Shining Prince (a wonderful introduction both to the Genji in particular and to the life of the Heian court in general), Murasaki portrays jealousy as the "greatest of human torments" (to use Morris's phrase)—what one might expect in a society organized the way hers was.

It is this that makes the novel so accessible to contemporary readers even though the surface features of Murasaki's world are about as different from our own as one can imagine. Edmund White noted how Heian literature could speak to men who moved in rarefied gay circles in pre-AIDS Manhattan and Hollywood also characterized by patronage, sexual promiscuity, and the tyranny of taste (with looks substituting for breeding). And, of course, the psychological and emotional effects of dependency— depicted with such penetration by Murasaki—will particularly resonate with many women. Jealousy for so many of Murasaki's characters arises not simply from fears of losing affection and of one's own deteriorating attractiveness, but from a realization—articulated or not—that the loss of the superior's attention spells forfeiture of status. Religious themes permeate the novel, albeit implied rather than expounded. The workings of karma are inescapable. Murasaki and her contemporaries believed the best days of their world were behind them (they were correct about that—the political and economic foundations of the Heian aristocracy were even then being undermined; it would forfeit its power less than a century after her death). They attributed the decline to the *mappō*—the Buddhist belief they were living in the era of the forgetting of the Law.

THE COLLAPSE OF THE HEIAN ORDER AND THE COMING OF FEUDALISM

Heian fell for pretty much the same reasons that polities everywhere collapse. The tax base shrank to the point where leaders could not carry out the basic functions of government: maintaining order and an essential framework for economic activity. And they could not cope with the core political problem of fostering a military establishment sufficiently robust to provide security while at the same time keeping it under control.

The aristocrats clustered in Kyoto were supported by *shōen*—usually translated as "manors" or estates—around the country from which they expropriated most of the rice crop. Rice formed the basis of the Japanese economy, as it would continue to do until the mid-nineteenth century, with rice being traded for other essentials. Growing numbers of these *shōen* were ostensibly granted what we would call tax-exempt status by the Court.

The central government as a result could no longer collect sufficient revenues to pay for its upkeep. It even lost the ability to coin money, meaning it could not transform what revenues it did collect into a medium of exchange. Barter replaced coinage. The Fujiwara found themselves with neither the underlying wealth nor the mechanism to pay for the services of the warrior clans that had theretofore secured the base of their power. Order collapsed on both the small scale—brigands plaguing highways; robbers menacing the streets of the capital itself—and the large as the warriors increasingly took matters into their own hands. The Fujiwara lost control of Imperial succession. Emperors allied with first this warrior clan and then that would begin to meddle in politics. Or, to put it differently, warrior clans would usurp the traditional prerogative of the Fujiwara in manipulating the Court to advance their own clan interests.

The waning years of the Heian saw the rise of the institution of the "cloistered Emperor," an ostensibly retired emperor attempting to control matters from a monastery, and in some cases actually doing so (e.g.,

Emperor Shirakawa who stepped down from the Throne in 1087 but shoved aside the usual Fujiwara regents in order to direct political matters himself during the reigns of the next three emperors).

The warriors—already, by late Heian, forming a distinct class that would eventually come to be known as *samurai* or "those who serve"— plunged the country into ever-wider civil wars, ostensibly over such matters as Imperial succession, but actually over power and control. The culminating Gempei War saw the two greatest of the military clans— the Taira (or *Heike*, using the Chinese reading of the characters) and the Minamoto (or *Genji*)—embroiled in a kind of epic struggle that would do for Japan what the War of the Roses did for Britain, ushering in a new political-cum-military order while serving as a source for innumerable plays, scrolls, epics, and other takes on the events by artists in various genres.

The iconic account of this war, the *Tale of the Heike*, is, together with the *Tale of Genji,* considered the cornerstone of Japanese literature. But while the *Genji* may be a sort of eleventh-century *Récherche du temps perdu*, the *Heike* resembles an *Iliad* or a *Song of Roland*—a vast epic of military derring-do, complete with valor, friendship, betrayal, and tragedy. Indeed, for sheer dramatic power and pathos, it would be hard to top the culminating scene of the penultimate chapter set at the decisive March 1185 battle of Dan no Ura as a boy emperor and his grandmother die while attempting to cast the sacred Imperial regalia into the waves. The battle took place in the straits of Shimonoseki that separate Japan's main island of Honshu from Kyushu. The Taira (i.e., *Heike*) at first seemed to have the upper hand until one of their generals betrayed them, revealing to the Minamoto the ship carrying the 6-year-old Emperor Antaku and his grandmother. She was the widow of the great Taira clan leader Taira no Kiyomori, who had been the architect of their power and the first warrior or *bushi (samurai)* effectively to become the ruler of Japan. The account of his rise and fall forms the heart of the *Tale of the Heike* and with the death of his widow and grandson, the ruin of all he had done for his clan was complete.

Significantly, the epic takes as its title the name of the losing side. One of the hoariest of Japanese cultural archetypes is the noble loser who fights on against hopeless odds, sustained only by loyalty and the purity of his devotion to the cause for which he is dying. Western movie audiences were treated to a dose of this with the film *The Last Samurai*, very loosely based on a famous incident in the late nineteenth century that saw a kind of last stand of the old feudal order. The sentiment is not completely foreign to Americans despite our adulation of winners; the career of Robert E. Lee fits the Japanese "noble loser" stereotype pretty closely, although, as Ivan Morris pointed out, if Lee had wanted to make it safely into the realm of Japanese immortal heroes, he probably would have done better to have died at Appomattox rather than living on into dignified old age.

Thus, while the "noble loser" archetype may not be limited to Japan, it has a particular hold over the Japanese imagination—sometimes to rather dark ends; *vide* the young *kamikaze* pilots sent in the waning days of the Second World War to certain death in fruitless attempts to forestall the inevitable. The *Tale of the Heike* does not end with the destruction of the Taira at Dan no Ura, but follows the tragic denouement of the general who won the battle—Minamoto Yoshitsune, younger brother of the Minamoto clan leader Yoritomo. Yoshitsune is depicted in innumerable plays, novels, and pictures as a slight, even effeminate boy who gains the affection and loyalty of the warrior Benkei after besting him in a fencing match. Benkei forms the original model for another enduring Japanese cultural archetype: the strong, dogged fighter—not much for words or any overt expression of emotion, but with a great heart and a fierce, dogged loyalty. Yoshitsune, meanwhile, is the archetypal doomed *bishōnen* or beautiful boy who dies young precisely because of his purity and virtue (significantly, in Kabuki performances, Yoshitsune is usually played by an *onnagata*, or actor who specializes in female roles). The relationship between the two forms one of the great romances of Japanese culture. After his glorious victory at Dan no Ura, Yoshitsune attracts the resentment and suspicion of his brother, the clan leader Yoritomo, who is quick to do away with anyone posing a potential threat to his own power. Yoshitsune is chased the length and breadth of Japan by Yoritomo's minions; Yoshitsune is abandoned by practically all his allies, except of course for Benkei. (In one heart-rending scene, repeatedly staged in Noh and Kabuki dramas and ultimately in a film of Kurosawa Akira, Benkei is forced to beat Yoshitsune in order to maintain the latter's disguise as a porter. This is enough to convince Yoritomo's police that the porter could not possibly be Yoshitsune.) The two are finally hunted down and trapped in a remote castle in the far north; Benkei singlehandedly keeps hordes of soldiers at bay while Yoshitsune commits ritual suicide with his wife and daughter inside. No soldier dares approach Benkei; like Boromir in the *Lord of the Rings*, he finally totters over dead from innumerable arrows. Yoritomo, yet another archetype—the cynical, scheming politician who will do anything and betray anyone to grab power—becomes the first ruling shogun of Japan.

It has become impossible to separate myth from history in all this. While these people all certainly existed, many of the exploits attributed to Yoshitsune and Benkei are clearly fanciful. Yoshitsune probably was an able commander, but he was almost surely not an angelic-looking youth with supernatural fencing skills (in certain Kabuki plays, Yoshitsune defeats Benkei at their first encounter by waving his fan in the air). Yoritomo was, however, just as nasty as he is often made out—killing off so many potential rivals that his line ended with his sons. He did, however, understand how to seize and hold power. For the first time in Japanese history, power would be exercised far from the traditional center of Japanese civilization in and around the Yamato plain where Nara sits. Yoritomo had made the town of Kamakura in the distant, wild east his base. Surrounded on three sides by steep mountains with a narrow opening to the sea, Kamakura seemed not only impregnable, it formed an excellent location for controlling access to Japan's largest plain, the Kanto. Yoritomo would start the process that would see the center of Japanese political and economic gravity shift from the areas in and around the Yamato plain in the west to the Kanto plain in the east where modern Tokyo is located. And he would create the institution that would control Japan for much of the next seven centuries—the Shogunate.

THE SHOGUNS

The barbarians of the title *Sei-i Tai Shō Gun* (barbarian-subduing generalissimo) were an aboriginal people known as the Emishi, or, later, Ainu who are related to the tribal peoples living around the Sea of Okhotsk. During the early centuries of Japan's existence as a nation, the Japanese shared their archipelago with the Emishi, gradually pushing them north and off the main island of Honshu altogether, where they mixed with the Ainu (what is Emishi and what is Ainu is still debated by anthropologists). Small groups of Ainu continue to exist today on the northern island of Hokkaido—not fully incorporated into Japan proper until the late nineteenth century. Outside of Hokkaido however, little trace remains of the Emishi or Ainu save for some place names (whenever the "p" or "b" sound crops up in the middle of a place name—Sapporo/Beppu—you probably have an Ainu or Emishi root) and some physical characteristics, particularly among people in northern Japan (more round eyes and hirsute men than you would find in China, Korea, or Mongolia) that point unmistakably to intermarriage in the past.

During the Nara and early Heian periods, however, the Emishi still represented a significant military challenge. Generals dispatched by the Court to deal with them were styled *Sei-I Tai Shō Gun*, and that was the title Yoritomo took for himself after he had effectively seized control of the entire country. Rather than replace the emperor and occupy the Throne, he set up what amounted to a second court in Kamakura—a court whose political legitimacy still theoretically rested on Imperial appointment. But in the manner of the founders of Nara who had cemented their power by commissioning a series of temples culminating in the great Buddha of *Tōdai-ji*, so the Shogunate at Kamakura would build its own temples and its own great Buddha, and, as their predecessors had done, consolidate financial control of the country.[6]

The parallels between the Imperial and shogunal courts even extended to matters of real vs. titular power. Just as Nara and Heian emperors rarely ruled in anything but name, real power on Yoritomo's death in 1199 passed not to his sons but to his wife Masako and her family, the Hojo, who established what amounted to a hereditary regency. In fact, Hojo Masako was arguably the single most politically powerful woman in Japanese history; she effectively ruled the country until her own death in 1225; she acquired the nickname *ama-shō-gun*, or nun-shogun (she had ostensibly taken the tonsure after her husband died). Thanks to the series of murders, executions, and betrayals begun by Yoritomo, the Minamoto line died out after Yoritomo and his two sons; the remaining Kamakura shoguns were figureheads selected by the Hojo from Fujiwara relatives or Imperial princes.

THE MONGOL INVASIONS, THE FALL OF KAMAKURA, AND THE ASHIKAGA SHOGUNATE

In 1274, the Shogunate confronted the greatest external challenge in Japan's history to date as Kublai Khan, grandson of the great Mongol warrior Genghis and the first Emperor of the Yuan or Mongol dynasty in China,

---

6. The Buddha image the Shogunate commissioned is the famous open-air statue that appears in all the tourist posters; the surrounding temple was washed away by a tsunami in 1498.

launched an invasion of Japan. Kublai Khan had already turned Korea into a vassal state and was mopping up the last resistance from the Southern Song dynasty in China. The first invasion of Japan failed, partly because of a great storm that sank much of the invading fleet (scholars today believe that the fleet might have withstood the storm had it been less hastily constructed—many of the boats were river craft not properly equipped for conditions at sea). But Kublai Khan would not give up so easily. After destroying the capital of the Southern Song in 1276 and eliminating the last of Chinese resistance to Mongol rule, he turned his attention again to Japan in 1281, this time dispatching two great fleets—one from Korea, as before, and one from China itself. They were to meet on Iki Island off the northern coast of Kyushu, and from there attack the Japanese main islands.

In the meantime, however, the Shogunate had been making preparations for a second invasion. A great wall had been built around Hakata Bay where the city of Fukuoka now sits and warriors mobilized throughout the country. They were able to harass the invaders using small craft and were again helped by a great storm that sank much of the invading fleet, stranding the tens of thousands of Kublai Khan's soldiers who had already landed. Cut off from sources of supply and reinforcements, most of them perished in the ensuing battles—Mongol casualties approached 100,000 men.

The defeat of the Mongol invasions had great repercussions—in the wider world, of course, since the Japanese punctured the myth of Mongol invincibility—but also in Japan itself. The events reinforced the notion of the Japanese-qua-Japanese; the great storms that had twice destroyed the invading fleets were labelled *kamikaze*, literally divine wind, a name that would be used again for the suicide bombers in the waning days of the Second World War. Most Japanese believed that the gods had indeed intervened to protect their country; among other things, Shinto shrines that had pawned land saw it returned at cost in gratitude for the seeming efficacy of the endless rounds of prayers they had made.

Prominent warriors who had fought for the Shogunate requested the usual rewards of land for their valor in battle, but the Shogunate had no lands to give them; its resources had been stretched to the limit in mounting the defenses. Discontent festered and factionalism increased, again much of it involving Imperial succession. For the only time in Japanese history, rival Imperial courts were established with succession at first alternating between the two before the arrangement broke down, leading to competing claims and open warfare. The most ambitious and able emperor of the times, Go-Daigo, is considered the founder of one of the lines, known as the Southern Court since Go-Daigo and his direct successors removed themselves from Kyoto and reigned from the hills of Yoshino some miles to the south. Much of this was linked to the declining reach of Kamakura. Go-Daigo had chafed against the power of the Hojo family and dispatched his ally, the general Nitta Yoshisada, to attack the city in 1333. The supposedly impregnable city fell to Nitta's onslaught; the leaders of the Hojo and their retainers—some 850 men—committed mass suicide and with it the end of the first of the ruling shogunates.

But in a fashion that was becoming typical, Nitta did not live to see his followers take power. He was defeated by another ambitious warrior, Ashikaga Takauchi, who proceeded to turn against the Emperor Go-Daigo, promote the rival Northern Imperial line, and establish the second of the three ruling shogunates—the Ashikaga or Muromachi Shogunate, named for the district of Kyoto where the Ashikaga set up their shogunal court. The successors of Emperor Go-Daigo renounced their rival claim to the Throne in 1392 and Japan was again ruled from a single capital—Kyoto—if indeed Japan could be said to be ruled from a single place. For behind this gaudy panorama of warriors, betrayals, sieges, battles, rival courts, and interminable struggles over both Imperial and shogunal succession, Japan was becoming a feudal country where real power was increasingly exercised by regional war lords rather than a central court or courts.

JAPAN'S "FEUDALISM"

There is more at stake in the designation "feudal" than simple semantics. The proper interpretation of these years of Japanese history became a fateful intellectual battle ground in the twentieth century, both in and outside Japan. Nationalist historians saw in the attempts of Emperor Go-Daigo to "restore" real power to the Throne a precedent for the Imperial system as they hoped it would evolve in Japan's modern period.[7] Meanwhile, much of Japan's intellectual establishment was in the thrall

---

7. Indeed, in 1911 an Imperial decree pronounced the Southern Court the legitimate line while emperors of the Northern Court were retrospectively labeled pretenders, creating some awkwardness when a man later appeared claiming direct descent from the Southern Court and arguing he had a greater claim to the Throne than Emperor Showa—or Hirohito as he is still known in the West—who traced his ancestry to the Northern Court.

of a particularly hidebound theoretical Marxism that postulated a priori a feudal period before any transition to capitalism could occur. Rivals schools argued whether early twentieth-century Japan had or had not yet undergone a complete capitalist transformation—one school arguing that feudal remnants were sufficiently strong to preclude an imminent socialist revolution—but both accepted that a feudal period had indeed occurred.

Anti-Marxist Western scholars led by Harvard Professor Edwin Reischauer (US ambassador to Japan under Presidents Kennedy and Johnson) agreed, but with a novel twist. Storming Cold War intellectual barricades in full battle cry against Marxist thinking, they argued that Japan was the only place in the world outside Europe that had experienced genuine feudalism; that Marx was thus wrong in postulating feudalism as a universal stage of human development, and that Japan's feudalism, far from being a harbinger of an ultimate socialist revolution, helped explain why Japan had, uniquely to that point among non-Western countries, become a fully developed industrial power. Implicit in this analysis was the notion that the end-point of Japan's historical trajectory would not be a Marxist utopia but liberal capitalism along American lines.

Both the Japanese Marxists and their intellectual opponents in the United States were correct that during the centuries after the collapse of the Heian order, Japan evolved a political setup that in some key respects did resemble European feudalism. In both systems, much of the power that determined what actually happened rested with warrior lords who controlled fiefs or domains; the lords in turn granted tenure over tracts of land in their fiefs to vassals who repaid the lords with pledges of service. The land was actually worked by peasants/serfs who were legally bound to the land and theoretically could not leave it (although in practice many did). The lords themselves pledged allegiance to monarchs of varying real power, although this allegiance—at least until the founding of the Tokugawa Shogunate in 1603—was both tenuous and fluid. A legitimizing spiritual power existed in parallel with the temporal; this supposedly spiritual power would also exercise some degree of temporal power.

In Europe, the lords were usually titled dukes, their allegiance to the Hapsburgs, the Capetians, the Plantagenets, or whomever could shift, while spiritual power rested with the Church. In Japan, the lords were called *daimyō*, their fiefs or domains were known as *han*, the "monarch" to whom they pledged nominal allegiance was the shogun, and spiritual/legitimizing power was held by the emperor.

Japan's feudal system had its formal beginnings in the dispatch by the Kamakura Shogunate of warriors known as *shugo* to supplement or replace the provincial governors that had traditionally been appointed by the Imperial Court. Unlike the governors of old, the *shugo*—or *shugo daimyō* as they came to be called—stayed in place and established in the old provinces what amounted to small kingdoms or *han*. Although these *han* were abolished in the late nineteenth century, borders redrawn, and the new units labeled "prefectures," consciousness of the original *han* remains strong in Japan. (One does not, for example, speak of the Kochi dialect but rather the Tosa dialect, Tosa being the name of the *han* that modern Kochi Prefecture replaced.) Most of Japan's regional capitals—Sendai, Hiroshima, Kochi, Kagoshima, Fukuoka—got their start as the *han* seats of their respective *daimyō*.

As the Muromachi period proceeded, the nominal authority of the Ashikaga shoguns shrank to the point that it scarcely extended beyond Kyoto and its surroundings. Particularly after the Onin War of 1467–77—a conflict that began ostensibly over shogunal succession and would culminate in the near complete destruction of Kyoto—the country degenerated into nearly continuous civil conflict as first this ambitious *daimyō* and then that attempted to expand the borders of his *han* or to bring other *daimyō* under his control.

Yet for all this terrible conflict, Japan's "medieval period" as the Kamakura and Muromachi shogunates are often known, was a time of cultural brilliance. Much of what we think of as Japan's "high culture"—Kamakura period sculpture with its startling realism, the Noh drama, the great ink paintings of the school of Shubun and Sesshu, the prototypical Japanese garden, the tea ceremony, and some of the most magnificent achievements in Japanese architecture—date from this era. And much of this brilliance, unlike that of the Heian period that preceded it or the Edo period that would follow, came in response to external stimulus—first from China and then from the West.

CULTURE AND RELIGION UNDER FEUDALISM

Traditionally, historians posited a sharp divide between the *kuge* or nobility-centered culture of the Heian period and that of the *bushi* ("fighting men") or *samurai* ("those who serve") who wrested political power from the Court with the establishment of the Kamakura Shogunate. But as with all supposed historical transitions, it probably seemed far less clear-cut to those who lived through it. Well before the end of the Heian, independent power centers had begun to appear in the provinces, and as we have seen, issues of Imperial succession and the status of the new power centers in the traditional legitimizing hierarchy continued to loom large after power had supposedly shifted to the shogun and the *daimyō*.

The same could be said of culture. The cultural hegemony of Kyoto continued unchecked; indeed it would not be seriously challenged until the founding of the Tokugawa Shogunate in 1603 and the rise of Edo, now known as Tokyo. But culture was nonetheless changing. While the *bushi* or *samurai* may have professed the most austere and ruthlessly militarized ethic—one that held loyalty and honor to be the ultimate standards of value and physical courage the highest virtue—they saw no conflict between this ethic and the inherited aestheticism of the Heian. Perhaps no warriors in history were ever so obsessed with the quality of their dress or their handwriting.

But just as aestheticism made its mark on the warrior, so did martial values begin to imbue Japanese aesthetics. The extravagance, brilliance, display, and—dare one say it?—essentially feminine ethos of the Heian arts was gradually transformed into a masculine (or at least martial) restraint, frugality, and concern with using the arts to penetrate to the essence of things—ink, paper, earth, rock, water, wood, and the unadorned sound of a lone flute. The rock garden with its handful of asymmetrically placed boulders and raked sand; the Noh theater with its masked actors, stylized gestures, and "set" of a single great pine; the tea ceremony held in a rustic hut with tea served in aged, cracked earthenware, the few splashes of ink on white, absorbent paper used to evoke the passage of the seasons—these typify the aesthetics of the Muromachi period.

Perhaps the most important catalyst in this aesthetic transformation was a Chinese import: Zen Buddhism. The Ashikaga shoguns had established relations with the new Ming dynasty (1368–1644) in China; paradoxically, the relations reflected a breakdown in the general order in Japan. Japanese pirates had become an increasing problem for China; the devastation they caused and the fear they invoked on the Chinese coast have been compared to terror of the Viking raids in Europe. The Ming appealed to the shogunate for assistance in controlling the pirates and for the only time in Japanese history, a Japanese ruler, Shogun Ashikaga

Yoshimitsu, would specifically declare himself a subject of the Chinese emperor and formally involve Japan in the Chinese tributary system. (Under this system, outlying states in China's cultural orbit pledged fealty to the Chinese Imperial Court with exports to China labelled "tribute.") Wealth and trade were undoubtedly Kyoto's underlying motives, not any desire to turn Japan into a Chinese satellite. But among other results—including the neo-Confucianism that would help shape Japanese political theory and governing ethos in subsequent centuries—was the introduction of Chán Buddhism, or, as it would be pronounced in Japanese, *Zen*.

Since Buddhism had taken root in Japan some eight centuries earlier, the religion had to all intents and purposes become Japan's faith, even though the indigenous Shinto did survive, albeit with liturgies and beliefs that were by then clearly derivative of Buddhist rites. But like religions everywhere that grow away from their founding impulses, institutional Japanese Buddhism had become top-heavy with doctrine, clergy, hierarchy, and worldly power.

Perhaps in reaction, two new strains began to win converts. The first group might be termed "faith-based" doctrines—so-called Pure Land sects introduced from China in the thirteenth century, and the Nichiren school launched by the Japanese monk of that name at roughly the same time. These sects stressed the personal faith of the believer. The obvious parallels with evangelical Protestantism extended to the classes of people attracted to them: merchants and other lower-class urbanites that had begun to cluster in cities such as Kyoto and Osaka in response to growing economic opportunity stemming from trade with the continent.[8]

Zen was the second of the strains that took root next to the Buddhism that had been inherited from Nara and Heian; rather than faith, it emphasized personal achievement of salvation or enlightenment through meditation and mental training aimed at ridding the mind of conceptual categories that stood in the way of an intuitive grasp of the essence of reality. The stress on arduous discipline and mental training had immediate appeal to the warrior/samurai class. Indeed Zen would effectively become the samurai religion.

---

8. Indeed, Nichiren's institutional descendants today—primarily the *Soka Gakkai* and other so-called "new religions"—still find their believers among groups similar to those attracted to fundamentalist Christian sects in the West: small shopkeepers and other members of the lower middle class not affiliated with a major company or bureaucracy.

The influence of Zen on Japan's high culture can hardly be exaggerated. Zen values—in particular, a stripping down to essentials together with sudden shifts in perspective aimed at triggering insight—came to permeate Japanese aesthetics and would continue to do so into the present day.

THE COMING OF THE EUROPEANS

Thanks to Marco Polo's mention of a far-off land where gold was said to be so plentiful that the temples and palaces were all covered with it, Europeans had, by the fourteenth century, heard of *Chipangu* (the Chinese pronunciation, from which our English word for the country stems). The reverse was not true, however, until a group of Portuguese landed on the island of Tanegashima, south of Kyushu, in 1543. Not knowing who these people were, the Japanese dismissed them at first as savages: *Namban-jin*, or Southern Barbarians. After all, they had arrived from somewhere to the south, they lacked the defining mark of any civilized person throughout East and Southeast Asia—the ability to read and write Chinese characters—they smelled bad, and they babbled on about some weird religion involving a god who had been tortured to death on a wooden cross.

But opinions changed quickly. Whatever the Japanese may have thought about the bathing habits of the Westerners, they couldn't help but be impressed by their ships, their navigational skills, and above all by their firearms. In the tumult of the times, the missionary efforts of the new foreigners fell on far more fertile ground than their first reception might have suggested. The Jesuit missionaries who followed the Portuguese traders six years later were subtle, adroit men with decades of proselytizing experience behind them, able to hold their own in any parrying with the indigenous Buddhist clergy. Their leader, St. Francis Xavier, had been one of the founders of the Jesuit order and is remembered as the great missionary to Asia; he had spread the Catholic faith from Goa to Malacca to Macao and finally to Japan. Thanks to a combination of Jesuit skill, the perennial Japanese fascination with anything novel, and a particularly favorable environment for a new faith—the near constant warfare and the resulting social and political tumult—within three decades of St. Francis' arrival, as much as a third of the population of the western island of Kyushu may have converted to Christianity. Meanwhile, up north, from the newly established *han* capital of Sendai, the *daimyō* lord Date Masamune dispatched an envoy to Rome. His craftsmen built a ship modeled on a wrecked Spanish vessel that had washed ashore near Sendai and sent it across the Pacific to Acapulco. Date's envoy Hasekura Tsunenaga crossed Mexico overland and then took another sea voyage from Veracruz to Europe where he was granted an audience with Pope Paul V. The crystal candlesticks given by the pope can still be viewed in the treasure house of a temple in the seaside town of Matsushima near Sendai—crystalline evidence, one might say, that Hasekura got back home.

Crystal candlesticks surely made an impression in a country that had never known glass, but that was hardly the end of the story. A veritable mania for all things Western swept Japan. A whole genre of painting—*Namban-e* or pictures of the southern barbarians—depicted the exotic foreigners in their pantaloons and strange helmets, and many Japanese began to copy the fashions. Dishes were adopted—*tempura* almost certainly stems from Portuguese cooking; before that time, the Japanese had never eaten deep-fried foods; indeed the word itself probably comes from the Portuguese word for time, *tempore*. The Portuguese influence extended into the language itself; the Japanese word for thank you, *arigato*, may have come from the Portuguese *obbligado*, and the Portuguese roots of terms such as *pan* for bread are obvious.

But the most important import was surely firearms. The Westerners arrived just as Japan's feudal period was irretrievably degenerating into incessant warfare. With the near-total collapse of Kyoto's ability to impose order following the Onin War of 1467, power shifted decisively away from a feeble Ashikaga Shogunate to the strongest of the *daimyō*. A naked and prolonged scramble ensued, culminating in successive campaigns by three great lords who succeeded finally in reimposing central authority on the entire country, thereby laying the foundations of the modern Japanese state. The crucial factor in their rise lay in their superior grasp of the military implications of firearms.

THE REUNIFICATION OF JAPAN

The names of the three lords who ended the fragmentation of Japan's feudal period are known to every Japanese schoolchild. The first, Oda Nobunaga (1534–1582), was born near present-day Nagoya as the son of a minor lord.

On the death of his father, he quickly grabbed his father's domain, using the hoary Japanese tradition of arranging for his rivals to be killed, including his younger brother. Indeed, Oda Nobunaga stands out even in a notoriously harsh age for his savagery and brutality. But there was no question of his military genius. Setting out on a course of conquest, he soon brought neighboring provinces under his rule and set his sights on Kyoto itself. He had no time for the elaborate pageantry of the traditional battle array that saw gorgeously attired samurai introduce themselves to their enemies before taking the field. Nobunaga understood that since the muskets of the era required so much time to reload, they had to be fired in sequence rather than simultaneously to maximize their effectiveness, and accordingly organized his soldiers in ranks. With his superior command of the use of firearms, Nobunaga's two-decade march to power culminated in the destruction of his most formidable enemies, the Takeda clan, in the pivotal 1575 battle of Nagashino. Nagashino suggests parallels to Agincourt in its demonstration of the transforming effects of a new technology on traditional warfare; in his 1980 film *Kagemusha*, Kurosawa Akira would stage one of the most famous battle scenes in cinematic history with a re-enactment of this battle.

Nobunaga's fascination with West was not limited to firearms. He befriended the Jesuit missionaries who mistakenly thought him the king of Japan (a painting of Nobunaga by a Jesuit is the first depiction in Western art of a Japanese); extensive records testify to their high regard for his military genius and skill as a political leader. There were even rumors that he was a secret Christian; although this is unlikely, the rumors may have been fed by his hatred of the traditional Buddhist establishment; as mentioned above, he finally and completely broke the power of the established Buddhist hierarchy, burning to the ground the great temple complex of *Enryaku-ji* on Mt. Hiei that overlooked Kyoto. In characteristic style, Nobunaga had every last one of its monks hunted down and killed.

Nobunaga's historical significance lies primarily in his destruction of the vestiges of so much of the traditional power structure. He seized Kyoto, emasculated all the remaining powers of the shogun, and eliminated much of the residual political influence of the Imperial Court, such as the adjudication of land disputes among major temples. By 1582, he had brought under his direct control about one-third of Japan, appeared to be intent on assuming the title of shogun for himself, and had, in classic fashion, begun to interfere in Imperial succession. But one of his vassals, Akechi

Mitsuhide, turned on him. Trapped in the precincts of one of Kyoto's temples, Nobunaga took his life in the way that had become established for warriors: disembowelment (*seppuku,* or, more crassly, *harakiri*—literally, stomach slitting).

Akechi arranged for an Imperial appointment as shogun. The appointment lasted all of thirteen days before Nobunaga's followers exacted their revenge. Chief among them was Toyotomi Hideyoshi, the second of the three great unifiers. Hideyoshi's origins could not have been more humble; he was the son of one of Nobunaga's foot soldiers, but his strategic brilliance and drive soon made him one of Nobunaga's closest advisors (later he would invent exalted origins for himself and change his original surname to the court title Toyotomi, or Bountiful Minister). Hideyoshi was Nobunaga's equal in his mastery of military tactics, but greatly his superior as a politician; he understood how much more effective honey could be than vinegar in catching flies. Instead of Nobunaga's reflexive resort to brutality and intimidation, Hideyoshi co-opted opponents and thereby succeeded in completing Nobunaga's conquest of Japan. In the process, he essentially laid the institutional foundations of the modern Japanese state. He set up sharp divides between samurai and peasant while specifying the duties and living arrangements for both. He granted *daimyō* privileges only on the basis of assurances of absolute loyalty, and instituted a nation-wide survey of all land under cultivation with a view towards a unified tax system that would translate all income into rice equivalents. He came as close to absolute power over the country as any single individual had ever enjoyed to that time.

But as if determined to serve as an object demonstration of Lord Acton's observation that absolute power corrupts absolutely, Hideyoshi began to exhibit delusions of megalomania. Suspicion and paranoia replaced his earlier magnanimity; with the birth of his son, he turned on his nephew who had formerly been designated his heir and had the poor man's entire household of thirty-one people down to small children publicly executed. He had himself named Imperial Regent and then *Taiko* (the title traditionally given to retired regents) rather than just Shogun. He launched two invasions of Korea with the announced intention of moving on to China, overthrowing the Ming dynasty, and placing himself on the Throne in Beijing's Palace of Celestial Purity. He sent letters to places such as Manila announcing his intention to conquer the entire world and suggesting to the Spanish governor that if he wanted to avoid the destruction of his provinces, he had best rush to Kyoto forthwith to perform obeisances at Hideyoshi's feet.

Hideyoshi's overseas adventures had prosaic as well as megalomanical-cum-romantic motivations; with all of Japan under his control, he needed to give his restless soldiers fresh places to pillage. But the invasions set a new standard for savagery that shocked both the Koreans and the Chinese and poisoned Japan's image in these two countries for centuries.[9] Meanwhile, at home, Hideyoshi forced the emperor to endure his execrable performances as a Noh dancer and transformed the austere rite of the tea ceremony into gaudy occasions for display. He fell out with Sen no Rikyu, the great master of tea who had previously been his cultural mentor and friend, forcing him to commit *seppuku*.

The most astute of Hideyoshi's lieutenants—Tokugawa Ieyasu—managed to stay clear of the Korean entanglements while busying himself with the consolidation of his control over the provinces of eastern Japan that he had been awarded by Hideyoshi as a reward for his role in a critical battle. These provinces included the great Kanto plain, the largest area in Japan suitable for the cultivation of rice, thus providing the economic base essential for political power. Choosing the small fishing village of Edo at the southern end of the plain as the site for his castle, Ieyasu emerged victorious in the inevitable struggles following Hideyoshi's death. He destroyed most of his rivals at the crucial battle of Sekigahara in 1600, had first himself and then his son proclaimed shogun, and eliminated the final threat to his rule in 1615 by laying siege to Osaka castle—then the greatest fortress in Japan (if not the world; historical records demonstrate unbounded admiration by the Jesuits for Japanese castle architecture and ready acknowledgment that it surpassed anything in contemporary Europe). Hideyoshi's son Hideyori, whom Ieyasu had pledged to support on Hideyoshi's death, had taken refuge in the castle after showing signs that he might grow into as astute a leader as his father had been; among other things, Hideyori had begun manipulating the Imperial Court to accumulate titles. Ieyasu, though, soon put a stop to that, issuing what amounted to orders that the Court devote itself to ceremony and protocol and not proclaim titles and promotions for

---

9. The effect of Hideyoshi's invasion of Korea would be far greater on that country than on Japan itself. Korea's Yi dynasty collapsed and, in many ways, the country never completely recovered from the carnage and devastation that Hideyoshi would leave in his wake. The Ming came to Korea's aid, but the strain on Ming resources probably contributed to the fall of the Ming a few decades later at the hands of the Manchus.

samurai and *daimyō*—that would be up to the Castle. Executing Hideyori and burning Osaka Castle to the ground was, of course, a betrayal (Ieyasu's forces weakened the defenses with a Trojan horse type of trick; they had agreed under cover of an ostensible truce to help reinforce the moats and instead filled them in). But it was to be the last such betrayal. The siege of Osaka Castle marked the end of a half-millennium of near constant warfare. Ieyasu turned Edo into what in a few decades became the largest city in the world and founded the regime named after him: the Tokugawa Shogunate. This regime gave Japan two and half centuries of peace and drew a thick curtain around the country that both separated it from the rest of the world and provided cover for the incubation of the modern Japanese state.

FIGURE 2. Kitagawa Utamaro *"Lovers in the Upstairs Room of a Teahouse"*. © Trustees of the British Museum, courtesy of the British Museum.

2

The Incubation of the Modern Japanese State

The beginning of Japan's modernization is usually dated to 1868. In that year, the last of the shoguns would formally "return power" to the Throne, ending Japan's two-and-a-half century experiment in quasi-isolation from the rest of the world. All but the most deliberately blind had, by that point, come to accept the need for radical change. Either Japan would be colonized by one or more of the Western powers or it must somehow muster the political will to overhaul its economy and society. That was the only way it could hope to engage, on something of its own terms, a world transformed by the industrial revolution; removing itself from that world was no longer an option.

By the end of the nineteenth century, it appeared that Japan had succeeded. Only Thailand and Ethiopia could join Japan in boasting that they had eluded a European imperialism that had brought the entire rest of the non-Western world under its yoke. Japan's success, however, went much farther. It had become a major imperialist power in its own right, complete with overseas colonies, heavy industry, and a modern military. Alas, forty-five years later the long-term price of the country's "success" would turn out to be defeat in war and a loss of political independence that has never been fully recovered.

Neither Japan's seeming triumph in the nineteenth century nor the subsequent catastrophe of the twentieth can be understood without grasping something of how Japan evolved during the centuries of Tokugawa rule. This is why many historians see 1603—the formal establishment of the Tokugawa Shogunate—as an even more important watershed than 1868; that is why the Tokugawa years are typically classed as "early modern" rather than "medieval."

All such distinctions are to some extent arbitrary; continuities running through 1603 were just as many and just as important as those running through 1868. Indeed, the latter year certainly *looks* like more of a real break with the past, if only because Japan's leaders began dressing like Westerners, throwing up some Western style buildings, and grafting onto indigenous arrangements imported institutions with Western labels. But if one has to choose, 1603 is the more important date. That was the year Japan accepted the key defining characteristic of the modern state system: the notion that the politically legitimate use of force is the prerogative solely of *national* governments—or to put this in other words, that the political powers of the state should be manifest at the national rather than the sub-national (e.g., fiefdom/*han*) or supra-national (e.g., empire) level. Before 1603, the legitimate use of force and the organization of economic affairs were as much at the discretion of the *daimyō* in their *han* as they were that of the ostensible seats of national power in Court or Shogunate. But from that year on, there would be no existential challenge to the legitimacy of centralized national power until Douglas MacArthur disembarked in Yokohama to begin the American occupation of Japan. The one real transfer of power that occurred between 1603 and 1945—the replacement of the Shogunate by the Meiji oligarchy—was, significantly, dressed up as a restoration and took place in accordance with existing legal procedures.

The year 1603 is also critical because that was when Japan began deliberately removing itself from the broader currents of world history, currents that would carry European technology, science, institutions, and political ideologies around the globe. As a result, a Japan that in the sixteenth century measured up well against its European counterparts by the usual criteria of national power—military, political, technological, and economic—would, by the mid-nineteenth century, have fallen behind in certain key respects. But perhaps, by way of compensation, Japan's seclusion fostered development of a highly distinctive national culture—culture defined not simply as art, music, language, and literature but as the sum total of political, economic, and social institutions; a culture that was markedly and increasingly different not only from the cultures of the West but from those of its closest neighbors.

THE SECLUSION OF TOKUGAWA JAPAN

Isolation as such was not the goal of the Tokugawa shoguns. Their concerns were stability, order, and fortifying the foundations of their rule such that no challenge could be mounted. The conventional rubric of the Tokugawa period—*sakoku* or "isolated country"—has been disputed by recent historians who document continued and extensive trade and cultural contact with Korea and China during Tokugawa times. The Japanese elite during those years continued to look to China as a source of cultural inspiration; the official governing philosophy of the Shogunate was rooted in the conservative Neo-Confucian doctrine that had emerged in the late Song dynasty under the twelfth-century philosopher Zhu Xi with its stress on the importance of a proper ordering of society through hierarchy. Japan's later contempt for Korea as an inferior, backward nation was not much in evidence during the Tokugawa centuries. Seoul sent periodic lavish embassies to Edo while the Shogunate maintained a presence in the southern Korean port city of Pusan. If anything, Korea's physical and cultural proximity to China gave Korean literati, artists, and scholars a special cachet in Edo. Meanwhile, the Ryukyu Kingdom of Okinawa and its neighboring islands—then an independent entity, albeit acknowledging dual tributary relations with both Beijing and the Satsuma *han* of southern Kyushu—acted as an important conduit of trade between China and Japan.

The Shogunate sought to isolate Japan not from its neighbors, but from Europe and specifically from Europe's religion—"seclusion" is probably a better word than "isolation" to describe Japan's foreign relations during the Tokugawa period. Europeans had, to be sure, introduced guns into Japan and we have already noted the decisive effect the guns had on the civil wars of the sixteenth century. But the Japanese had quickly absorbed the technology and begun manufacturing their own firearms; they were soon copying European ships as well. Early seventeenth-century Japan was no Aztec Empire that could have been conquered by a handful of determined Spaniards. Even had Japan not been halfway around the world from Europe, it would have presented a formidable military challenge to a France, England, or Spain seeking to colonize the country, something the Europeans themselves recognized with their appreciation of Japan's castle architecture and the fighting quality of its samurai. The threat Europe represented was not technological or military—not at that time. It was ideological.

Speculation on whether Japan might, after all, have turned into a Christian country—and what could have flowed from that—is one of the more intriguing historical counterfactuals. The initial Japanese enthusiasm for Christianity was probably greater than that in any other Asian country, an enthusiasm that was reciprocated, *vide* St. Francis Xavier's famous comment that the Japanese were the finest non-Western people he had encountered. Early inroads by the Jesuit missionaries led the period after their arrival to be labeled "Japan's Christian century," and although their success lasted well short of a century, an observer of the time might reasonably have concluded that Japan was a candidate for full national conversion to Christianity.

Some believe that Oda Nobunaga's early death was a factor in the failure of Christianity in Japan, for Nobunaga had been fascinated by what he had learned from the Jesuits and was impressed by their demeanor and erudition; he was also, as we have seen, implacably hostile to the established Buddhist clergy. The persecution of Christianity only began with Hideyoshi's paranoia and culminated in the Tokugawa obsession with threats to stability. Admirers of Nobunaga include two of Japan's most influential living politicians—former prime minister Koizumi Junichiro, and Ozawa Ichiro, architect of the rise to power of the Democratic Party of Japan. They share the belief that Japan may have erred after Nobunaga, cutting itself off from so much of what would happen in subsequent centuries.

Whatever speculation one can make about a Japan in which Nobunaga survived another twenty years, the wars of religion in Europe played a central role in turning Japan's elite against Christianity. Hatreds between Protestant and Catholic precluded any conceivable joint front among competing Christian confessions. With the arrival of Protestant Dutch traders in the late sixteenth century anxious to grab a share of Portugal's theretofore lucrative hold on Japan's foreign trade, the Japanese were soon hearing how Jesuits and Dominicans formed the thin edge of Iberian imperialism, of the downfall of the Aztec and Incan empires—and, closer to home, of the colonization of Malacca, Macao, and the Philippines. Will Adams, the English captain of a Dutch ship that ran aground in Kyushu in 1600, turned out to be a particularly influential voice, becoming a confidante of both the first Tokugawa shogun, Ieyasu, and his son, Hidetada, the second Tokugawa shogun. As a Protestant in the service of the Dutch who had seen action in the defeat of the Spanish Armada, Adams offered a very different take on events in the wider world from that of the Jesuits. Ieyasu granted Adams a small fief and an official appointment; some 360 years after his death in 1620, he became the central figure in a best-selling pot-boiler of a historical novel complete with an American television mini-series based thereon ("Shogun").

Implacable Jesuit condemnation of pederasty also hurt efforts to convert Japan's elite to Christianity. Pederasty had become so institutionalized among the *daimyō* and the samurai that comparisons have been made with ancient Athens and Sparta; the practice drew the harshest denunciations from Jesuit missionaries, which in turn did not endear them to many among Japan's ruling elite.

The missionaries made their deepest inroads among ordinary people—downtrodden peasants who had neither the resources nor the inclination to indulge themselves with page boys, not to mention parry metaphysical speculations. The core Christian message of love, forgiveness, and the prospect of a better time in another world helped the religion spread like proverbial wildfire among people who had known little but misery and constant warfare. It was this that so alarmed the Shogunate; that and the idea implicit in the Christian message of an order independent of and transcending existing political arrangements. The notion that one could and should render separate forms of tribute to "Caesar" and to "God" struck Japan's guardians of its new regime as profoundly subversive.

This was not simply a matter of bigotry. The incessant warfare of the preceding centuries had made the right to rule the pre-eminent political question of the times—as it would indeed continue to be into our own era. While a greatly weakened and circumscribed Throne continued to serve as the ultimate token of political legitimacy, the claims of competing *daimyō* and other power centers had to be silenced if Japan was to know peace. This was accomplished not simply through displays of overwhelming force, although the Tokugawa would, over the course of three days, parade some 100,000 troops through the streets of Kyoto after the battle of Sekigahara to emphasize the total nature of their victory and the futility of further opposition. But shogunal officials obviously believed that overt intimidation was not enough. They encouraged the deliberate inculcation of an ideology that identified anything beyond the existing political order as a challenge to the very notion of legitimacy; a challenge they hoped to place beyond the pale as an offense against the natural order of things. This helps explain both the warm reception accorded Neo-Confucian doctrines and the zeal with which Japan's rulers attempted to stamp out any sign of Christian sympathies.

Japanese Christians found themselves subject to persecution of a ferocity that invites comparison with what took place in the Roman Empire before the conversion of Constantine. It was more than a simple ban on worship. All foreign missionaries were ordered out of the country on pain of death. The persecution would reach its peak in 1637 when tens of thousands of converts took refuge on the Shimabara peninsula near Nagasaki. Onerous new taxes played a role in what happened, but religious conviction formed the core of the rebellion against the Shogunate. The converts held out for months under the leadership of a charismatic young Christian, Amakusa Shiro. Their resilience paradoxically reinforced the Shogunate's belief that this was a dangerous religion that must be wiped out. With the fall of the castle where they had taken refuge, tens of thousands were slaughtered and tens of thousands more throughout the country hunted down and executed or forced to recant their faith.

In the succeeding decades, nothing so agitated shogunal officials as signs of Christian sympathies; anyone suspected thereof was required to perform ritual degrading of Christian symbols. Punishment for refusal was usually crucifixion. Nonetheless "hidden Christians" managed to survive for two and half centuries, secretly handing on their faith from generation to generation. In a final grim twist to the saga, the largest concentration of their descendants in Japan was wiped out in 1945 by the atomic bomb dropped on Nagasaki.

TOKUGAWA OBSESSION WITH ORDER
AND STABILITY

All Japanese were divided by birth into four classes: the samurai on top, followed by peasants, craftsmen, and merchants—the last, since they contributed nothing of tangible value, held to be largely parasitical.[1]

---

1. A fifth class of supposed untouchables also existed; these were people who engaged in ritually impure but necessary occupations—tanning, for example, or the disposal of the dead. Although class distinctions were formally abolished in the late nineteenth century, prejudice against the descendants of these people continued for some time and even lingers on today; they form one of the world's more interesting minority groups—their social and economic indicators display a

Each class had specific restrictions and obligations. Samurai, being the most obvious source of potential unrest, were required to pledge absolute fealty to their lords or *daimyō*. The *daimyō* or *han* system that had reached its organized culmination under Hideyoshi was left untouched. Already between them Nobunaga and Hideyoshi had destroyed most other power centers (the clerical establishment principal among them); Ieyasu finished the job by ending the Court's ability to make any kind of appointment involving the *daimyō* or samurai.

All of Japan save for those areas under direct control by the Shogunate (about a fifth of the country, albeit including some of the agriculturally richest land) plus small reserves for the Court and shrines and temples, were divided into *han* ruled by *daimyō*. But the *daimyō* were not equal.

The *han* that each *daimyō* ostensibly ruled varied enormously from what amounted to a handful of villages and fields to great provinces the size of small countries (e.g., the Maeda *han* on the Japan sea coast with its *han* seat at Kanazawa). Even more important was the relationship with the Tokugawa. Hereditary vassals of the Tokugawa (*fudai daimyō*)— typically, descendants of those who had fought alongside Ieyasu at Sekigahara—were awarded *han* near major routes that led to the great cities of the realm: Edo, Osaka, and Kyoto. Descendants of *daimyō* of the major *han* that had been established well before Sekigahara and who submitted to Tokugawa rule only thereafter were known as *tozama* or outside lords. They included the Date of Sendai, the Asano of Hiroshima, the Shimazu of Satsuma, and the Mori of Choshu. Rather than attempting to break the power of these great lords, Ieyasu had wisely co-opted them. Shogunate officials long suspected that if and when any challenge to Tokugawa rule occurred, it would come from one of these "outer" *han* or *tozama*. They were right about that—the Shogunate was finally overthrown by samurai who hailed from three of the outer *han*: Satsuma, Choshu, and Tosa (modern Kagoshima, Yamauchi, and Kochi prefectures). In the meantime, *tozama* were largely frozen out of positions in the ruling bureaucracy. Required to pass their youth in Edo, as adults they could spend only alternate years in their "home" castle towns, and while there, had to leave hostages in Edo. These measures effectively neutralized the *daimyō* lords themselves as sources of subversion. The men

divergence from those of the wider society similar to that of minorities in other places, but they are ethnically, religiously, and culturally indistinguishable from other Japanese.

from the outer *han* who came together to overthrow the Shogunate in the 1860s were lower ranking samurai, not their *daimyō* lords.

To be sure, the restrictions on where and how one could live were hardly limited to *daimyō*. The Shogunate maintained a network of spies and secret police throughout the country. Checkpoints studded the roads used by travelers. Sumptuary restrictions were imposed on every household in every class. Samurai had the theoretical right to cut down any member of the lower orders for any reason with the swords that only they were permitted to carry, and the samurai themselves could be ordered to commit *seppuku* (*hara-kiri*) for the tiniest signs of disloyalty to their lords. Members of the lower orders who violated any of myriad laws were subject to banishment or crucifixion, the latter being the one Christian import enthusiastically adopted by the authorities.

The Shogunate granted a monopoly on foreign trade to the Dutch East India Company ("VOC") as a reward for Dutch help in driving out the Catholics (Dutch ships had participated in the shelling of Shimabara). But VOC officials were confined to a small island in Nagasaki harbor and only allowed out on special occasions, including an annual visit to Edo to pay respects to the shogun. With this one exception, all contacts with the West were banned. Any Westerner found in Japan other than the officially approved Dutch were subject to execution—an increasingly sore point with the Western powers as the growth of whaling and other ocean-bound activities meant more seamen fleeing shipwrecks off the coasts of Japan. No Japanese who went farther abroad than the Ryukyu Islands was allowed to return home on pain of death, save for members of the occasional official missions to China and Korea.

Meanwhile, the firearms that had played such a critical role in the establishment of Tokugawa rule disappeared. Possession by all but a handful of shogunal officials became illegal and manufacturing ceased. One would have to look long and hard to find a similar case of a country deliberately turning its back on an important new military technology.

ECONOMIC AND SOCIAL CHANGE

The Shogunate wanted to lock into place forever the power relations that prevailed after the fall of Osaka Castle in 1615. Every member of society from the most despised untouchable all the way up to the emperor himself was supposed to occupy his or her specified niche in a complex hierarchy, bound by an intricate web of duties and obligations to others. But while the Tokugawas succeeded in creating a formal structure of power relations that lasted with very little modification for the 265 years of their rule, this formal structure masked almost continuous change.

True, Tokugawa Japan was a very oppressive place. Probably no large society in history before the coming of modern surveillance technologies experienced more pervasive repression. And the repression worked. For over two centuries the Shogunate confronted no serious domestic political challenge, while enjoying outstanding success in ferreting out and punishing deviance. Features of social control that are familiar today—mass media, "security theater" checkpoints at transportation hubs, plainclothes police busying themselves with what people are thinking—can be identified in embryo in Tokugawa Japan earlier than perhaps anywhere else on earth.

But all this repression did deliver one overwhelming benefit to Japan's people. At a time when Europe endured a trajectory of violence from the Thirty Years War to Waterloo while subjecting the rest of the planet to imperial rapacity, Japan basked in peace. That peace extended effectively to freedom from violent crime as well as freedom from marauding soldiers. The Tokugawa peasant may have been ruthlessly exploited in a political order that saw *han* and shogunal officials openly debating just how much they could squeeze from him before he would be unable to live; but he did not have to fear that bands of soldiers would seize his crops or burn down his hut. Urban craftsmen may have been packed into flimsy housing subject to fires so frequent they were known as "flowers of Edo," but the streets were probably safer than those of any contemporary city in the world.

Partly as a result, Japan's population nearly tripled to some thirty million people—pretty much the limit imposed by an essentially autarkic economy employing premodern agricultural practices. By the early eighteenth century, Edo boasted more than a million inhabitants, making it the largest city in the world, while Osaka and Kyoto had populations of, respectively, more than half a million and 300,000, comparable in size to contemporary London and Paris.

With this population growth came economic growth. Tokugawa thinking on economics saw agriculture (and fisheries) as the sole source of genuine wealth, but without understanding quite what they were doing, the Japanese during those centuries developed economic institutions that were as sophisticated as anything in contemporary Europe—in some cases, more so; arguably the first real futures market anywhere in the world, for example, grew up in Osaka in the network of warehouses where *daimyō* pledged their future rice crops for cash.

Tokugawa paranoia acted as the unwitting midwife for many of these institutions. Particularly important was *sankin kōtai*, or the requirement that the *daimyō* spend alternate years in Edo while leaving wives and children behind when they went back "home." The practice made Edo a great city, for it was not simply a seat of government with a single ruling court but a whole patchwork of "courts"—all of which had to be supplied with both necessities and luxuries. (Needless to say, *daimyō* felt they had to maintain appearances; Edo literature is rife with tales of the households of poorer *daimyō* from small *han* reduced to penury in order to keep up with what is expected.) In modern Tokyo, one can still trace the pattern of many of the old *daimyō* estates. While the artisans and merchants crowded into the flat lands in the eastern parts of the city (the *shitamachi* or downtown), the *daimyō* estates were clustered in the hilly areas around Edo Castle (now the Imperial Palace) where the shoguns lived. Institutions occupying large tracts of land today in these areas—universities, major hotels, parks—typically sit on the sites of former *daimyō* estates.

The endless processions back and forth between Edo and the *han* capitals necessitated a whole infrastructure of travel: a nationwide complex of roads, inns, portage facilities, ferries, harbors, and supply depots. Both the processions and the Edo estates had to be financed, which in turn gave birth to sophisticated financial instruments such as the rice futures market mentioned above. Rice formed the basis of Tokugawa finance with each of the *han* classified according to its expected annual output of rice. Taxes were collected mostly in the form of rice, and members of the entire samurai class (about 6 percent of the population) were awarded annual stipends in the form of rice. But the size of the rice crop varied from year to year with the vagaries of the weather, leading to the Osaka futures market and to other forms of financing based on pledges of future rice crops.

The emergence of complex financial arrangements and the need to manage long supply chains in turn greatly empowered the merchant class. Merchants may theoretically have been the lowest of the four official classes, but as the decades went by, more and more wealth flowed into their coffers. Osaka, the center of the nationwide rice trade, was the mercantile city par excellence, and many of the great names of Japanese business—Sumitomo, Nomura—can trace their roots to the Osaka merchants of the era.

Meanwhile, the samurai—theoretically the ruling class—were suddenly deprived of any real reason for being. In the decades immediately after Sekigahara, large numbers of them thronged into Edo and the major castle towns. In a manner comparable to the swashbuckling dandies of Shakespeare's time or the glamorous gangsters who fostered today's hip-hop, these crowds of raffish youths helped give birth to the cheeky, popular art forms that formed the Tokugawa period's most enduring contribution to world culture. The Kabuki theater, the *ukiyo-e* or woodblock prints of the "floating world" of brothels and teahouses, the *haiku* dashed off at the spur of the moment—these have their origins with all these young men with time on their hands flocking into the newly burgeoning cities of seventeenth-century Japan.

But crowds of young men with time on their hands also form the world's most reliable ingredients for political disorder, particularly when they are armed and see themselves as society's pacesetters. The Shogunate headed off the danger by turning them into bureaucrats. The hordes of samurai officials used by the Shogunate and the *daimyō* to staff their offices would, in turn, carry paper pushing to a degree unseen until the rise of modern totalitarian regimes. Some of this could actually be useful; Jared Diamond notes that census-taking extended beyond people to trees. In an autarkic country that built almost exclusively out of wood with vast cities subject to periodic fires, this made a lot of sense. Every tree in the country was classified according to its suitability for timber with careful monitoring put in place to ensure that demand for timber was constrained by sustainable supply. Diamond sought to make the point that human beings have in the past demonstrably coped with environmental constraints—that is, we are not inevitably condemned to the fate of Easter Island where all the trees were cut down. But all this tree counting, along with myriad other activities, also served to mop up and neutralize potentially subversive "warriors"—who, at least as warriors, were totally superfluous by that point.

There was, in fact, hardly any occasion for samurai to put their martial training into practice. As the actual experience of battle receded into the mists of history, the ethos of the samurai became paradoxically ever more rigid and militaristic, with stress on absolute loyalty to the superior, preparedness to carry out any order even at the risk of death, and a disdain for softness and physical comfort. The last was politically useful as relative economic circumstances for the samurai class progressively worsened. Tied to fixed incomes derived from rice stipends in what at least during the first century and a half of Tokugawa rule was a rapidly growing economy, samurai had to watch as their supposed social inferiors raked off most of the benefits of economic growth. Many were left clinging only to their status.

But it was not just the austerity; the whole samurai ethic—the disciplined, unquestioning response to any order, the personal rectitude, and contempt for moral or physical laxity—served just as well to shape a compliant bureaucracy as it had originally done to form a vigorous military. The ethic did, however, put the samurai increasingly at odds with what was obviously, in the merchant class, a commercial bourgeoisie in embryo.

Many seeming contradictions of contemporary Japan that so puzzle the outside world can be traced to the gap between the formal institutional structure of Tokugawa Japan and what was actually going on. For example, in late twentieth-century Japan, the world confronted some of the most dazzling business successes of all time emerging out of a country that simultaneously served as a byword for rigid, faceless bureaucracy. But this is less puzzling when one notes precedents in the great Osaka merchant houses and in an increasingly ossified samurai class. It is also in the Tokugawa period that we can find the roots of a culture that, on the one hand, would carry loyalty and self-abnegation to seemingly crazy degrees—the samurai cult of self-immolation, the suicide missions of Japanese soldiers in the Second World War, the contemporary company men working themselves to death—while, on the other, generating wave after successive wave of zany, subversive art culminating in the bizarre video games, *hentai* (animated features of sexual perversions), *manga*, and wacky fashions of our own time.

The Japanese themselves were naturally aware of these contradictions; a whole vocabulary grew up to describe the clash between the facade maintained for the sake of social peace to which everyone gave lip service (*tatemae*) and the reality going on underneath that could not be articulated except, perhaps, with trusted confidantes over bottles of sake (*honne*). Or the conflict between socially mandatory obligations to superiors, creditors, households, and the like (*giri*) versus spontaneous human feelings (*ninjo*)—love between a shop attendant and a prostitute, for example, that leads to mutual suicide, or a father forced to sacrifice his own child to protect the son of his lord.

These contradictions may have made for a society with huge amounts of tension, but they also made wonderfully fertile material for artists in all genres. Thanks to widespread literacy (upwards of 30 percent of the population with even higher percentages in the cities), economic growth, and technologies that allowed for cheap production and dissemination of printed matter, Tokugawa Japan saw the birth of what was arguably the world's first mass culture—that is to say, a culture known to and partaken of by people in most walks of society. The high culture inherited from the Heian and feudal periods—Noh drama, *tanka* poetry, ink painting—continued into the Tokugawa years, particularly among the samurai and the old nobility in Kyoto. But most of the population—including many of the samurai themselves—was turning for entertainment and edification to the newer art forms taking shape in the great urban centers.

POPULAR CULTURE

We have already noted that much of the tone of Edo period mass culture was initially struck by the hordes of young samurai set adrift by the final victories of the Tokugawa. But over time, it was the rising merchant class that increasingly supplanted the samurai as arbiters of taste. Ground zero for the mass culture that developed were the licensed pleasure quarters—Edo's Yoshiwara and Kyoto's Shimabara being two of the most famous. Samurai were theoretically banned from entering the quarters, but the prohibition was rarely enforced; most samurai simply dispensed with the swords that marked them as samurai when they entered the quarters. There they mingled with merchants and other commoners in the one place in Japan where class distinctions ostensibly disappeared.

What drew them all was sex. Sex served as the not-so–hidden root, the energy source behind the brilliant efflorescence of popular culture during the Edo period. Later, when the Japanese began taking their cues from priggish Westerners, the origins of such quintessentially Japanese art forms as Kabuki and *ukiyo-e* were deliberately obscured—particularly when Westerners began going gaga over Japanese prints and other artifacts of Edo popular culture, which had theretofore been seen as little better than trash by Japan's elite.

But ironically Kabuki started as a sort of early seventeenth-century equivalent of pole dancing. A former shrine maiden by the name of Izumo no Okuni began organizing troops of young women on the banks of Kyoto's Kamo River to dance and act out simple plays in pantomime. Okuni herself was particularly popular when she would appear on stage as a handsome youth. Everyone understood that the girls were available later for private dalliance for those with the means to pay. Fights broke out among the young samurai who were the principal patrons (indeed the word *kabuki* actually comes from a verb that had been applied to these young men meaning something like "being weird" or "offbeat"). Of course, anything that smacked of disorder attracted the attention of shogunal officials, and they promptly banned women from the stage. Not missing a beat, Okuni simply substituted boys, which in the pederasty-soaked samurai culture of the early seventeenth century, hardly damaged business. It may actually have helped since, featuring boys rather than girls, the Kabuki attracted the attention of the third shogun, Iemitsu, a notorious pederast, who arranged for command performances. With his death in 1651, however, and samurai now brawling over boys instead of girls, the Shogunate restricted the stage to males over the age of 15.

It was from that point on that the Kabuki matured into the great theater we know today, drawing much of its inspiration and plot lines from the *bunraku* or puppet theater taking shape in Osaka at roughly the same time. Kabuki's most famous actors—particularly the *onnagata,* or men who specialized in female roles—created around them a culture of celebrity comparable to that generated today by rock stars or by the *castrati* who dominated Baroque opera.[2] Their only rivals as trend-setters were the geisha who reigned supreme over the floating world of the licensed quarters. For as both economic and cultural power passed from samurai to merchant, the cult of the boy (*wakashu*) that had prevailed in the early years of the Tokugawa period was gradually edged aside by that of the accomplished courtesan—the geisha. Geisha literally means "arts person" and women who aspired to that position were trained in mastery of a whole gamut of art forms—singing, dancing, poetry—and of course

2. The dichotomy between the high culture of the Noh and the popular origins of Kabuki bears comparison with that Richard Taruskin noted between the high-minded opera first created by circles of nobles in sixteenth-century Florence and the popular opera that emerged in Venice.

conversation. They were not "just" or even primarily prostitutes and their physical favors could only be purchased by the wealthy—and then after a period in which a patron was required to prove himself worthy.

But the geisha were perched at the top of what was, in the final analysis, a world in which sex was traded for money. Pretty young girls from peasant families were essentially sold into the pleasure quarters at the age of 6 or 7 (technically, they were not sold but had to work off contracts of sufficient severity that they were for all intents and purposes indentured sex workers). A girl showing aptitude as well as looks was trained in all the arts befitting a geisha, usually via an apprenticeship. At age 13 or 14, she would undergo ritual deflowering by a man who would have paid a handsome sum for the privilege. If she continued to demonstrate skill and preserve her beauty, she could aspire to the heights of the floating world as a geisha. Otherwise, she would drift down into more common prostitution.

But while there is no getting around the reality that the floating world was ultimately about sex and that it rested on the ability and willingness of people with money and power to exploit others for sexual pleasure, it did produce enduring art that set the tone for an entire civilization. Just as the almost breathless aestheticism of the Heian aristocracy had, some 600 years earlier, served as a kind of counterbalance to the rampant promiscuity of the times, so did the style, taste, and sheer panache of the floating world offset the exploitation on which it was based. (Many of the geisha—and the less exalted common run of prostitutes—often adopted as namesakes characters in the *Tale of Genji*, albeit often in jest.) The underlying economic and power relations may have been pretty much what one finds today in the fleshpots of Bangkok or Hamburg, but they made a contribution to world culture that, if such a thing as a balance sheet for civilizations can be imagined to exist, must be entered into the accounts opposite that which made it possible.

It was not just a matter of the wealth flowing into Japan's cities and the ability of both the *nouveau riche* and established status-holders to exploit poor peasant girls. Among other things, it is by no means clear that the life of a girl back in the village was in any way less onerous than that of her sister sold into the houses of the Yoshiwara. Rural girls who stayed home could look forward only to back-breaking dawn-to-dusk labor at the mercy of whatever uncouth peasant her parents decided was a proper mate for her.

More broadly, the understanding of marriage and Tokugawa thinking about the nature of sexual desire provided the conceptual space in which

the floating world and its arts flourished. Marriage was a political institution—a contractual alliance between families. While there was no notion of
female equality, a man could not disgrace his wife by divorcing her simply
because he no longer found her sexually attractive; that is, there was no
counterpart to the contemporary practice by which successful men dump
their wives of several decades in favor of trophy bimbos. Instead, it was
expected that a man who could afford it would enjoy sex on the side—
everything from the modest shopkeeper's occasional visit to a prostitute
up to the wealthy merchant patronizing a geisha. Since respectable married women stayed home (the formal Japanese name for a wife is *okusan*,
which literally means "honorable interior"—i.e., the person who manages
the home), "society" grew up around the courtesan—the geisha. The old
samurai culture had looked down on sexual escapades with women, seeing
such practices as a softening and feminizing, but the newly ascendant merchants gloried in the luxury and titillation that only the presence of women
could provide. While there have been other times and places in human history where courtesans played important social roles, few cultures in history
rivaled Tokugawa period Japan for the way in which almost all social and
cultural trends revolved around the geisha-dominated floating world.

It is true that the samurai was supposed to eschew the company of
women while Buddhist priests saw sexual desire as an obstacle on the path
to enlightenment, which is why both groups tended to treat dalliance with
boys as superior to that with women and would become bywords for ped-
erasts. But sexual desire in and of itself was not held to indicate human
kind's fallen state. For example, women as well as men were expected to
have sexual feelings—there was nothing comparable to the Western cult of
the Virgin or the Victorian notion that sex is something women don't really
like. True, women had far less freedom than men to indulge those feelings,
and adultery was severely punished, but some women (if they could afford
it and get away with it) also visited prostitutes. (A saying among male prostitutes of the time was that they spent their days on their backs and then
turned themselves over when the sun went down, a reference to their female
clients who had to be back home by dark.) Women also enjoyed the erotic
novels and prints that formed the mainstay of Edo popular print culture.

But men who lacked the resources to frequent the floating world
consumed even more of these materials. Timon Screech has argued that
more than half the famous *ukiyo-e*—literally, "pictures of the floating
world"—that would so dazzle the Western eye when they flooded into late

nineteenth-century Europe were explicitly erotic. They were intended as substitutes for people who could not afford direct experience of the pleasures of the floating world or, like samurai women, were for reasons other than money unable to avail themselves of those pleasures. Scholarship has only recently established these points, not only because the Meiji establishment tried to hide the origins of *ukiyo-e* once they realized how popular they had become in Western artistic circles, but because the more explicit of these prints had become literally illegal in post–World War Two Japan with the passage of blue laws that forbade the depiction of unadorned genitalia. The relaxation in the 1990s of these laws made it possible to establish what Screech has done: that the great effusion of Edo period erotic printed matter was the product of a culture that saw no intrinsic problem with sexual desire per se, but in which the opportunity to indulge it directly was limited. Because of *sankin kōtai*—the pilgrimages of *daimyō* back and forth to Edo—there were far more men than women living in Edo at any given point. Most of the women who did live there lacked either the freedom or the money to satisfy their sexual feelings directly. So both men and women resorted to the auto-erotic.

Screech has also noted that Edo period pornography—and that is what it was—stands out in any catalog of global erotica for its lovingness, its romance. In Edo period Japan, almost all sex occurred between two unequal parties in situations where at most one party desired it; the other was doing it usually because she had no choice (prostitution; arranged marriage). Even the one seemingly widespread exception—pederastic affairs among samurai—tends to support the point. While samurai youths could freely accept or reject older lovers—and even seek them out—they were not expected to take any pleasure from the anal sex that it was assumed would follow. They were supposed to put up with the pain in return for the guidance, friendship, and mentoring they would receive.

Edo period pornography thus emphasized what was greatly desired but unattainable for most people: genuinely loving, reciprocal sex. This may be one reason why so much of it is also great art. It is worth dwelling for a moment on a print like Utamaro's *Lovers in the Upstairs Room of a Teahouse*, which forms the frontispiece to this chapter. It is one of the most famous of the *ukiyo-e*. But what it literally shows—and wonderfully so—is sexual passion and arousal in the context of a loving, romantic relationship. There is nothing in the Western canon quite like it. To find loving sexual ecstasy depicted with such superlative faithfulness, one has to turn in Western art to music like Berlioz's *Romeo et Juliette* or Wagner's *Tristan und Isolde*, and even in these cases one is dealing with forbidden and dangerous sex.

Nothing is forbidden or dangerous in the Utamaro print; it's just beyond reach for most people. Most handling of reciprocated romantic love in Edo period literature, as opposed to visual art, treats it as a tragedy—a disruptive emotion that brings *ninjō* (human feelings) into direct conflict with *giri* (duty). The most famous playwright of the Edo period, Chikamatsu Monzaemon (1653–1724), explored this theme over and over again. His heroes are typically anti-heroes: shopkeepers and prostitutes falling hopelessly in love with each other with terrible consequences all around.

Here again we see the beginnings of mass culture in that these tales spoke to all walks of society. And just as samurai could be riveted by depictions of desperate lower-class urbanites—something unthinkable, for example, to aristocrats of the Heian period—so could money-grubbing merchants find themselves pulled into a nationwide obsession over the fate of samurai from a minor *han* whose old-style loyalties seemed to serve as a rebuke to the increasing pre-eminence of commercial values.

THE TALE OF THE 47 RŌNIN

In 1701, one of the Shogunate's senior officials humiliated and insulted the young *daimyō* of a small *han* near Hiroshima. The official may have expected a bigger gift than the *daimyō* could afford, he may have lusted after the man's beautiful young wife, he may have secretly coveted the *han*'s landholdings, or he may just have been a nasty person who enjoyed snobbish gloating over the discomfort of an untutored provincial who did not quite know all the rules (the official was responsible for giving instruction on ceremonial rituals). Whatever; the young *daimyō* was sufficiently provoked that he drew his sword and slightly injured the official. The drawing of a sword inside the shogun's castle was a capital offense; not only did the young man have to commit *seppuku*, but his heirs were disinherited and his *han* merged into another. Forty-seven of his retainers formed a secret pact to avenge their lord. Since shogunal police would be on the alert for something like this, the retainers had to cover their tracks, which they did by ostentatiously pretending to lose themselves in the licensed quarters and abandon all sense of honor. Once they had succeeded in deflecting suspicion, they came together, attacked the Edo estate of the official, and beheaded him. They then proceeded to their lord's tomb (still a site of pilgrimage today in a temple in Tokyo), placed the head on the tomb, and then turned themselves in to the police.

The entire country was thunderstruck; the tale of these forty-seven *rōnin* (masterless samurai) almost instantly assumed the character of a national myth and would resonate down through the centuries up to and including the assassinations of the 1930s that helped drive Japan into fascism. The incident certainly put the Shogunate on the spot. The forty-seven *rōnin* were guilty of the gravest of offenses: the killing of a high shogunal official. But conservatives in the Shogunate, obsessed with what they saw as the decline of traditional samurai virtues at the expense of self-serving greed and extravagance, could hardly help but note that the actions of the forty-seven served as a paradigmatic example of precisely these virtues. Instead of executing the forty-seven like common criminals, the Shogunate ended up allowing them to kill themselves in the honorable samurai fashion: *seppuku.*

The incident became fodder for artists and writers, culminating in the great 1748 *bunraku* and Kabuki play *Kanadehon Chūshingura* (*The Treasury of Loyal Retainers*). Performances, like those of *Messiah* in the West, would become annual events akin more to religious rituals than entertainment.

But the immense popularity of the play—and the way in which the incident on which it was based captivated the whole country—did point to what would become the single largest political-*cum*-ideological contradiction for the Shogunate in its last century. Its governing constitution, as it were, of rectitude, loyalty, and a stable hierarchy was increasingly at odds with what people could see all around them. With the ever-growing pressure of that contradiction came a gradual loss of legitimacy that called into question the capacity of the Shogunate to cope with developments beyond Japan's shores—developments that were becoming harder and harder to ignore, developments that posed a formidable threat to Japan's existence as an independent polity controlling its own affairs.

COMMODORE PERRY'S "BLACK SHIPS" AND THE DEATH KNELL OF THE TOKUGAWA SHOGUNATE

The second coming of the Western powers—beginning with Perry's 1853 and 1854 visits—famously precipitated the fall of the Tokugawa regime. Japan was no longer dealing with a comparative handful of traders and missionaries, as it had some three centuries earlier, but with peremptory demands from powerful countries that were in the process of carving up the entire planet among them. It was obvious the Shogunate was not up to the resultant challenge. But it was not the Westerners who actually over-threw the regime; it was groups of low-ranking samurai from the outer *han*. While their rage at what they saw as the pusillanimous response of the Shogunate to the insolent "barbarians" contributed to their sense that conditions had become intolerable, that was hardly the limit of their dissatisfaction.

They were at least as distraught at the erosion of samurai privilege, at the lavish living of wealthy merchants and corrupt officials, and at the utter misery they saw around them following a series of crop failures in the 1830—misery that included their own straitened circumstances. The beginning of the end for the Tokugawa, typically assigned to Commodore Perry's 1853 visit, can just as easily be dated to 1838. In that year, an Osaka samurai official by the name of Oshio Heihachiro led a motley group of insurrectionists in burning much of Osaka to the ground. Violence on this scale had not been seen for some two centuries. Although the rebellion was soon snuffed out—Oshio and his followers either killed themselves or underwent the most gruesome of executions (the bodies of those who had not survived torture were pickled in salt and hung on crosses)—Osaka's central position in commercial networks meant that all Japan was soon aware of what had happened. And it was not just the rebellion itself that shocked, it was the kind of people involved: a rabble of samurai, desperate peasants, and even untouchables. It was the seemingly complete break-down of any proper sense of hierarchy in the people Oshio led as much as the incident itself that horrified the country. In the context of wider events—the series of bad harvests; the ominous rumbles from beyond Japan's shores—the incident was a harbinger of collapse.

Oshio was a follower of the Ming philosopher Wang Yangming (1472–1529) whose most famous statement is "To know and not to act is not to know." Wang's emphasis on the unity of thought and action put his philos-ophy at odds with the dominant Neo-Confucianism of both Qing-dynasty China and Tokugawa Japan. The radicalism implicit in Wang's writings would make him an inspiration to a whole series of reformers in late nineteenth- and early twentieth-century East Asia.

Oshio's failed insurrection may seem to have had little to do with the Western world. Inspired as it was by thinking that may have been heterodox but was nonetheless East Asian in origin, it represented a crisis that arose from contradictions inherent in the Tokugawa polity. The most important we have already noted: the regime had brought an end to the incessant civil wars of the preceding centuries by freezing in place a hierarchy of power relations. In an example of dialectic forces at work, that very stability fostered developments that over time undermined it—in particular, the coming of great cities and the new classes of wealth-holders they spawned. This contradiction might eventually have brought down the curtain on the Shogunate, West or no West. But it was Tokugawa autarky that helped pull the rope, particularly given the contrast with what was going on in Europe, where international trade acted as a great spur to technological and military advances.

Edo period Japan's most dramatic growth—in population, in urbanization, in cultural flowering—took place in the first century of Tokugawa rule, culminating in the Genroku Era (1688–1703), long considered a kind of Golden Age. As the eighteenth century proceeded, urban growth ran up against what amounted to the limits of autarky: in the absence of significant trade with the outside world, the larger cities began to stagnate. Absent foreign sources of supply, the occasional bad harvest brought on famine. With the samurai dependent on income extracted from the countryside, attempts to squeeze money from destitute peasants gave rise to more and more cases of peasant riots labelled *ikki*. Although such incidents decreased in the early nineteenth century after surging in the eighteenth, bad times returned in the 1830s and seemed linked to the growing dread of developments beyond Japan's shores. Distant tremors from the American and French revolutions were felt in Edo; legends grew about figures such as George Washington and Napoleon. Probes by Russian ships into the southern Kuril Islands and on the coasts of Hokkaido itself meant that the Shogunate could no longer relegate Japan's northern frontier to a minor concern appropriate to an indistinct area fading off into distant lands that had long been nothing more than a source of trade in herring and pelts with primitive people. Meanwhile, the worldwide growth of whaling meant inevitable encounters between Japanese coastal shipping and foreign vessels.

But it was the Opium Wars of the 1840s and 1850s together with the inauguration of the Treaty Port system on the China coast that most shocked Japan's elite. Since earliest times, China had always loomed as the great superpower over the horizon. There may have been no formal relationship between Edo and the Qing dynasty, but to see China humiliated, to see its major ports occupied and administered by barbarians from the West, made it obvious to even the most willfully blind that a great shadow had begun to fall over East Asia, one that Japan could not escape.

THE "REVOLUTION" OF 1868?

In the process of overthrowing the Shogunate, the new leaders who seized power in 1868 destroyed a number of Japan's central governing institutions. They abolished the *han* that long pre-dated the Tokugawa Shogunate (and, one could argue, had helped to give it birth), redrew the old *han* borders, and appropriated for themselves the significant powers the *han* capitals had previously enjoyed over local affairs. They expropriated *daimyō* holdings, eliminated formal class distinctions, and commuted samurai annual stipends into one-time lump-sum payments that ended the automatic claims samurai had had on the state. They imported new institutions from the West with dizzying speed—everything from universal schooling and male conscription to joint-stock companies, limited liability banks, parliaments, courts, and currency backed by precious metals, not to mention the latest science and technology and even Western clothes and ballroom dancing. If these upheavals did not collectively add up to a revolution, it is hard to imagine what would.

But simply labeling these events a revolution obscures a critical matter in understanding everything that has taken place since then. Marxists contend that real revolution only occurs when one class overthrows another, and one need not be a Marxist to point out that this is precisely what did not happen in the 1860s. Instead, elements on the fringes of the existing elite—the lower-level samurai from the outer *han* of Choshu, Satsuma, and Tosa—staged what was effectively a *coup d'état* in order to counteract an existential threat to the collective independence and discretionary power of Japan's ruling class. Seen this way, the Meiji Restoration is closer to a counterrevolution than what happened in France in 1789 or Russia in 1917. It is perhaps best understood as a desperate, inter-elite power struggle with very high stakes. It would be the first of several such power struggles over the next century and a half, each of which involved elements of Japan's ruling class grabbing power from other elements in order to forestall what they saw as a devastating loss of control by Japan's elite over not just the country's direction but the very ability of the country to manage its own affairs.

This naturally leads to the question of whether an actual class-based revolution might have been possible in the 1860s, or to put this differently, why Japan did not undergo a genuine bourgeois revolution during the Edo period and achieve capitalist transformation on its own. As we have seen, many of the necessary preconditions were in place—in particular, sophisticated economic and financial institutions, widespread literacy, great cities, and what was obviously, in the merchant class, a bourgeoisie in embryo. The merchants had demonstrated they were capable of accumulating and deploying the capital necessary for an industrial takeoff.

Some of the answer to the question of Japan's failure to produce a home-grown bourgeois revolution may lie in the genius with which the Tokugawa authorities co-opted potential sources of opposition, a feature of Japan's political culture that survived the demise of the Shogunate and remains critically important right into the present day. The authorities were not only aware of the growing financial leverage the merchant class had over the samurai and *daimyō*, it also troubled them since it contravened their sense of the proper order of things. But rather than attempt to interfere directly in merchant affairs, thus potentially provoking the kinds of reactions to absolutist power that served as the crucible for the formation of the European bourgeoisie, shogunal authorities largely left the merchants alone—provided, and this is the key point, that merchant guilds and other relevant institutions exercised self-policing. The self-policing served to keep merchant activities within implicit bounds that precluded open challenge to existing power relations. Unable to appeal to ideas such as the inviolability and sanctity of property rights, the merchants lacked a conceptual apparatus that might have allowed them to contemplate any such challenge on their own.[3] The Neo-Confucian political theory that underlay Tokugawa rule posited the existing hierarchy itself as the source of political legitimacy or, to put this in other words, there was little notion of an order transcending existing political arrangements that conferred legitimacy on those arrangements. Even

---

3. Another example of this characteristic way of co-opting rather than attempting to eliminate potential trouble-makers is the way in the early decades of the Edo period that the authorities dealt with the banditry that plagued the *Tōkaidō*, the great highway running between Edo and Kyoto. Bandits were given the tacit right to organize and run prostitution and gambling establishments as long as they kept the peace. Police in the modern era have dealt with street crime in pretty much the same way, allowing the yakuza to organize and profit from theoretically illegal activities provided they kept young hoodlums off the street.

European absolutism—"the divine right of kings"—contained within its very formulation the notion that the rights of monarchs derived from a source of greater authority; kings themselves were not divine.[4] But in Japanese political thinking, duly constituted political authority is *itself* divine—a notion that while evident as far back as the sixth century had been encouraged by the Tokugawa in order to render unthinkable any challenge to their rule.

This notion would survive the demise of the Shogunate and create all kinds of mischief in the twentieth century. A clue to the tenacity of the hold it has on the Japanese political imagination can be found in the immense popularity of the television program *Mito Kōmon*, a serial that ran for over a thousand episodes from 1969 to the end of 2011, making it by far the longest-running such program in world history. (Even smash-hit Japanese TV programs typically run for only two to three seasons with the possibility of a resurrection a season or two later.) Each episode follows the same arc. Mito Kōmon himself, a former vice-shogun, travels the length and breadth of Japan in disguise as a retired merchant, accompanied by two sidekicks. They encounter evil-doing—typically by gangsters in league with corrupt officials or samurai gone to seed who are oppressing decent local folk. After a series of outrages clearly calculated to stir the viewing audience, some sort of sword fight occurs and at the climactic moment, Mito Kōmon reveals who he actually is by unveiling his *inrō* (a small case) embossed with the official seal of the Shogunate. The bad guys, who outnumber Mito and his little group of proverbial regular and guest-star white hats, invariably sink to the ground in awe and terror. It does not take an advanced degree in theology to see that what is being served up here is a kind of political myth with Mito Kōmon in the role of an avenging angel whose tolerance for injustice finally reaches the snapping point.

Of course, in many times and places, people have blamed intractable problems not on the basic political order but on those who would change or undermine it. Nor are the Japanese alone in thinking that if we can just get rid of self-seeking operatives and corrupt officials—we call them "special interests" today—then the will of the people or God's plan or the Imperial Mind, as the case may be, can shine forth clearly and righteousness will

---

4. This of course had been the original sticking point between the Jews and the early Christians on the one hand and Roman governors on the other. While the followers of Abraham were prepared to recognize the divine source of political authority, they believed that worship itself is properly directed only to God.

reign. But the notion that the political order *itself* is divinely constituted and thus beyond question has been particularly ingrained in Japan. That made it conceptually as well as practically difficult for Edo period merchants to set up self-governing entities comparable to the Hanseatic League or the Italian city–states that created the seedbeds for capitalism in Europe. The closest they came was probably Sakai, a port city adjacent to Osaka that was governed by councils of merchants. But unlike their counterparts in Europe, the merchants of Sakai were unable to place any limit on the theoretical power of monarchs—shoguns/*daimyō*—or require that monarchs submit to the rule of any kind of law. As a result, even though the Shogunate was increasingly dependent on financing arranged by the great merchant houses, the Shogunate retained the power to expropriate merchant property. This never gave rise to anything resembling revolutionary sentiment among the merchants, however, since the primary outlets for merchant earnings were loans to the *daimyō* and the Shogunate. While the threat of expropriation was always there, and the merchants had no means of procuring, much less enforcing, any kind of judgment on a *daimyō* who refused to honor his debts, *daimyō* were reluctant to do so since they knew they would have difficulty raising future loans. The merchants thus ended up as tacit allies of the shogunal order; their own prosperity was completely wrapped up in its survival.

THE FALL OF THE SHOGUNATE

The chink in the Tokugawa conceptual armor lay in the ultimate source of its political legitimacy—Imperial appointment. An appointment granted by the Throne could theoretically be revoked—never mind that neither the original 1603 appointment of Tokugawa Ieyasu as Shogun nor the 1868 revocation of the title from his descendent Tokugawa Yoshinobu had anything to do with an actual policy decision freely arrived at by a sitting emperor. Commodore Perry's demands for trade and refueling privileges for American shipping had triggered a scramble by the other leading Western powers to stake out claims of their own on a potentially lucrative new market that seemed, like China, ripe for exploitation. Shogunal officials—by then aware that any resort to arms would end in abject defeat—attempted to placate the Westerners not simply with trade agreements but with concessions on extraterritoriality. Collectively known as the Unequal Treaties, they were almost as bad as those signed a decade or so earlier by the Qing dynasty, save that the British did not win the right to push narcotics on the Japanese.

These treaties and the sudden appearance of swaggering foreigners dictating this and that naturally led to rage on the part of many, particularly hot-headed young samurai from the outer *han*. They began meeting in secret and forming networks. They seized on the ancient institution of the Throne as a means of cloaking what was in fact sedition in order to make their plots conceptually palatable—to themselves, probably, as much as to anyone else. The Court itself for the first time in centuries became politically involved. Emperor Komei (1831–1867) sympathized with the anger of these young samurai at the Shogunate's capitulation to Western demands. The Shogunate, concerned about the latent threat from the Court, engineered a marriage between the emperor's sister and Shogun Tokugawa Iemochi, which neither the emperor nor his sister desired. But Edo was unable to prevent Kyoto from issuing an order that the "barbarians" were to be expelled from Japan.

Unlike the shogunal officials—who were keenly aware by then of the military power that backed up "barbarian" demands—neither the emperor nor the young samurai who had egged on more radical elements of the old nobility had any real notion of what Japan faced. An English merchant in the Satsuma *han* capital of Kagoshima was murdered in 1862; a few months later, gun batteries on the coasts of Choshu shelled foreign shipping in the Straits of Shimonoseki between Honshu and Kyushu. The British retaliated by burning Kagoshima to the ground; shortly thereafter, Choshu's batteries were destroyed by joint action of American, British, French, and Dutch ships.

While many radicals continued to agitate for change under the banner *Sonnō, Jō-i* (Revere the Emperor and Expel the Barbarian), these direct confrontations with Western military power led to a more realistic assessment of Japan's situation. A paradigmatic figure of the age is the young samurai Sakamoto Ryoma. Sakamoto had been born into a line of well-to-do saké merchants in the outer *han* of Tosa. His family had bought its way into the lowest ranks of the samurai in return for bringing fallow land back under cultivation.[5] Sakamoto had been sent to a Confucian school

---

5. Despite the official rigidity of class distinctions, there was a good deal of actual fluidity. Wealthy merchants could sometimes purchase titles in the lowest rank of the samurai class: the *gōshi*, literally rural samurai. The *gōshi* also included the highest stratum of the peasantry who were allowed the samurai privilege of carrying swords.

typical for boys of his class, but showing little aptitude for academics and finding himself a target for bullies, he allowed his sister to persuade him to enroll instead in one of the new fencing academies that were springing up in response to the turbulence of the times and the provocations of the "barbarians." For this, he moved to Edo and at the academy fell in with some of the most radicalized of the young samurai, who recruited him to become what today we would call a terrorist operative. On his first mission, he set out to assassinate a high shogunal official. The official had been charged with overhauling Japan's naval defenses and establishing a naval training school as part of the Shogunate's attempts to cope with the challenge from the West. When Sakamoto burst into his house, the official succeeded in persuading the young hothead to hear him out before killing him, and then managed to convince Sakamoto that something had to be done to prepare Japan to deal with the world in which it found itself; that killing the people who were trying to do this was not the solution to Japan's problems.

In a phenomenon not unknown elsewhere, Sakamoto experienced a kind of conversion, switching from passion-fueled rage against these new barbarians and the "traitors" who were trying to mollify them, to curiosity about the West (he seemed to have been particularly intrigued by American ideals of political equality among all men) and a conviction that Japan's problems lay with its governing structure—that it had what amounted to two rulers and two courts. Wanted by the shogunal police, Sakamoto fled Edo for Kagoshima, where he played a critical role in forging an anti-shogunal alliance between the two great western *han* of Satsuma and Choshu, traditionally enemies. Sakamoto was assassinated in Kyoto just months before his dream of a single unified government came to fruition with the resignation of the last shogun and the official "return" of power to the new young emperor, known posthumously as Emperor Meiji.

Sakamoto's career, writ large, is the story of what happened to Japan in those years. Faced by an overwhelming external threat, the country first reacted with rage and denial. Once it became obvious that that would lead to nothing but Japan's loss of independence, the country embarked on a radical change of course, overhauling its institutions and desperately trying to learn what it could from the outsiders in order to equip itself to meet the threat.

Despite—or because of—its concessions to foreigners and its incoherent reform efforts, the Shogunate's palpable inability to cope with that threat cost it its legitimacy. Order collapsed. Mobs of people began dancing in the streets of the major cities chanting *eei ja nai ka* (isn't it good) in the belief that money was dropping from the sky. Faced with such manias, not to mention open rebellion from the outer *han* in Japan's west, the Shogunate imploded. It happened with remarkable lack of bloodshed—the worst of it stemming from samurai in northern Japan who believed, correctly, that they would be frozen out of the new power structure and who took a further eighteen months to subdue after the establishment of Japan's new government. But the relative lack of bloodshed and the obvious need for a change of course allowed Japan's new rulers to take control in accordance with existing legal procedures, such as they were, by "returning" nominal power to the emperor. While no emperor had actually enjoyed uncontested rule over Japan for well over a millennium, the claim to have "restored" power to the emperor gave Japan's new government an almost immediate legitimacy. The gap between the fiction of direct Imperial rule and the reality of government by self-appointed oligarchs who exploited that fiction for their own ends would, a half-century later, help set the stage for the greatest catastrophe in Japanese history. But for the time being, it gave Japan's new leaders the political authority they would use to transform their country in a single generation into a major power capable of taking on Western imperialism at its own game and winning.

FIGURE 3. Portrait of Iwasaki Yataro, the Founder of Mitsubishi and the Father of Modern Japanese Industrial Organization. Courtesy of the Mitsubishi Archive.

3

"Restoration" to Occupation

The small group of able men who saved their country from colonialism and turned it into a major industrial and imperial power are usually called the Meiji leaders after the emperor in whose name they ruled. They bear comparison with the Founders of the United States or the Young Turks who took a moribund Ottoman Empire and made it into modern Turkey. Because most of them were so young in 1868, many lived into the twentieth century and reigned over Japanese politics as *genrō* or elder statesmen, effectively exercising the right to choose Japan's prime ministers until well into the 1930s. As the list of their names and backgrounds in Appendix A suggests, they came mostly from either Satsuma or Choshu; two other key figures were drawn from the ranks of the Kyoto-based nobility. (A possible comparison could be drawn with the dominance among the American Founders of men from Massachusetts and Virginia.)

The Meiji leaders faced three urgent and intertwined tasks. They had to build a military strong enough to act as a deterrent to Western imperialism. They had to assemble the capital and technology needed to turn their country into an industrial power sufficiently advanced to equip that military. And they had to create the institutions necessary not only to accomplish these other tasks but to convince the West that Japan had accumulated the prerequisites for membership in the club of countries that were to be taken seriously. That meant not only a credible military—preferably evidenced by victories in imperialist wars waged on weaker lands—but also such institutions as parliaments, courts, banks, monogamy, elections, and, ideally, Christian churches, not to mention familiarity with Western ways and appearances in such matters as architecture, dress, sexual mores, and table manners. It was only by governing as the leaders of a convincing imitation of a modern imperialist nation that these men could persuade the West to revise the Unequal Treaties and thereby wrest back control over their country's tariff regime and security apparatus from the Europeans.

Fortunately, they had examples. Satsuma and Choshu had already sent delegations abroad before the Restoration, but beginning with the 1871–73 Iwakura Mission under the leadership of the Court noble of that name, the new leaders and their most able subordinates fanned out across the Western world, seeking the most appropriate models for whatever they needed. From Britain came shipbuilding, naval organization, central banking, railroad technology, and the new outward trappings of the monarchy; from France, jurisprudence, fortification know-how, and medicine; from the United States, modern agriculture, development policies for frontier areas such as Hokkaido, and public education; from smaller lands such as Sweden and Switzerland, lessons in how weaker countries could deploy military strength sufficient to deter more powerful neighbors.

But the greatest teacher was Prussia—or, as it would become, Bismarck's Germany. Germany presented a particularly apt model since it too had been met with the classic "late" or "catch-up" developer challenge amidst the need to forge a unified nation out of a hodgepodge of minor states and principalities. German thinking on state-led industrial development became conventional wisdom among the Meiji leaders. The writings of the German economist Friedrich List were particularly influential; List had been a great admirer of the regime of protective tariffs and explicit subsidies to industry implemented in the young United States by such figures as Alexander Hamilton and Henry Clay; in his *National System of Political Economy* he advocated comparable policies for his own country. This book was translated into Japanese, complete with an official introduction from the governor of the newly established Bank of Japan, and it circulated widely among members of the Meiji elite.

But while the Meiji leaders enthusiastically followed German ideas on the primacy of industry and bank-centered industrial groups, they faced a horrendous challenge of capital accumulation much worse than anything Germany had had to contend with. Although the great merchant houses had largely bankrolled the Restoration itself and some would survive Japan's transformation into an industrial economy,[1] the Meiji government could not wait for the rise of an organically formed bourgeoisie to lead industrialization. Aside from being far too slow for a country that sought to hang onto its independence in the colony-grabbing, imperialist world of the late nineteenth century, turning over control of economic outcomes to a merchant class would have necessitated both conceptual and political revolutions. The formal existence of a *de jure* ruling class may have been abolished along with the "samurai" designation of its members, but in a country where political legitimacy was completely wrapped up in notions of hierarchy, precedent, and heritage, it was probably inevitable that former samurai would largely end up running things. Meiji government leaders took over shogunal and *han* enterprises, started some of their own, and then, after discovering they really did not know how to run them, proceeded to sell controlling stakes in these enterprises to their former samurai associates at what amounted to give-away prices. It was a bit like what would happen in Russia after the collapse of the Soviet Union, except that Japan's insiders were usually motivated by the strong, almost existential desire to save their country rather than to line their pockets. *Fukoku Kyōhei* (Rich Country, Strong Army) was their battle cry.

IWASAKI YATARO AND THE BIRTH OF MODERN JAPANESE INDUSTRIAL ORGANIZATION

A good example of how things worked can be seen in the career of Iwasaki Yataro, listed in Appendix A as the greatest industrialist to emerge in Meiji Japan. Iwasaki had been a minor samurai official from Tosa, the same *han* that produced Sakamoto Ryoma, whom we met in the preceding chapter. After the Restoration, Iwasaki acquired the rights to the *han* trading offices in Osaka and Nagasaki. (The major *han* had maintained offices in Nagasaki as well as Osaka in order to procure essential foreign goods.) With the abolition of the *han* system, Iwasaki changed the name of the

---

1. Sumitomo and Mitsui were two of the most famous Edo period names that successfully made the transition.

trading office to Mitsubishi. In 1875, the Meiji government turned over thirty ships free of charge to Mitsubishi together with some operating subsidies. The ships had been assets of a failed shipping company the government had set up in response to foreign inroads in Japan's coastal shipping. Iwasaki used his ships to help put down the 1877 rebellion led by the estranged Satsuma general Saigo Takamori,[2] and as a reward, received further privileges.

Being the gifted visionary he was, Iwasaki was able to convert these initial grants into the foundations of the one of the world's great business empires. But he also introduced a significant innovation into the organizational structure of Japanese industry, one still visible and important today. The Meiji leaders had followed the German practice of placing banks at the center of industrial groups, with banks, instead of bond and stock markets, serving as the primary providers of investment capital to industry. But rather than have banks take equity stakes in the industrial companies, equity of both banks and industrial concerns should, in Iwasaki's view, be held directly by those who ultimately controlled the industrial groups. It is to Iwasaki's innovations that we can trace the origin of the distinctive Japanese form of industrial organization known as *zaibatsu*. The form survives today in the Korean *chaebol* such as Samsung and Hyundai, modeled as they were on the prewar Japanese *zaibatsu*. In Japan, after the Second World War, the *zaibatsu* families were stripped of their holdings, and *zaibatsu* re-emerged as *keiretsu* or *guruppu gaisha* (group companies) with majority stakes in group companies owned by other companies in the group rather than a controlling family; many of today's great names in Japanese industry and finance are still affiliated with these groups.

Back in the Meiji period, the central position of banks in the industrial groups controlled by members of Japan's tightly knit elite meant that first claim on scarce financial resources went to "strategic" industries which, in the late nineteenth century, still carried the original connotation of industries needed to equip a modern military. But that did not solve the problem of how the capital to build these industries would be accumulated, much less how Japan could finance the imports of capital equipment necessary to run its new factories. In the late nineteenth-century world, gold-backed financial instruments were the only universally acceptable means of

2. The incident formed the basis for the film *The Last Samurai.*

settling obligations arising from cross-border trade, which meant that somehow or other, Japan had to accumulate financial capital in the form of gold if it was going to build an industrial base. Alas, during the final years of the Shogunate, Japan had lost much of what gold it had had; the domestic gold/silver exchange ratio of 1/5 was so far from the generally prevailing 1/15 ratio outside Japan that savvy foreigners, spotting the opportunity for hugely profitable arbitrage, snapped up Japan's gold at this grotesquely undervalued rate. Meanwhile, the Unequal Treaties prevented either the Shogunate or the new Meiji government from using tariffs to halt the rapid drain of gold out of the country.

There was, of course, no such thing in those days as a World Bank or foreign development aid to which Japan could turn. There were, however, foreign loans typically floated in the City of London—the sorts of loans that had largely financed the building of the North American railways. Japan would follow in America's footsteps, taking down a loan in London to pay for its first railroad. But Bismarck had specifically warned Iwakura of the danger of relying on foreign financing in an era when the price of default could include the arrival of the British Navy seizing assets in lieu of unpaid principal and interest. Matsukata Masayoshi, who became finance minister in 1881, saw this happen to countries such as Egypt and Turkey. He had been present when Bismarck warned Iwakura of the consequences of foreign borrowing. Matsukata resolved to repay the loan that had been taken down, and from thenceforth to take Bismarck at his word.

CAPITAL ACCUMULATION AND THE OUTWARD FORMS OF CONSTITUTIONAL GOVERNMENT

But if capital would not be raised overseas and the Unequal Treaties prevented Japan from restricting imports to conserve capital at home, the only way to accumulate enough of it to have any prayer of achieving "Rich Country, Strong Army" was to squeeze yet more out of Japan's long-suffering peasantry. If wages, prices, and living standards can be made to fall far enough, a capital surplus can be generated irrespective of a country's tariff regime, something that was first demonstrated by David Hume in the 1740s and has been intuitively understood since then by every government from Hamilton's United States to Bismarck's Germany to Stalin's Russia desperate to build an industrial base sufficient to field a state-of-the-art military.[3]

Pushing wages and living standards down, however, only works when peasants and workers do not fight back. Matsukata implemented a set of deflationary policies that succeeded in generating the capital surplus needed to repay the loans his predecessors had taken down and to provide his friends like Iwasaki with funds to import essential capital equipment. The price, however, was the closest Japan came until the late 1940s to an actual rebellion-from-below, in the form of the Freedom and People's Rights movement.

Much of the climate for the movement had already been laid by ex-samurai who had seized on the democratic notions that had inevitably begun circulating in Japan with the wholesale imports of other artifacts of Western culture. Some of these men may have simply been acting out of resentment at the way in which almost all positions of power had been grabbed by men from Satsuma and Choshu (many of the movement's early leaders, including Itagaki Taisuke, came from Tosa), but whatever their motivation, they fingered the lack of institutions of representative democracy as a key explanation for Japan's backwardness. With the deflationary policies and new taxes put into effect by Matsukata, the movement spread to the lower ranks of society. Hundreds of thousands had seen their land holdings expropriated when they were unable to pay land taxes; facing destitution and loss of their ancestral holdings, farmers staged violent protests in places such as the Chichibu district west of Tokyo, then a major center of sericulture.

The Meiji leaders reacted to these threats by agreeing to establish Japan's first modern constitution—the so-called "Meiji Constitution"— and a parliament, known as the Diet. These institutions not only helped mollify some of the democratic agitation, they also served as tangible evidence that the country was building the institutional apparatus of a modern state.

---

3. Hume's theory, known as the price-specie flow theory (or model), is considered the first important principle of economics as a systematic science. Hume showed that if a country on the gold standard acquired gold through trade surpluses, the country's money supply would increase, causing its export prices to rise, eventually leading to a fall in exports. Meanwhile, imports would become cheaper. A trade deficit would result, gold would flow out of the country, and—unless governments intervened—prices and wages would fall to the point that the cycle would resume. Hume's point was that governments need not fear a loss of gold provided wages and prices are allowed to fall.

THE SINO-JAPANESE WAR OF 1895

Even more convincing evidence to Westerners that Japan had to be taken seriously as a modern state, however, would be victory in war, and the obvious target was a disintegrating Qing dynasty. Korea was the ostensible *causus belli*; since the 1870s, the Meiji leaders had split not so much over the incorporation of Korea into their orbit—that was seen as inevitable—but whether Japan was "ready" to launch the necessary invasion. In fairness, Tokyo had legitimate strategic concerns, given the mad scramble of the time for colonies. With an erstwhile anti-imperialist power such as the United States gobbling up Hawaii, Puerto Rico, and the Philippines; with little lands such as Belgium that were barely countries themselves raping and pillaging their way through Africa; no one who mattered was going to give Japan any brownie points for being, in Woodrow Wilson's phrase, "too proud to fight." A German military advisor sent by Bismarck had warned Tokyo that Korea was a "dagger pointed at the heart of Japan." Korea had traditionally maintained a formal tributary relationship with Beijing, but as a moribund Qing dynasty was unable to resist increasingly blatant incursions by the Western imperialists, Tokyo worried that Korea's dependence on China and its inability or unwillingness to begin the reforms that might conceivably have preserved its independence made Korea a tempting target for Western colonization. If Korea was inevitably going to fall into someone's orbit other than China's, Tokyo was determined it would be Japan's. Opinion in Korea itself was split between those who favored the traditional relationship with China and those who saw what was happening in Meiji Japan as a model for their own country. The assassination in Shanghai of a pro-Japanese Korean in 1894 and the mutilation of his remains when they were shipped back to Korea provoked waves of hostility in Japan that helped determine the timing of the invasion. Japan insisted that China join Japan in demanding Korean "reforms"; when China predictably refused, Japan went to war.

The Japanese made mincemeat of the Chinese. They defeated the Chinese army near Pyongyang while chasing the Chinese navy out of the Yellow Sea and then sinking it in the Shantung harbor where it had taken refuge. Within a few months of the war's start, the Chinese sued for peace.

The war had all kinds of effects. It served as the death knell of a Chinese imperial system that had lasted for more than two millennia.

With the Qing brought low by people the Chinese had long regarded as scarcely more than half-civilized pirates, the dynasty saw the last of its prestige crumble. Japan's victory triggered a final rush for "concessions" by the European powers[4]; the Boxer Rebellion broke out in 1898 in response. The bloody suppression of the Rebellion and the capture of Beijing by the so-called Eight-nation Alliance of imperialist powers (including Japan) set the stage for the collapse of the Qing and the establishment of the Republic of China in 1911.

Meanwhile, huge Chinese gold reparations awarded to Tokyo in the settlement of the 1895 war finally ended the harrowing balance of payments problems that had hobbled Japan since the last days of the Shogunate. Japan got itself some colonies: Taiwan, the Penghu islands off Taiwan's west coast, and the Liaodong Peninsula to the northwest of Korea with its strategically located city then known as Port Arthur. Local Taiwanese, proclaiming an independent Republic of Formosa, fought on for another five months, but by October 1895, resistance to Japanese occupation had ended. Russia, with its own designs on China, persuaded Paris and Berlin to join Moscow in forcing Tokyo to give up the Liaodong Peninsula. The Triple Intervention, as it was called, tried to compensate Japan with more money, but Tokyo was not mollified. Russia won itself a twenty-five-year "lease" of the Liaodong Peninsula and, just as Tokyo had long feared, began moving to replace China as the dominant power on the Korean peninsula.

THE RUSSO-JAPANESE WAR OF 1904–1905

The Triple Intervention reminds one of a pride of lions moving in on a kill that a naive young leopard has made, but the leopard was learning fast. Tokyo signed the Anglo-Japanese Alliance of 1902, firmly anchoring itself to the superpower of the time, signaling that it too could play power politics and high-stakes diplomacy, while giving itself the freedom to prepare for war with the country it now saw as its greatest threat: Russia. The Unequal Treaties that had been signed under duress in the waning days of the Shogunate were renegotiated; Tokyo regained full control of its tariff

---

4. Americans may remember from their high school history textbooks a compensating call from Washington for an "Open Door" that would allow all the imperialist powers to gorge together on a single Chinese dish rather than carving it up with each power getting its own share.

regime and ended extraterritoriality. Japan's emerging stature—financial, military, industrial, cultural—enabled it to raise the money overseas to wage the Russo-Japanese War of 1904–5. Organized by Jacob Schiff of the American Jewish investment bank Kuhn Loeb, the financing marked Wall Street's debut as an international financial center. Schiff had been incensed by the treatment of his co-religionists at the hands of the Czarist police, but he also trusted Japan's credit.

Japan's victory in the Russo-Japanese War was, if anything, even more striking than its triumph ten years earlier over the Qing. For the first time since the fall of Constantinople, a non-Christian, non-Western power defeated the forces of a Christian nation. Both the Japanese Navy and the Army acquitted themselves brilliantly, with the Navy sinking much of the Russian fleet off the coast of Korea while the Army's battles on the Korean peninsula culminating in the siege of Port Arthur led to Japanese mastery on land. Some of the consequences of the two wars were similar; like the Qing, the Czarist regime never recovered its prestige; its defeat set the stage for the 1917 revolution. Meanwhile, just as Tokyo had picked up Taiwan as a spoil of the earlier war, so the 1905 settlement finally put Korea into its orbit. Tokyo had to use an ugly trick to force the abdication of Korea's King Gojung in order legally to convert Korea into an outright colony, but the trick was probably no worse than what the United States had done in 1893 to overthrow Queen Liliuokalani and incorporate Hawaii into the American Empire. Japan was behaving pretty much according to the standards of the time; more to the point, in fewer than forty years, the country had transformed itself from a weak, tottering polity into the pre-eminent nation-state of Asia and the first non-Western country in centuries that the Great Powers had to admit into their ranks. But the bill for that transformation had not yet been paid in full; it turned out to be far higher than anyone at the time could have imagined.

THE MEIJI ROOTS OF JAPAN'S MODERN TRAGEDY

Any account of what went wrong would have to start with the penetration of the countryside by the institutions of a militarized state capitalism. The *daimyō* and Shogunate may have squeezed the peasantry mercilessly during the Tokugawa centuries, but in the final analysis, all they really cared about was stability and taxes. As long as taxes were collected and

order maintained, villages and rural areas were largely left alone to organize their own affairs.

But the coming of Meiji saw what amounted to a forced proletarianiza-
tion of the peasant class and its incorporation into the military-industrial
polity the Meiji oligarchs believed essential to preserving Japan's independence. As we have seen, the countryside formed the primary source of the
capital expropriated to finance the building of an industrial base. The peasantry also served as a vast labor pool; young women in the tens of thousands worked in the silk-spinning factories that produced Japan's largest
earner of foreign exchange in the late nineteenth century. (Tens of thousands more were sold into the brothels of the major cities—one Edo period
practice that continued with little change, although the cultural brilliance
of Edo's floating world had been considerably dimmed by a Meiji Japan that
found it all a bit embarrassing.) Meanwhile, semi-annual migrations of
men from farm to city and back replaced the annual processions of *daimyō*
to and from Edo, as peasant workers flocked into the factory towns and
cities during the winter months when their paddies and fields lay fallow.

The Meiji leaders had deliberately set about incorporating the peasantry
into a single national polity that would replace the *han* and class-based
mosaic of the preceding centuries. But success in this project required
systematic efforts to substitute a new political and conceptual framework
for the web of local institutions and cultural mores that had knit together
life in the rural parts of Japan during the Edo period. Otherwise, fierce,
sometimes violent resistance (noted above in the People's Rights movement) threatened to sabotage the project. A key ideological prop of the
new framework was the notion that Japan is an innately harmonious society, operating on consensus, whose political and economic arrangements
have divine sanction stemming from the will of a god—from the emperor.
Thus overt opposition to political and economic arrangements is not only
"un-Japanese" but an existential rebellion against a sacred order.

Constructing such a framework was no easy task, even if the groundwork had been prepared by the Neo-Confucian worship of hierarchy that had been such a critical component of the political ideology of
Tokugawa Japan. But the Meiji leaders had tools that their predecessors
had lacked: universal public education and universal male conscription.
With the possible exception of the nationwide land tax that had been used
to squeeze the capital for industrialization from the countryside, perhaps
nothing was so hated as the introduction of conscription in 1873. Peasant

families had been resigned to the periodic corvée labor that had been required during the Tokugawa centuries, but to see their sons taken away from them engendered huge bitterness.

Hated it may have been, but conscription—and universal public education—largely achieved its ideological purposes in indoctrinating the peasantry (and their children off in the factory towns and cities) into the new ethos thought essential for a great modern nation. To be sure, this ethos was built on the existing foundations of the traditional rural stress on frugality, endless labor, and a communal approach to problem solving (the last essential to rice cultivation and the concomitant maintenance of the network of irrigation canals and drainage ditches needed to flood and drain paddies at the appropriate times of the year). The Meiji leaders mixed into these timeless rural verities, however, the samurai virtues that had been their own inheritance even though these were foreign to much of rural Japan. Like farmers everywhere, Japanese peasants had traditionally loathed militarism and war. The notion of a young man cheerfully slitting open his stomach after avenging a slight to his lord would have struck many peasants as bizarre and ultimately unfilial; young men were expected to be loyal to their fathers and they demonstrated that loyalty by working until they dropped and siring sons of their own. The samurai ethos itself had ossified to the point of caricature during the Edo period as samurai retreated into ever more histrionic displays of self-sacrifice and hyper-stoicism as compensation for living in a society where such virtues had become in fact meaningless. But with Japan suddenly facing both external military and domestic civil threats, these virtues were dragged out of their Edo period museum and refashioned to suit not just a modern military but a militarized society.

Almost every aspect of life took on a military coloring. Boys went off to school in uniforms derived from what Prussian cadets wore. For the first time on a large scale, girls joined boys in school, where they were taught that the highest aspiration for a girl was to become "good wife, wise mother" with the implication that her ultimate aim should be to produce soldiers to fight and, when called on, die for their emperor. The emperor himself was recast as a military figure; from the days of Heian and before, the emperor had been a cultural and religious personage—apart from and at least nominally superior to the warrior caste. No more. The emperor now appeared regularly in uniform and became the ultimate focus of that supreme military virtue: unquestioned loyalty.

This was a conscious political construct. Bismarck had advised the 1871–73 Iwakura Mission that Japan needed a focus for national feeling: a deliberate inculcation of patriotism that would transfer loyalties previously centered on family, village, region, or local lord to a national level. This was, of course, the great project for nineteenth-century Germany, as it would become for Meiji Japan. Japan's ruling classes had always had a consciousness of themselves as Japanese—and of Japan as a nation in a world of nations; as was noted in the first chapter, this forms a key reason why Japan could adopt so easily to the sovereign territorial ideal of the Westphalian system. Japan's ruling classes did not require the huge conceptual leaps of their counterparts in such places as Beijing or Istanbul to grasp what they needed to do to fit their country into a world order in which both political authority and political legitimacy rested with national governments.

But such consciousness of "Japaneseness" had been largely limited to the upper classes. Even among most of their members, loyalty to *han*, *daimyō*, or shogun had often taken precedence over loyalty to "Japan." That was certainly the case among the peasantry. A critical mission of Meiji was smashing those loyalties and replacing them with nationalism and emperor-worship.

One measure we have already noted: the breakup of the old *han* and the redrawing of the political map of Japan into the modern *ken* or prefectures. The result was no federal system with powers distributed among national and regional centers. While many of the old *han* castle towns—Sendai, Hiroshima, Kochi, Kagoshima—were, to be sure, reincarnated as prefectural capitals, they forfeited almost all the power they had enjoyed over local affairs to the great bureaucracies taking shape in Tokyo. Meanwhile, the Meiji government took direct aim at the traditional fabric of Japanese religion. Despite Oda Nobunaga's persecution of the Buddhist clerical hierarchy late in the sixteenth century, Buddhism itself had continued to be thoroughly intertwined with Japanese cultural life during the Tokugawa era. Indeed, shogunal officials had turned to the nationwide networks of Buddhist temples in their efforts to ferret out and destroy Christian sympathies. All Japanese had been required to register with their local temples which had thus come to function as something like local registrars. All samurai and well-to-do merchants sent their sons to temples for schooling, as did the *gōshi* or "rural samurai" (the top stratum of the peasantry that had been allowed to carry swords) and some of the better-off peasant families.

With the militarization and universalization of education under Meiji, however, the state wrested control of education away from the temples at a time when the sudden obsession with defining the "Japanese" at the expense of the foreign cast a shadow over Buddhism. Japan did, in Shinto, have an indigenous faith of sorts, but after more than a millennium in which Buddhism and Shinto had functioned effectively as a single religion (albeit with a plenitude of sects), pulling the two apart proved, in theological terms, to be almost a hopeless exercise—but not in patriotic or national terms. Buddhist temples were stripped of much of their wealth, required to separate from the Shinto shrines with which they had usually been affiliated, and pushed aside as the central religious institutions in the lives of most Japanese. In their place, the Meiji government instituted so-called "State Shinto" centered on worship of the Imperial House. While the edifices of this effectively new religion may have looked like pure, minimalist re-creations of traditional architecture in which Chinese and Korean influences were eliminated to the extent possible (Tokyo's Meiji Shrine is a good example of the style), their ceremonial functions were effectively modern: inculcating nationalism and other virtues considered essential for a unified, authoritarian polity. The social and political functions of leading shrines such as Meiji and Yasukuni were far closer to those of the Nazi Thingplaz or the Palaces of Atheism in the Marxist polities than to those of genuine churches or temples serving the spiritual needs of congregants. State Shinto was a deliberate political construct, inculcating the notion that the state itself had the highest command on human loyalty; that it embodied eternal principles.

Meanwhile, what of Christianity? Meiji leaders understood early that the prohibitions against Christianity would have to be lifted if Japan was to be accepted as any kind of equal by the West. And they could hardly avoid noticing that the countries on which they were now trying to model their economic and military institutions all professed one or more of the Christian confessions. A number of Meiji intellectuals did experiment with the religion and some became genuine converts. Christian missionaries were, after a 250-year hiatus, permitted again to evangelize in Japan. This time, the Catholics came mostly from France rather than the Iberian Peninsula, and they were joined by Orthodox from Russia and Protestants largely from the United States. The efforts of these late nineteenth- and early twentieth-century missionaries resulted in a plethora of schools, universities, and hospitals, many of which continue to thrive today and are among the best of their class in Japan.[5] Unlike the situation three centuries earlier, however (or, for that matter, the contemporary situation in Korea), Christianity made few inroads among ordinary people—it was thought of as something for a small, Westernized elite.

The fate of religion during the Meiji period—the destruction of much of the existing fabric tainted as "un-Japanese," the construction of what was effectively a new religion made up of supposedly "pure," native traditions, and a fascination among a small elite with a Western import that left a large institutional footprint—serves as a template for wider developments. Meiji was simultaneously obsessed with defining what was "Japanese" while trying to obscure the historic continental roots of so much of what made Japan what it really was, at the same time tearing off and gulping down huge chunks of Western culture that ended up being only half-digested. The result was a kind of schizophrenia both about the rest of Asia and about the West, a schizophrenia that turned out to have deadly political consequences.

Attempts to identify a supposedly pure Japanese culture had predated Meiji; they were particularly associated with the Mito School named for a city to the north of Edo that featured a famous academy devoted to nativist learning. The influence of the Mito School itself was tied up with the growing awareness in the last decades of the Tokugawa that Japan's seclusion could not be sustained. But in the wake of the Restoration, the obsessions of the Mito School acquired a seemingly new relevance.

Japan had always defined itself in relation to Chinese civilization; as noted in the first chapter, the distinctions among what is "Japanese," what is imported, and what has been made over from original Chinese models extended into the very fabric of the language itself. Almost reflexively, questions of native vs. import had always been framed with reference to China.

But now there was a new external frame of reference in the form of the Western powers, a group of countries that posed an existential threat to Japan's control of its own affairs that China never had. What made things even trickier was the persistence of the old frame, still unavoidably there, down to the very characters used to write Japanese. Japan's collective

---

5. Empress Michiko is, for example, a graduate of a Catholic girls school, arguably the most prestigious such school in the country. No one finds this remarkable; to understand the implications for the sociological reach of Christian institutions in modern Japan, try imagining a Prince Philip or a Kate Middleton having graduated from a Buddhist, Hindu, or Muslim academy.

reaction to these new realities can remind one of an immigrant or parvenu desperately trying to conceal his origins. As the Meiji era proceeded and the ambitions of its leaders came to fruition, growing contempt for the rest of Asia became more pronounced and would reach pathological levels after Japan's triumph in the 1895 Sino-Japanese war.

The reaction of Fukuzawa Yukichi to Japan's victory is revealing. This admirable man whose portrait today graces the 10,000 yen note was arguably the most important intellectual of Meiji Japan, a visionary who founded Japan's leading private university and a tireless promoter of "enlightened" Western ideas from science and education to representative government and a free press. He famously called upon Japan to "leave Asia" with the implication that it should seek to join the West. He characterized the war as one "between a country which is trying to develop civilization and a country which disturbs the development of civilization"; on receiving news of the victory he "could hardly refrain from rising up in delight."

Paralleling this contempt for Asia was an emulation of the West that could reach absurd levels—calls to abolish the Japanese language in favor of something written with Roman letters, for example, or the construction of a fancy pavilion in central Tokyo where the elite gathered for European-style balls. Mixed bathing was banned while (almost wholly ineffectual) laws were passed against male homosexuality, cross-dressing, and the practice of keeping official concubines. The Kabuki was separated from its long-standing association with male prostitution and some of its actors began appearing on stage in white-tie-and-tails. Eating meat became a mark of distinction.[6] Meanwhile, at the very time the Meiji government was promoting State Shinto and emperor-worship as ostensibly pure Japanese rites untainted by foreign associations, traditional rural shrine festivals featuring mobs of naked young men and boys chasing after fertility symbols while women staggered around carrying huge phalli were treated like some dark family secret. All this half-understood aping of the West at a time of busy hiding of anything that might reek of Japan's cultural links with continental Asia or its own indigenous bawdy past went

6. During the Edo period, the killing of four-legged creatures had been prohibited; the famous Japanese dish *sukiyaki* was a Meiji period attempt to make beef palatable to people who were not used to eating it. Indeed, there is a whole category of Japanese cuisine known as *yōshoku*—literally, Western food—that isn't Western at all but rather Meiji reworkings of European dishes. Other famous *yōshoku* dishes include *tonkatsu* (deep-fried pork cutlet, *katsu* being the Japanese pronunciation of cutlet), *omu-raisu* (omelet draped over rice), and *karei-raisu* (rice with curry—a Japanese version of Anglo-Indian food).

under the rubric *bunmei kaika* (civilization and enlightenment)—a slogan as redolent of Meiji as *fukoku kyōhei* (rich country, strong army).

The great mid-twentieth-century novelist Mishima Yukio captured all this when he compared Meiji Japan to "an anxious housewife preparing to receive guests" hiding away anything she might think could detract from the image of the "immaculate, idealized life" with which she hoped to impress her guests. In his novel *Spring Snow*, Mishima would portray with unsparing accuracy the world of the small Westernized elite of late Meiji down to the billiard tables, snifters of brandy, and suits cut in perfect imitation of what one could find on London's Seville Row. (Indeed, the old Japanese word for a Western-style business suit is *sebiro*, derived from Seville Row.)

Spring Snow is the first in a tetralogy of novels Mishima wrote at the end of his life about the fate of Japan in the twentieth century. The second, *Runway Horses,* depicts the inevitable reaction to so much fawning over the West by a small elite: the rise of an extreme fanaticism centered on the national essence, national polity, and the Person of the Emperor. This fanaticism would slip out of political control of those who had designed it as a means of assuring peasant loyalties and destroy their legacy.

What was ironic about the whole business was that all the obsessions with what it meant to be Japanese, the essence of the national polity, and the position of the Japanese "race" in the global hierarchy owed at least as much to Western racial theorizing and the crude social Darwinism of such writers as Count Gobineau and Herbert Spencer as it did to the intellectual inheritance of the Mito School or earlier Japanese thinking on such matters. In his ugly and hugely influential 1850 pamphlet *Judaism in Music*, for example, the German composer Richard Wagner had argued that great art could only emanate from those who had grown up organically within a given culture; that any political arrangement that cut people off from the deepest wellsprings of their culture would give rise to false and inauthentic art. From an artistic standpoint, Wagner may simply have been articulating an early version of the "gotta be black to feel the blues" notion, but the political ramifications of the widespread sentiments to which he gave voice were both profound and disastrous.[7]

7. They may have included the modern state of Israel. Theodore Herzl, the founder of the Zionist movement, accepted Wagner's core contention; if his diaries are to be believed, he conceived of a separate state for Jews where they could once more be proudly and unabashedly Jewish at a performance of Wagner's opera *Tannenhauser*. It is no accident that Wagner, whose aesthetic is about as un-Japanese as it is possible to get, is revered by legions of Japan's classical music lovers.

This was all catnip to Meiji Japan. Of course, it is obvious in retrospect why so much of this theorizing about race and culture would emerge out of a Germany where building a modern nation-state out of the wreckage left behind by Napoleon and the breakup of the Holy Roman Empire was a project, not a given. It is also obvious why it would exert such a baleful influence on a Japan where gloating over military triumphs and its acceptance into the club of Great Powers barely concealed raging insecurity about whether the country really did measure up—coupled with an inability to acknowledge or grieve openly about the sacrifice of so much of Japan's traditional culture.

NATSUME SOSEKI'S *KOKORO* AND THE MEIJI LEGACY

The most profound attempt to grapple with what had happened to Japan during the Meiji decades—the killing off of so much of the past without the ability to discuss it—can probably be found in the 1914 novel *Kokoro*, widely acknowledged as the masterpiece of the greatest of the early twentieth-century Japanese writers, Natsume Soseki. The central figure in the novel—an older man known only as *Sensei* (teacher/master)—carries with him a dark secret: the suicide of his best friend decades earlier for which he blames himself. But he can only discuss the incident and his guilt in the form of a long letter that serves as the third part of the novel.

Commentators universally agree that Soseki wanted *Sensei* to represent the Meiji era that had just ended, while the best friend and his suicide stand, respectively, for traditional Japan and what was lost so the country could survive. (The young man to whom *Sensei* sends the letter symbolizes the new Taisho era that was then just beginning. The era was named for the emperor who succeeded Meiji in 1912 and who would in turn be the father of the man the West would come to know as Emperor Hirohito.) Overshadowing the novel—and referred to many times therein—is the suicide of General Nogi Maresuke, one of the great heroes of the Russo-Japanese War, and the personal tutor and mentor of young Prince Hirohito. Nogi committed *seppuku* in the traditional samurai manner following the death of the Emperor Meiji. Nogi may well have been anguished by the tens of thousands of lives (including that of his second son) lost in the siege of Port Arthur that he commanded, a battle that would provide the world a gruesome foretaste of the horrific, grinding trench warfare of

World War I. Whatever private demons may have assailed Nogi, however, both his suicide and the manner in which he carried it out electrified the country and helped serve as a catalyst for the murderous fanaticism that would gather strength over the following decades.

As the history of the last century tells us—or even, alas, a glance at the evening news—prewar Japan had no monopoly on hatred; hysteria; an ugly, jeering nationalism; or any of the other monsters unleashed by modernity. But while these afflict all modernizing societies to a greater or lesser degree, they slipped out of political control in Japan in the specific ways they did because of the yawning gap between political reality in Japan and the fictions with which that reality was described and understood.

Such gaps, of course, exist everywhere outside middle school civics texts. But what arguably made Japan unique was the existence of not one but two sets of fictions about the way the country was governed—one inherited from the past and one imported from the West. The fiction imported from the past was that of imperial rule; that from the West the notions of constitutional government and the rule of law. The latter had been instituted partly in response to the threat of the People's Rights movement and the agitation of people such as Itagaki for some form of representative government. Most of the impetus, however, came from the expectations of the Western world. Modern countries were supposed to have parliaments and courts; in the much the same way their people were supposed to eat meat with knives and forks and eschew mixed bathing.

If Japan was supposed to have parliaments, political parties, and courts, then Japan would have parliaments, political parties, and courts. But as we have seen, the men who seized power in 1868 did so under the rubric of "restoring" direct imperial rule, and most of them were not about to accept any constitutional limits on "imperial" decision-making, irrespective of whatever facades they needed to construct to convince the countries that had imposed on them the Unequal Treaties that they had become a fully modern land.

In setting up an apparatus of courts and legislatures, the Meiji government was not creating a constitutional monarchy along British lines. While the British government may style itself "Her Majesty's Government" and enter into treaties or pass laws in Her Majesty's name, it is now universally understood that a British monarch has no actual power to overrule Parliament or an English court—that any attempt to do so would create an immediate constitutional crisis that a monarch could not survive.

No such situation existed in Japan, and while the possibility was latent in the existence of such institutions as a National Diet (Parliament) and a judiciary, the Meiji leaders took deliberate steps to ensure that these institutions could not interfere in—much less overrule—"imperial" decision-making.

YAMAGATA ARITOMO AND A BUREAUCRACY BEYOND POLITICAL CONTROL

The key figure in all this was Yamagata Aritomo, usually styled the father of the modern Japanese military. E. H. Norman described Yamagata as "the perfect military bureaucrat" noting that he "detested above all political parties of any stripe. . . any movement organized to represent the interests of people at large, no matter how inadequate or restricted, stirred his fiercest animosity." Yamagata's critical step in "creating and maintaining the structure of military autocracy" eliminated any possibility of parliamentary oversight over key bureaucratic appointments. Yamagata specifically arranged for an "imperial message" that critical matters dealing with the staffing of the bureaucracy be the province of the Privy Council, which theoretically served at the pleasure of the emperor.

But, of course, the emperor was not actually making appointments or decisions. The Taisho Emperor, who reigned from 1912 to 1926, was probably feeble-minded, and while that was certainly not true of his oldest son, known today in Japan as the Showa Emperor and in the West as Emperor Hirohito, Hirohito had grown up understanding that the emperor did not make policy. This understanding stemmed both from the historical role of the emperor as a legitimizing figure "above politics" and the notions of constitutional monarchy floating in from Europe. (Only on three occasions is Hirohito known to have intervened decisively in policy matters—in 1936 to suppress an uprising by rightist officers, in 1941 when he instructed Tojo Hideki to form a cabinet, and in 1945 to end the war.)

As long as formally unacknowledged but actual decision-making power lay with the "Sat-Cho" clique—the ex-samurai from Satsuma and Choshu who had overthrown the Shogunate—the central flaw in Japan's governing structure could remain hidden. But once these men began dying off, it became fatal.

Karel van Wolferen has identified this flaw as the lack of a center of political accountability. Such a center can be a democratically elected political party, a politburo, a dictator, or even a hereditary monarch. But the key here is that the individual or individuals who constitute the political center—who make and implement decisions that determine a country's goals and the means to reach them—must account for what they are doing, if not to an electorate, a disinterested judiciary, or an independent press, then at least to themselves.

As the *genrō* (elder statesmen—i.e., the Meiji leaders who survived into the twentieth century) began retreating from active policy-making into groups such as the Privy Council who could veto decisions without being required to bear the consequences, the stage was set for colossal political irresponsibility. That irresponsibility would culminate in the prosecution of a land war in Asia that lacked any plausible scenario for victory and to a direct attack on an overseas power with an industrial base ten times larger than Japan's. The end-result would be precisely what the Meiji leaders had attempted to forestall: the loss of Japan's control of its own affairs.

THE CATASTROPHE

Given the destruction, misery, and death that Japan would rain on its neighbors and ultimately itself, one is inevitably tempted to counterfactuals. If the Meiji government had not hidden from the Japanese people the actual situation at the end of the Russo-Japanese War, would the curdling of public opinion against the United States have gotten started?[8] If Woodrow Wilson had not insisted on the deletion of clauses from the Versailles Treaty calling for an end to racism or if the US Congress had not passed the blatantly racist 1924 Immigration Act could Japanese have come to believe something other than that the Western democracies would

8. Although Japan's military triumphs had been indisputable, the war had not been won when Japan agreed to the peace settlement brokered by Theodore Roosevelt. The Meiji leaders saw what their successors three decades later did not—that total victory on the battlefield was beyond reach. Japan's bankers also signaled Tokyo they wanted Japan to settle with Moscow. But rather than explain why Japan did not receive an indemnity as it had ten years earlier from the Chinese, the government allowed the notion to take hold that the Treaty of Portsmouth that had ended the war was another Triple Intervention; that one more time, Western countries—this time, the United States—had intervened to rob Japan of what its soldiers had died for on the battlefield.

never see them as equals? Could the very real shoots of party politics and representative institutions that began to flower in the 1920s—aka "Taisho Democracy"—have conceivably matured into robust checks on militarist power grabs if the external economic and security environment had been less hostile? If an earthquake had not leveled much of Tokyo in 1923, setting the stage for a financial crisis four years later—a crisis that devastated both rural areas and the urban working classes—would fanatics have had a harder time recruiting ordinary Japanese into their grandiose projects? Behind all of these lies the biggest question of them all: if the major powers had not immolated their economies in fruitless attempts to re-create the vanished pre-1914 global monetary and financial order, precipitating a global depression that sucked Japan into its maw, could the country have avoided the slide into fascism?

While there can be no final answer to these questions, the central flaw in Japan's governing setup was not corrected after the Second World War. We will return to this issue in the next chapter; for our purposes here, it is sufficient to note that Japan's experience since 1945 demonstrates that the lack of a center of political accountability is not in and of itself inconsistent with a far more benevolent political order than that which prevailed before the war. But such benevolence is possible in a political setup lacking a center of political accountability only when the most potentially disruptive of issues—the conduct of foreign relations, arrangements to provide for national security, and the distribution of economic power—can be sidestepped. The peculiar situation of the immediate postwar decades did indeed permit Japan to sidestep those issues—a matter, again, we will take up at some length in the next chapter—but they were both unavoidable and unresolvable in the crucial decades during which the grip of the Meiji leaders loosened and finally disappeared. Instead, Japan came increasingly to resemble a murderous arena without umpires in which victory went to the most ruthless, the most fanatical, and those most ready to resort to force, whether that be in the form of provocations abroad or the murder of political opponents at home.

Again, Japan was not unique in those fateful decades in falling under the sway of thugs, in elevating hatred and brutality to national fetishes. Japan could hardly, in any case, have avoided the tidal waves unleashed by the greatest avoidable catastrophe in human history: the First World War. Nominally fighting on the allied side, Japan had done rather well for itself in the war, running its factories full-stop to meet orders from the belligerents and picking up some German colonies afterwards. Even the devastation of the 1923 earthquake could hardly compare with what had happened to the economies of France, Germany, or Russia because of the war. And while Japan, like so much of the rest of the world, succumbed to the fetishization of the gold standard and the economically devastating attempts to re-create pre-1914 parities (in November 1929, Japan returned to the gold standard and a forced appreciation of the yen to the prewar rate of ¥2/$1 triggering an immediate deflationary recession), it came to its senses sooner than most, going off the gold standard in 1931. The efforts of the finance minister of the time, Takahashi Korekiyo, to stimulate the Japanese economy even earned him the nickname "the Japanese Keynes."

Whatever the myriad horrors committed in the emperor's name, they ultimately pale beside those of the Nazi and Soviet regimes. Japan never murdered millions of its own citizens simply because of their religion or their supposed class background. Nor, despite the atrocities committed in China and Southeast Asia or the abominable treatment of prisoners of war, was there anything quite comparable in scale to German behavior in the siege of Leningrad or the suppression of the Warsaw uprising. The closest was probably the saturation terror-bombing of Chongqing in 1939 and the rape of Nanjing two years earlier in which Japanese soldiers went on a weeks-long rampage after the fall of what was then the capital of China, killing tens of thousands in cold blood.[9] But the Nanjing massacre was not official policy; it represented, rather, what can happen in the absence of policy.

Nanjing writ large points to what was unique to Japan's political setup in the way the country joined the general global descent of the times into barbarism and moral bankruptcy. Unlike the Nazi concentration camps or Stalin's gulags (or for that matter, the March 1945 American firebombing of Tokyo or the atomic bombings of Hiroshima and Nagasaki five months later, or the Bengal famine of 1943), the atrocities committed by the Japanese did not typically result from specific policy decisions made by central governing authorities. This is not an attempt to whitewash Japanese behavior, to excuse the depravity of the xenophobic intellectuals of the time with their endless paeans to Japan's divine mission, or to make allowances for the inhuman brutality which became par for the course in

9. The infamous medical experiments conducted on several thousand Chinese and Russians by the notorious Unit 731 would, alas, also serve as an outstanding example in the annals of atrocities.

the Japanese Imperial Army—both in the treatment of its own soldiers and in the treatment of foreigners. But it is critical in grasping both what happened during these decades and the historical ramifications, ramifications that extend into our own time, that we make the attempt to be clear on the causes of the disaster.

A crazed, leering madman of a dictator is not one of those causes. Allied analysts kept trying to find a Japanese equivalent of a Hitler or a Mussolini and for a while they settled on Tojo Hideki, the commander of the notorious Kwantung Army in China and later the prime minister who authorized the attack on Pearl Harbor. (Technically, Tojo recommended the attack to the emperor who then—reluctantly, it is said—authorized it.) While no one would mistake Tojo for St. Francis of Assisi—he was a xenophobe and a militarist—neither was he a Goering. Tojo had not hijacked the organs of the Japanese state in pursuit of a maniacal vision; he was a conscientious solider carrying out what he thought was his duty and was distinguished from many of his contemporaries only by being more obviously skilled at the bureaucratic infighting that led to his appointment as prime minister. If Tojo did not fit the demonic bill, and since the mayhem Japan had unleashed had been carried out in the name of the emperor, perhaps, then, Hirohito was the ultimate villain. But this was even more transparently absurd. While the emperor may not have been the shy, pacific recluse of postwar construct, neither was he some sort of latter-day Genghis Khan bent on world conquest.

Rather than engage in a fruitless hunt for an agent or agents who led Japan to disaster, the analyst does better to remind him- or herself that there never was any break in the continuity of Japan's governing institutions in the decades leading to the war—nothing like the Reichstag Fire Decrees or Mussolini's March on Rome, not to mention the Bolshevik storming of the Winter Palace or the 1911 and 1949 revolutions in China. The closest was the February 26, 1936 Incident in which a group of radical young Army officers attempted to seize power and succeeded in assassinating several leading business executives and cabinet ministers (including the finance minister Takahashi mentioned above—his "crime" had been advocacy of some restraint on military spending). The uprising was suppressed and its ring-leaders executed on the direct intervention of the emperor with the explicit support of then-General Tojo.

The uprising represented the culmination of what might be called the politics of intimidation and assassination. Absent responsive institutional channels in which nationalist radicals in the Army and elsewhere could influence policy, outraged by corruption in high places at a time of grinding rural poverty, nourished by a noxious stew of national socialism, emperor-worship, and racialism, they resorted to a characteristic East Asian political phenomenon: histrionic displays of nationalism and xenophobia in order to embarrass sitting govern-ments. This phenomenon is more visible today in China and South Korea than in Japan, but it was the only acceptable way to express op-position to policy in prewar Japan. And because the young men were "pure"—i.e., untouched by the "sordid" money-grubbing of commerce or horse-trading of normal politics—they commanded a great deal of popular support.

An obvious parallel exists not only with China and Korea but also with Islamist radicals today in Muslim nations, not simply in the tactics of terror and intimidation, but also the sympathy commanded in the wider population. The religious zeal and "purity" of the agitators forms, after all, such a contrast to the compromised worldliness of ruling elites. But unlike at least the first generation of Islamist radicals—or, for that matter, anti-Japanese demonstrators in China and Korea today—Japan's young agitators of the 1930s had at their disposal duly constituted means of physical coercion. They were not outsiders; they were embedded within the existing power structure. But it was a power structure in which real, as opposed to formal, mechanisms to settle disputes had disappeared with the dying off of the Meiji leaders. The result was end-less, debilitating, and even murderous power struggles. The paralysis in Tokyo was so great that not only did the Navy and the Army separately exercise veto power over policy and even the makeup of governments, but were at constant loggerheads with each other. The high commands in Tokyo could not control hotheads in the field who effectively made their own military decisions and had demonstrated that they were pre-pared to kill superiors who showed insufficient zeal or reverence for the "Imperial Will."

It was in this atmosphere of fear and intimidation, where the cost of raising even the mildest objections to some young zealot's harebrained pro-posal could be life itself, that Japan sank ever deeper into the morass of an endless land war in China against an enemy that could not be defeated, no matter how many battles were "won" or how much land was (temporarily) seized. Ultimately, the capacity to make reasoned policy judgments collapsed altogether, leading Tokyo to authorize a direct attack on the United States that the very architects of the attack understood was ultimately suicidal.

Three things ultimately stand out in any attempt to identify the roots of what happened: adventurism and imperialist ambitions in China, fear of the Soviet Union, and admiration for the Nazis. Americans tend to see the US war with Japan in the Pacific as the central event of the times. While the American victory over Japan did, to be sure, bring an end to the entire series of conflicts known collectively as the "Second World War," for the Japanese, the Pacific War—as the war with the United States is often known in Japan—is more like a disastrous sequel to the more important war: the "Greater East Asia War" fought with China.[10]

Japan had joined the Western powers in the scramble for concessions in China in the waning years of the Qing dynasty. When the First World War distracted the attention of the West, restraint on Japanese adventurism all but vanished. In 1915, Japan issued the infamous Twenty-One Demands that would have effectively established Japanese hegemony in China and turned China into a Japanese protectorate. Partly because of pressure from the United States and Britain, some of the demands were withdrawn, but they signaled the extent of Japanese ambitions. They also midwifed the birth of modern Chinese nationalism.

Despite the outpouring of national feeling in China unplugged by the Twenty-One Demands and their partial retraction, the failure of the Republic of China to impose a unified national government left the Japanese opportunities for all kinds of mischief. China dissolved into warring fiefs controlled—or not controlled as the case may be—by various warlords, many of whom were nothing more than gangsters prepared to do deals with Japan's own adventurers.

The key player in widening the conflict was the Kwantung Army. Established in 1906 for the purposes of protecting Japanese lives and property in Manchuria, the Kwantung Army had, by the 1920s, effectively become a force unto itself. Yamagata's machinations had removed any accountability or oversight of the Army—the Army reported directly to the emperor, which meant in practice that it reported to no one.

---

10. The Chinese also—and understandably—see their war with Japan as the central theater of the wider war. While the United States did ultimately crush the Japanese, the suffering in China by every measure was orders of magnitude greater than what the United States endured.

In September 1931, radical officers in the Kwantung Army staged an explosion on a railroad near Mukden in Manchuria. Having manufactured a pretext, the Army then proceeded to take over Manchuria and turn it into what amounted to a Japanese colony, although they established a puppet regime ("Manchukuo" or "Country of the Manchus") nominally under the sovereignty of the last of the Qing emperors, Pu Yi. The League of Nations demanded that Japan leave Manchuria; the Japanese walked out of the League as a result.

Manchuria became the most important of the Japanese colonies, serving as something of a laboratory for experimentation with economic methods that would be perfected in the postwar era in Japan proper. The economic misery of the times had convinced many Japanese—as it would many others in the world, most notably the Nazis in their search for *lebensraum*—that without additional territory, without captive markets and sources of supply, they were doomed. The economics of liberal capitalism posits free trade and comparative advantage as the sources of wealth. But liberal capitalism had been discredited by the Great Depression which hit Japan as hard as it hit anyone, and in Japan's case had started two years earlier with the financial crisis of 1927.

The great ideological competitor of the corporatism-*cum*-fascism implemented on such a thoroughgoing scale in Manchuria was not liberal capitalism, seen by ruling circles in Japan as on its death bed, but Marxian socialism embodied in Stalin's Soviet Union.

The hatred and fear of Communism in general and Stalin in particular has to be factored into any analysis of what happened. "Manchukuo" was held to be a critical bulwark checking Soviet designs on China. Apologists for Japan's wartime actions[11] will point to China's anarchy of the time as an open invitation to Soviet meddling. The most important consequence in China of the war itself may have been to bring the Chinese Communist Party to power, but the Kuomintang (literally, National People's Party) against which the Japanese would, after 1937, wage open war was also organized along Leninist lines and advised and assisted by Moscow throughout the 1930s.

11. They still exist in Japan and include the current prime minister Abe Shinzo, whose grandfather, Kishi Nobusuke, was first economic czar of "Manchukuo," then minister of munitions in the wartime cabinet, and would emerge as the key architect of the postwar Japanese political order.

THE MARCO POLO AND NOMONHAN INCIDENTS

These two incidents determined the future course of the war. In July 1937, fighting erupted on the Marco Polo bridge outside Beijing between Nationalist Chinese troops and small groups of Japanese solders (under earlier treaties, the Japanese and other foreigners had the right to station small groups of soldiers to protect their legations in Beijing proper). This incident was almost certainly an accident—it was not deliberately staged, as Mukden had been. But it was the spark that lit open war between the Nationalist Chinese under Chiang Kai-shek and the Japanese.

Things might have worked out differently had it not been for a less well-known incident that occurred two years later. Believing Stalin was the real enemy, many in Japan's high command were eager to "strike north." The Red Army handed the Japanese their first real defeat of the wider war in 1939 when the two armies met and fought at the Mongolian border town of Nomonhan (Mongolia had become a Soviet satellite.) The Russians sent the Japanese reeling; casualties on the Japanese side numbered over 25,000. In the wake of the Nazi-Soviet pact signed later that year, Tokyo and Moscow also signed a non-aggression pact. Hitler would, of course, famously violate the Nazi-Soviet pact, but both Tokyo and Moscow continued to honor the Japan-Soviet pact until the days immediately after Japan's acceptance of the Potsdam declaration in August 1945 that formally ended hostilities between the Allied powers and Japan. Fearful that he would not get his share of the spoils, Stalin grabbed two large Japanese islands and a group of smaller ones off the coast of Hokkaido.

But we are getting ahead of our story. The cumulative effect of the Marco Polo and Nomonhan incidents was to turn Japanese military attention back to China itself.

From then on the continued prosecution of the war became a matter of an inability to walk away from sunk costs, of strategic blindness concealed—for a time—by tactical success, of an unwillingness to acknowledge the reality that Japan's aims could not be achieved under any plausible scenario (particularly once Hitler had launched his own strategically blind invasion of Russia). Japan's strategists could not conceive of acknowledging error, much less walking away from it—among other things, even talk of retreat invited assassination. Instead, China proper had to be invaded to secure the all-important Manchurian colony. The British and French colonies in Southeast Asia had to be taken over to secure the sources of supply necessary for the China invasion. The United States had to be knocked out as a potential combatant, since it was threatening an embargo unless Japan gave up its designs on China and Southeast Asia.

The Japanese Imperial Army achieved tactical victory after tactical victory in China. But while the Army may have had no intention of being sucked into a protracted land war, that is what happened. It kept looking for a knockout blow that would destroy the Chinese will to resist, but after each "victory," the "defeated" Chinese soldiers would simply melt into the cities or the countryside. This was one reason why the scale of atrocities grew: ordinary Japanese soldiers began seeing enemies everywhere.[12]

The Imperial Army did finally "win" in China. In the Ichigo offensive of 1944, an operation on a scale that dwarfed even the contemporaneous Battle of the Bulge (and with more momentous consequences), the Army finally succeeded in breaking the back of the Nationalists. But those who walked into the resulting power vacuum were not the Japanese. They were Mao Zedong's Chinese Communist guerillas.

PEARL HARBOR, SURRENDER, AND THE LEGACY OF WAR

The last chance to avoid the wider war occurred in the fall of 1941. The prime minister of the time, Prince Konoe Fumimaro, a direct descendent of the Fujiwara, whom we met in chapter 1, had been attempting to avoid the looming confrontation with the United States. The signing of the 1940 Tripartite Pact among Germany, Italy, and Japan had frightened Washington with visions of a Eurasia wholly under Axis control. Ruling Japanese circles had been smitten by Nazi successes; enamored of the way Hitler had revived the German economy, many in Tokyo hoped that the British, Dutch, and French colonies in Southeast Asia would fall into their laps, removing their grinding anxiety over the sources of supply for their troops in China. Tokyo ignored warnings by its diplomatic attachés on the ground in Europe that the Nazi invasion of Britain was not a sure thing.

Meanwhile, the Roosevelt White House feared the consequences of Burma, French Indochina, and the Dutch East Indies falling under

---

12. If this sounds familiar to Americans who came of age during the Vietnam War, that's not a coincidence.

Japanese control. The Americans began signaling that Japan must end its designs on the European colonies and leave all territory seized in China beyond the original South Manchurian colony. And they had a credible threat to back up its demands—an embargo of essential oil supplies.

Many in Tokyo—including the emperor himself and Tojo Hideki, the former commander of the Kwantung Army and by that point the army minister—believed that Japan was being confronted by a choice that would require it to give up its designs on the continent or wage war on the United States. Konoe, having failed to convince Washington that its demands would lead to war, submitted his resignation. The emperor instructed Tojo to form a cabinet; from that point on the outcome was no longer in doubt.

A vast literature exists on what subsequently happened: the attack on Pearl Harbor, the fall of Singapore, Nanjing, and Manila, the battles of Midway and the Coral Sea, the capture of Iwo Jima and Okinawa, the fire-bombing of Japan's cities and the final awful climax in the atomic bombings of Hiroshima and Nagasaki. The events are known to anyone with an interest in the history of the time. It is a long tale of atrocities and horror (and heroism) equaled in barbarism and misery only by contemporary events in Europe.

But aside from the broader lesson of what can happen when power is unrestrained by political oversight, there are three points to take away. The significance of these three points for what has happened since 1945 will become clear in the chapters to follow.

The first point to be emphasized was the brilliance of Japan's battle-field tactics and the arrogance of the Western powers in consistently and repeatedly underestimating Japanese capabilities, whether that be in the refusal to believe that Japan had the capability to launch the attack on Pearl Harbor or to move with lightning speed down the Malay peninsula and to take Singapore from the north—or for that matter, that the Japanese would deploy a fighter aircraft superior to anything the West had in its armories.

The Japanese were also blinded by their misreadings of their enemies. They believed the Chinese were such an inferior, backwards people that they would not fight on and could be compelled to surrender; that the Americans were decadent and would collapse under the force of a strong blow. They assumed foreigners could never understand Japan so the possibility that the Americans had broken the Japanese code need not be considered. But the difference between these two sets of misunderstandings is revealing—the Japanese consistently misread the motives and resolve of their enemies while the West consistently misread Japanese capabilities.

Second, the war was not ultimately some audacious gamble on Tokyo's part. Japan's leaders felt they were being dragged into it. In a famous article that appeared during the Tokyo War Crimes Trial after the war was over, the great Japanese political philosopher Maruyama Masao wrote: "During the war Allied observers generally assumed that, since Japan had deliberately embarked on a large-scale war against the two most powerful countries in the world, she must have set up an organization and formulated plans based on a reasonably clear forecast of the future. It is no wonder, then, that the Allies should have been more and more amazed as the truth of the matter dawned on them." The truth, he would go on to explain, was that Japan's wartime leaders saw the whole period as a "sort of natural disaster, a convulsion of nature, eclipsing all human powers." He would note that "the men who held supreme power in Japan were in fact mere robots manipulated by their subordinates, who in turn were being manipulated by officers serving overseas and by the right-wing *rōnin* (masterless samurai) and ruffians associated with the military. In fact, the nominal leaders were always panting along in a desperate effort to keep up with *faits accomplis* created by anonymous, extra-legal forces." Or to put this in other words, the ultimate cause of the war—or at least Japan's part in it—was not a concentration of power in the hands of a usurper, but a diffusion of power that had slipped out of control.

Finally, the war saw the realization of Japan's ostensible aims while destroying any hope of achieving the complete control of its own destiny that was Tokyo's actual motive. The official line out of Tokyo was that Japan had started the war in order to end colonialism and drive Western imperialism from Asia. With one real exception, Japan succeeded in these aims. As Churchill himself feared it would, the fall of Singapore spelled the effective end of the British Empire. The French limped back into Indochina after 1945, but were kicked out for good less than a decade later, and if the United States had not tried like some latter-day King Canute to resist the tides of history, that would have been the end of the colonial story there as well. The Dutch were thrown out of the East Indies as the Indonesian archipelago was then called. Meanwhile, in China, as Zhou Enlai once put it, without the Japanese, there "would have been no new China." Even America's only formal colony in Asia, the Philippines, would, under the pressure of the events of the time, receive *de jure* independence.

Only Japan itself and its former colonies of Taiwan and Korea—or at least the southern half of the latter—would be locked indefinitely into the US defense perimeter, relying on the United States for security and with foreign policies subject to veto in Washington. The whole trajectory of Japanese history from the seclusion of the country under the Tokugawa to the desperate battles of 1945—control of Japan's own affairs without ideological, military, or economic domination by foreigners—had come to ruin. After 1945, Japan would find itself under occupation; an occupation that in many crucial ways has never ended.

FIGURE 4. The Assassination in 1960 of Hard-line Socialist Leader Asanuma Inejiro. Photograph by Nagao Yasushi; courtesy of Mainichi Shimbun.

4

The Miracle

Three reasons help explain the sobriquet "miracle" for Japan's postwar re-emergence. The first and most obvious reason lies in the growth rates themselves. Between 1955 and 1971, Japan achieved the highest real economic growth rates of any economy to that point in history. The second reason is the overall transformation of the country in a little over two decades from a ruined, bombed-out shell to the world's number two industrial and economic power. It seemed miraculous at the time because this transformation was effected not—as in Stalin's Soviet Union—by expropriation, famine, and murder, but by what appeared to be democratic, non-coercive means. Japan's transformation not only eliminated poverty in the country but brought economic security to most Japanese, together with universal health care and education, all in a demonstrably peaceful society with free elections and free speech.

Finally, no one at the time—inside or outside Japan—had an adequate theoretical explanation of just how Japan had done it. Japan's experience did not fit any of the dominant development paradigms of the era, whether Marxist, Keynesian, or the policies that flowed from so-called "dependency theory" then in vogue among Third World elites. Marxists called for a revolutionary state to seize the commanding heights of the economy on behalf of the proletariat in order to accelerate capital accumulation; no revolution happened in Japan and the government left the economy largely in the hands of nominally private enterprises. Keynesians prescribed proactive government measures such as deficit spending to stimulate economy-driving demand; Japan usually ran balanced budgets during the "miracle" years while domestic demand as a percentage of GDP was below that of other countries at comparable levels of development. Meanwhile Japan was not given the option of following the examples set by India's Jawaharlal Nehru, Argentina's Juan Perón, or Tanzania's Julius Nyerere who attempted to spark economic takeoff by building their own industries to supply their own markets and thereby—it was hoped—reduce their "dependence" on the industrialized world. The terms on which the American Occupation ended in 1952 inextricably bound Japan to the United States; it "depended" completely on the United States for capital goods, markets, and an internationally acceptable currency.

But if Japan did not follow any of the development recipes on offer at the time, neither did it revert to a version of Victorian or laissez-faire economics. The Great Depression had, in any case, temporarily discredited laissez-faire; its development doctrines—sound money, balanced budgets, price-setting by markets rather than bureaucrats, and free cross-border movement of goods and money—would be reincarnated in 1989 as the "Washington consensus." But if Japan had not, as we saw in chapter 3, bought into this approach during the late nineteenth century when laissez-faire enjoyed intellectual hegemony, Tokyo was certainly not going to implement laissez-faire in an era when it seemed to have lost its cachet for good. Key prices in the postwar Japanese economy—for money, labor, foreign exchange, technology transfers, and capital equipment—were set if not exactly, by bureaucratic decree, then certainly not by market forces. Market forces were permitted to operate unchecked only in areas of the economy deemed non-critical. Markets for corporate control, for labor, and for financing were tightly constrained or eliminated altogether. Direct investment by foreigners (buying Japanese companies or establishing greenfield operations in Japan) was permitted only in exceptional circum-stances, while cross-border portfolio investment (purchases of Japanese securities by foreigners and vice versa) and trade in goods and services was closely monitored and controlled. Most industries were cartelized, with cartels policed both by members themselves and by elements of the bureaucracy.

It was this lack of any theoretical explanation for what Japan's policy makers and business leaders were doing as much as the results themselves that gave what happened a miraculous aspect. The Japanese were as surprised as anyone; true, Ikeda Hayato, prime minister from 1960 to 1964, had famously called for an "Income Doubling Plan," but this was at least initially regarded as so-much grandstanding (actually, Japan would succeed in doubling income two years ahead of Ikeda's target). Chalmers Johnson wrote that the Japanese themselves were first made aware of the "miraculous" nature of what they were achieving by a long 1962 article in the British magazine *The Economist* that was translated into Japanese as a best-selling separate book under the title *Odorokubeki Nihon* (Amazing Japan). Johnson began his 1982 book *MITI and the Japanese Miracle* with an account of the reaction to the *Economist* article; his book represented the first systematic attempt by a Western scholar to explain what had happened in Japan. Johnson himself located the source of the "miracle" in what he termed "the institutions of high-speed growth" that had come together in the mid-1950s to form the platform for economic takeoff.

Johnson's insistence on the primacy of an institutional explanation for the "Japanese miracle" made him something of an outlier in the intellectual climate of the time. The early 1980s saw the ascendancy in the academy of such notions as rational choice, perfect information, and the efficient market hypothesis that not only presupposed, with classical, laissez-faire economics, that free markets represented the royal road to economic prosperity, but that all economic and political questions should best be approached with the assumption that human beings are rational decision makers attempting to maximize their well-being ("utility" is the technical term) in response to prices which by their very nature incorporate all possible information.

Needless to say, the Japanese experience represented an uncomfortable anomaly for this mode of inquiry, and, predictably, various attempts were made to discount the importance of the institutions Johnson had identified. When the Japanese economy hit a bad spot in the road a decade after Johnson's book came out, a veritable "I told you so" chorus rose from partisans who had once belittled the institutions of high-speed growth and were suddenly quick to proclaim how they now interfered with Japan's "recovery."

A straightforward defense of an institutional explanation for the "Japanese miracle" was complicated, however, by various ideologically motivated Japanese attempts to place some of these institutions beyond investigation by assertions that they resulted not from conscious political design but were inimitable outgrowths of Japanese culture. This was particularly true where issues of economic power were involved; examples include lifetime employment, company unions, and "consensus management" that were explained away as organic outgrowths of an ineffable Japaneseness. When combined with the eclipse within the American academy of the institutional approach, the net effect was to render scholarly investigation of the sources of Japan's economic performance unusually fraught with ideological controversy. Japan's track record thus tended for a time to radiate an aura of something beyond normal powers of understanding (i.e., miraculous).

As Japan began to experience significant economic difficulties, however, just when its neighbors—first Korea, Taiwan, and Malaysia, and then China itself—started to adopt many of these very institutions of high-speed growth, the aura of mystery began to recede. The "Japanese Economic Miracle" was succeeded as a sobriquet in the Western imagination by the "East Asian growth model" that was said to involve an export-led economy and the accumulation of large dollar surpluses, together with the vague implication that—like the Japanese experience—it would only work for a limited period of time before its contradictions caught up with it.

It is certainly true Japan accomplished something unprecedented in the 1955–1971 period. It is also true that the force of Japan's example ultimately counted for more than all the development theories of Right and Left floating about two generations ago; that having seen what Japan had done, other countries wanted to understand and do it too. There was, however, no recipe book.

Johnson himself had stressed that Japan's successful structuring of the institutions of high-speed growth came about only through a long historical process of trial-and-error. Much of what gave birth to and shaped the "Japanese Miracle" lay in the peculiar—even unique—circumstances in which Japan found itself in the years just after the war. While those circumstances might appear to be a one-off confluence, Japan's response to them determined not only much of its own subsequent history, but that of the rest of the world—most importantly, in strengthening and perpetuating a global political and financial order that revolved around the hegemony of the United States. Japan's experience in the postwar decades thus critically affected the circumstances in which other countries—China not least among them—would subsequently negotiate their own passages to modernity, matters we will take up at some length in later chapters. For the moment, however, we turn to the roots of what happened in the circumstances of the immediate postwar decade.

THE EXCEPTIONAL CIRCUMSTANCES
OF THE POSTWAR DECADE

There is nothing particularly unique about recovery from defeat; many countries have done it and emerged stronger than they were. Yoshida Shigeru, Japan's most important prime minister in the immediate postwar decade, had in fact attempted to console his fellow Japanese with this very observation. West Germany's *wirtschaftswunder*, achieved during the same decades as the Japanese economic miracle, demonstrates that Japan's "miraculous" recovery was not even unique among those nations defeated in the Second World War.

But unlike Germany carved up by four victorious allies, Japan had to engineer its recovery while occupied by a single power—a power that was initially determined to remake the country but lacked either the stamina or the knowledge to do so. Before it got very far with this project, it was distracted by other priorities and it drafted Japan into the service of those priorities. Japan had little choice in the matter. As the Occupation went on, it became clear that the United States did not intend to let Japan go its own way; that the price for a restoration of even nominal sovereignty would include incorporation into the US defense perimeter, at least the appearance of support for American geopolitical and ideological goals, and concrete evidence that leftists could and would be kept away from the levers of power in Tokyo.

For much of Japan's ruling elite, this was an acceptable trade-off, particularly when it became evident that the United States was willing and even eager to leave domestic power alignments basically untouched provided Japan remained nominally in the "capitalist" camp. To this day, the United States has managed for Tokyo what fully independent governments typically take care of for themselves: providing for security and conducting foreign relations. Japan's failure to recover full sovereignty after the formal end of the Occupation stuck in the craw of both the Left and the Right in Japan. The Left feared being dragged into American military adventures and drafted into Washington's hegemonic designs; the Right believed that the country had been emasculated by the constitution imposed by the Americans with its famous Article 9 mandating pacifism. While there were elements of truth to both critiques, Yoshida, who had negotiated the San Francisco Peace Treaty that brought a formal close to the Occupation, argued that he had the gotten the best deal he could for Japan, which was probably correct.

Whatever the long-term consequences of the terms on which the Occupation ended—and they are with us to this day—they did allow ruling elites to put behind them the debilitating and murderous struggles of the preceding decades that had brought on the disasters of the 1930s. Defeat and occupation had removed from Japan's control the fundamental political matters that had provoked those struggles. Security was no longer Tokyo's responsibility. Relations with the continent—the supreme "foreign policy" issue for all of Japan's recorded history—had been taken out of Tokyo's hands. Whatever they may have thought privately (and it was not just the Left that deplored American blindness), Japan's officials meekly had to fall in line with Washington's refusal to have any dealings with the new People's Republic of China. Japan was a bystander in the division of the Korean peninsula, and while there were sympathizers in Tokyo with both Seoul and Pyongyang, all Japan could do from a practical point of view was act as a supply base for the US military.

The only real issue still open for contention was the economy, and in the ruined landscape of the late 1940s, no one could possibly disagree that the country's overwhelming priority had to be reconstruction. The militarists seen as directly responsible for the war had been discredited and the bureaucracies they had commandeered—most importantly, the Imperial Army and the Naimusho (Interior Ministry) that had concerned itself with social control—were either broken up or disbanded altogether. Aside from a handful of men like Tojo executed by the Occupation as war criminals, most of the rest of the men who had been in power during the war years either moved back into the shadows of Japanese politics as power brokers and fixers (often in cahoots with the criminal underworld), or like Kishi Nobusuke, who had been Minister of Munitions in the Tojo cabinet and served as prime minister from 1957 to 1960, they remade themselves into champions of economic growth and the US–Japan "Alliance."

Such men, joined by moderate conservatives such as Yoshida who had been shunted aside during the war years (or kept low profiles in fear of their lives), emerged as the dominant power holders in post-Occupation Japan. But the process was not automatic. Even though the Occupation's Supreme

Commander, Douglas MacArthur, was a traditional Republican, many of the civilian officials who initially joined him from Washington were ardent New Dealers who saw a chance to effect a democratic transformation of Japan more complete and thoroughgoing than anything they had been able to accomplish at home. One of the first things they did was free thousands of political prisoners, including many leftists. The sudden re-emergence of a Japanese Left embarrassed thousands more intellectuals, teachers, and erstwhile labor activists who had publicly recanted their leftist sympathies during the previous decades. Perhaps as psychic compensation for the guilt they felt, many became militant partisans of socialist thought. Members of the Japan Communist Party who had refused to recant their beliefs during the war years were greeted as heroes when they were released from prison. Given the misery of the times, the emergence of profiteering on black markets by well-placed insiders and the huge resentment this sparked, it was probably inevitable that the country would be gripped with revolutionary fervor. By May 1946 waves of demonstrations (including a notable one that month against the food rationing system) wracked the country; two years later, Japan actually elected a socialist government.

All this scared Washington, occurring, as it did, during the beginnings of the Cold War. Stalin's Soviet Union had signaled it had no intention of retreating from those parts of Europe its soldiers had overrun in the concluding months of hostilities. Knowledgeable insiders in the State Department were warning that it was only a matter of time until Mao Zedong's guerilla armies entered Beijing in triumph. While these men paid for their prescience with their careers when later smeared by red-baiters such as Joseph McCarthy and Richard Nixon for the "loss" of China, they contributed in the mid-1940s to a sense that the United States faced an implacable, monolithic foe—and one that appeared then to be on the right side of history. The economic cataclysm of the Great Depression had not been forgotten, and with the ending of the economic stimulus provided by war, many feared capitalist economies would fall back into an economic trough while Communism proceeded from strength to strength.

It was against this background that Japan's conservative elites first deployed tactics that would be used again and again right down to the present in order to maintain their control of outcomes in Japan. Their overwhelming priority at the time was to enlist the Occupation on their side in their effort to prevent a leftist takeover of Japan and to preserve as much as possible the power relations that had characterized the prewar period.

Their tactics involved the manipulation of American opinion by playing on American fears and, as Yoshida privately acknowledged, the "beautiful misunderstandings of the Americans."

As the latest news can readily attest, every country that relies on or wants something from Washington learns how to do this—how to flatter and influence American power holders. But the Japanese arguably take a back seat only to the Israelis at the skill with which they play this game. Part of the reason is that they have a lot of practice. The ability to manipulate and soothe the more powerful constitutes the golden road to success in Japan, beginning in the kindergarten classroom and extending to the highest corridors of government and business. Any foreigner who has ever dealt with a Japanese from a position of power, whether negotiating a tawdry encounter in a cheap cabaret, dining at a good Japanese restaurant, or being solicited for a major order by a Japanese company, will understand how seductive Japanese people can be. People learn from infancy how to seduce, since any mother who expects her child to succeed in Japanese society will almost instinctively teach him or her how to carry it off. There is naturally a whole vocabulary for this in Japanese; many words even lack precise English equivalents—*amae*, for example, which labels behavior intended to induce feelings of indulgence on the part of the more powerful by pretending to push boundaries. The ubiquity of seduction is one of those phenomena that gets shoved under the label "Japanese culture"—which it is, but that does not tell us very much. It almost certainly stems from the power relations that prevailed during the centuries of Tokugawa rule when samurai had the right to cut down any commoner for any reason.

Seductive tactics writ large first became part of Japan's foreign policy apparatus during the early Meiji period when Japan had to use every tool it could command to preserve its independence. After 1945, with independence lost and hundreds of thousands of Communists and their sympathizers marching in the streets, the challenge facing the power holders was even greater. Fortunately for them, they could count on the American penchant for confining relationships to established elites, to people who can speak English well, have been educated in American schools, and know how to act in ways that disarm Americans. MacArthur's vanity and self-importance also helped; ensconced as he was in the office building across the moat from the Imperial Palace that the Occupation commandeered for its headquarters, this man who had more power over what happened in Japan than any single person since the early Tokugawa shoguns never met any Japanese outside the very top echelons of Japanese society, never tried to find out for himself what was actually going on, and was particularly susceptible to the kind of obsequious flattery that the Japanese could deliver with such unrivaled skill. On top of that, China experts in the State Department succeeded not only in keeping "old Japan hands" out of Tokyo, but in driving away from the Occupation the cadres of bright young men who had been trained by the US military during the war in the Japanese language. The State Department's "China crowd" as they came to be called were enraged at the way the Japanese had behaved in China and they feared that those who knew too much about Japan might be inclined to go easy on Japan's business and military elites. With their leftist political sympathies, the "China crowd" had concluded a priori that these elites were responsible for the war. They were probably correct to be suspicious of the prewar ties between the "old Japan hands" and the moderate conservative elite around Yoshida that re-emerged after the war, but the net effect of their victory in Washington's bureaucratic battles was to deprive the Occupation of any independent means of ascertaining what was actually going on in Japan. As John Dower wrote in his magnificent history of the Occupation *Embracing Defeat*, "From top to bottom, [MacArthur's] 'super-government' in Tokyo reflected an aversion to area specialists as such. . . at the level of daily operations (it) appears deliberately to have excluded most individuals who possessed even slight credentials in Japanese matters." Dower uses the term "super-government" to describe the Occupation since—under these self-imposed circumstances—it had no choice but to rely on the existing Japanese power structure to carry out day-to-day policy.

In all fairness, the conservatives had good reason to fear the Communists. Even if the Japanese Left did not take its marching orders from Moscow, the Kremlin did nothing to discourage that impression. It went so far as to openly criticize Nosaka Sanzo, the founder of the Japan Communist Party and one of its key leaders during the late 1940s, for being "gradualist." (After the fall of the Soviet Union, KGB documents came to light revealing that Nosaka had in fact engaged in espionage for the Comintern.) Stalin's troops, in direct violation of the nonaggression pact signed with Tokyo, had declared war on Japan and would no doubt have proceeded to attack Hokkaido had Japan not surrendered to the United States. The Soviet declaration was as important as the atomic bombs in precipitating the surrender; if the surrender had happened even a few weeks later than it did, Japan would probably have ended up like Korea and Germany, divided into Communist and non-Communist sectors. (Instead, the Russians had to content themselves with the southern Kuriles, seized after Japan had announced its surrender.) As it was, over a million Japanese soldiers stationed in northern China and northern Korea were taken prisoner by the Soviets and condemned to slave labor in appalling conditions for upwards of five years; tens of thousands died in captivity.

Widespread hatred and fear of the Soviet Union in Japan thus had a solid basis, and it was amplified by the 1948 Soviet-engineered *coup d'état* in Czechoslovakia and the descent of the Iron Curtain over Eastern Europe. But fearful as they may have been of Soviet designs, the conservatives were even more agitated by the very real democratic reforms that the Occupation succeeded in introducing, culminating in a constitution that was, if anything, more progressive than its American counterpart, including as it did explicit guarantees of gender equality and provisions for workers' rights, not to mention the famous foreswearing of war. General Headquarters, or GHQ, the universally used acronym for the Occupation, had initially instructed the Japanese government to prepare drafts of a new constitution; when it became clear that the government had no intention of coming up with anything that would meet American expectations, GHQ took matters into its own hands, writing much of the constitution itself.

Part of the problem was that Japanese jurists who had initially been given the job of rewriting the Meiji period constitution were steeped in the Prussian legal tradition that saw law as something intended to buttress and clarify state power, not as an instrument to enable citizens to hold rulers to account. Part of it was simply that Japan's conservatives did not believe in real democracy; it subverted the hierarchical notions that seemed to them part and parcel of being Japanese, hierarchy enjoying a quasi-sacred aura in their conceptual universe as the only alternative to anarchy and barbarism.

The resulting constitution, admirable as it may be, however, suffered from a flaw that has dogged it to this day—it appeared to have been imposed on Japan. The people who did the imposing may have had the best of motives, but ultimately it smelled foreign; the language itself in places reads like a somewhat awkward translation.[1] The constitution has thus ended up

---

1. The conventional interpretation of the constitution as something entirely imposed by the Americans on Japan has been challenged recently by the journalist Tachibana Takashi, who demonstrated in a 2008 article in the now-defunct Japanese magazine *Gekkan Gendai* that substantial parts of the constitution were actually taken from a draft constitution drawn up

not as Japan's ultimate governing legal document, but in the grand political Japanese tradition as a somewhat blurred and compromised token of legitimacy, hoisted about erratically like a portable shrine by competing contenders for power. This is most famously obvious with Article 9 that explicitly forbids Japan from acquiring "war-making potential." In direct violation of these words, Japan today maintains the world's fifth largest military, but the very same officials who ignored the constitution in appropriating funds for Japan's euphemistically termed "Self-Defense Forces" were quick to trot it out in deflecting US requests for more direct military cooperation from Japan. (The proverbial ink was barely dry on this document before the United States regretted forcing Article 9 on Japan; it has been well on sixty years now since Washington first started urging Japan to contribute more to US military efforts.)

Similar points could be made about other aspects of the constitution—the locus of sovereignty, for example. The constitution is quite clear that sovereignty lies with the Japanese people, but a strong residual sense exists to this day—at least among older people—that the ultimate locus of sovereignty continues actually to be the Imperial House. Legislative authority is vested by the constitution in the Diet, but for much of the postwar period, powerful bureaucracies enjoyed legislative, executive, and judicial authority in areas under their purview; they were quite obviously subject to only token parliamentary oversight. The constitution could—and often has been—invoked in bureaucratic and other power struggles, but it has rarely been accepted as the final word on a given matter.

The fate of the constitution writ large describes the fate of the Occupation. GHQ staffers started out with the best of motives, but depriving themselves of the means to reach their natural allies among the Japanese—labor leaders, intellectuals, women's rights advocates—and over time replaced by those more concerned that Japan be anti-Communist than it be democratic, GHQ ended up effectively as a partner of the old conservative elite it had been set up to supplant. Both would end up using each other.

After the short-lived socialist government, the conservatives won the 1949 election and at the encouragement of GHQ, instituted a "Red

by liberal Japanese lawyers and journalists during the Taisho era (1912–26). This evidence has been largely suppressed, however, since it does not fit the conservatives' contention that the constitution was "imposed" on Japan. See discussion in chapter 11.

Purge" that would see upwards of 13,000 suspected Communists and Communist sympathizers driven out of government and business. Meanwhile, the prisons were emptied of those who had run wartime Japan and the Truman White House, fretting at Japan's continued drain on the US Treasury, dispatched a Detroit banker, Joseph Dodge, to Tokyo with the hopes he could staunch the red ink. His "Dodge Line" imposed economic austerity, complete with tight money, a fixed exchange rate, and an end to deficit spending. All this collectively acquired the label "Reverse Course" (both the Red Purge and the Dodge Line) and the Japanese Left to this day sees it as a betrayal of the initial democratic ideals of the Occupation.

This is not to say that GHQ completely failed in its early objectives. Once institutions are implanted in a body politic, even as a nominal cover for actual power relations, they can serve as stubborn—even subversive—reminders of the purposes for which they were originally conceived. Meiji period imports such as parliamentary government and the rule of law, initially introduced into Japan as a sop to Westerners and local agitators "infected" with Western ideas, had already demonstrated to Japan's traditional elite their potential for subversion; we noted in the previous chapter Yamagata Aritomo's devious and tireless machinations to insulate the bureaucracy from the oversight and accountability implicit in the idea of parliamentary government. Now, the conservatives were confronted with a new and even more disturbing set of institutions, institutions whose birth had been midwifed by the power of the US military. Yoshida himself would concede the partial success of the Occupation's reformers when he acknowledged that the conservatives intended to get rid of these institutions once Japan regained its independence, but then found they couldn't, not altogether. Japan's power holders would figure out ways to hobble labor unions, a free press, universal suffrage, *de jure* female equality, a radicalized cadre of teachers determined never again to train their students for cannon fodder, and the whole notion of a government staffed by *public* as opposed to *imperial* servants. But the inherent ideas were sufficiently robust that they continued to act at least as softeners on arbitrary exercises of power. Labor militancy was broken, but not until large, well-established companies came around to guaranteeing the economic security of their core employees. Reporters for Japan's quality papers are to this day forced to act more like stenographers than journalists, but plenty of boisterous, unruly media exist beyond the established papers and television networks, and only a handful of topics are genuinely off-limits.[2] Elections may not determine policy in Japan, but no government can openly flout popular outrage for long. Women's *de facto* as opposed to *de jure* equality has been a long time coming, but the trends have continued to run in that direction. Japan's students are taught the basics of democracy and parliamentary government while many teachers fought decades-long trench warfare with some success against the whitewashing of the past and the remilitarization of the curriculum. To be sure, many policy decisions are still made without much accountability, and prosecutors in Japan tend to see themselves not as servants but as masters of the law, using their extraordinary discretionary powers to decide which laws will be enforced and which will be winked at. Japanese police, however, are generally courteous, professional, and helpful, and few Japanese citizens need fear arrest for what they think or read.

Nonetheless, the Occupation failed to achieve the democratization of Japanese society that its early officials had worked for. As John Dower explains, "Contrary to the practice of direct military government adopted in defeated Germany, this occupation was conducted 'indirectly'—that is, through existing organs of government. This entailed buttressing the influence of two of the most undemocratic institutions of the pre-surrender regime: the bureaucracy and the throne."

GHQ's treatment of the Throne was more than just a failure to clarify the status of the emperor in postwar Japan or to establish a constitutional monarchy along British or Scandinavian lines. Even before the war had ended, Washington had made the a priori decision that the emperor was not be held accountable for anything that had happened during his rule; the orientalist and condescending view prevailed that Japanese society would collapse if the emperor were forced to abdicate.

To be fair, American motives were partly rooted in the sense that the Occupation should not be some sort of Carthaginian peace of pure vengeance. Many Japanese did genuinely believe that the emperor held Japan together; uncritical American acceptance of this notion formed part of a wider American desire to "democratize" and "reform" rather than destroy Japan. But lacking any nuanced understanding of just how the Meiji leaders had woven an essentially modern nationalist myth out of this ancient token of political legitimacy, the Occupation could square

---

2. With the newly passed Official Secrets Act rammed through the Diet late in 2013 by Prime Minister Abe, this may change.

"democratization" with the decision to leave the emperor in place only by constructing a fiction of Hirohito as powerless and otherworldly, wringing his hands helplessly as bad guys seized power and did wicked things in his name. The only alternative the Americans could conceive of—that the emperor had led his country the way Hitler or Stalin had led theirs—was transparently not the case. That he was neither a passive bumbler nor in control of events, that his socialization and both the conceptual and actual world he moved in acted as very real constraints on his freedom of action, that he was neither blameless nor the ultimate villain—such considerations were too subtle for the Manichean mindset of the time.

Before it became clear that GHQ intended not only to preserve the Imperial Institution but to shield the emperor from any form of accountability, it had been widely assumed in defeated Japan that while the Throne would probably survive in some form or another, Hirohito himself would abdicate in favor of his young son Akihito, with one of his brothers serving as regent until the boy came of age. Not only was there abundant precedent for imperial abdication, as we saw in chapter 1, but the resignation of titular leaders to "take responsibility" is standard procedure in Japan when things have gone wrong. But GHQ would not only encourage Hirohito to stay on the Throne, it would use its formidable powers to censor any discussion of the emperor's role in the events of the preceding decades.

This created huge cognitive dissonance in the wider population. People who had been indoctrinated from early childhood with notions that the emperor embodied the highest sacred values and that one should be ready to lay down one's life for the emperor were suddenly instructed not to consider the possibility of any link between these notions and the misery they saw around them. GHQ essentially told them to repress the past rather than to re-examine the disaster in order to understand what had gone wrong in order to ensure it never happened again. It is entirely and understandably human to want to forget a miserable past, to turn the page and get on with new realities. This is what happened in Germany (or, for that matter, in the United States after the Vietnam War). But a younger generation coming of age in Germany would finally force that country to come to terms with its past; this never happened in Japan—in large part because the Japanese were not allowed by GHQ to debate and discuss what had actually taken place.

The ramifications were first obvious in the Tokyo War Crimes trials, the tribunals modeled on the Nuremberg Trials set up to ascertain the guilt or innocence of those accused of leading Japan into war. As Dower wrote, "the most flagrant control of evidence involved the prosecution's single-minded campaign to insulate the emperor. The tribunal was distinguished not only by the physical absence of the emperor and the careful exclusion of any sustained references to him, but also by the absence of testimony by him. The manipulation of 'victors' evidence' to save him had no counterpart in Nuremberg and received no challenge from the defense in Tokyo." As a result, the proceedings degenerated at times into something close to a farce. The men indicted as so-called "Class A War Criminals" closed ranks to protect the emperor; only on one occasion did they slip up when Tojo testified that it was inconceivable to have taken action contrary to the emperor's wishes. Joseph Keenan, the chief prosecutor, used the Imperial Household Agency to get a message to Tojo in prison inviting him to retract the comment, which of course he did.

The trials ended up being dismissed by many (and not just the Japanese) as "victors' justice"—show trials that had little or nothing to do with arriving at any real understanding of what had led to the horrors of the preceding decades. It was not just the deliberate distortion of history that occurred at the trials, distortion that was carried out not simply with the connivance but at the actual orders of GHQ. It was also the double standards they embodied. US Air Force General Curtis LeMay, who conceived and ordered the firebombing of Japan's civilian population, was at least as much a war criminal as Generals Yamashita Tomoyuki and Honma Masaharu, who were executed for atrocities committed in the Philippines. The United States has never had to answer for Hiroshima and Nagasaki. One can make an argument—morally stretched and convoluted as it may be—for the atomic bombing of Hiroshima, which was an important naval base and had been the center of Japan's military infrastructure. But Nagasaki was simply a gratuitous atrocity.

Most Japanese quite rightly, thus, came to see themselves as victims. They had not asked for the war; while most of them had, to be sure, supported it with varying degrees of enthusiasm, they had never had any real choice in the matter. The most commonly encountered epithet in the postwar decades for the war among ordinary Japanese was "stupid." It had been stupid to think one could win any kind of meaningful victory in the tar pit of China; it had been stupid deliberately to poke a vastly stronger United States in the eyes. But ordinary Japanese were never invited to examine the causes of this stupidity with a view toward preventing a repetition;

indeed they were actively encouraged by both their conquerors and the Japanese Right to bury memories of what had happened. The Right nursed its wounds, fulminating against postwar "democracy," descending into violence and intimidation against teachers, liberals, and socialists.

Japan's neighbors, acutely aware of all this, remain to this day suspicious of Japan. They see a country wallowing in self-pity that has never reckoned with the causes of the vast human suffering inflicted on Asia. They note the way Japan's power elite continues to wink at right-wing whitewashing of the past—the struggles over official textbooks, the museums glorifying the war, the sound trucks roaming the streets of Tokyo blaring militarist songs. To give a sense of what this is like, imagine the reaction in Europe if periodic battles surfaced every few years over the wording of officially approved textbooks in German schools that omitted any references to the Holocaust and described the invasion of Poland as an "incursion." Or a museum near Germany's most important historical monument containing displays glorifying the rise of the Nazis, displays from which *Kristallnacht* and the concentration camps had been carefully excised. Or thugs in SS uniforms driving sound trucks around the streets of Berlin and Frankfurt shaking nearby office buildings with ear-splitting renditions of Nazi slogans and songs while the police stand by demurely.

While the Chinese Communist Party has at least as much blood on its hands as Imperial Japan, what most specifically galls China and Korea is the lack of any unequivocal statement from the Japanese government along these lines: (1) this is what happened; (2) it was mostly our fault; (3) we give absolute assurances it can never happen again; (4) you can trust these assurances because of irrevocable institutional changes.

Germany succeeded in making essentially these statements in ways that have reassured its neighbors, but Tokyo never has. It could not do so without calling into question the underlying legitimacy of the Japanese polity. As we noted in the previous chapter, Meiji fostered two contradictory political fictions used to legitimize one truth—respectively, the fiction of parliamentary government, the fiction of direct Imperial rule, and the reality of control by the Sat-Cho clique. It wasn't quite like that in postwar Japan. The GHQ-imposed constitutional democracy was much more than a fiction and a substantial segment of the population wanted Japan to be what it claimed to be—a democracy with sovereignty placed firmly in the Japanese people. But while many of Japan's power holders were content to use this construct to render their government legitimate in the eyes of the world (the Occupation and the terms on which it ended really gave them no choice), they have never fully accepted the constitutional, democratic basis of its legitimacy. They continue—without being explicit in the matter—to fall back on notions of Japan as a unique, holy land centered on the Imperial House as the ultimate source legitimizing their political power. Since this was also the theoretical source of legitimacy in the prewar setup, an unequivocal statement that the disaster could never happen again could not be made and would not be credible if it were.

In contrast to Germany, the question of where the legitimate right to rule lies was, thus, not resolved by Japan's defeat, occupation, or the imposition of the postwar constitution on the country. The absence of a resolution to this fundamental political question can create the conditions for murderous, catastrophic disorder—as we saw in prewar Japan or, for that matter, are witnessing today across the Middle East. Governing could nonetheless function smoothly in postwar Japan because of assumption of actual power over policy by the other of Dower's prewar undemocratic institutions buttressed by Occupation policy: the bureaucracy.

Bureaucratic rule is almost an oxymoron. Bureaucrats are essential to a functioning political order, but they cannot ultimately run countries—they require political guidance. The endless struggles that are endemic to bureaucracy have dominated Japanese policy since 1952, but they have not yet proved fatal to postwar Japan for two reasons: because those bureaucracies with the means of physical coercion at their disposal had been broken up or eliminated in the early years of the Occupation. The endless struggles that are endemic to bureaucracy have dominated Japanese policy-making since 1952, but they have not yet proved fatal to postwar Japan because those bureaucracies with the means of physical coercion at their disposal were broken up or eliminated in the early days of the Occupation. As we have seen, the United States took on responsibility for Japan's security and has, since 1945, exercised veto-power over its foreign relations. Those elements of the bureaucracy left standing after the Occupation's re-ordering of Japan's governing arrangements could thus devote themselves primarily to economic matters. Since these bureaucrats were charged with managing economic recovery rather than matters of war and social control in a world where practically everyone agreed that economic recovery had to be the country's first priority, they could function without political direction– and function well, at least until the 1970s when necessary adjustments to Japan's economic model could not be made because of a lack of political leadership enjoying full legitimacy to carry them out, a matter we will take up at length in later chapters.

The Left and Right phases of the Occupation, to coin a term, might as well have conspired to enhance the power of Japan's economic bureaucrats. The zealous left-leaning reformers of the early Occupation accepted the Marxist contention that the causes of war lay in capital's control of the instruments of coercion, and capital's use thereof to maintain power to determine economic outcomes. This thinking led Occupation officials to disband the Imperial Army and Imperial Navy and to break up the all-powerful Naimusho (Interior Ministry) that had had control over the police, the courts, and local affairs. But they also set about socializing private concentrations of wealth, most importantly, the great prewar *zaibatsu*. The owners of Mitsubishi, Mitsui, Sumitomo, Yasuda, and others like them were stripped of their holdings.

Without understanding what it was doing, GHQ had removed one of the key counter blocks to untrammeled bureaucratic power. The *zaibatsu* owners had been at best lukewarm supporters of the war. Targets of assassination and intimidation by the fascists of the 1930s, never trusted by the bureaucrats who ran Japan's war economy, these men had understood that Japan's policies were bad for business, or at least their business. Meanwhile, the bureaucrats who had mobilized Japan's economy for war—the so-called *Kakushin Kanryō* or "Reform Bureaucrats"—were influenced by the corporatist thought that lay behind the "national socialism" of the Nazis and the Italian fascists. Tracing its intellectual heritage back to the same Hegelian foundation as Marxian socialism, this strain of thinking sees the primary purpose of economic activity as the enhancement of state power and is perennially suspicious of the "selfishness" of private capitalists driven by the profit motive.

While the Reform Bureaucrats could not avoid working through the great *zaibatsu* in Japan itself, they had done their best to exclude them from a colonial Manchuria that had been used, as we noted in the preceding chapter, as a kind of experimental laboratory for a planned, bureaucratically directed economy. Many of the great names of Japanese business that do not trace their institutional heritage back to the old *zaibatsu*—Hitachi, for example, or Nissan—got their start as bureaucrat-sponsored entities in Manchuria.

With the *zaibatsu* transformed by GHQ into what were essentially bureaucracies themselves susceptible to direction from the economic ministries, the direct heirs of the Reform Bureaucrats in these ministries—most importantly, Finance and Munitions (quickly renamed International Trade and Industry)—may have surveyed in the mid-1940s a ruined economy, but it was one over which they enjoyed power even beyond that they had

had during the war years. Coming on top of the evisceration of other competing institutions—the *zaibatsu*, the military, the Home Ministry—the Dodge Line finished the job of turning over to these bureaucrats the tools they needed to run the economy. Dodge was able to impose what no Japanese government at the time could politically have done: fiscal austerity, balanced budgets, and a credible fixed exchange rate.

During ordinary times, such a policy mix (as we saw in southern Europe in the early 2010s) could have been a recipe for widespread misery and even revolution. But these were not ordinary times. The Korean War broke out in 1950, and the Americans began placing waves of orders for all the goods other than weapons themselves that they needed to supply their soldiers. And they paid for the goods in dollars. The Japanese spoke of the orders as "manna from heaven." The export surge coming on top of the Dodge Line created a kind of best-of-all-possible economic stage on which Japan could rebuild its ruined economy. The dollars pouring into Japan enabled the country to order the capital equipment needed to restart its industries without relying on foreign direct investment, thereby ensuring that ultimate control of the economy stayed in the hands of Japanese.

The Korean War came to an end shortly after Japan recovered its *de jure* independence with the signing of the San Francisco Peace Treaty. Two unwritten conditions of the treaty—that Japan follow American policy in having nothing to do with the People's Republic of China and that Tokyo provide credible assurance that left wingers be kept away from the levers of power—were characteristically used by the Japanese to extract indulgence from Washington. With their historically largest markets in continental Asia effectively closed, Tokyo pleaded for unrestricted access to the American market without reciprocal access to Japan by American industry. Japan's diplomats argued that with the end of the Korean War, Japan needed another source of dollars, but that its own industries were too small and fragile to withstand American competition. Meanwhile, Japan's conservative elites procured covert help from the CIA in merging the country's disparate conservative groups into a single Liberal Democratic Party ("LDP"). While, to paraphrase Voltaire, this entity was neither liberal nor democratic, nor a conventional political party and hardly ever could command more than 50 percent of the popular vote in subsequent elections, it succeeded in its mission of providing political cover both for bureaucratic control of the economy and for Japan's continued incorporation into the US defense perimeter. (We will have a lot more to say about the LDP and Japan's electoral politics in the final two chapters.)

The United States was only too happy to comply. It was not just for fear of a left-wing Japan. Although the leftist tide had begun to recede from its high-water mark in 1946–48, Tokyo had learned how to scare Washington with dark warnings about the dangers of the socialists unless the United States cooperated with this trade issue or retracted that request for overt military cooperation.[3] But the United States also needed Japan for ideological reasons as a showcase for a vibrant "capitalist" democracy to set against the siren songs emanating from Moscow and Beijing—never mind that Japan's postwar economic methods would stretch the definition of "capitalism" to its breaking point.

It is here that we find the unique circumstances of the early 1950s setting the stage not simply for Japan's economic miracle of subsequent decades but the East Asian growth model as a whole. Japan was essentially given no choice but to turn to the US market in order to export its way out of the economic ruin of the war. We noted above that many newly liberated developing countries of the time were touting "import substitution"—the nurturing of locally owned industry to free themselves from dependence on their former colonial masters. But this was not an option for a Japan caught in an inescapable American embrace. Instead of trying to wean itself from dependence on the United States, Tokyo would turn that dependence to Japan's advantage, creating and perfecting institutions that would foster industries and companies capable of generating high levels of dollar earnings—dollars that at least in the early decades of economic takeoff were rationed and controlled by the economic bureaucracy to propel the country forward.

POLITICAL AND CULTURAL FOUNDATIONS FOR HIGH-SPEED GROWTH

Japan's overall economic strategy in the postwar decades centered on the exploitation of experience-curve dynamics. American statisticians during the war years had discovered a statistically robust correlation between increased volume of production and reductions in manufacturing

---

3. At one point when President Eisenhower's secretary of state, John Foster Dulles, was in Tokyo pressing for more military spending from Japan, Yoshida sent a private message to the socialists indicating this would be an excellent time for a large and noisy demonstration against American "imperialism."

costs: costs declined in a predictable fashion with given increases in volume. The concept was popularized in the 1960s by Bruce Henderson, founder of the Boston Consulting Group. But the Japanese had already been using the notion for a decade to drive their economy.

The origins of this construct in the dynamics of a war economy is not a coincidence. A war economy harnesses nominally private economic entities to the pursuit of centrally determined goals. One of Japan's most important economic historians, Noguchi Yukio, has argued that the institutional origins of the postwar Japanese economy lie in measures implemented in 1940 to place the entire economy on a war footing—measures such as the organization of production cartels and the rationalization of the financial system—with industries deemed critical to the war effort receiving priority access to funds. The Occupation's unwitting expansion of the ambit of the economic bureaucracy served to cement and institutionalize these measures. As the Occupation ended, it was a relatively simple matter for the bureaucrats overseeing economic strategy to redeploy the tools at their disposal from military objectives to the goal of capturing as many dollar earnings as possible in export markets.

Experience curve dynamics permitted Japan's export champions to set prices below present production costs and thus to capture market share abroad. Thanks to patient financing, businesses could accept the resultant losses on the assumption that future increases in volume would bring production costs below sales prices, permitting them eventually to recapture the losses. But ensuring that those increases in volume did indeed happen required predictability, which in turn presupposed what the prominent financial analyst Mikuni Akio has labeled the socialization of risk in the Japanese system. Those businesses sufficiently well connected and deemed "strategic" directly benefited from public policy aimed at reducing risk—political, social, economic, financial, and market—to the individual enterprise.

Japan was, however, starting with an important inherited advantage, since predictability was already so highly prized. Particularly in any kind of interaction away from immediate family and close friends, Japanese people exhibit an appreciation of routine and a horror of the unexpected that can strike Westerners as verging on the pathological. People deliberately send all kinds of both verbal and nonverbal signals indicating where they stand in society and how they accordingly expect to be treated. This accounts, for example, to rituals connected with the Japanese business meeting such as the exchange of calling cards that give the two parties the opportunity to ascertain the relative status of the opposite side. Rank and hierarchy among a group of Japanese business executives or government officials is instantly obvious to other Japanese from the way they arrange themselves in a car, restaurant, or meeting room, to the floor plans of their offices and the language they use with each other. The bar hostess, the housewife, the schoolboy, the executive, the academic, the construction worker, the engineer, and the artist all dress in characteristic ways that enable others to size them up at a glance. The resultant predictability of social interactions in Japan assumes the aura of ritual.

The predictability of social life in Japan is another of those features that is commonly and correctly labeled "Japanese culture" as if this were the end of the matter, and, again, it almost surely stems from the power relations of the Tokugawa period when stepping outside an accepted frame of reference could mean loss of life. Under the force of the so-called stagnation of the last twenty years—more on that later—some of this predictability may be breaking down, and it has long provided wonderful opportunities for comedians and artists. During the "miracle years" of the 1950s and 1960s, however, this inherited, ingrained social predictability provided a solid foundation for the panoply of financial, corporate, and market institutions designed to socialize and distribute risk rather than leaving it to individual entrepreneurs or companies.

But it was not just "culture." Cementing the foundations of Japan's race for high-speed growth were political developments that in retrospect proved to be as important as external circumstances and inherited mores. We have already noted how various conservative groups were merged in 1955 with covert CIA help into an overarching Liberal Democratic Party that, with one brief exception in 1993–94, would control the formal levers of parliamentary government, including the Cabinet and the office of the Prime Minister, until 2009. The LDP never functioned like a European party with an explicit platform based on an explicit ideology; for most of its history, it was divided into well-recognized factions that did not originate in ideological or policy differences but were rather political machines led by a series of powerful operators, machines that distributed patronage and political favors. The LDP resembled in some key respects the US Democratic Party before the McGovern reforms of 1972. Like the famous machines of Richard J. Daley's Chicago, Tom Pendergast's Kansas City, or James Michael Curley's Boston, LDP factions acted as groups of power brokers mediating between the central government and their various constituencies, delivering votes in return for patronage and pork that they extracted out of the bureaucracy. But the LDP's electoral base, unlike that of the mid-twentieth-century US Democrats, lay not in the urban working and lower middle classes, but in rural areas of the country. LDP tentacles extended deep into the countryside with important local positions such as post office chief awarded to those with LDP connections. Meanwhile, LDP politicians secured rural living standards in a political and highly visible manner by identifying themselves with the rural public works spending and the protection from cheaper imports of rigged, cartelized markets for farm products.

In the process, they neutralized one of the great potential sources of resistance to the postwar Japanese polity. The economic strategy of the postwar years with its privileging of export champions inevitably resulted in the passage of power and wealth from the countryside to the city, the farm to the factory. Periodic, system-shaking bouts of rural unrest dated as far back as the *ikki* or peasant uprisings of the Edo period. The People's Rights movement of the 1880s had stemmed from the rural resistance to Meiji policies of extracting capital from the countryside to finance Japan's first round of industrialization. Rural Japan had been the source of much of the anticapitalist, rightist agitation of the 1920s and 1930s; farmers had borne the brunt of the deflationary policies of the time aimed at putting Japan back on the gold standard, and their misery had been exploited by rightist agitators. Japan's postwar political setup, however, would finally end all this by securing rural livelihoods once and for all, *provided that rural districts voted reliably for LDP candidates.*

Since parliamentary representation did not change even when large numbers of people began moving from the countryside into the cities, a vote in a rural district came to count for anywhere from three to five urban votes.[4] This quid-pro-quo thus saw rural areas of Japan providing a stable national political framework in return for "compensation" as the political scientist Kent Calder has put it—compensation in the form of protectionism and public works spending for the reality that small farmers and local businesses had no real place in Japan's overall postwar economic strategy. The arrangements may have succeeded only in delaying

---

4. A parallel could be drawn in the dominance of the US Senate by voters from lightly populated states, but that dominance is limited to one house in a bicameral legislative setup that sees the executive elected independently; in Japan's case, the rural segments of the electorate have until very recently effectively controlled both the legislature and the cabinet, if not policy which largely originates out of the permanent bureaucracy.

an inevitable loss of population and vitality in Japan's rural areas, but they were sufficient to provide political stability during the decades of postwar transition to a fully industrialized, developed economy.

LDP politicians thus emerged as key power brokers in the postwar setup, obtaining favors from the bureaucracy in return for providing the bureaucrats with a stable political environment in which they could determine and carry out policy. The politicians' role was not limited, however, to arranging compensation for costs imposed by Japan's overall economic strategies. Prominent LDP politicians were also expected to mollify one or another element of the Japanese power structure when concessions were required to maintain American indulgence. But perhaps their most critical role was negative: to block any move toward real as opposed to ceremonial political oversight over the bureaucracy. The LDP lockhold on the Diet precluded substantive political input into key bureaucratic appointments or any meaningful requirement that bureaucrats explain and justify to politicians what they were doing. The formal apparatus of constitutional government left behind by GHQ did allow for the institutional possibility of a disciplined and able group of politicians capturing control of the Diet and from there moving on to form a cabinet that might try to impose political control over the bureaucracy. In the early 1950s, the most credible scenario along these lines involved politicians from the Left, and it was precisely to forestall any such event that the LDP had been formed in the first place. As the decades passed and the threat of leftist electoral victory receded, however, the LDP came to serve as the ramparts of a political setup that became increasingly and obviously dysfunctional with the lack of a political center that could overhaul Japan's economic model in response to the new realities of the late twentieth century. When a disciplined and able group of politicians did finally emerge, determined to construct for their country the center of political accountability that Japan had lacked since the demise of the Sat-Cho clique, they came not from the Left but largely from within the ranks of the LDP from which they had walked out to start new political parties.

But we are getting ahead of our story by some four decades or more. The initial creation of the LDP by no means spelled an end to the Japanese Left. The consolidation of the "1955 system"—the rubric applied to Japan's postwar political setup reflecting the founding year of the LDP—effectively blocked leftist access to power through the electoral system. So the Left took to the streets. Labor unions, amalgamated into a nationwide federation, launched waves of strikes. Union members together with other elements of the Japanese Left—women's rights advocates, Left political parties, anti-nuclear activists empowered by a 1954 incident in which Japanese fisherman had been exposed to radioactive fallout from a US thermonuclear test—staged huge demonstrations when LDP politicians attempted to revise the constitution or pass laws greatly expanding police powers to suppress opposition. The demonstrations were sufficiently overwhelming that the laws were never passed and the constitution remained intact, despite the LDP's majority in the Diet.

Events reached their peak in 1960. Upwards of a million people flooded into the streets of Tokyo to protest Prime Minister Kishi's ramming through the Diet the revision to the US–Japan Security Treaty. The original treaty, signed in 1952 in what amounted to a prerequisite for an end to the Occupation, had been valid for only eight years. The 1960 revision codified Japan's status as a US dependent in perpetuity, since the revised treaty's terms called for automatic renewal barring request for a change by one side or the other. The United States would continue to enjoy unrestricted access to a string of bases throughout Japan that Tokyo would help pay for. The United States would come to Japan's aid if Japan were attacked without any reciprocal obligation placed on Tokyo. (The official line out of Washington maintains that the quid-pro-quo lies in the American bases in Japan.) To put things bluntly, the terms of the treaty established that while Japan might not be a colony of the United States, neither was it an ally. It was more akin to a protectorate, free to manage its own domestic affairs, but required to defer to a foreign power on questions of security and foreign relations—and with an obligation to pay for its own subordination.

The hundreds of thousands of demonstrators opposed not simply the quasi-permanent relegation of Japan to "subordinate independence" under American hegemony that the treaty represented. They were also outraged at the patently undemocratic way in which the treaty had been renewed by men with blood on their hands. Kishi had, after all, been imprisoned as a suspected war criminal. He had been the economic czar of "Manchukuo" and had then served as Minister of Munitions in the wartime cabinet headed by Tojo Hideki. To secure the renewal of the treaty Kishi had called a snap, late-night vote and brought police onto the floor of the Diet; the police literally carried the speaker to the podium through crowds of bellowing opposition members.

The events surrounding the treaty renewal consolidated the return of the men who had been at least partly responsible for the horrors of the 1930s, men who had clawed their way back into power by selling their country out to the United States—or at least it seemed that way to millions of Japanese.[5] A visit by President Eisenhower to sign the renewed treaty had to be cancelled when a car carrying his press secretary who had come to Tokyo to work out the details was surrounded and nearly overturned by angry crowds.

Meanwhile, labor militancy culminated that year with a ten-month strike against Mitsui and Company at the company's Miike coal mine in Kyushu. With roots going back far into the Edo period, Mitsui was arguably the most famous name in Japanese business. The strike was ultimately about control of the workplace. Mitsui had sought to fire some 2,000 of the most activist union members and substitute its own house union for the union that had been built by the local miners.

The local union was seen as a "major threat to industrialists nationwide" and the resultant strike "dubbed 'total war between labor and capital.'" At one point, nearly 10 percent of the country's police force was dispatched to the site of the strike because of the attendant violence; tens of thousands rallied at the site in support of the strikers while the company hired goons to break up the demonstrations, resulting in the death of a striker and some 1,700 injuries.

The Left lost. The strike was broken. The Security Treaty was renewed. But the Left's defeat was not total. True, Mitsui succeeded in substituting its own docile company union for the trade union it had broken, thereby setting a national trend. But from that point on, major Japanese companies would accept the obligation to provide for the lifelong economic security of their core male employees and the ability to do that became an overriding corporate goal, far more important than quarterly earnings or the company's stock price. Well-established companies were effectively prohibited from firing people, even when they proved to be a problem of some sort or the company was in financial distress. With the concession of this core Left demand—economic security—labor militancy gradually morphed into a kind of ritual. Occasional half-day work stoppages were carefully staged to avoid slowing down critical production, and every May

---

5. Their suspicions would be confirmed when evidence came together decades later that the CIA had played a critical role in the electoral politics of the 1950s—see discussion in chapter 10.

Day the streets were filled with disciplined ranks of workers carrying flags in a parade-like atmosphere. It was all part and parcel of an emerging nationwide routine that saw company unions in key industries negotiate annual wage increases that then served as a benchmark for the country as a whole. The increases invariably reflected general economic conditions, and the factory floor ended up with what amounted to a guaranteed cut of any general improvement in the Japanese economy.

Meanwhile, Japan's "alliance" with the United States had been placed beyond challenge. But Eisenhower's visit was cancelled and Kishi resigned. He was replaced by Ikeda Hayato who, as much as any single person, deserves the title "father of the Japanese economic miracle." Ikeda may well be the most underrated economic policy practitioner of the twentieth century; it is only a slight exaggeration to say he is to export-led high growth what David Ricardo and Robert Peel were to free trade and comparative advantage or John Maynard Keynes and Franklin D. Roosevelt to proactive demand management. Ikeda had risen from within the ranks of the most elite of Japan's postwar governing institutions, the Ministry of Finance. He had an unrivaled view not only of the workings of the Japanese economy in their totality but of how Japan could harness the dollar-centered global financial order of the postwar world to spur high-speed growth through the meshing of foreign exchange and monetary policies.

Ikeda had already worked out most of his ideas and had put them into practice by the time he became prime minister; he had served as both finance minister and minister of international trade and industry in several postwar cabinets. On becoming prime minister, he seized the political opening created by the demoralization of the Left and the exhaustion of the country as a whole with what had come to seem endless political turmoil. Confident of the tools at the disposal of the bureaucracy, he announced his famous plan to double Japan's income within a decade, implicitly calling for his country to turn from political to economic struggle. His call resonated. With the spread of the salaryman culture of the large corporations that we will consider in the next chapter, as Japan achieved and surpassed Ikeda's goals, the humiliation of defeat and Japan's subordination to the United States would be, if not exactly forgotten, then placed into the shadow by pride at Japan's stunning economic achievements.

Washington cooperated in soothing the wounds left by the struggles that had culminated in 1960. The incoming administration of John F. Kennedy appointed Harvard professor Edwin Reischauer as ambassador to Japan.

Reischauer created a sensation. Handsome and genial, he had grown up in Japan as the son of one of the high-minded Protestant educators who flocked to Japan in the late Meiji period; he spoke Japanese, had a Japanese wife, and worked tirelessly to deflect the anti-American feelings that had boiled over with the renewal of the Security Treaty (he also took it upon himself with considerable success to shape American views of Japan).

For its part, the Left retreated into the academy and the increasing ritualism of the Japan Socialist Party ("JSP"). Forming the leading "opposition" party with no prospect of taking power, striking rigidly doctrinaire poses that had little to do with the actual concerns of most voters, the Socialists ended up as a *de facto* pillar of the postwar system by blocking the emergence of a genuine opposition. In October 1960, a knife-wielding nationalist 17-year-old schoolboy in school uniform had assassinated the uncompromising hard-left leader of the JSP, Asanuma Inejiro, on live television. While Asanuma's murder may have engendered some sympathy for the JSP, it also, with its deliberate echoes of the violence of the 1930s, helped stir waves of revulsion at the seemingly endless conflicts that had paralyzed so much of the country for the previous decade. A moderate faction of the JSP walked out to form its own centrist Democratic Socialist Party of Japan; the JSP would never again represent a serious electoral challenge to conservative hegemony.

The Communists, paradoxically, were less rigidly Marxist than the Socialists and continued from time to time to function as real gadflies, but they were never strong enough to be more than that. The Communists appealed primarily to the urban lower middle class of shopkeepers and small businessmen, but more of these people were attracted to the Komeito or Clean Government Party, founded in 1964 as an offshoot of Soka Gakkai, the largest of the "new religions" as they came to be known. These religions fused elements of the Nichiren Buddhism we encountered in the first chapter with the proselytizing tactics of evangelical Protestantism; their followers were primarily city dwellers who had been left out of the emerging salaryman culture of the large corporations. The religions gave these people a sense of belonging and, with Komeito, at least some voice in the corridors of power. Komeito functioned for all intents and purposes as an ally of the LDP,[6] doing for urban

---

6. Much of the Japanese media, hostile to Komeito, contends that the price of Komeito's support for the LDP has long been preservation of the tax-exempt status of any kind of "religious" foundation and, specifically, no investigation into the financial affairs of Ikeda Daisaku, the vastly wealthy third president of Soka Gakkai who built it into one of the most formidable institutions in Japan.

shopkeepers and small businessmen what the LDP did (more effectively) for farmers—providing enough "compensation" for their dwindling economic and social status that they were neutralized as a potential source of unrest.

Marxian professors continued to rule the academic roost in the social science faculties of the great universities. Like the pagan philosophers of the late Roman Empire who imparted a veneer of civilization to the Church Fathers, these professors trained the young men who would go on to assume positions of power in the great bureaucracies, banks, and corporations, often after a few years in college affiliated with ostensibly radical groups of student "revolutionaries." As the 1960s proceeded, the protests launched by these groups became larger, noisier, and ultimately more violent, perhaps reflecting examples abroad and the growing mayhem in Vietnam. It was impossible to hide the reality that Japan was the most important external supplier of the US military while the streets of Saigon hummed with Japanese motorcycles and small cars. The students were genuinely exercised about this—and about Japan's overall subordination to a United States they saw as imperialist and reactionary. But their demonstrations never posed any kind of existential threat to the Japanese power structure. With the groups of demonstrators arranged in rows that reflected seniority and the relative prestige of the universities from which they came, the student groups were as hierarchical as the society they were protesting. The protests gradually ran out of steam; some former students, it is true, would remain drop-outs, opening jazz cafés in funky urban neighborhoods or taking up organic farming in the countryside. Most, however, would return to the slots that had been marked out for them in the Japanese power structure from the moment they passed the grueling university entrance examinations, with those from the most elite schools—Tokyo and Kyoto Universities—taking charge of key institutions in the "emerging Japanese superstate." After all, whatever else they might have picked up during their years of tutelage under Marxian professors, they had obviously absorbed the key Marxian insight that it is the pace and nature of economic change that drives human history.

With the real political question of who has the right to require what of whom settled (if not for good then at least for the time being), with the most potentially divisive issues taken out of its hands altogether, embedded in stable external security and financial frameworks, Japan could single-handedly prepare to sprint forward in the most astonishing lunge for prosperity in human history. The country's dazzling success would bring on its own challenge up to and including the destabilization of the global framework that had made it possible, challenges for which Japan would be much less well equipped to cope. But all that was in the future. For the moment, it was time to get to work.

FIGURE 5. Ikeda Hayato, Father of the Economic Miracle, Is Voted Prime Minister on the Floor of the Diet. Courtesy of Hokkaido Shimbun.

5

The Institutions
of High-Speed Growth

In the previous chapter, we saw how politics, culture, and external circumstances came together in the fifteen years after 1945 to provide a framework that allowed a set of institutions to propel the Japanese economy into the highest growth rates ever seen to that point in history. Since the late 1960s, these institutions have come under increasing strain and some of them barely function now. But they are all still around in one form or another. Furthermore, they were selectively copied by Japan's neighbors as these countries sought to replicate the "Japanese miracle" themselves. They are worth understanding.

Some of these institutions date from the war years, some took shape farther back in Japan's past, and some were postwar constructions. All, however, were harnessed to overall national goals: first, recovering from postwar devastation; then, accumulating sufficient reserves of foreign exchange to free Japan from balance of payments constraints; and finally, building a wholly integrated modern industrial economy that would reduce as much as possible dependence on unpredictable foreigners. As noted in the previous chapter, predictability underpinned the emerging Japanese postwar economic model. But predictability could not be guaranteed, not in a country that could at best feed one-third of its population without imports or in which domestic energy sources were so limited. Furthermore, Japan's elites had, by 1960, largely accepted the reality that for the foreseeable future, their country would have to function essentially as a protectorate within an American-led world order—and the United States could prove disturbingly unpredictable. Japan's post-1960 economic and foreign policies would thus be driven by the need to contain and control Japan's vulnerability to the unpredictability that came with inevitable dependence on the outside world.

JAPANESE CORPORATIONS

A survey of the institutions of high-speed growth should properly start with corporations since they were the entities that actually produced the goods and services of the Japanese economy. While small businesses were sometimes organized as single proprietorships or partnerships, the limited liability corporation (*kabushiki gaisha*) was the near-universal legal construct for larger businesses. A few companies were privately held (the drinks company Suntory, for example) but most larger companies were publicly traded. Japanese companies were thus legally constituted just like their Western counterparts: contractual edifices with residual profits and residual ownership of corporate assets resting with equity holders after all parties with legally enforceable claims (customers, employees, suppliers, creditors, tax officials) had been satisfied.

But this legal construct tells us practically nothing about the way Japanese companies actually behaved. Common discourse in Japan and reams of Japanese language management literature treat the company not as a contractual construct but as an organic institution akin to a family, tribe, or religious foundation. Much of this literature maintains that Japanese corporations are natural outgrowths of the Edo period *ie* or household. It is true that Edo period economic organizations were, like their counterparts in China or pre-modern Europe, largely family-based. It is also true that both peasant and merchant households in Edo period Japan differed from their European and Chinese counterparts by regularly incorporating people who were not biological or marital relatives but nonetheless held reciprocal rights and obligations in the *ie*. They formed "part of the family" and were recognized as such both in the households themselves and by the wider society. But the "company as family" notion in modern Japan was much less an organic outgrowth of Edo period institutions, not to mention "Japanese culture," than it was an ideologically driven response to the labor militancy of the immediate postwar period discussed in the previous chapter.

That history did not, however, reduce the hold of the "company as family" notion on the mindset of Japanese managers, particularly when it was reinforced by laws and bureaucratic oversight that made it practically impossible to fire anyone. The Japanese manager saw his principal charge as the strengthening and survival of his company as an institution. Short-term profits were incidental or even trivial and certainly did not determine an individual manager's compensation or standing in the company. What counted was his contribution to helping the company provide for the economic security of its core employees, present and future. That, in turn, was a function of market share, product or service quality, technological leadership, cost control, and the maintenance of good relations with entities that could affect the company: banks, politicians and bureaucrats, suppliers, customers, trading companies, universities (to ensure a steady stream of high-quality recruits)—even, in some cases, organized crime. Particularly during the early years of the high-growth period, companies that demonstrated the ability to seize market-share overseas, thereby procuring dollar earnings, enjoyed a privileged position in the Japanese economic hierarchy.

Japanese companies came in several varieties. Some, notably those with names like "Mitsubishi," "Sumitomo," "Mitsui," or "Yasuda" in their corporate titles, had been spun off from the prewar *zaibatsu*, reconstituted in the postwar period as *keiretsu* or, as they are more often known in Japan, *guruppu gaisha* ("group companies"—the term *keiretsu* being more commonly used in Japan to refer to clusters of suppliers around a single large company).

A second type, as we noted in the previous chapter, consisted of companies started or encouraged by the Reform Bureaucrats in the decades leading up to the war (Nissan and Hitachi are two famous examples). These companies had had few *zaibatsu* ties; in early postwar decades, they tended to look for financing to the Industrial Bank of Japan rather than to the former *zaibatsu* banks.

Many other companies that had been founded by technologically gifted entrepreneurs in the prewar period—Toyota, for example, or Matsushita (now Panasonic)—proceeded to become first-tier companies in the postwar era. Other such companies settled into a *keiretsu* as suppliers to large companies such as Toyota and Matsushita that sold durables directly to end-users. Some major companies got their start only in the postwar period. Sony, Honda, and Kyocera are three famous examples. They often had a harder time than older firms, since they had to prove themselves to the Japanese establishment before they received the access to credit and, most crucially, to allocations of foreign exchange that were automatically available to the more established corporate champions.

But irrespective of their origins, all these companies were systematically protected from the threat of takeover or pressure to maximize short-term profits. Meanwhile, their shareholders were constrained from exercising any voice in the management of corporate assets. Equity shares were a source of dividend flows and played ceremonial functions in cementing business alliances; they were not, in practice, instruments that conferred any degree of corporate control.

Well-established Japanese companies enjoyed predictable and comparable financing and labor costs. While they could not fire their core employees, neither did they have to fear that their employees would leave for higher wages elsewhere. No one would hire these men, at least for comparable jobs in comparable firms.

INDUSTRIAL ASSOCIATIONS AND THE CONTROL OF COMPETITION

Competition was controlled. While competition to establish beachheads in new businesses could be ferocious (two of the most famous historical examples: Honda and Yamaha over motorcycles; Sony and Matsushita over the video cassette recorder), "excessive competition," as the Japanese liked to call it, was usually stymied through informal guidelines disseminated via industrial associations that were essentially cartels. They form another of the key high-growth institutions. They were particularly important in Japan since there was no market in corporate control that could force companies to abandon money-losing businesses. Nor did Japanese companies use profit-driven yardsticks such as return on investment ("ROI") or return on equity ("ROE") to help them determine which businesses they should enter and which they should exit. Given the absence of such yardsticks, Japanese companies sometimes found themselves locked into economically destructive competition—destructive not just for their own businesses, but for the economy as a whole. Corporate obsession with "face," with institutional survival, and with job security made it almost impossible for companies to accept reductions in market share, not to mention exiting businesses in which they had established positions. This is where the associations stepped in. They established unwritten rules that allowed also-rans to preserve jobs and market share. (Yamaha neither went bankrupt nor exited the motorcycle business after "losing" its battle with Honda over the domestic market.) The industrial associations were particularly important in coordinating and policing informal agreements about prices and supply chains, agreements that would be illegal under US antitrust law. These agreements allowed weaker members to survive, thereby protecting employment levels, and were also effective in blocking imports. Companies that defied these agreements, which theoretically lacked the force of law, could find themselves subject to intolerable pressures, which is why examples of defiance are relatively rare.[1]

In the long run, the recoiling from "creative destruction" that forms an indispensable part of market capitalism would prove deadly to some Japanese industries—consumer electronics, for example, when confronted after 1990 by nimble competitors from overseas such as Apple and Samsung. But during the high-growth years, the industrial associations helped ensure that the sharpest competition was directed outwards, where a mixture of Japan's labor practices, financing, and the skills of its workers proved definitive in the drive for global market share.

EMPLOYMENT PRACTICES

Employment practices formed a third institution of high-speed growth, one totally bound up with Japanese corporate behavior and the unwritten rules of Japanese economic life. The most important of these practices, so-called "lifetime" employment, was not actually for life; it referred to a corporate commitment to the economic security of core male employees. No real labor market existed in postwar Japan; an attempt by an ambitious

---

1. Two of the more famous cases: Sumitomo Metals which in 1965 attempted to defy a collective agreement on production cutbacks decreed by its association, the *Nihon Tekko Renmei* (Japan Iron and Steel Association); and Lion Petroleum, which in 1984 attempted to import refined gasoline from Singapore rather than relying on Japanese refineries. Both were forced to back down.

entrepreneur, Ezoe Hiromasa, to create one in the late 1980s brought on one of the largest political scandals in postwar history, a story we will look at in more detail in chapter 10. The scandal illuminated the unease of Japan's political and economic elites at any tampering with employment practices that had not only worked so well for Japan economically but also had an important political dimension. The deliberate suppression of a labor market coupled with supposedly paternalistic employment practices had suppressed—at least for the time being—any return to the class-based activism of the immediate postwar years. Japan's elite had not forgotten the struggles of the late 1940s and 1950s over control of the workplace.

Blue-collar male workers were hired on graduation from high school; white-collar males, on graduation from college. While companies competed fiercely for quality male recruits, this competition did not extend to wages or benefits, all of which were essentially identical across industries and companies at given levels, with the one exception of subsidized housing—only well-established companies offered this extremely valuable perk, in and of itself enough to explain the appeal of such companies to potential employees over start-ups and other smaller firms. The employment window in Japanese organizations for young men with management-track ambitions opened only once: on graduation from college (exceptions existed for some technical specialists who were expected to obtain graduate degrees in subjects like metallurgy before seeking jobs). Miss it, and there was no second chance; there was nothing comparable in Japan to the "find yourself" years between college and serious work in which the offspring of the American elite indulged.

Both first-tier and other companies hired women as well as men. But women were almost universally relegated to classic pink-collar jobs. Known as "office ladies" or OLs, they were typically required to wear uniforms, expected to marry after a few years, and then to leave the company on becoming pregnant.

A young man joining a firm as a management-track hire spent the first decade or so of his working life rotating through most of the firm's functional areas—sales, operations, finance, human resources. New assignments were usually announced shortly before the end of the fiscal year in March, leading to a common sight in Japan as March 31 approaches: streets clogged with moving vans as employees and their families prepare for transfers to new cities. Sometimes men who had demonstrated unusual aptitude were sent for a year or two to top universities overseas for specialized graduate training in subjects like management. That was one of the few tangible signs that a man had done well, for gaps in salaries and titles did not start to appear for at least a decade after a given group of recruits joined a company. Promotions began when a man was in his late thirties or early forties; from then on, as the management pyramid narrowed, men who did not make it to the next level would be assigned positions with a firm's affiliates or suppliers. These men would continue to be looked after by the original firm's *jinjibu*—human resources department—until their final retirements, and even beyond.[2]

These employment practices also prevailed in the public sector. Bureaucrats retiring from their ministries and landing jobs in the companies they once regulated formed a practice known as *amakudari* or "descent from heaven."

EDUCATION

The education system provided the raw material directed by the all-powerful HR departments (*jinjibu*) of corporations and the bureaucracy. Education in Japan had four purposes: equipping graduates with the literacy and numeracy demanded of a developed, industrialized economy; socializing Japanese children in the attitudes and behavior expected of highly bureaucratized economic organizations; acting as a sorting mechanism in selecting boys eligible for potential future membership in Japan's political and economic elite (and, to a lesser extent, sorting out the girls who would qualify to be their wives); and, finally, constructing the foundations for social networks that would serve crucial purposes in later life in the key senior management task of binding organizations to each other.

Occupation era reforms and the radicalization of the Japan Teacher's Union had succeeded in transforming only the outward forms of education inherited from the prewar era. GHQ had imposed the 6-3-3 system then coming into vogue for American schooling (six years of primary school followed by three each of middle and upper secondary; it still prevails in Japan today, even though the United States has moved to a 5-3-4

---

2. In certain industries that demanded high levels of expertise acquired only through years of experience, functional groups within the firm might be responsible for hiring a man and keeping him employed through his working life. The coal department in a major trading company, for example, might well be staffed by "lifetime coal men."

system) but the academic content remained largely what it had been under the prewar system, minus the overtly xenophobic elements of "patriotic" education. Japan's prewar high schools had been modeled on their German equivalents and, like the German *gymnasien*, completed a student's general education, with the university years devoted entirely to the study of specialized subjects such as law or medicine. Despite the Occupation reforms, the postwar Japanese high school continued essentially to finish the student's general education, although the task had to be crammed into fewer years than had been true before 1945.

Japan's middle- and high-school students in a particular school all followed the identical curriculum, one that in an academic school emphasized Japanese language and mathematics but with plenty of history, basic science, geography, and English (vocational schools naturally stressed more "practical" subjects). Students spent an entire academic year in the same classroom; teachers, not students, moved back and forth between class periods.

Schools were Spartan, no-nonsense places. While most public primary schools were open to both boys and girls, many secondary schools were single-sex. Students themselves rather than custodial staff were typically held responsible for keeping their classrooms neat and orderly. Younger boys often wore trim navy shorts straight through the winter while older teenagers still donned the modified German cadet uniform of the prewar years, complete with stiff celluloid collar. Girls' uniforms—and uniforms were common in primary schools; universal in secondary—were usually some form of sailor suit.

The emphasis on a disciplined, uniform appearance and the acceptance of discomfort formed part of wider pedagogical goals at least as important as numeracy and literacy: *gaman*, or the ability to endure and fulfill demands without complaint, and the suppression of individuality in favor of the group. Internalization of some of this discipline was necessary in order to master the fiendishly difficult written Japanese language.[3] But internalization of the discipline meted out in Japanese schools was also required of anyone expecting to function smoothly within Japanese

---

3. Written Japanese requires some six to nine times the amount of time and effort to achieve real literacy that English, Spanish, or German do; because the Chinese characters used to write Japanese have different readings depending on context, mastery of written Japanese requires more sustained effort than even Chinese does.

organizations as an adult. It was certainly necessary to pass the entrance examinations into high schools and universities.

These grueling, all-day examinations formed the one unavoidable gateway that had to be traversed by any Japanese boy who expected a life of status and privilege. (There was one way out of these exams: enrollment in a primary or secondary school affiliated with a university. The best Japanese private universities as a result saw ferocious competition for entrance into their expensive lower schools.) The pinnacles of Japanese society—policy positions in the major ministries, editorships of the top newspapers, the executive suites of the leading banks, trading companies, and manufacturers—were effectively closed to those without undergraduate degrees from Japan's top universities with the University of Tokyo *primus inter pares*. (*Tōdai*, to use the Japanese acronym, has no affiliated lower schools; no one matriculates without passing the entrance exam.) Even well-established second-tier companies rarely hired anyone for a management track position without a college degree. This was not simply because a degree assured employers that a graduate was literate, numerate, and had demonstrated the ability to endure the years of privation and effort necessary to pass the entrance examination. It was also because the connections formed at university would prove critical to anyone promoted into the ranks of upper-middle management and above. Beyond a certain point in many Japanese organizations, job content became almost entirely a matter of working through and strengthening a firm's (or a ministry's) external relationships. Even an otherwise capable man would have been at too much of a disadvantage in building all-important "human networks" (*jinmyaku*) had he not graduated from a good school.

It is for this reason that the academic content of the undergraduate years was so unimportant, if not irrelevant. To be sure, students who planned careers in fields such as medicine, the sciences, and law—or who expected to become academics themselves—needed to study. But for the others, grades hardly mattered and professors rarely failed students, even if they did not show up for class. It is a mistake, however, to term the Japanese undergraduate years a "vacation" as is often said. The undergraduate years were (and are) the time when an ambitious young man was expected to build a network of human connections that would sustain him in later life. This was done principally through membership in an undergraduate "club" and, in his senior year, through the seminar (*zemi*) in which he enrolled. A major responsibility of a Japanese university professor was arranging suitable introductions to employers for his *zemi* students.[4]

The ideal employment candidate for a position in a top Japanese organization was a good-looking, well-spoken young man graduating from a major university who had served as the captain or the manager of a team ("club") in a team sport such as baseball, soccer, or rugby. That he had graduated from a top university meant he had had the smarts and *gaman* (ability to endure) necessary to pass the entrance examination. That he had been on a sports team meant not only that he had health, stamina, and strength but that he had internalized the strict hierarchical relations that prevail in most Japanese team sports. That he had been captain—a position chosen by his teammates—meant he could command respect and affection from others. Companies did not worry about how much history, economics, or physics he had mastered in college. They would see to it that he was taught what he needed to know in order to do what would be required of him.

THE FINANCIAL SYSTEM

Employment practices and the educational backgrounds of employees helped Japanese companies plan for the long term in their assault and conquest of foreign markets, but equally important was the financial system. Postwar Japanese finance had its roots in the institutional innovations of the Meiji period discussed in chapter 3 that saw banks acting as the principal providers of investment capital to *zaibatsu* firms. But postwar Japanese finance assumed the final shape it did because of events in two critical years: 1927 and 1940. In 1927, Japan endured a financial crisis that in many ways served as harbinger of the global crisis of 1929–1931. The Japanese bond market imploded and essentially disappeared from that point forward as a significant source of corporate finance. Meanwhile, scores of weaker banks went under, and in stepping in to rescue those banks left standing, the Ministry of Finance ("MOF") assumed what amounted to direct control of the banking system.

---

4. The coming of the Internet has reduced somewhat the importance of the *zemi* in finding jobs.

In 1940, the MOF would use that control to put the financial system on a war footing. A war economy poses two exceptional challenges to policy makers: directing credit toward enterprises for the non-market purpose of munitions manufacturing and managing the concomitant destruction of savings without ruinous inflation. (Since armaments are never sold, directly or indirectly, to households, they do not generate cash flows that can be used to retire the debt taken on to finance their manufacture.) The MOF's control of the banking system allowed it easily to steer credit toward munitions makers. But avoiding ruinous inflation proved a bigger hurdle. To get around it, the MOF issued bonds to finance the proceeds paid to armaments manufacturers, forced household savings into deposit-taking institutions, and then required those institutions to buy the bonds.

It was a relatively trivial matter in the postwar period to redirect bank credit from "strategic" industries (as in munitions makers) to "strategic" industries (as in companies with demonstrable capacity to export)—in many cases, these were the same companies with production lines reconfigured to churn out consumer durables rather than weapons. But ensuring there was enough credit to begin with was a tricky problem in a desperately poor country whose savings had been wiped out.

Most countries confronted with this problem—how to finance development without sufficient domestic savings—will opt to accept foreign investment. That is what China did in 1978 after Deng Xiaoping consolidated his control of that country. That is what the United States did in the nineteenth century when it relied on capital raised in the City of London to finance the building of its railroad network.

But the Japanese were determined not to allow any significant part of their economy to fall under the control of foreigners. The Japanese authorities had initially been backed up in this determination by left-leaning GHQ officials, and they continued and even strengthened the exclusionary policies once the Occupation ended. But if a poor country is unwilling to accept foreign investment, then if it expects to grow, it must conserve and rationalize every spare unit of savings it can command.

Here is where the genius of such men as Ikeda Hayato proved crucial. They devised monetary and financial oversight policies that would marshal the unique structural features of Japanese finance into the creation of a credit pump that provided Japan's export champions with the patient financing needed to mount and sustain assaults on foreign markets. Many of these policies involved a reworking of wartime financing methods: forcing household savings into deposit-taking institutions, then requiring those institutions to buy government-issued financial instruments.

Household savings were encouraged by every conceivable means. The only way a family could reasonably expect to acquire its own home—not to mention pay school fees and put aside money for retirement—was through careful management of household finances and regular saving. About one-third of typical salaries were paid as semi-annual bonuses, teaching housewives to manage the household's expenses on two-thirds of its income. Bonus season saw blizzards of promotions from banks and the post office (essentially a large bank the disposition of whose assets was controlled by the MOF) encouraging people to put the bonus money on deposit. Interest income was not taxed, but no deductible existed for mortgage interest payments.[5]

During the early years of the high-growth period, however, the sum total of household savings was not enough to finance the capital investment needed by Japanese industry to mount assaults on foreign markets. The gap was filled by meshing monetary policies with bank oversight.

Japan's banks were divided into three groups. Group one consisted of thirteen so-called "city banks" (*toshi ginkō*) descended from prewar *zaibatsu* banks. With their headquarters in one of the three major metropolitan areas (Tokyo-Yokohama, Osaka-Kyoto-Kobe, and Nagoya), they were the primary providers of investment capital financing to the *guruppu gaisha*—companies with names like Sumitomo and Mitsubishi in their corporate titles. These banks also provided the day-to-day financing of production and trade (i.e., working capital financing) to many large established companies. The second group consisted of three so-called long-term banks, the biggest and most prestigious of which was the Industrial Bank of Japan. These banks provided investment capital financing to corporate champions such as Nippon Steel or Nissan that were unaffiliated with a particular *guruppu*. Finally, there were some sixty-plus regional banks (*chihō ginkō*) that served as the pre-eminent financial institutions in Japan's prefectural capitals where they financed local businesses.

In any well-developed national banking system, banks will sometimes find themselves with more deposits than they have lending opportunities

---

5. The Occupation had scarcely ended when the MOF instituted measures that forced households that still had stock market holdings to sell them or sustain huge losses. Until the 1980s, the stock market was seen as a dangerous casino. People put their money into the bank, not the stock market.

and vice versa. But in the high-growth years, the city banks were always short of funds.[6]

Why were the city banks perennially short of funds? Banks are supposed to manage their assets and liabilities closely to prevent structural shortages from happening. But in Japan, the credit pumps the city banks made available to industry consisted almost entirely of short-term evergreen loans that were never expected to be paid back but renewed indefinitely. The Japanese had a term for it: "overloan." The banks made up the gap between their deposit base and their loan book with direct credit provided by the BOJ.

Pumping newly created credit directly into the banking system is something central banks are only supposed to do in times of emergency. Even then, as the brouhaha over the Federal Reserve's "quantitative easing" in the wake of the 2008 financial crisis suggests, it is fraught with controversy. It is certainly risky for a country whose currency is not yet "hard," a currency that is not accepted as a global settlements and reserve currency and is not backed by sufficient levels of international reserves to render it credible. This is a fair description of Japan's financial situation at least in the early years of the high-growth period. Excessive credit creation by a developing country central bank usually invites inflation and a collapse in the currency's external value as local elites, understanding what the central bank is up to, quickly dump their holdings of domestic financial instruments in favor of hard currency holdings abroad.

But in Japan the tactics worked. Japan's leaders could rely both on external capital controls that made it technically illegal to transfer wealth out of the country, and on the social cohesion that rendered it unthinkable among those who knew what was going on. Even so, the tactics carried risk since the credit did not stem from cash flow generated by current assets. Rather, credit was created out of nothing to finance assets that did not yet exist, assets that would ultimately have to generate future returns sufficient to make credible the credit created to finance them. This alone explains the emphasis on predictability, on controlled competition. Japan's elites needed to be sure that the credit they were conjuring up out of thin air went to finance assets that would generate a sufficient level of dollar

6. The three long-term banks, which did not take deposits, financed themselves with issues of five- and seven-year debentures, the market for which—if one can call it a market—was set and controlled by the MOF.

earnings in export markets to keep the engines of the Japanese export-led economy running. The Japanese themselves described the setup as a bicycle that must be kept running lest it tip over. The belief on the part of Japan's policy elite that it could indeed keep that bicycle upright and moving fast underlay Ikeda's promise that he could double Japan's income in a decade.

THE BUREAUCRACY

Here, then, is where we finally come to the critical role of the bureaucracy as the central coordinating institution of high-speed growth. Highlighting this essential feature of Japan's high-growth economic machine invites controversy. The ideological foundations of neo-liberalism pronounce, a priori, the very existence of a bureaucracy capable of "outguessing" markets to be impossible—or at best, able only to engineer a crude, Stalinist type of industrialization in the context of a totalitarian political order. Thus, attempts to belittle or dismiss the central coordinating role of the Japanese bureaucracy fall back on the same examples trotted out over and over again—Sony's long wait for allocations of foreign exchange to import prototypes of the transistor, Honda's defiance of MITI's attempts to engineer a consolidation of the Japanese automobile industry—in order to reinforce the notion that bureaucrats can never outwit markets.

But this misses the point. Ideological preconceptions may account for much of the perennial downplaying of the central importance of the Japanese bureaucracy in the economic miracle. But misconceptions about the Japanese bureaucracy and how it operated also play a role. The Japanese bureaucracy was not limited to the ministries, and even the economic ministries themselves rarely functioned in a "do this, do that" command-and-control mode. The economic ministries worked in a collaborative fashion with major companies as well as bureaucracies outside the formal government such as the *Keidanren*, or Federation of Economic Organizations (the national amalgamation of the industrial associations discussed above), and the *Keizai Dōyūkai* (once known in English as the Organization for Economic Development; now called the Japan Association of Corporate Executives). Furthermore, the great business combines, particularly those in the *guruppu gaisha* (Sumitomo, Mitsui, etc.) where they owned shares in each other, functioned far more like bureaucracies than like profit-seeking business enterprises. They were not driven by "greed and fear" (i.e., profit opportunities and the threat of bankruptcy); among other things, large established Japanese companies effectively did not go bankrupt while "excessive" profit making was seen as socially suspect. Instead, like bureaucracies anywhere, these companies responded to expectations generated by the sociopolitical system in which they were embedded.

This collective Japanese bureaucratic elite demonstrated the character of a hive-mind or swarm intelligence, zooming in on particular industries for targeting and then bringing forth the corporate champions that would mount the assaults on foreign markets. To be sure, there were outliers from time to time—Sony and Honda being, as noted, the two most famous cases—and, occasionally, disputes over the appropriate industry (the most contentious was probably over automobiles), but there was usually little discord; the choice of a given industry for targeting seemed obvious. Typically, the industry in question was a critical upstream industry that Japan "had to have" (steel, for example, or machine tools) or the industry had high fixed costs and high barriers to entry (earth-moving equipment/complex consumer electronics) or both (semi-conductors). In a high fixed-cost business, financing and employment practices proved definitive over the long haul, since Japanese companies could sustain losses for the time needed to establish a pre-eminent global market share. Foreign competitors, under pressure from financial markets to show steady profit growth, would surrender markets rather than swallow the losses needed to compete with the Japanese, while high barriers to entry discouraged new competitors once the Japanese had established themselves.

The collective nature of the Japanese economic juggernaut—famously labeled "Japan, Inc."—suggests that Japan's was more akin to a socialist than a capitalist economy, and indeed Japan has been called the most successful socialist economy ever. Such a designation is superficially plausible, given that corporate control was never subject to market forces, nominal "owners" had next to no say-so in management decisions, and, as noted above, key prices—for money and labor in particular—were removed from market influences. But labeling the Japanese economy socialist is ultimately no more helpful in understanding how things actually operated than assuming that Japan had to be a conventional market-capitalist economy since, after all, it had been successful. Unlike the leaders of Leninist command economies, Japan's business and economic elites were acutely sensitive to market developments. Companies acted like finely honed antennae in seeking out opportunity, or, to continue our "hive" metaphor, like swarms of bees or ants that set forth to locate food sources. Given the way the entire setup was financed, Japan could not afford to make many mistakes, particularly during the early high-growth years. Assaults were launched only after every conceivable bit of technological and market data had been accumulated, only after a corporate champion or champions had emerged from trial heats in the protected domestic market, and only after a collective determination had been made that the industry in question was one which Japan could conquer.

The system began to sputter after Japan pulled equal to the other leading developed economies; once that happened, it was no longer obvious what industries should be pursued. (Significantly, the last major foreign industry targeted by "Japan, Inc." was mainframe computers; Japanese companies went after IBM in the early 1980s, not realizing the ground on which the whole computer industry rested was about to shift.) And then, other countries would learn to play the Japanese game—South Korea arguably followed Japan's economic methods the most closely, and the Korean electronics giant Samsung now makes more money than the top 10 Japanese electronics firms put together.[7]

But all that was in the future. During the high-growth years, the collective Japanese bureaucratic "hive" had a string of successes in picking off industry after industry: textiles, shipbuilding, steel, radios, color television, earth-moving equipment, film, machine tools, cameras, watches, fax machines, printers, and copiers, not to mention motorcycles and automobiles. The result was to catapult Japan into the front rank of the world's industrial powers; by 1968, two years ahead of Ikeda's announced goal, Japan had indeed doubled its 1960 per capita income and had become the world's second largest economy.

THE "MANAGEMENT OF REALITY"

Other institutions contributed to what happened—the police, for example, that helped keep Japan's cities free of violent crime (sometimes via tacit cooperation with the *yakuza*, the Japanese mob, that absorbed otherwise

---

7. To be sure, much of these profits stem from the domestic monopolies Samsung enjoys in such non-related businesses as shipbuilding and steel.

incorrigible youths and kept them off the streets while providing services that were technically illegal—prostitution, gambling—but could not be eliminated) or the so-called "new religions" that gave a sense of belonging to the urban lower-middle class that had been left out of the emerging salaryman culture of the large corporations. The most important of these other institutions, however, were charged with what Karel van Wolferen has labeled the "Management of Reality."

Reality management consisted of a cluster of institutions and practices that ensured that everybody who mattered acted in predictable ways, often manifest in seemingly deliberate, collective decisions not to notice contradictions. A good example is working hours. On the surface, people work eight-hour days and, when overtime is required, companies are supposed to compensate workers with extra pay. And indeed, come 6 p.m., heating or air conditioning goes off, the gates to office buildings and factories close, cleaning crews begin their evening rounds, and skeleton night-time security staff report for duty. Subways, buses, and trains run on reduced schedules.

Yet no one has gone home (or at least no men have gone home). All the lights are on and everyone continues to work until 9 p.m. or so if it is an ordinary day, and midnight or beyond if times are busy. Small side doors see streams of people leaving office buildings after 10 p.m. while late evening subways may be even more crowded than they would be during the next morning's rush hour. Admittedly, such scenes are less common today than when the Japanese economy was chugging along full-throttle, but during those years, everyone "knew" that the ordinary workday was about twelve hours—and much longer at busy times such as fiscal year-end—even though for reporting purposes it was eight.

Japan was not, of course, the only country where people worked long hours. No one who expects to make it on Wall Street or in Silicon Valley goes home at five o'clock. But in those places, long hours are openly acknowledged—and openly compensated. In Japan, a whole elaborate fiction existed—buttressed, significantly, by corporate record-keeping and official reports sent to and from the Ministry of Labor—that most everyone worked only the theoretical forty-hour weeks. When one had to discuss the extra hours, euphemisms such as *saabisu zangyō* ("service" or free, i.e., uncompensated, overtime) were employed.

This kind of thing is everywhere in Japan. When someone is visibly incompetent in a Japanese organization, the person is not fired, but everyone "knows" without it being spelled out that the person has to be watched and any critical task is quasi-automatically double-checked or done by someone else. Yet there will be no formal indication that the person is unsuitable for the job. Japan's trade negotiators would regularly point to low official tariff rates to demonstrate that their country's markets were open to all comers, but companies "knew" they were not supposed to import, and if they "forgot," the relevant industrial association would remind them. Parliamentary proceedings might give the casual observer the sense that public policy emerged out of legislative debates. But both the questions being asked by one set of politicians and the answers read out by another were written by bureaucrats. That did not mean, however, that a minister could absent himself from a parliamentary review any more than a Japanese executive could miss a board meeting, even though in both cases everyone knew that whatever it was being debated had already been decided.

One might even go so far as to say that success in Japan was determined by one's ability not to notice contradictions—or to put this in other words, to figure out how to behave in any given situation without it being spelled out. Of course, this is another feature of "Japanese culture" inherited from a centuries-old political setup in which the formal trappings of power differed dramatically from the reality. And naturally, there is—again—a whole vocabulary in Japanese to cope with these things; we have already noted the distinction between *tatemae* (the constructed reality to which everyone pays lip service) and *honne* (what is actually going on); someone who fails to pick up on the unspoken reality is said to be unable to read the *kūki* (literally, the air) or is accused of being *rikutsuppoi* (a logic-fetishist)—not a compliment in Japanese.

But while the Japanese power holders could rely on cultural mores in getting people to move with programs that were not spelled out, they still needed some means to disseminate the unspoken reality. The most important of these were the quality press, television, and advertising.

Control of both information and its interpretation in Japan invites parallels with the way in which the economy was controlled. Unlike the situation in Cuba or the Soviet Union, there was no rule against starting a new business in Japan. A budding entrepreneur who conceived a new technology was not prevented from trying to market his invention. But the whole system worked to push him into the arms of an established company or trading house; if he tried to stay independent, he found he could not raise money or even get meetings with potential customers. The moment he conceded to the unspoken reality and took up a position in the *keiretsu* of a major company as a supplier, markets and capital opened up to him—at the price, of course, of loss of independence.

The examples of mavericks such as Sony and Kyocera are the exceptions that prove the rule. They had to prove themselves overseas before they were accepted by the Japanese economic establishment. And significantly, as the decades went by, the number of exceptions dropped off. There would be no Japanese Apple, Cisco, Microsoft, Intel, Google, or Facebook riding the IT revolution to worldwide fame and profit. (We will look at the emergence of such companies as Softbank and Rakuten in chapter 8.)

A similar dynamic prevailed in the realm of ideas and information. No one was arrested for writing or saying things that contradicted the agreed-to story.[8] But one was inevitably marginalized. The flow of news was controlled by *kisha kurabu* (reporters' clubs)—cartels of journalists covering major news sources such as politicians, ministries, and the police. Only members of the established press could join these clubs, and if they filed stories that contradicted the unspoken agreement on how a particular piece of news was to be presented, the reporter and his newspaper could find himself frozen out of future scoops, which is why stories covering major economic and political developments in the leading dailies can read like carbon copies of each other. The system also explains how the media could turn suddenly like a pack of hyenas on a particular politician or business leader—they all would have held back until the signal was given that the man had become open game, a signal that typically emerged from the public prosecutor's office via leaks to the relevant *kisha kurabu*.

The quality press and NHK, the publicly supported television network, thus essentially determined what was news and how it was to be presented. Meanwhile, television serials and popular movies signaled middle-class families on the unspoken norms people were expected to adopt at home, in the office, and at school. While family breakdown, school bullying, company skullduggery, or sexual escapades could be depicted in entertaining and even lurid ways, the causes invariably ended up pointing to a

---

8. That may change with the railroading in December 2013 through the Diet of a new law ostensibly aimed at controlling secrets but in practice giving the government essentially unlimited powers to arrest and imprison anyone—including journalists—revealing anything the government does not want revealed.

housewife neglecting her husband and children, a man neglecting his job, or a schoolchild neglecting his or her studies—or with anyone who tried to assert resistance to the demands of family, school, or workplace. Of course, something similar prevailed in other countries as well; one would have to look long and hard for genuinely subversive content in the American television programming of the 1950s. But there was nothing quite comparable in Japan to the underground rumblings during that decade of the American "beats," rumblings that would burst forth in the 1960s in the songs of musicians such as Bob Dylan, in films such as *The Graduate*, in television programs such as *Rowan and Martin's Laugh-In* with their frontal attacks on important political institutions in American society. Of course, Japan spawned dissidents and others deeply unhappy with the contemporary order, but the marginalization of dissidence into ritualized, harmless protest was a process carried out in Japan far more effectively than in countries such as the United States, Britain, and Germany.

In Japanese popular culture, political institutions—companies, schools, bureaucracies such as the police—came off as ultimately benevolent; any institutional wrong-doing was inevitably the result of "bad apples." Pretty, dimply pop stars—*aidoru* (idols)—were stamped out in assembly-line fashion by powerful agencies such as Johnny's Jimusho; these boys and girls would prance about on television for a few years lip-synching bouncy songs, exuding a kind of non-threatening, puppyish sexuality, before staging "farewell concerts" and then disappearing back into regular life.[9]

The mainstream media was also kept in line by Japan's oligopolistic advertising business, dominated by the behemoth Dentsu, the world's largest advertising firm, that during the high-growth years raked in from one-fifth to one-third of all the advertising spending in Japan. In the immediate postwar years, Yoshida Hideo, who built Dentsu into the power it became, had made his firm into a such a refuge for men who had held positions in colonial Manchuria that its headquarters was nicknamed the Second Mantetsu Building, a reference to the former headquarters of the Manchurian Railways. Many whom Yoshida employed had been key figures in the war-time propaganda bureaucracy, including the former head of the military thought police. Yoshida was rewarded by a grateful

---

9. Now and again, those who demonstrate real talent will resurface as adults, usually as actors rather than singers.

Japanese government with the political protection and favoritism needed to establish Dentsu's dominance over the Japanese media.

"Reality management" thus served to delineate to all but the most obtuse (or "un-Japanese" as they might be called) what was permissible and what wasn't. Of course, the dynamic exists in other places. As George Orwell once wrote: "At any given moment there is an orthodoxy, a body of ideas which it is assumed all right-thinking people will accept without question. It is not exactly forbidden to state this or that or the other, but it is 'not done.'. . . Anyone who challenges the prevailing orthodoxy finds himself silenced with surprising effectiveness." But perhaps no power holders outside the Japanese elite had ever been so effective in delineating orthodoxy, to paraphrase Orwell, or in silencing dissent without resort to overt coercion. What made it even more remarkable was that much of the orthodoxy was never made explicit; it was just "in the air"—the *kūki*.

FIGURE 6. The Kyoto Tower Hotel from the Grounds of the Toji Temple. Courtesy Photolibrary Kabushiki Gaisha.

6

Consequences

Intended and Otherwise

By the mid-1980s, it appeared that the institutions of high-speed growth had succeeded beyond even the dreams of their designers. Current account deficits had disappeared by 1966, freeing Japan from balance of payments constraints. In 1968, Japan passed West Germany to become the world's second largest "capitalist" economy. Japan appeared to suffer a drastic setback with the OPEC oil price hikes and the 1973–75 recession, but the country astonished the world by bouncing back far more quickly than any other developed economy. By 1976, Tokyo had pushed inflation and unemployment down to levels that induced sputtering envy and incomprehension in Washington, London, and Paris. Japan took in stride the further spike in energy prices in the wake of the 1979 Iranian revolution, and was not far into the 1980s when it could credibly boast of industrial parity or supremacy in practically every key sector—the only significant one left to conquer was computers. The dream that had obsessed Japan's power holders since the fall of the Tokugawa Shogunate—reducing dependence on foreigners to levels where the outside world no longer really needed to be taken into consideration in charting economic and political outcomes—seemed within grasp. Japan depended on the outside world only for commodities and a few finished goods such as commercial aircraft that for political reasons Tokyo had decided not to target. True, Japan still relied on the US military to protect its vital sea lanes and as a deterrent to a visibly declining but still menacing Soviet Union. But Japan had emerged as the principal foreign financier of the American external and government deficits; the so-called Reagan Revolution that allowed the United States to finance a rapid military buildup without concomitant tax increases was pretty much paid for by Japan. It was that buildup that finally convinced Moscow it could never win an arms race with Washington. Meanwhile, by paying for it, Tokyo bought itself security without the risks of putting the means of coercion at the disposal of one or more elements of its own bureaucracy.

It had all been possible because the institutions of high-speed growth worked the way they were supposed to. Japan's bureaucratic hive-mind made scarcely any mistakes in identifying industries to target and conquer. With patient financing and a literate, numerate workforce socialized into doing whatever it took to establish supremacy, Japanese corporate champions racked up one success after another. While the demands on the workforce could seem almost infinite, economic security had become a given. No one starved, and anyone who played by the rules could expect a decent, middle-class life, albeit with cramped living quarters, long crowded commutes, and little to no vacation time. National health insurance gave everyone access to affordable care, public education ensured universal literacy in the world's most complicated written language, and the risk of violent crime was essentially zero.

THE COSTS

But there were costs. Some of them—horrendous levels of industrial pollution, for example—could be dealt with, and were. In the late 1950s, the air in Tokyo and Osaka had become some of the world's worst; twenty years later, it had been cleaned up. Others problems, however, proved more intractable.

One of the most serious lay in the cheapening and coarsening of Japanese culture, in both the arts-and-literature sense of the word and in the wider meaning. This was harder to see—and much harder to reverse—than industrial pollution, although there was at least one fully visible and, to choose a modifier deliberately, concrete manifestation: the defacing of Kyoto. Kyoto had been burned to the ground during the Onin War of the late fifteenth century, but Hideyoshi and the Tokugawa shoguns had lavished attention on the city, restoring and even surpassing its former glory. They may have had political motives—demonstrating the legitimacy of their rule—but they left behind them one of the crown jewels of human civilization. Kyoto had largely been spared the ravages of prewar industrialization, and Franklin Roosevelt had been persuaded that its architectural and cultural legacy was too precious to destroy in bombing raids.

But the institutions of high-speed growth would succeed where the US Air Force had been blocked. The process started with an eyesore of a garish tower built in 1964 that wrecked the wondrous symmetry of Kyoto's skyline with its acre-on-acre of sloping roofs punctuated here and there by the graceful pagoda or temple gate. From then on, there was no halting the vandalization—blocks and blocks of magnificent traditional townhouses—*machiya*—and shops torn down to be replaced, not by brilliant examples of modern architecture, but by the ugly, banal buildings and utility poles with their tangles of wires that characterize so much of the contemporary urban Japanese landscape. Aesthetes, lovers of the past, and abbots of the great temples howled in protest, but their voices counted for nothing. Implacable inheritance taxes forced families to sell their ancient homes; in the accounting system used by the authorities that captured the price of everything and the value of nothing, the gardens and wonderful old structures were worth more converted into nondescript office buildings and drab apartment blocks. True, the famous temples were off limits to the ongoing destruction and with the designation of several UNESCO world heritage sites in the city, small areas around these sites were finally set off as special neighborhoods for preservation. These still give a sense of what Kyoto had been like as recently as the early 1960s. But the fabric that had made Kyoto was all but irretrievably torn. Kyoto today resembles a once-lovely woman who has had acid thrown in her face; you can still make out enough to tell that she had been a great beauty, but it is a melancholy act of mental reconstruction.

Kyoto writ large describes what happened to so much of Japan in the high-growth years—to both its natural and historical/cultural inheritance. Vast swathes of what had been an incredibly beautiful country were ruined beyond redemption. Forests were chewed up and replaced by monotonous plantations of *sugi*—Japanese cedar trees. Seawalls of giant concrete tetrapods wrecked more than half the country's coasts. Every single river of any size was not simply dammed repeatedly but often lined with concrete.

The assault on nature was so overwhelming that it could seem like some monster out of science fiction; indeed the lurid, nightmarish backgrounds of so much Japanese *anime* are drawn directly from the hideous sprawl that characterizes so much of modern Japan.

Japan's traditional art forms—Kabuki, Noh, ink painting, flower arrangement, tea ceremonies, gardening—all survived, as did the historic popular culture embodied in village and neighborhood festivals (*matsuri*), in folksongs (*minyō*), and in crafts (*mingei*) produced by artisans for everyday use by ordinary people. But as high growth kicked into gear and ordinary Japanese people were sucked into the new mass culture of television, pop songs, and baseball, traditional folk arts lost much of the spontaneity that had so delighted Western visitors to Japan a century earlier.

Meanwhile, Japan's most significant postwar contributions to mainstream world culture were largely made before the high-growth period got underway. In the first two postwar decades, Japanese directors would bring to the screen some of the greatest masterpieces in the history of cinema: films such as Ozu Yasujiro's *Tokyo Story* and *Sōshun* (Early Spring), Mizuguchi Kenji's *The Life of Oharu* and *Sansho the Bailiff*, and Kurosawa Akira's *Seven Samurai* and *High and Low*. Novels such as Mishima Yukio's *Confessions of a Mask* (1949), Dazai Osamu's *No Longer Human* (1948), Kawabata Yasunari's *Snow Country* (1948), and Tanizaki Junichiro's *The Key* (1956) featured protagonists, isolated by the disruption of the immediate postwar years, descending into self-destructive sexual obsessions. But while these novels may have been bleak and even harrowing, there was no doubting their stature; Kawabata would receive the Nobel Prize for literature in 1968, largely on the strength of *Snow Country*.

But as the salaryman norms of the large corporations spread throughout society, such searching explorations of the human condition were increasingly pushed aside by forms of entertainment that amounted more to cheerleading or mind-numbing relaxation from work and social pressures than to art.

BASEBALL AND THE EMERGENCE OF SALARYMAN CULTURE

Work-related matters absorbed most of the time and emotional energy of the salaryman. Dressed within the narrow boundaries permitted by Japan's business culture—a dark blue or gray suit with white shirt and tie in the winter; a short-sleeved shirt, dress slacks, and tie in the sweltering summer months—he endured long commutes in packed trains to offices that no matter what the industry or company had the same open floor plan. This floor plan might as well have been an organization chart come to life: columns of six to eight desks facing each other with the senior managers sitting farthest from the door at the head of each column. The seating arrangements conveyed rank with the clarity of military insignia.

The salaryman rarely got home before midnight. Free evenings were usually spent out drinking with work colleagues. Other men in a man's work group formed the main sources of emotional support and human connection. Even if they didn't, the man was expected to act as if they did. Most salarymen got married at some point—marriage being an unspoken requirement for advancement into middle management and above—but the salaryman saw his wife only late at night or on those weekends that were not taken up by company outings or, as he advanced up the corporate ladder, by golf dates with customers or suppliers. "Love marriages" (*renai kekkon*) became increasingly common during the high-growth years, although many marriages were still arranged in the traditional fashion with bride and groom barely knowing each other on the wedding day. But with the workplace taking up most of the waking hours and emotional energy of the salaryman, passion faded from many marriages even when it had been there to start with. Many salarymen thus found even sexual release in the company of their workmates rather than with their wives. On a typical evening during the high-growth years, the streets of districts such as Tokyo's Shinjuku or Osaka's Namba were clogged with groups of salarymen staggering about on their way to *Toruko* ("Turkish baths" later renamed *soppurando* [soaplands] after protests from the Turkish embassy) or to seedy cabarets where oral sex could be had under the table from the waitresses. A law prohibiting prostitution had been passed in 1956 after agitation from Japan's first female parliamentarians. The Yoshiwara—the old center of Edo's courtesan culture—was ostentatiously shut down in the wake of the law's passage. But with that exception, the law was about as effective (or about as rigorously enforced) as eighteenth-century laws still on the books in the United States prohibiting any sexual position other than the missionary.

Even at the height of salaryman culture in the 1960s and 1970s, only some one-third of Japanese men qualified as full-fledged salarymen— that is to say, men covered by "lifetime" employment protocols working in white-collar jobs for salaries in established Japanese companies. But salaryman norms pervaded Japanese life and held sway over both the blue-collar workforce and those with white-collar jobs in smaller, less stable firms. Men with blue-collar jobs in established companies were governed by most of the same employment and compensation conventions as their white-collar counterparts, while the only way a small company could look credible was if its office workers acted and dressed like their counterparts in larger, more established firms.

A prime tool in spreading salaryman culture throughout Japanese society was an imported American sport: baseball. Baseball had been introduced into Japan in the Meiji period and caught on when Japan's leading secondary school (later absorbed into the University of Tokyo) adopted the game. Baseball was the first team sport played in Japan—traditional Japanese sports such as sumo, judo, and kendo involved one-on-one competitions—and it has remained far and above the most popular. It proved curiously well-suited to Japan. Unlike team sports such as basketball and soccer, with their continuous action and simple strategies (if complex tactics), baseball involves stop-and-start play and elaborate decision trees at any given point in the game. This provides opportunities for a great deal of debate both in and off the field before a consensus emerges. The rhythms of baseball thus reflected and embodied the rhythms of Japanese organizational life. And in Japanese baseball as it emerged in the high-growth period, the salaryman found a symbolic apotheosis.

Television, the tabloid press (*suppottsu shinbun*, i.e., "sports newspapers"), and comics (*manga*, often highly lurid and thus aimed at and read by adults more than children) may have been as important as baseball in inculcating and spreading the norms of salaryman life. But it could be hard to tell where baseball left off and the media began. For much of the control over both Japanese baseball and the media that interpreted the world for the salaryman and the would-be salaryman lay with a single great corporate bureaucracy.

That name of that bureaucracy—the greatest media empire in Japan—was the Yomiuri Group. We noted in the previous chapter the critical importance of the advertising firm Dentsu in the "management of reality" that ensured the Japanese were pulling together in one direction during the high-growth years. The Yomiuri Group was perhaps even important. Yomiuri boasted the largest-circulation newspaper in Japan (if not the world), a major television network, a slew of magazines from *suppottsu shimbun* to high-brow journals, real estate enterprises, a symphony orchestra, a large amusement park, and a host of other smaller businesses. But its crown jewel was its baseball team, the Yomiuri Giants, the team that dominated Japanese baseball during the high-growth years. Not even the New York Yankees or Manchester United have enjoyed the hegemony over their respective national sports that the Giants did over Japanese baseball. During the baseball season, it could seem that television consisted of one continuous Giants baseball game. Of course, this wasn't literally true, but the *suppottsu shimbun* devoted endless copy to the ups and downs of the Giants.

The rules of Japanese baseball are essentially the same as those in the United States. No American fan would have the slightest difficulty in following a Japanese game. (The biggest difference is probably that Japanese baseball allows for ties.) But as with corporations and politics, content was another matter.

Unlike the idiosyncratic culture heroes who emerged out of American baseball—Babe Ruth, Willie Mays, Sandy Koufax, Joe DiMaggio—avatars of Japanese baseball during the high-growth period—Nagashima Shigeo, Oh Sadaharu—were quintessential team players, they played for one team, the Yomiuri Giants, and they never haggled over their pay, accepting what was offered. Japanese baseball practice emphasized not the development of individual skills, but generalized effort and suffering, to the point that managers were eventually accused of ruining talented players by pushing them past their breaking points. This directly reflected the core principle of Japanese HR management: that overcoming obstacles was a matter of visible effort and teamwork, that what gave Japanese business its edge was its superior teamwork and the selfless work ethic of its people—their toughness (*konjō*) or *gattsu* ("guts") to use a favorite Japanese coinage.

Just as entrance into the upper reaches of Japanese business and government came through grueling years of effort culminating in the university entrance examination, the road to Japanese professional baseball led from the schoolyard to middle- and high-school teams and, finally, the national annual high-school baseball tournament held at the Koshien stadium near Kobe. Even today, Koshien (as the tournament came to be called) has a quasi-sacred aura; no other "amateur" sports event comes anything close to the nationwide interest and passion evoked by Koshien. The closest American comparison would be college bowl games like the Rose Bowl and the Sugar Bowl. But unlike the United States, with its glorification of the winning teams and their greatest individual players, in Japan it is often the losers that provoke the greatest reaction. Every year, millions are transfixed by the sight on television of teams of weeping boys who have given their last ounce of effort and devotion.

Most of the great names of Japanese baseball emerged out of Koshien, with the best usually ending up with the Yomiuri Giants. Of course, the Giants had to have some competition for their victories to be credible; other teams could not just be complete pushovers. The ideal game or season would see the Giants eke out a hard-fought victory (or championship). Adulation of the Giants was so great that it was said you could tell on a given morning whether the Giants had won the previous evening by simply looking at the faces of salarymen streaming into any of greater Tokyo's hundreds of commuter train stations on their way into work. To be anything other than a rabid Giants fan in any of the great private and public sector organizations headquartered in Tokyo was to invite suspicions of deviance and worse.

The great exception lay in and around Osaka. Osaka's home team, the Hanshin Tigers, engendered a level of devotion that could exceed that of the Giants. But it was devotion to a perennial loser; predictably, the Tigers were often compared to the Boston Red Sox and their rivalry with the Giants to that between the Yankees and the Red Sox. Of course, the Tigers' status as noble losers fulfilled one of the hoariest of Japanese archetypes. But perhaps even more to the point, the lopsided rivalry symbolized the ultimate pre-eminence of Tokyo and the surrounding Kanto area at the expense of the Kansai of Osaka, Kyoto, Kobe, and Nara. Ever since the founding of the Kamakura Shogunate, the center of gravity in Japan had been moving inexorably eastwards. Yet until the high-growth era, Kansai had hung on. Throughout the Edo period and well into the twentieth century, Osaka had been Japan's mercantile city par excellence while Kyoto remained the repository of traditional Japanese culture and values. But the final victory of Tokyo's bureaucratized ways saw Kyoto and Osaka descend into little more than glorified provincial cities.[1] The vandalization of Kyoto noted above had given it the look of just one more banal prefectural capital. Meanwhile, all the great Japanese businesses that had grown up in

---

1. To be sure, modern Kyoto has spawned some the most innovative companies in Japan, whose names include Nintendo, Kyocera, Omron, and Wacoal; unlike many of their counterparts with Osaka roots, the Kyoto-bred companies typically stay in Kyoto.

Osaka—the Sumitomos, Nomuras, Sharps, Torays—would open what they often called "2nd" headquarters in Tokyo, and it was obvious over time where the real power had come to lie.

Thus, the hegemony of the Giants over not just Japanese baseball but the whole mental life of the salaryman—his dreams, his struggles, his identification with a winner—symbolically embodied the power of Tokyo's bureaucratized organizations as they consolidated their control of Japanese economic and social life in the high-growth period.

It is common knowledge today that the pre-eminence of the Giants—indeed, the whole structure of Japanese baseball and its place in salaryman culture—has been, if not shattered, then at least seriously challenged. The way in which that happened, beginning with the departure of the great pitcher Hideo Nomo in 1995 to the Los Angeles Dodgers followed by the defection of a stream of top Japanese players to the American major leagues, has a lot to say about the fate of other Japanese organizations since the collapse of Japan's so-called bubble economy in the early 1990s. Japanese boys now dream of playing for the Yankees or the Red Sox, and major league games in which Ichiro Suzuki or Hiroki Kuroda appear often draw bigger television audiences in Japan than do Giants games. While the Japanese business world has not exactly seen defections along the lines of those of Nomo, Ichiro, and Kuroda, just as the eyes of the sports-mad young now shift toward America, callow geeks today crave iPads and iPhones rather than Sony's latest products. Meanwhile, the sense of mission that pervaded the economy's elite command and control posts at MOF and MITI in the high-growth years has been replaced by the endless bureaucratic grind of allocating shrinking benefits to an aging population in an economy that seems to have lost its edge.

The roots of what happened can be traced in part to the way the institutions of high-speed growth would change the lives of a very large group of people who had had no say-so in the way those institutions were formed: Japanese women. For while Japanese blue-collar workers, salarymen, farmers, small business owners, shadowy Far Right fixers, ambitious politicians, and the University of Tokyo-bred mandarin class that staffed the upper reaches of Japanese finance and the official bureaucracy had all had their input during the 1950s when the institutions of high-speed growth assumed their final shape, women were not represented. And the consequences of their exclusion—both for them and for the men they married and the children they raised—would prove incalculable.

JAPANESE WOMEN IN THE HIGH-GROWTH ERA

Japanese women have never, unlike their Western counterparts, been placed on pedestals. No Japanese man ever stood up when a Japanese woman came into a room simply because she was a woman. If anyone ever held a chair for her or opened a door for her, it was not because of her status as a woman. Other things being equal, she deferred to men; a proper Japanese wife was expected always to walk a step behind her husband. Every public gesture she made, every word she uttered (and the language with its separate verb endings and pronouns for women almost made this automatic) was expected to demonstrate submissiveness and a consciousness that she stood lower in the vast Japanese hierarchy than men of her age, breeding, and class. It may have been oppressive—indeed it was—but Japanese women did, as a result, have one advantage over their Western sisters: they never had to contend with the notion that they were some kind of expensive bauble.

For they had their roles, and within those roles they held some degree of power. Women managed household affairs. Of course, they were expected to show outward deference to their husbands—a Japanese proverb went something to the effect that when young, a woman should defer to her father, as an adult to her husband, and in the twilight of her years, to her oldest son. But it was a standing joke that in many families women actually controlled what happened. Women oversaw household finances, the education of the children, and often the care of the husband's aging parents.

Japanese husbands turned over their salaries to their wives; women granted husbands an allowance from which he was expected to pay for his lunch, clothes, and the all-important nights out with his workmates. A stock figure of Japanese fiction from the Edo period to the present is the hard-pressed wife maintaining appearances in straitened financial circumstances, juggling this and that so well that the husband is scarcely aware of how bad things are. The ditsy-brained housewife of 1950s American television out on shopping sprees while her husband is chained to a desk at home piled high with tax returns and unpaid bills had her closest Japanese counterpart not in the *oku-san* ("wife") but in the Japanese husband who knew nothing of household finances other than his salary and what his wife doled out for his allowance.

Women had traditionally played out their socially defined roles embedded in extensive kinship and neighborhood networks of other women. But with the coming of high-growth and salaryman culture, external circumstances changed drastically, even as expectations for women barely moved. There was no Betty Friedan who would articulate for Japanese women the novel situations in which so many of them found themselves as high-growth accelerated—situations for which their upbringing had not really prepared them. Married women were still assigned the management of household finances, the education of the children and, in many cases, the care of the husband's parents. But fewer and fewer women were living in the rural villages or settled urban neighborhoods of yore. Particularly if their husbands were salarymen, they were most likely to be housed in the early years of their marriage in cheaply constructed, cramped apartments in one of the thousands of housing blocs—*danchi*—that sprang up in dense clusters on the edges of the major cities in the postwar decades. A dream of most salarymen and their wives was to escape the *danchi* into houses of their own and many of them—particularly if the men were working in large, established companies—would finally succeed in amassing the funds necessary to do it. This was a key reason why management of household finances was so important: mortgage credit was scarce and expensive. Japanese women played a pivotal role in marshaling the savings that financed the economic miracle; if they wanted their own houses, they had no choice. The alternative was to fall into the hands of *sarakin*—literally, "salary finance"—money lenders with extortionate interest rates and extensive links to organized crime. The more lurid magazines ran endless stories of attractive housewives forced into prostitution to pay off money lenders; while there was surely some literary license at work, these stories were rooted in financial circumstances that resonated with their readers. But even when the salaryman's family made it into their own house, it would be small, built of the cheapest materials, and separated by inches from the houses around it.

There was thus never any real privacy and women often found themselves in the worst of all worlds: trapped in tiny quarters with demanding children without any help in raising them from the children's father or from older relatives, saddled also perhaps with the care of an aging mother-in-law.

The typical postwar young Japanese woman thus had only one real source of support: other women just like herself. Her husband, after all, came home only to sleep, and on those occasional Sundays he had off, he had neither the knowledge nor interest to help or advise her. Her mother and aunts might be sympathetic, but they were likely to be in another part of the country, and having grown up in a different world, had limited insight into the problems she faced. And while naturally friendships could and did develop among the women of the neighborhood, the media tended to emphasize backbiting, gossip, and competitiveness, if only because it made for better copy. That competitiveness tended to revolve around two things: the status of the husband—both his position itself and the position of his company—And how well children were doing in school, in particular, how well they did on entrance examinations.

Legends grew up around rites of passage for the salaryman's wife such as *kōen debyu* ("park debut"). This referred to the first time that a mother took her toddler to the neighborhood park. Typically, any given park would already have a well-established group of mothers who looked after their children while they played. Would the new mother fit in? Would she be accepted by the group? Or ostracized because of something wrong she said to the more senior women or because her child was dressed oddly or misbehaved toward the other children?

The preparation of children's *bento* (box lunch of steamed rice and a variety of side dishes) was another matter fraught with anxiety. In many schools, Japanese children were expected to bring their lunches and eat them at their desks. Even the youngest children were sensitive to the quality and presentation of the *bento*; an intense competitiveness could develop over just how beautifully presented, tasty, and nutritionally balanced a given *bento* might be. Teachers would also join in the evaluation of the *bento*.

Relationships between teachers and mothers were fraught with tension on both sides. Teaching may have been a relatively well-paid and socially prestigious occupation, but with it went grueling hours and endless demands as teachers were seen as responsible not just for imparting knowledge but also for discipline, for counseling, for standing *in loco parentis* for their charges. Teachers did not hesitate to intervene in situations where they believed a mother's discharge of parental duties was inadequate— and the criteria by which mothers were judged included such things as the quality of the *bento*, the way the child was dressed, and the child's language and behavior both in and out of class.

Parent Teacher Associations ("PTAs") were the institutional vehicle that brought parents and teachers together. Like baseball, PTAs formed another imported American institution soon deployed for purposes of social control in ways that would have been unrecognizable across the Pacific.

Japanese PTAs were organized on a school-by-school basis; membership was essentially involuntary and any mother who cared about her child would have to become involved. PTAs displayed all the characteristics of other Japanese organizations—endemic factionalism masked by endless harping on harmony and cooperation, and passive-aggressive tactics wielded with such skill that they practically gave new meaning to the term. But while men could sometimes escape from the all-enveloping tensions of the workplace—if only by drowning them in cheap whiskey and the ear of a sympathetic hostess—Japanese mothers lived with the pressures of children, mother-in-law, and PTA all the time. There was no relief for her in alcohol, or at least none socially sanctioned. Women lived in the same *danchi* or neighborhood with the other PTA women and shopped at the same stores. Whatever they may have thought about the demands of the PTA on their emotions and on their time, they were held hostage by their love for their children.

As time went by, increasing numbers of younger Japanese women looked at the lives of their mothers and older sisters—and the way those lives were portrayed in the media—and simply decided to opt out. The design of the institutions of high growth had unwittingly placed the salaryman's wife in what millions of women came to see as a trap. And the very success of those institutions gave them the means to avoid the trap. The result was the collapse of the Japanese birth rate.

During the early years of the high-growth era, the only real alternatives to marriage for young women was either the "water trade" (*mizu shōbai*), as the euphemism had it, or an unfashionable, despised spinsterhood. The proper life course for a Japanese girl from the same social stratum that produced the salaryman involved two years at a junior college where she was expected to pick up a smattering of skills useful in the low-level pink-collar jobs to which she could aspire. On graduation, she should still be living at home with her parents; established organizations were reluctant to hire women living on their own. On entering the company, she donned a uniform and became an office lady or OL. She was supposed to serve tea, prepare documents, and perform other menial tasks suitable to the "office flower," as she came to be known. Unlike her male colleagues, she typically left the office at the formal close of the working day. She probably enrolled in evening and weekend classes in matters thought important for housewives—tea ceremony, flower arrangement, perhaps the art of donning and wearing a kimono properly.

The theme running through all the variations of these years—or at least the theme that was supposed to be running through them—was the search for a suitable husband. An ideal candidate would be a young man in another section of the same company. Companies encouraged such marriages since the wives would already have been socialized into the company ethos and be aware of and reconciled to the demands the company would make on the husband's time and energy. But if no suitable mate could be found inside the company, a man found via a go-between in the tradition of the arranged marriage or perhaps introduced by a schoolfriend would be perfectly acceptable provided he was a permanent employee (*sei-shain*) in an established company or had a position in a public sector bureaucracy. Economic security was overwhelmingly the most important qualification on the male side of the marriage market; on the female side, it was a mixture of looks, family background (no scandals among close relatives), manners/breeding (the right schools, "wifely" accomplishments such as tea ceremony), and a spotless reputation.

The marriage window lasted about six years, opening on a young woman's graduation from junior college at 19 or 20. A saying popular during the high-growth years compared young women to the special cakes eaten on Christmas Day.[2] The number 26 was said to be a bad one for both young women and Christmas cakes. Companies would not actually fire women who failed to find husbands, but they were typically shunted into clerical positions that practically spelled "old maid."

The other track open to young women was the water trade, the new euphemism for the modern reincarnation of the Floating World of the Edo period. Geisha in the old style still existed but they had become museum pieces. Their patrons were wealthy gentlemen more interested in the classical Japanese arts—music/dance—than in risqué repartee with beautiful, trend-setting young women. The real descendants of the great Edo courtesans of Utamaro's prints were to be found in the exclusive night clubs of Tokyo's Ginza and Akasaka where elegant hostesses entertained Japan's business, financial, and political elite. These women facilitated the

---

2. Christmas is not a religious holiday in Japan or even a legal holiday at all, but a mish-mash of secular customs adopted from the West and enthusiastically pushed and modified by the entertainment and retail industries. The ubiquitous "Christmas Cake" may have its origins in the French *Bouche de Noel* or the English plum pudding, although there is nothing exactly like it in the West.

building of the all-important *jinmyaku* (networks of human relationships). Sex was always in the air, but rarely explicit.

Only the most accomplished of the women of the water trade, however, made it to such exalted places. Girls were no longer sold by their families into the water trade, as their prewar and Edo period predecessors had been. But the lure was very great for a girl from a poor or single-parent family—or who had done badly in school or had gotten into trouble with boys. The more beautiful, intelligent—and ruthless—she was, the greater her chances of making it into the rarified clubs that catered to Japan's elite where bills could run into the thousands of dollars for a group of executives or politicians who spent two hours drinking and chatting with the hostesses. Far more common was the run-of-the-mill club that catered to the ordinary salaryman where the bills for an evening's entertainment ran into the hundreds rather than thousands of dollars—still picked up by the company (salary differentials among men at the same level in the same company did not exist, but top performers were often rewarded with lavish expense accounts). After a few years in one of these clubs, a woman who had not made it to the top (i.e., become the *mama-san*), would leave and perhaps start a bar of her own.[3] She sometimes raised the capital from her patrons at the previous establishment. She might hire a girl or two just starting out and go into business. These *sunakku* could be found clustered around the commuter stations; men had to pay out of their own pockets for the drinks at these places, so they were far more reasonable than the clubs in the city centers.

Girls who lacked the combination of looks, smarts, and connections to find their way into the clubs ended up in the lower reaches of the water trade—in the "pink cabarets" where fondling and oral sex could be had under the table or in the *toruko* (a.k.a. soaplands) mentioned above. These establishments were usually under *yakuza* control; life for their young employees was about as pleasant as one might imagine.

Six years as an OL followed by decades trapped in a *danchi* or tiny house with an absent husband and demanding children might have seemed unappealing, but it was better than providing sexual services under the

---

3. These bars were called *sunakku*—from the English "snack" or snack bar. A law passed in the 1950s had required bars to shut down early; a loophole existed for places that served food as well as liquor. So the bars renamed themselves *sunakku*, posted menus of food items that were rarely available, and everything went on just as it had been.

table to drunken salarymen. But then as the decades went by, other alternatives began to open up.

University entrance examinations had always been evaluated blind, so women could—and increasingly did—make their way into four-year degree programs in the universities. True, a full bachelor degree for a woman counted for worse than nothing with many Japanese companies; many companies actively discriminated against women with degrees from four-year colleges, and, as we have seen, the educational content behind the degrees often mattered little to such companies anyway. But some ambitious young women nonetheless went about educating themselves. Partly under international pressure, some companies began offering management track positions to young female recruits. And foreign companies in Japan, realizing that well-educated Japanese women represented an underutilized resource, began hiring them in considerable numbers. Japanese men tended to shun foreign companies; they were thought to lack job security and had little social cachet in Japan.[4] But for women, foreign companies represented opportunity lacking at Japanese companies. HR managers at foreign companies were known to say the company generally got a better deal with a Japanese woman than with a man, other things being equal.

But the coming of the *kyaria ooman* ("career woman") track did nothing for the Japanese birthrate. Some Japanese and many foreign companies may have been prepared to give women jobs that had previously been reserved for men, but they were not willing to treat them differently. Part of the whole lifetime employment settlement that had arisen out of the struggles of the 1950s had been a quid-pro-quo which allowed companies to make essentially any demand of time and commitment on core male employees in return for economic security. That commitment could not be squared with the competing demands of children, aging parents, and household management. It was precisely to free men from these competing demands that the expectations of marriage and family had evolved—men's roles in the family had been reduced to that of funds provider. If *Papa* could take the family on a three-day vacation once a year or play catch with his son on the occasional Sunday afternoon, that was nice, but it was not strictly required. Revealingly, the Japanese term for this kind of activity is *fuamiri saabisu* ("family service")—the meaning of the English

4. The one exception during the high-growth years was IBM Japan, which carried the status of a major Japanese firm.

word "service" having changed in Japanese to imply an extra that is freely given without expectation of return.[5]

While increasing numbers of women did take the *kyariia ooman* track, more of them continued to flock into the OL positions. But then they simply refused to stay with the program and get married. They were not paid particularly well—salaries for OLs ran only about three-fifths those of men—but since they continued to live at home, their expenses were much lower. In the early years of the high-growth period, this would not really have been a pleasant option; parents would not have had much room for adult offspring while women who failed to marry were seen either as whores or dried-up old maids.

But all that began to change. As Japan became richer, houses got a little larger. Lifestyle possibilities opened up for single women that would have been unthinkable earlier. Women found themselves with the disposable income to dress well, travel abroad, and eat in nice restaurants with their friends, as long as they stayed single. Young—or, increasingly, not-so-young—single women became Japan's most important trend setters in fashion, the arts, and cuisine, playing a role in Japan similar to that performed by yuppies, chic gay men, and metrosexuals in places like New York and London.

It was not exactly women's liberation or the rise of feminism; the upper reaches of Japanese politics, finance, business, media, academia, and both the popular and high-brow arts remained overwhelmingly male preserves. But there was now a third route for Japanese women alongside the prostitute/courtesan/hostess of the Floating World/water trade and the proper daughter (*ojōsan*)/dutiful wife and mother. A glance at a few of Tokyo's tens of thousands of restaurants on a given Friday evening can convey what happened. In one kind of restaurant—the ubiquitous *izakaya* where the diners sit at the counter scarfing down traditional Japanese eats while guzzling beer, sake, or *shōchū* (a distilled spirit)—the customers will be almost all men, ties askew, drunk or doing a good imitation thereof, puffing away on cigarettes in a frat-house atmosphere of male camaraderie with *enka* (a kind of blues or Japanese country music) blaring away on

---

5. A waitress in a restaurant giving a customer a small treat the customer has not ordered will, on placing the tidbit in front of the customer, say "*saabisu desu*" ("this is a 'service'") indicating that the customer will not be charged for the item. *Saabisu* was, as noted in the previous chapter, the term applied to after-hours work that was neither compensated nor officially recognized.

the speakers. If a woman is present, she is probably an older waitress who can give as good as she can get with bawdy comebacks to the men's innuendo. Meanwhile, across the street in a fashionable new Italian or French restaurant, the customers will be groups of women beautifully dressed in the latest fashions, sipping chilled white wine and picking at the dainty dishes set in front of them while baroque string concerti or modern jazz plays discreetly in the background. The only visible males will be waiters with soulful eyes, perfect haircuts, and exquisitely polite explanations of the menu.

Such developments horrified Japan's old guard, particularly when the consequences of Japan's tumbling birth rate began to sink in. "Parasite singles" became the label of choice for these women. The media portrayed host clubs where dandyish young men catered to women in mirror images of what went on in the hostess clubs. Lurid tales began to circulate of discotheques where women went to pick up hunky black American soldiers looking to supplement their pay with some hustling on the side. Organized tours of horny Japanese men going to Korea or the Philippines for sex holidays had never elicited much comment, but now that they were joined by groups of Japanese women headed for Thailand or Bali for no-strings sex, paroxysms of anguish could be found in the media. The underlying message that many young women took from these howls of rage was not, however, how horrible all this was, but that it had become possible for women to meet their sexual needs outside marriage in ways that did not damage their reputations in the only circles where reputation mattered to them: other women like themselves.

MATSUDA SEIKO

Probably the greatest single heroine among these women was the pop star Matsuda Seiko. She took the Japanese entertainment scene by storm in the early 1980s just as the nationwide passive-aggressive rebellion by so many Japanese women against the lifestyles that had been carved out for them was beginning to take shape. *Seiko-chan* was probably the closest Japan has ever come to producing someone like Judy Garland, Barbara Streisand, or Madonna. But while these American entertainers found many of their followers in the emerging American gay subculture, Matsuda Seiko's rabid fans were drawn almost entirely from the ranks of single Japanese women working at an office in the day, living at home, and spending their free time with their girlfriends. Unlike the demure girl stars of yore,[6] *Seiko-chan* flaunted her three marriages and string of trashy boyfriends. Dressed in mock school-girl attire, she belted out the cloying songs thought appropriate for Japan's young *aidoru* ("idols") but in such an over-the-top manner it was clear the whole business was a mockery—*burikko* was the slang term that popped up for a woman who adopted the fake-innocent approach of which *Seiko-chan* was the acknowledged queen. The *burikko* presented herself with an artificial cuteness that might fool clueless males, whether those be fathers, potential boyfriends, or pompous pontificators of *Nihonjin-ron* ("theory of the Japanese" beloved by nationalist intellectuals). But it was transparently an act, or at least transparently so to most Japanese women.

The hand-wringing at the refusal of growing numbers of women to behave the way they were "supposed" to usually failed to acknowledge either the initial trap that the institutions of high-speed growth had set for so many women or how changing economic circumstances had made that trap more and more obvious to girls. Of course, many young women continued to long for marriage, for family, for children. But more and more of them were unwilling to walk into the trap set for them unless they could see their way out of it. That meant marriage to a man who was a second son, thus not responsible for care of aging parents, who would soon be making enough money that he could afford a nice house. Japanese companies and the Japanese bureaucracy were slow, however, to modify compensation and employment practices that might have made a lot of sense for a country with Japan's 1955 demographic and economic profiles, but made less sense by 1975 and no sense at all by 1995. Power holders would react to changing circumstances not by revisiting the social compact that had emerged out of the 1950s, but by tinkering at the edges—by hiring fewer men for "lifetime" positions, by bringing in part-timers at sharply reduced wages to do the work that had been previously assigned to junior men. Many of those part-timers were young single women or older married women returning to the workforce. Thus, young women saw an

---

6. The contrast between Matsuda Seiko and the greatest female pop idol of the 1970s, Yamaguchi Momoe, reveals a great deal about changing gender roles and expectations. Beautiful, demure, and utterly sincere, Momoe "retired" after a few years on the stage to marry actor Miura Tomokazu, a specialist in "straight man" roles, and has stayed out of the media ever since. Momoe's fan base consisted mostly of would-be salarymen.

ever-smaller pool of young men who could offer them the benefits of marriage and family while holding out hope of escape from the trap marriage and family seemed to entail. More and more of the marriages that did take place were childless; DINKS ("double income no kids") may have been an American acronym but it described accurately enough another route that began to open up out of the salaryman/*danchi* housewife trap—for men as well as for women.

By 1975, the Japanese birthrate had fallen from over the four live births per woman of the late 1940s to below two (replacement level). In 2005, it reached an historical low of 1.26. The collapse of the birthrate counts as one of the most momentous consequences of the failure of Japan's institutional response to drastically changing economic circumstances. Those changing circumstances stemmed in part from damage to the global economic framework that had permitted the institutions of high-speed growth to function the way they did. But since this damage was first experienced outside Japan, the risks to Japan's way of doing things were not initially obvious to Japanese. And when the risks did finally become obvious, Japan's elite felt powerless to do anything about them other than try as hard as they could to re-create the circumstances under which the institutions of high-speed growth had been so successful in the first place.

THE INSTITUTIONS OF HIGH-SPEED GROWTH AND THE GLOBAL ECONOMIC FRAMEWORK

Japan's economic model involved the systematic, targeted conquest of industries at particular points on the value-added ladder, beginning with textiles in the early 1950s and moving up into industries demanding ever more capital and technological inputs. On a microeconomic level, Japan's success spelled the loss of jobs in direct competitors abroad of the Japanese, and, in many cases, the disappearance of those industries altogether in foreign countries. This had political consequences. Those consequences might not matter much in the wider scheme of things when the competitor was, say, a consumer electronics maker in a small European country like the Netherlands. But when the industries falling to the Japanese onslaught were located in the United States, the consequences could not be avoided. Not only did the relationship with the United States form the bedrock of the postwar Japanese political order, the entire global economic system that had emerged in the wake of the Second World War pivoted around the openness of the American market. A United States that abandoned free trade in the wake of the loss of industry after industry to Japan would bring on the collapse of the global economic order—and with it, the Japanese system as it had emerged in the postwar period.

To be sure, savvy politicians might neutralize protectionist pressures in ways that allowed things to go on as they had been for awhile, and the 1970s saw a series of cosmetic trade agreements and "market opening" measures that allowed politicians to preen on television about solving this or that trade problem without really changing anything fundamental. But the swelling financial imbalances resulting from the emergence of Japan's trade surpluses posed an immediate and deadly threat to the rigid architecture of the Bretton Woods system, a threat that could not be made to disappear with political posturing and meaningless trade agreements.

Japan's surpluses took financial form in an influx of foreign reserves into the Japanese banking system, mostly denominated in US dollars. But the Japanese did not redeem their dollars for gold, as they had the right to do under the Bretton Woods system. They simply allowed them to accumulate, using a variety of tactics to isolate these reserves and thus head off the domestic inflation and concomitant export price hikes that the textbooks would have predicted ("sterilization" is the technical term for what the Japanese did). Perversely, the inflation happened inside the United States. The double "guns and butter" whammy of Lyndon Johnson's Great Society programs and the Vietnam War pushed the demand side of the American economy beyond what the supply side could provide, leading—as any student doing his or her homework in a freshman economics course could predict—to inflation and trade deficits.

Under the Bretton Woods system which, among other things, fixed the exchange rate of the yen to the dollar at 360 and the dollar to gold at $35 to the ounce, such imbalances were supposed to be resolved in one of two ways. Either the Bank of Japan would exercise its right to present its accumulated dollars to the United States in exchange for gold, forcing the United States to reduce its imports or see its gold supplies disappear, or else Tokyo and Washington would negotiate a reset of the yen/dollar exchange rate to a level sufficient to bring the Japanese surplus/US deficit back into balance.

But neither of these happened. Japan was not the only country accumulating dollars and some of these other countries—France in particular—exercised their right to exchange dollars for gold even when Washington tried hard to dissuade them from doing so. But Japan never did, thus automatically helping to finance the swelling US trade deficit. The United States tried to persuade Japan and the other surplus countries—notably West Germany—to revalue their currencies against the US dollar, and while the Germans would reluctantly agree (after extracting some concessions on restoring German control over NATO troops stationed in their country), Tokyo refused to listen.

Why wouldn't Japan listen? Why couldn't Japan be persuaded to help take steps to make obviously needed repairs to a global economic framework from which the Japanese had benefited as much as anyone? The answer comes down to three things. First, in Tokyo's view, Japan had faithfully kept its side of the postwar bargain that had ended the Occupation and cemented the US–Japan Security "Alliance." No leftist had been allowed to get anywhere close to the real levers of power. Tokyo had loyally continued to pretend that Chiang Kai-shek's regime in Taipei was the legitimate government of all of China and kept its misgivings over US policy in Vietnam to itself, even when tens of thousands of Japanese students were marching in the streets in protest against the war. The Japanese archipelago continued to serve as the lynchpin of the American military presence in East Asia. And hadn't the Americans *wanted* Japan to become prosperous? Wasn't Japan a useful example in Washington's ideological struggles with Beijing and Moscow for the attention of emerging developing country elites? Why should the Japanese be asked to tinker with a formula that had worked so well for them in keeping their side of the postwar bargain?

Second, it was hard for Tokyo to believe that the United States was really in economic difficulty. The Japanese elite could not easily wrap their heads around the notion that things they did in what they still saw as their weak, broken homeland were really affecting lives and politics in the country that within living memory had reduced their cities to rubble.

Finally, there was no one in the postwar political setup in Japan who had the authority to force an overhaul of the way things were done, even if some believed that the time for adjustments had come. The Ministry of Finance actually went out of its way to suppress any discussion in the financial press of the possible benefits to Japan from a stronger yen.

By the time the crisis began to peak, Richard Nixon had become president. He had won a close election in part because he had promised relief from Japanese textile imports to an industry that employed thousands of voters in what were then two critical swing states, North and South Carolina.[7] Nixon thought he had delivered on the promise by extracting a commitment from then-Prime Minister Sato Eisaku to curb Japan's textile returns in return for a nominal restoration to Japan of sovereignty over Okinawa. Sovereignty was theoretically restored—we will have a lot more to say about what happened on Okinawa in the last chapter—but the Japanese textiles kept coming; like his predecessors and successors, Nixon was to discover that Japanese prime ministers do not have the power to deliver on commitments of the sort Nixon thought he had obtained from Sato.

Nixon reacted by threatening to pull the plug on the Bretton Woods system. He unilaterally closed the gold window under which the United States had been "obligated" to redeem for gold dollars held by foreign central banks, demonstrating one more time that great powers cannot be constrained by treaties that lack enforcement mechanisms against acting in what they see as their national interest. He refused to reopen the window until exchange rates had been reset to reflect what Washington viewed as fair. And he took direct aim at Japan, imposing a 10 percent surcharge on Japanese imports into the United States. As if that wasn't enough, news began to emerge of negotiations between the White House and the Beijing government that would eventually lead to Washington's abrogation of its formal diplomatic relations with Taipei and recognition of the People's Republic of China as the legitimate government of all of China. Tokyo had not been informed.

The result was the greatest shock to the Japanese polity since the Battle of Midway when Tokyo insiders first grasped that the war had been lost. The Japanese media collectively labeled Nixon's announcements and the revelations of the negotiations in Beijing as the "Nixon shocks." Among other things, the residue of the shocks helped bring to power new types of politicians in Tokyo, politicians skilled at extracting concessions out of the bureaucracy in order to deal with restive interest groups that needed to be mollified if Washington's demands were to be met.

But no one—whether bureaucrat or politician—envisioned fundamental overhaul of an economy structured around export success and the accumulation of dollar surpluses. The Japanese participated in the Smithsonian

---

7. In 1968 the states of the Old South were no longer solid Democrat but not yet solid GOP.

Conference of December 1971, at which exchange rates were reset while $38 to the ounce became the new price at which the United States "would not sell gold" as the wits put it. Tokyo played its hand skillfully, negotiating a new yen/dollar rate that was neither as strong as Washington had wanted or as strong as Japan was prepared to accept.

The re-jiggered Bretton Woods survived less than two years, destroyed by the OPEC oil embargo of 1973 and the Watergate crisis. Nixon had no political capital left to police or defend the fixed rate system; the world staggered blind into a new financial framework of floating exchange rates and a final end to any link with gold, a framework that no one had designed or planned for.

The world wrote Japan off. The country was almost completely dependent on imported energy. But in the teeth of what was then the worst global economic recession since the 1930s, Japan exported its way back to prosperity more quickly than any other country. By 1976, Japan was back on track.

This time, there were no fixed exchange rates to prevent adjustments to trade imbalances without politically fraught negotiations. Academics such as Milton Friedman had predicted that floating rates would lead to the disappearance of severe trade imbalances; currencies would rise and fall in accordance with trade and investment demand. But Japan's imbalances did not disappear with the advent of floating rates, they got larger. The incoming administration of President Jimmy Carter accused Tokyo of "dirty floating," a reference to secret interventions by the Bank of Japan to keep the currency at a pre-determined rate. Under international pressure, the Japanese abandoned dirty floating and the yen rose to a postwar record. In 1971, it had cost 360 yen to buy a dollar; by July 1978, it only cost 177 yen.

The flip side of a stronger yen was a weaker dollar; faith in the US currency appeared to be collapsing. It had lost two-thirds of its purchasing power in less than a decade. Carter's hand was forced into appointing hard-money man Paul Volcker as Chairman of the Federal Reserve. Owing nothing politically to Carter, Volcker set about doing what he thought necessary to defend the US currency, raising interest rates to the point where demand in the United States collapsed—a recession—and investors were again willing to hold dollars.

Many of those investors were Japanese. Japan had been a member of a secret four-party rescue effort for the dollar in the summer of 1978.[8] The double blow of the Iranian revolution of 1979 and the Volcker recession in

8. The others were West Germany, Switzerland, and Saudi Arabia.

Japan's largest market brought on a slowdown in the Japanese economy and, for two consecutive quarters that year, Japan would experience its last trade deficits until 2009.

But faith in the dollar had been restored, thanks in large part to the enthusiastic response of Japan's institutional investors to Volcker's interest rate hikes, helped by a Ministry of Finance that liberalized the foreign exchange control law in 1980 (under the revised law, Japanese financial institutions no longer needed to seek prior approval before making investments overseas). Ronald Reagan was elected in the United States on a tax-cutting platform. He pretended that cutting taxes would actually increase tax receipts; maybe he even believed it, but the results of his so-called Reagan revolution were to open up what were then the largest peacetime deficits in American history. In the process, Reagan and his advisors demonstrated something they surely had not intended to do: that Keynes had been right. Provided it can be financed, the quickest and most reliable way to revive a moribund economy is to run a large government deficit.

In 1978, it had not been clear that the United States had much room left to finance larger government deficits. But thanks to Paul Volcker's interest hikes and the willingness of the Japanese to hold dollars, that was no longer an issue. Reagan's deficit spending did exactly what Keynes would have predicted, and by 1982, the US economy was roaring back.

A last golden age began for Japanese exporters. With the US Treasury offering to pay double-digit interest rates, worldwide demand for US government securities soared. The dollar spiked in value—against the yen, of course, as well as other major currencies As the US economy revived and Americans began spending again, they bought Japanese goods: Sony Walkmen, Panasonic VCRs, Sharp televisions, Toyota cars, Fuji film, Nikon cameras, Nippon Steel bars, Honda motorcycles, Yamaha pianos, Komatsu steam shovels, Ricoh copiers, Seiko watches, Casio calculators, Fujitsu computers, Hitachi semiconductors; the list went on and on. In retrospect, these years would prove not quite the disaster to American industry they seemed to so many back then; the ruthless weeding out of American industry by the high dollar and high interest rates caused capital to flow into new companies whose names scarcely anyone had heard of outside the geek world: Microsoft, Apple Computer, Cisco, Intel, and Sun Microsystems.

At the time, however, anyone predicting that American companies—companies from the land of the overpaid, the lazy, and the shoddy as the Japanese increasingly came to think of the United States—would, thirty years later, dominate the high-tech sector with operating systems and protocols everyone would have to use would have been thought mad. No one in their wildest dreams—or their worst nightmares—could have predicted that by that time the world's most desirable consumer electronic gadgets would be made by a company whose headquarters were in Cupertino, California. Instead, the political pressure to do something about what seemed the destruction of American industry at the hands of the Japanese—much of that pressure emanating from inside the Republican Party—became overwhelming.

Reagan's first term had been dominated by ideologues who refused to consider the notion that governments could intervene in markets with positive results. As one of them put it, "The proper value of the dollar is what the markets say it is." But Reagan's second term would bring more ideologically flexible men into positions of power over economic policy. Convinced for both patriotic and political reasons that something had to be done (they were concerned over the erosion of the US industrial base; they feared giving a potent political issue to protectionist Democrats), and believing that currency levels explained trade imbalances, they browbeat Tokyo into agreeing to join in a coordinated series of interventions aimed at breaking the back of the super-strong dollar.

This time, unlike 1971, they found a response in Tokyo. In the person of Nakasone Yasuhiro, Japan had one of its most formidable postwar prime ministers. He was worried about the ongoing damage of the trade imbalances to the US–Japan relationship. And unlike fourteen years earlier when the MOF had actively squelched talk of a stronger yen, key elements inside the bureaucracy had come to agree with Nakasone that perhaps it was time for Japan to overhaul its economic model. The country's runaway success now threatened its most important foreign relationship. With Japan seemingly poised to become the world's "headquarters economy," with dominance of virtually every key industrial sector now either secured or within its grasp, it was time for change. Tokyo would work with the Washington to realign the currencies of the two countries. Even more importantly, measures would be taken to find drivers other than exports for the Japanese economy.

But that task would prove impossible.

Part Two

The Shackles Trap
Today's Japan

FIGURE 7. The Red-Light District Kabukicho and the Skyscrapers of the Shinjuku in Tokyo in 1986, the First Year of the Bubble Economy. Courtesy of Hokkaido Shimbun.

7

Economy and Finance

Japan's "bubble economy" of the late 1980s was, in many respects, the greatest financial bubble ever, even when measured against the recent housing and derivatives bubble in the United States. The valuations assigned to land in late 1980s Tokyo reached levels so preposterous that in one widely noted comparison, the Imperial Palace grounds were "worth" more than the whole of Canada. The price of shares and the per-share earnings of the companies that issued them lost any discernible relationship to each other. As the bubble swelled, well-connected Japanese businesses found themselves pressed to issue bonds that they were told would "cost" them less than nothing. They were promised by their bankers that if they "borrowed" this money, they would never have to pay it back, and until the "borrowing" matured, they would be "charged" a negative interest rate. Never having to pay back money you have borrowed while receiving a nice little stream of payments during the life of the loan is something even all the Americans who were snookered into dubious mortgages during the US bubble might have envied. To be sure, like their American counterparts who found that their too-good-to-be-true mortgages were precisely that, the Japanese corporate treasurers who availed themselves of this ostensibly "free" money would discover later that it wasn't free at all. But that was not clear at the time, either to them or to the bankers who concocted the transactions. Both bankers and corporate treasurers believed the Tokyo stock market could only move in one direction: up. That was what made the money in these deals seem "free," just as the mortgages hawked to American homeowners appeared to be great deals—provided, that is, you could convince yourself that housing prices would never fall.

That is what defines a bubble—a general divorce of asset prices from the cash flows those assets can plausibly generate, whether those cash flows be rents or corporate earnings. The bubble keeps on growing because most everyone believes that "something" has happened that will allow asset prices to rise forever. For a while, it does not seem to matter that asset holders can repay the financing taken down to purchase assets only by selling them to a "greater fool" at a higher price than was paid for them. Who cares that the cash flow the assets generate is insufficient by itself to service the debt? The American economist Hyman Minsky, who famously modeled the progress and aftermath of financial bubbles, maintained that the appearance of this "Ponzi financing," as he called it, is a sure sign that a bubble is spawning

The Japanese bubble certainly fit Minsky's description. It also conformed in many other ways to the classic parabola of a financial mania followed by a panic, a crash, and, finally, a prolonged aftermath mixing stagnation with outright recession. The initial fuel for the Japanese mania came, as Minsky held it always does, from excess credit creation. As the mania gathered steam, it sucked in more and more people who, seeing their neighbors becoming rich without effort, were determined also to get in on the game. Well-placed insiders concocted stories that convinced not only outside investors but also—and most importantly—themselves that "this time is different," to paraphrase the title of an important book on financial bubbles. Fraud and wholesale corruption increasingly marked political and economic life, blurring the lines separating the legitimate from the criminal. These features of the Japanese bubble were entirely in keeping with the history of financial manias.

The Japanese experience on the way down was as easily recognizable to students of "manias, panics and crashes"—the title of another important book on the subject—as it had been on the way up. There was a clear "Minsky moment" when the mania peaked and the scales began to fall from the eyes of many; that "moment" was brought on, as it typically is, by a sudden realization that new financing would not be available to bid up asset prices any further. (The Minsky moment in the Japanese case occurred on Christmas Day, 1989—not a holiday in Japan—when the Bank of Japan sharply raised interest rates.) The resultant collapse of values could not be confined, as many initially predicted, to shadier financial institutions with links to criminal elements. Eventually—and inevitably— the core institutions of the financial system were swept up in the general "revaluation of values," presenting policy makers to make the stark choice of bailing out the very institutions that had fomented and facilitated the mania or standing by and watching the financial system implode and take the general economy with it. Millions lost their life savings, profound political realignments were set in motion, and received wisdom long accepted by both elites and ordinary people found itself called into question. The most important elements of received wisdom that had to be junked in the Japanese case were the notions (1) that land prices in Japan could never fall and (2) that the Ministry of Finance ("MOF") had the will and the ability to support both real estate and equity prices plus all the financial institutions under its sway.

The bubble had its origins in the 1985 revaluation of the yen/dollar rate mentioned at the end of the preceding chapter. The way the story unfolded—the mania itself, followed by the implosion of the bubble and the long deflation in its wake—has helped strengthen the theoretical edifice used by scholars and analysts to understand the progress and aftermath of financial bubbles in general. In large part we can thank the economist Richard Koo. Following his close study of the Japanese economy of the 1990s and his extrapolation of the lessons drawn therefrom to the history of other bubbles, he coined a new term for what happens to economies in the wake of a bubble: "balance sheet recession."

A BALANCE SHEET RECESSION

Koo argues that a balance sheet recession typically follows a crash precipitated by the implosion of a far-reaching financial mania. A critical mass of companies find themselves either technically bankrupt or close to it because they took on financing during the mania to purchase assets whose values have collapsed. Liabilities thus exceed the value of corporate assets, the technical definition of bankruptcy. But many of these companies are still going concerns, since they continue to generate positive cash flows from their core operations. Their creditors will be reluctant to close these companies down and seize their assets, since the assets cannot command the prices necessary to retire the financing taken down to acquire them in the first place. (Think of the American homeowner who has mortgaged a house now worth less than the amount of the mortgage.) Companies in such situations will use any profits they can extract from operations to pay down debt rather than expand or invest in new lines of business, and their bankers will help them get away with it rather than forcing them to declare bankruptcy, since, after all, that is the only chance the banks have of being repaid.

But since so many companies find themselves in this situation, demand dries up. No one is placing orders for new equipment or factories; no one is hiring new workers. Everyone is just desperately trying to pay down debt—that is, to repair their balance sheets. A balance sheet recession is a classic case of the fallacy of composition. What makes sense for the individual enterprise destroys the prospects for a general recovery. Loose monetary policy—the usual remedy for the garden-variety slow-down—is useless in a balance sheet recession; no matter how low interest rates are cut or how much additional money central bankers try to push into an economy, companies will not borrow more funds for any purpose other than refinancing existing loans at lower rates. Money thus accumulates in vast stagnant pools of liquidity.

Koo extrapolated from the Japanese experience of the 1990s both backward to the Great Depression of the 1930s and forward to the Great Recession that began in 2008 to produce his theoretical explanation for what happens to economies in the wake of a financial mania. (In 2009, it was millions of American households rather than Japanese companies that found themselves trapped by assets—their homes—that were worth far less than the financing they had taken down to pay for them.) Koo's theories help us to understand such matters as the length and intractability of the Great Depression, the inadequacy of the stimulus package enacted in the opening months of the Obama administration, the failure of employment rates in the United States as of this writing to return to politically safe levels (safe for incumbents, that is), and the near-absence of inflation in the United States today despite very loose monetary policy. If Koo is right, then not only did the Japanese experience conform in most crucial ways to the standard historical model of "manias, panics, and crashes," it serves as a paradigmatic example for other comparable phenomena.

THE JAPANESE DIFFERENCES

No one could argue, however, that every country's experience of the mania-panic-crash-balance sheet recession parabola is identical, even if they all follow a recognizable pattern and even if what happens in one can help shed light on another. For despite the general conformity of the Japanese bubble and its aftermath to that of the standard model, and despite the light Japan's experience sheds on other bubbles at other times, there are some crucial differences that set Japan's "bubble economy" apart—even from others that appear to resemble it closely.

What is distinctive about the Japanese bubble is not simply the tautological observation that it happened to the Japanese in the 1980s rather than the Dutch in the 1670s, the Thais in the 1990s, or the Americans in the 2000s. The most important distinction that separates the Japanese bubble from others can be found in the motives of those responsible for starting it.

Minsky maintained that the origins of financial bubbles lie in what he called an exogenous shock, something that causes investors to re-evaluate their understanding of the potential for return in certain classes of assets. An example of an exogenous shock is an important technological breakthrough that promises economy-wide transformation. A famous case of such a shock is the coming of railroads in the mid-nineteenth century that helped lead to the great crash of 1873 when too much money had flowed into too many harebrained schemes to build railroads.[1] Other cases include the twin advent of the automobile and the radio that helped set the stage for the Great Depression, and the "killer app" of the Internet that led to the dot.com bubble of the late 1990s.

Exogenous shocks need not be technological; they can include wars or the sudden appearance of new sources of credit (gold and silver from the New World flowing into Spain in the sixteenth century; investors piling into Mexico in the wake of the passage of NAFTA). But in all these cases, the key word is "exogenous"—that is to say, something that happened outside the realm of established economic processes and policies.

In the Japanese case, however, the shock was not exogenous. It was deliberately administered. The shock grew out of the shared understanding

---

1. Anthony Trollope would portray what bubbles and their aftermath do to values and social cohesion with his fictionalized treatment of the railroad bubble in his 1875 masterpiece *The Way We Live Now.*

of all significant power holders in Japan that the key to Japan's "miraculous" recovery from the devastation of war had been its mastery and commercialization of manufacturing technology. Japan had lost the war, so it was thought, because its technology had been inadequate. The story since the end of the Occupation had been the construction and perfection of an industrial juggernaut that had secured for Japan what it had lacked on the eve of the war: across-the-board supremacy in virtually every key industrial technology.

That juggernaut was, by 1985, seen by the most far-sighted people in Japan to be under threat. The threat was both political and economic. The political threat was manifest in a rising tide of anti-Japanese sentiment in the United States that appeared to Tokyo to endanger the US–Japan relationship. By the mid-1980s, virtually all Japanese believed—even if they did not say so publicly (and many did)—that the United States had fallen into a cycle of debt, dependence, and decline from which there was no easy escape. Yet at the same time, the United States was as essential as ever to the Japanese political and economic order. It provided a security umbrella without which Japan would have had to confront again the existential question it had managed to sidestep since 1945: how to defend itself in a dangerous world while bridling a military establishment sufficiently robust to undertake that defense. And the United States did more than help assure Japan's security. The Americans also provided the political framework that permitted a genuine global economy to function, a framework within which Japan had been able to build and steer its juggernaut. Key elements of that framework included a universal settlements and reserve currency in the form of the US dollar, and a global open trading system. No alternative to either the security umbrella or the political framework that the United States provided for the global economy seemed plausible to Japan's power holders at the time.

Meanwhile, the economic threat to the Japanese juggernaut lay in the decline of the buying power of the country's overseas markets. Since the late Meiji period, the principal driver of the Japanese economy had been exports—not so much as in the percentage of Japan's GDP accounted for by exports (exports from small trading countries such as the Netherlands and Singapore would inevitably count for a much higher percentage of their overall economies than would exports from large economies like Japan's). Rather, competition in export markets had been the principal spur to technological advance and the achievement of economies of scale. Corporate profitability and access to credit had largely been functions of success in export markets. But by 1985, with Japan heading for what appeared to be a commanding position in virtually all important manufacturing technologies, how could other countries pay for Japanese goods? With the Japanese making seemingly everything of real value, the day seemed imminent when demand from overseas would be insufficient to sustain the juggernaut.

That day had been postponed by an undervalued yen—first, with the fixed rate under Bretton Woods that had given Japan such an advantage during the immediate postwar decades, then the "dirty floating" of the mid-1970s, and, finally, the peculiar circumstances of the Reagan Revolution that had resulted in a temporary surge in the value of the dollar.

Many in Japan simply expected that the government would continue to do what was necessary to maintain a cheap currency. But the more observant understood that this would only buy a limited amount of time, and in any case was becoming more and more untenable politically as Washington latched on to the "unfair" yen/dollar rate and Tokyo's supposed currency manipulation as the explanation for the loss of its industrial base at the hands of Japanese competition.

The solution that key Japanese politicians and bureaucrats conceived was threefold. First, Japan would work with the United States (the Germans, the British, and the French agreed to participate as supporting actors) to bring down the value of the dollar and raise that of the yen. Second, Tokyo would take other steps to ease political tensions with Washington, signing a series of trade agreements that removed some of the more obvious conflicts while encouraging Japanese companies to begin moving production facilities to the United States in order to reduce the employment losses in the United States stemming from Japan's trade surpluses.

Finally, the financial authorities in Tokyo began laying the groundwork for a shift away from exports as the principal driver of the economy. The obvious candidate for the new driver was investment. A wave of investment spending on spanking new factories would consolidate Japan's position as the world's headquarters economy while offering the prospect of replacing exports with plant and equipment investment in the economic driver's seat.

The usual recipe for sparking an investment boom is cheap credit, and the Japanese authorities were both willing and able to provide it after the September 1985 agreement reached with the Americans to engineer a rise in the value of the yen (the agreement is known as the Plaza Accord since it was negotiated at New York's Plaza Hotel). Cheap credit was also politically useful—much of the Japanese business community was so outraged by the Plaza Accord that the business-bureaucrat-LDP coalition that had provided political stability in Japan since 1960 threatened to come unglued. The Finance Minister who had helped negotiate the Plaza Accord, Takeshita Noboru, got himself an unwanted nickname ("Minister High Yen") and became so unpopular for a while he was advised to curtail campaign appearances. Cheap financing went some distance in mollifying corporations facing the sudden threat of a super-strong currency in their export markets.

But cheap credit in and of itself is not enough to spur plant and equipment investment. It can just as easily end up as inflation or in spasms of conspicuous consumption. The Japanese authorities believed, however, that they had the tools to ensure the waves of credit went where they were supposed to. Those tools consisted first of various means that had heretofore allowed the authorities to target and set general prices for real estate.[2] The second set of tools stemmed from the unique structure of Japanese corporate finance discussed in chapter 5. Japanese companies typically raised funds for investment in plants and equipment not from stock and bond markets but from banks in the form of short-term loans that were perpetually renewed.

By both taking steps to boost land prices and by taking the lid off quantitative restrictions on bank lending, the authorities hoped to ensure that much of the extra credit being created would go directly into plant and equipment investment. But as the investment boom gathered steam and unwanted side effects began to appear, the authorities were reluctant to step in to call a halt, particularly after the October 1987 New York stock market crash, which was both triggered and stopped in Tokyo. The announcement of the August 1987 trade statistics showed that despite a near-doubling of the exchange rate of the yen against the dollar since the Plaza Accord of two years earlier, the size of the bilateral US–Japan trade deficit had barely changed. Americans were beginning to learn that the explanation for Japan's structural trade surpluses was a lot more complex

---

2. The most important of these were measures such as agricultural-use designations that suppressed markets in urban real estate, and arbitrary assignment of prices for tax and reporting purposes.

than currency misalignments; that, among other things, nothing could force Japanese companies to give up recently acquired market share just because their profit margins had started dropping. (As we have already noted, profits in the Japanese system were historically of minor importance; what counted was technological leadership and market share.) But in the meantime, the numbers scared Japan's institutional investors with the prospects of another round of dollar weakening. They dumped US government securities, causing the prices to fall; that is, the yields on these securities rose, in fact they rose into the double digits. When American investors realized they could earn over 10 percent a year on US government securities, they sold their equity holdings for bonds, precipitating the stock market crash. The crash threatened to go global, but the Japanese authorities, with a few well-aimed informal directives to Japanese securities companies, were able to stop and then reverse the global rout. They followed that up by strong-arming Japanese institutional investors to return to dollar bond markets, thus halting the widespread flight from the dollar. They backed up their actions by widening the credit floodgates yet farther. All this extra credit, coming on top of the waves that had already been financing an investment boom, helped Japan to increase its already substantial dollar holdings, in the process stabilizing the American currency.

That was not all the extra credit did, however—there were inevitable spillovers. One was alluded to at the beginning of this chapter: the deals that gave Japanese companies what they thought was free money they would never have to pay back. It seemed to Japanese corporate treasurers that they were being paid to build new facilities. (The "free" money was contingent on ever-rising stock prices.[3]) With all this "free" money

3. These deals involved issues of dollar bonds with warrants attached giving the warrant holders the right to buy shares of the issuer at pre-determined prices set generally slightly above the prevailing stock prices. The warrants were detached from the bonds and sold to Japanese investors. The bonds carried very low coupons and were sold in Europe at deep discounts to bring the yields on the bonds in line with market rates. Most everyone in Japan expected that the warrant holders would exercise their rights to buy stock at the pre-determined price, allowing the issuer to use the proceeds to repay the bond holders. (Standard corporate finance theory argues that the sale of additional equity has a cost, since it dilutes the value of existing equity, but in Japan the claims of equity holders to pro-rata shares of corporate profits and the residual value of corporate assets are almost entirely theoretical.) Since the coupons on the bonds were so low, the issuers could enter into currency swap agreements to cover the coupon payments that actually resulted in small yen receipts to the issuers—thus the perception that the principal was "free" and carried negative interest rates. With the collapse of the bubble and the Tokyo stock markets, the warrants became worthless, forcing the original issuers to raise new sources of financing to repay the bond holders.

sloshing around, companies could erect lavish new headquarters as well as state-of-the-art factories. Meanwhile, millions who held tiny plots of land found themselves rich, and proceeded to act like such people will, throwing money about in as conspicuous a fashion as possible. Millions of others, seeing this all around them, went into debt to purchase assets that were soaring in price. With banks practically begging small businesses to borrow at rock-bottom rates and asset prices doubling every few months, it seemed like a sure thing.

Such phenomena mark all financial manias as they reach their peak. But a critical difference in the Japanese case was that many of the people who were actually driving the mania were not themselves the ones getting rich. They were acting the way they did because they thought that was what they were supposed to do in order to further shared national goals. The contrast between the wholesale corruption of Wall Street in the final stages of the housing-derivatives bubble of the 2000s and the behavior of Japanese bankers at the peak of the late 1980s bubble is revealing. Yes, the greatest names of Japanese banking were in cahoots with the criminal underworld. But the individual bankers themselves were not typically the ones who were personally benefitting. They involved themselves in schemes to inflate share prices and did other deals with gangsters because they thought that by doing so they were helping their institutions and their country.

Of course, they were wrong, but this matter of motive is crucial in understanding both how the bubble ended and the aftermath. The Japanese authorities were perfectly aware of all the side effects of the bubble and they were not happy about them. They had not sparked the boom to enable spoiled *narikin* (nouveau riche) to tool around the streets of upscale urban neighborhoods in fancy German cars on their way to restaurants where waiters would sprinkle gold-leaf on their *foie gras*, or to allow company executives to trade golf-course memberships that ran into the tens of millions of yen. But the events of 1987 had convinced the authorities they had the tools to cool things down when needed without provoking a crash. So they waited to do so until they were sure that the dollar had stabilized, that the US economy had recuperated from the 1987 stock market crash, that the relationship with the United States was back on a solid footing, and that the consolidation of Japan's manufacturing supremacy was complete.

By the fall of 1989, all this seemed in place. The 1988 presidential campaign in the United States had unnerved many in Tokyo; it looked as if the

Democrats might nominate Richard Gephardt running on a protectionist, anti-Japanese platform. But the election was won by George H. W. Bush, the kind of moderate Republican with whom the Japanese political elite had long been the most comfortable. It seemed that after all there would be no significant political opposition in the United States to the emergence of what scholars and analysts on both sides of the Pacific were increasingly calling the "Nichi-Bei" or "G-2" global economy—that is, a global economy where the really significant decisions would be made by the two economic superpowers, the United States and Japan. The Americans would continue to provide security and a global currency while supplying commodities (wheat, corn, soybeans) and certain "soft" economic goods (movies, for example, or popular music). Japanese companies such as Sony and Matsushita could acquire major stakes in Hollywood, the global capital of popular culture—thus guaranteeing streams of content for their televisions, VCRs, and Walkmen—while other industrial companies were assured that when necessary they could buy up the emerging technologies that the Americans still seemed to be so good at spawning, allowing Japan to play to its core competency in commercializing them. Enough Japanese plants would be located in the United States to keep employment levels at politically acceptable levels in America, and the Japanese would leave to the Americans a couple of key manufacturing sectors such as commercial aircraft that had extensive overlap with defense industries, although Japanese suppliers would provide much of the value-added in these sectors. Tokyo and Washington would work together to manage global currency and trading frameworks while Washington would continue, with extensive Japanese financial support, to act as the global policeman.

With the political and economic aims of the bubble economy apparently in place by the summer of 1989, the side effects were becoming ever-more worrisome. The rivers of cash inundating Tokyo allowed criminal elements and outsiders to challenge established power holders in ways that frightened them. The most important incident was probably the scandal referred to in chapter 5 that saw the attempt by an ambitious entrepreneur to replace traditional Japanese employment practices with a genuine labor market, a market whose infrastructure would be provided by his company, Recruit. The bubble had provided the cash that Ezoe Hiromasa, Recruit's founder, had used to bribe a whole roster of important politicians.

It was time to call a halt to all these excesses, and the authorities set about doing so in a very systematic way. Again, this was a critical difference with other financial manias—not that the mania finally peaked and crashed; that happened to Japan as well. The difference was that the mania was deliberately stopped.

The mistake the Japanese authorities made lay in the belief that since they seemed to have been in control during the surge, that they could also control the aftermath—achieve a "soft landing" rather than a crash. This belief was not stupid. They did have formidable controls, and those controls were sufficient to keep the Japanese economy from sliding into depression and perhaps, even more remarkably, to avert a general banking panic of the type that almost always follows a collapse in values, particularly a collapse as great as the one that Japan would experience in the wake of the bubble. The crash did happen in Japan, but it happened in slow motion, allowing the country to avoid a complete meltdown of the financial system and the impoverishment of millions.

But although it may have unrolled in slow-motion, there was a crash. In the two decades after the mania peaked, Japan grew slowly or not at all. Its ruined banks retreated from global markets, and the great names of Japanese finance were swallowed up in a series of mergers. There may have been no breadlines and there weren't any beggars to speak of, but horizons seemed to shrink. Young men graduating from even the top schools could no longer automatically find secure employment, and people began to speak of a "lost generation." The price of bailing out the financial system and preventing a general depression turned out to be far higher than anyone had anticipated. That price included the largest cumulative fiscal deficit in the developed world. Perhaps most disconcerting to Tokyo, the much vaunted technological/manufacturing supremacy that had appeared to be within Japan's grasp would prove to be if not exactly an illusion, then vastly overhyped.

AVOIDING DEPRESSION: THE BAILOUT OF JAPAN'S FINANCIAL SYSTEM

The Japanese implemented two sets of policies to avoid the depression that might have seemed inevitable given the magnitude of both the crash and the mania that preceded it. The intellectual godfathers of these policies—Walter Bagehot and John Maynard Keynes—would certainly have understood what the Japanese authorities were doing and would probably have criticized them only for being less consistent than they should have been.

Bagehot famously advised financial authorities that their most important responsibility during a financial panic is to ensure that credit continues to be available by acting as lenders of last resort. Banking panics wreak their greatest havoc when even sound financial institutions have to close their doors because frightened depositors or other funds providers withdraw their cash; banks are forced to liquidate their portfolios—calling in loans—and businesses cannot obtain credit. Then orders are cancelled, people are fired, and the economy goes into a tailspin. To prevent this chain of events, central bankers must step in to keep credit flowing.

Bagehot's book *Lombard Street* was published in 1873, but it was clear as late as 2008 that not all its lessons had sunk in. In what has been called the single greatest avoidable policy error since the days of Herbert Hoover, the George W. Bush administration stood by while the American investment bank Lehman Brothers collapsed. Lehman Brothers, it is true, was not precisely the type of bank Bagehot had in mind when he was writing *Lombard Street*. It did not take deposits or make loans. But it was the second largest commercial paper house in the United States and stood at the center of the markets in which banks exchange short-term obligations with each other (the "repo" markets). Commercial paper had become the most important source of working capital financing for American companies while repos, as they are known, provided crucial liquidity to the banking system and to Wall Street. The freezing of these markets in the wake of Lehman's collapse all but guaranteed that the US economy would implode.

The Japanese authorities never made this kind of mistake. Although they were criticized repeatedly for being late in recognizing the full scale of Japan's banking problems, for keeping too many failed financial institutions for too long on life support, they succeeded in what had to be their number one priority: preventing a widespread panic that would see money drain out of the financial system with a concomitant breakdown of the machinery that kept credit flowing in the economy. They faced a daunting task because the financial system was, in fact, bankrupt; the collective value of its assets was far lower than the amount of money supporting the system.

In such circumstances, it would have been entirely rational for individual depositors to take their money out of the bank lest that bank be forced to close its doors before depositors could get their hands on it. Monetary statistics show that there was indeed a fair amount bleeding of this sort around the edges; a lot of people did liquidate their deposits— bought gold or securities denominated in foreign currency—or even stuck their cash in a safe.

But that bleeding never turned into a full-scale bank run. In what was by some measures the greatest financial collapse in history (albeit one that happened in slow motion), not a single depositor in a Japanese financial institution lost money. As a result, people kept their money in the banks— or, to be precise, enough of them did to keep the system afloat. Things came closest to actual meltdown in the fall of 1997 when a series of major banks and securities companies failed within weeks of each other. The MOF stepped in to ensure that all depositors in these institutions were made whole (legally, the MOF was only required to underwrite deposits of up to ¥10 million, about $100,000 at the time.) The MOF then proceeded to ram two bank bailout packages through the Diet, the second of these the largest single peace-time government expenditure in history: the ¥72 trillion package that passed the Diet in October 1998. This is about the same size as the TARP legislation enacted by the US Congress almost exactly ten years later to bail out the US financial system, but in a Japanese economy less than two-thirds the size of the American. The bank bailout package was no more popular in Japan than TARP would be in the United States; indeed, the prime minister of the time, Hashimoto Ryutaro, had to resort to a time-honored Japanese practice, *gaiatsu* ("pressure from abroad"), to provide the necessary political cover. The *gaiatsu* came from a well-publicized telephone conversation with US President Bill Clinton, arranged by Treasury Secretary Robert Rubin, in which Clinton supposedly jawboned Hashimoto into taking the necessary measures. Rubin was sufficiently frightened by the possibility of a meltdown of Japanese banking—and what that would do to global finance—that he helped stage the needed piece of political theater.

The financial system was pulled back from the precipice; a general meltdown that would take Japan and the world down with it had been avoided. But that did not solve Japan's problems or return the economy to where it had been in the early 1980s.

MISTAKEN ASSUMPTIONS AND THE BLOWING
OPEN OF JAPAN'S FISCAL DEFICIT

Japanese bankers had operated under three assumptions, all of which turned out to be, if not false, then inoperative in the wake of the bubble's implosion. The first of these assumptions was that well-connected Japanese companies do not go bankrupt. Second, one could safely lend to companies that were not so well connected provided they offered land as collateral, since land always held or increased its value. Third, no institution under the protection of the MOF would ever be allowed to fail.

After the implosion of the bubble, however, not only was the MOF unable to protect all the institutions under its purview, but almost every major Japanese financial institution either disappeared or merged into another. One famous bank, the Long Term Credit Bank of Japan, even came under the control of foreigners who restructured it and renamed it the Shinsei Bank. No depositor may have lost money and "life time employment" for permanent employees in established banks continued to be a given (much to the wider public's disgust). But careers were ruined.

Then, in July 2000, the Sogo Department Store went bankrupt—or to be precise, the financial lifelines that had kept this otherwise bankrupt company alive were withdrawn. The Japanese media treated it as a seminal event; enormous black-bordered headlines ran in even the quality papers. The treatment was appropriate, for Sogo's collapse demonstrated that no one was safe anymore—that the Japanese system was in danger of unraveling. Sogo had been supported by both the bureaucracy and the financial community even though, as the president of the Industrial Bank of Japan ("IBJ"), Sogo's "main bank," would acknowledge, it was common knowledge by 1994 that not only did Sogo's liabilities exceed its assets—the definition of bankruptcy—but that its cash flow from operations had turned negative.

The Sogo bankruptcy spelled the end of IBJ's independence and with it the structure of postwar Japanese finance. IBJ had been the great establishment bank, set up to channel long-term investment funds to the champions of the economic miracle; with its disappearance, it was clear anything could happen.

All the key assumptions held by Japanese bankers were revealed to be empty. Bankers did not know how to act or what to do. Japanese banks were not used to doing Western-style credit analysis—running pro-forma projections under various scenarios to test whether loans could be serviced and repaid even in stressful times. Nor had they built up their own capital structures to allow a certain percentage of loans to go bad; after all, who needed capital when bankruptcies were either not supposed to happen or were supposed to be covered by collateral, principally land. Banks had provided ever-green financing to Japanese industry, financing that needed only to be rolled over rather than repaid. The financing had been made available on the basis of real estate collateral, the company's historical track record, and its standing within the Japanese power structure rather than bankers' assessments of the viability of business plans.

That didn't work anymore. So essentially banks quit lending to any but the most well-connected and prosperous companies (i.e., companies that did not need the money). And they called their outstanding loans in, exacerbating the problem of the balance sheet recession. As one frustrated businessman of my acquaintance during the late 1990s blurted out, "I need a bank, not a safe deposit box!" His company had contracts and orders from the government itself, but that was not enough for his gun-shy bankers. All they would do for him was process his payments to suppliers, provide an account to which his customers could remit funds, and keep his cash for him. They wouldn't extend a yen of credit.

Instead, banks took their depositors' money—and the bailout money they received from the government—and used it to buy Japanese government bonds ("JGBs") and other government financial instruments (e.g., bills issued by the Bank of Japan). Interest rates on deposits were even lower than the yields on JGBs, enabling banks to earn a small positive carry on their JGB holdings.

A meltdown of Japanese finance may thereby have been prevented, but with the financial system not playing its proper role in the economy and with businesses in any case looking to pay down debt rather than expand, demand had to come from somewhere if the economy was to avoid spiraling downwards into a depression. That demand would come from overseas and, ultimately, from the Japanese government itself.

John Maynard Keynes had called upon governments to use deficit spending in order to spark an economy back to life when nothing else would work. In a garden variety recession, one brought on by the normal workings of the business cycle, monetary policy alone (cutting interest rates to the point that businesses believe they can earn profits by using borrowed funds to invest in new facilities) can restore economic vitality. But when businesses refuse to borrow or banks refuse to lend—or both—then the government has to step in. Otherwise, savings are destroyed.

This may not be intuitively obvious—given what is going on inside the United States and Europe today, it clearly is not—but when households and businesses are paying down debt, when they are collectively saving more than they are spending, the difference will show up as an increase in the funds flowing into the financial system—that is, as deposits or other claims on financial institutions. The financial system has to do something with this money. So the money goes into one of two places: overseas (banks lend abroad) or into some form of government paper. There is no alternative if savings are to be preserved at a time when households and businesses are paying down debt.

SETTING THE STAGE FOR THE ASIAN FINANCIAL CRISIS

Japanese banks may have been unwilling or unable to lend at home, but they would still extend credit to foreign financial institutions, particularly after the so-called Tequila crisis of 1995/96. This crisis initially had little to do with Japan; a flood of funds into Mexico after the passage of NAFTA spawned a bubble in that country. When the bubble collapsed, it took the Mexican economy down with it. Usually, the IMF steps in—after all, the IMF was set up in part to deal with just such crises. But early in 1995, the IMF's coffers were too low. Mexico was seen as America's problem, so it was up to the United States to top up the IMF funding. But the Republican Party had just taken control of the House of Representatives after a forty-year hiatus. Seeing the opportunity to embarrass the Clinton administration, Republicans linked hands with Left Democrats who distrusted the IMF to block the necessary funding.

The result was a global currency crisis as the dollar went into free fall. A United States that could not or would not bail out a Mexico in its own backyard would mark the end of US hegemony over global finance. But Treasury Secretary Robert Rubin found a way around the congressional obstructionism, a way that allowed the US Treasury to pump some $50 billion into the IMF without Congressional approval. The crisis ended. The dollar stopped falling.

Except against the yen. The yen continued to climb, breaking post-war records, even at one point shattering the ¥80 to the dollar rate. At this point, many Japanese companies could not even cover their variable costs with export sales—that is to say, they were losing money with every item they sold. The pressure on the government to do something became overwhelming.

The MOF went outside the usual order of bureaucratic succession and brought in maverick Sakakibara Eisuke to fill the crucial position of Director General of the International Finance Bureau. Later crowned "Mr. Yen" by the media, Sakakibara got the nod because of his purported friendship with Larry Summers, then Deputy Secretary of Treasury. (Sakakibara had been a visiting professor in the Economics Department at Harvard when Summers was on the faculty there.) Sakakibara flew to Washington in June 1996 and convinced Rubin and Summers that they had to help him bring down the yen, otherwise a bond market panic might ensue as Japanese institutional investors were forced to sell off their holdings of Treasury securities. With a presidential election only six months away, the White House could ill-afford anything like that. The Americans agreed to Sakakibara's proposal. Joint interventions executed in August had the desired effect, both in bringing down the yen/dollar rate and in calming the bond markets.

But these events sent another—perhaps inadvertent—message to the markets: that the United States and Japan had both the will and the ability to control the yen/dollar rate; to ensure that it would take at least ¥100 to buy a dollar. This kind of mistake had been made before. After the currency crisis of summer 1978, Japanese investors had convinced themselves that the Japanese and US government would never again allow the yen/dollar rate to fall below ¥180/US$1. They had piled into US Treasury securities as a result, financing the Reagan Revolution, only to lose their shirts (in yen terms) when, after the Plaza Accord, the rate plunged past ¥140/US$1.

But memories in the financial markets are notoriously short. This time, it was the foreign bankers and hedge fund operators who would make the mistake. The August 1996 intervention had been so successful that they believed Washington and Tokyo had both the will and the ability to see to it that the ¥100/US$1 barrier would never again be breached. So they did something foreigners had rarely before been willing to do: they borrowed huge quantities of yen without any hedge.

The business came to be known as the yen carry trade. The idea was to borrow in yen at the rock-bottom interest rates on offer, then flip the borrowing by lending it on in a higher interest currency such as the US dollar or the Thai baht, and capture the difference in interest rates. It is a slam-dunk, *provided the yen does not strengthen*—which of course it would ultimately do. In the meantime, the yen carry trade helped spawn bubbles in such markets as that for Bangkok real estate. When the trades abruptly unwound in the summer of 1999 as the yen soared in value in the wake of Russia's default on its debt, they brought on the most acute financial crisis of the postwar era until 2008. The crisis culminated in a bailout organized by the Federal Reserve of the prominent American hedge fund Long Term Capital Management. The bailout was needed to prevent a general financial panic, since so many leading banks had lent money to this hedge fund.

But for all the damage abroad, the lending to foreigners by Japanese banks that fueled the carry trade helped the Japanese economy, both directly and indirectly. It gave the banks some place to put their money. And it financed investment booms in countries such as China and Thailand, booms that would help provide a long-term solution to Japan's post-bubble woes by increasing export orders in those countries for Japan's capital goods.

But that was not enough for the time being to keep the Japanese economy from tipping into depression. That would require government spending—and spend the Japanese government did.

JAPANESE GOVERNMENT SPENDING

Richard Koo contends that between 1990 and 2005, the Japanese government bought itself two quadrillion yen worth of GDP growth (some $2–2.5 trillion dollars depending on the exchange rate used) with 460 trillion yen of deficit spending—in other words, one yen of spending bought 4–5 yen worth of GDP. Koo maintains that this was a fantastic bargain; that without it, the Japanese government would have sunk into a profound depression.

The problem is that the counterfactual is not obvious—either to voters or even to policy makers. Koo's advice, following that of Keynes before him, is that governments have to keep spending until an economy has fully recovered. But this is difficult to do, because what policy makers and voters see is the spiraling debt, not what would have happened had the money not been spent.[4] Koo points to the United States in 1937, the United States and Europe today, and, of course, Japan since the bubble. Policy makers—and voters—confronting growing levels of debt are tempted by the first signs of an economy coming back to life to address the spiraling debt problem by raising taxes or cutting spending—or both. What they often fail to grasp is that this makes even the debt problem worse because employment levels stop rising. Tax receipts fall and businesses continue to hoard cash. Japan's policy makers certainly did not see it; as soon as the economy began showing sporadic signs of life, the MOF pushed a hike in the consumption tax through the Diet in 1996. This tax hike sent the economy promptly back into a tailspin, leading directly to the peak of the bank crisis in 1997 and the huge bailout package. Depression had been avoided, but at higher cost than had been necessary.

What made things worse was that the political setup in Japan dictated that all the money that had to be pumped into the economy could not be used in ways that would have done the most good: spending aimed directly at improving the living standards of the urban middle class. Programs such as a complete makeover of Japan's urban housing stock would have directly created hundreds of thousands of jobs and indirectly stimulated demand by providing space for consumer durables. But given the balance of political power in Tokyo, the money inevitably went instead into lavish infrastructure spending in declining rural areas, much of it for white elephants—airports practically in sight of each other; recreational centers in dying towns—that saddled localities with operating deficits as far as the eye could see. The spending did, as Koo points out, keep Japan from tumbling into depression, but that is pretty much all it did—and at the price of drastic worsening of Japan's fiscal situation. (Again, it must be stressed that Japan's fiscal situation would have been yet worse if the money had not been spent; but it would be a lot better today if the money had been spent

---

4. One of the hardest things to make people understand is that in circumstances such as Japan's in the 1990s or America's in the 1930s or post-2008, deficits would actually have been greater had the government not primed the economic pump with fiscal stimulus (i.e., with deficit spending). The reason lies in collapsing tax revenues and the automatic stabilizers (e.g., unemployment insurance) that all developed countries have. By buying GDP with deficit spending, a government also buys itself tax revenues and, ultimately, lower aggregate spending, since more people are working and paying taxes than living on the dole. When 1 unit of deliberate spending buys 4–5 units of GDP, this trade-off is worth it, even in narrow fiscal terms, not to mention the costs in human misery and stunted potential that fiscal stimulus avoids.

intelligently rather than simply thrown around—*baramaki* as the Japanese call this kind of boondoggle spending—in ways that ensured capture by entrenched interests rather than deployment for the wider good.)

To be fair, the MOF has reasons to worry about the spiraling debt that is the legacy of the spending that kept the Japanese economy out of depression. This debt has reached the highest levels in the developed world as a percentage of GDP. Even more worrisome, the amount of the debt is equal to 93 percent of total household assets vs. 41 percent in the United States—in other words, paying the debt off in one go would require almost all of the accumulated holdings of Japan's households. Furthermore, Japan's looming demographic crunch means that the number of working-age Japanese left to support retirees will fall below the crucial three-to-one ratio. The MOF has been desperate to overhaul the structure of Japanese taxes before that happens.

Fortunately, there is plenty of room to increase tax revenues without economically destructive effects. Before the consumption tax was instituted, most Japanese tax revenues came from taxes on large, profitable companies and from income taxes imposed on salaried workers. The latter taxes may be heavy, but politically they are almost invisible, since they are deducted from paychecks before salaries are received. The families of Japanese salaried workers do not go through the annual American ordeal of filing tax returns; they are not required unless one has significant sources of outside income, which most salaried workers do not.

It has been obvious for two decades now that this system was becoming untenable, both politically and economically. Demographic changes spell the eventual end of the compensation structures that emerged out of the labor struggles of the 1950s. Market forces in employment have not yet swept all before them, but they are increasingly a reality. We will look at this more closely in the next chapter, but the fiscal implications are clear: Japan can no longer rely so heavily on income taxes from salaried workers. To be both politically fair and economically effective taxation has to be universalized, with all Japanese paying their fair share of taxes, not just salaried workers.

The great source of untaxed income in Japan is the earnings of farmers, single proprietorships such as doctors' clinics, religious institutions, and small businesses—principally construction companies—that run their books in such a way that they report little taxable profits. But these groups form a critical element of the political structure that has given the MOF such freedom to determine policy. The MOF has long feared that if it went after them directly, that protection could crumble.

Instead, in order to universalize taxation, the MOF has opted for consumption taxes. There is nothing in principle wrong with a consumption tax; arguably, it is the fairest and most efficient way to raise tax revenues. But it is bitterly opposed by broad swathes of the Japanese population— with good reason, as we shall see in chapter 10 that covers Japanese politics.

Furthermore, a consumption tax hike has an immediate deflationary effect. Rate increases should properly take place only during times of strong economic growth fueled by robust demand. It has been more than two decades now since Japan enjoyed such a situation.

Rather than wait until such a recovery happens and institute the tax at the appropriate turn of the business cycle, however, the MOF opted first to introduce and then raise the tax rate whenever it was politically possible to do so. The MOF had a political opening in 1996, but the results, as we have seen, were disastrous. It would be sixteen years before the political stars were properly aligned again. This time, the MOF was more careful, pushing a tax rate hike through the Diet late in 2012 that was to take effect only if certain conditions are met. (The government deemed that these conditions had been met and the hike went into effect on April 1, 2014.) And the MOF succeeded in coupling the rate hike with something equivalent to the US Social Security number that will make it far harder going forward to hide income as so many single proprietors and the owners of other small businesses have historically done—in the future, if things go as planned, people will be unable to open bank accounts without providing this number.

Again, the MOF's actions are far more than a bureaucratic power grab. The MOF has real and justified fears, chief among them that JGB rates will rise before the deficits come under control. If interest rates on JGBs were to climb even into the 2 percent range, Japan's fiscal deficit would become unsustainable in the absence of spending cuts, higher tax revenues, or both.

Japan has been suffering from deflation now for over fifteen years. This is generally regarded as a bad thing; it is certainly bad for economic growth, conventionally defined. Deflation did, however, permit the Japanese government to run up very high deficits without provoking a bond market crash. Since, as we have seen, businesses were not investing domestically— and banks were too shell-shocked about lending in any case—much of

Japan's corporate and household savings were channeled via the financial system into JGBs and other government instruments.

But deflation may be ending. The government of Abe Shinzo, elected in 2012, has taken direct aim at deflation. Whether its efforts succeed or not—at this writing, it is too early to tell—the demographic winds are at the government's back. In the Japanese compensation system, the peak earning years are the early fifties. The baby boomer bulge has now passed that peak and is drawing down savings. Aggregate household savings are falling as a result. In the meantime, most corporations have completed the de-leveraging process and have long since repaired their balance sheets. As a smaller group of younger workers begins to move into the peak earning years, they may be able to bid up wages. They may begin spending, particularly on housing.

Japanese domestic demand may thus finally begin to revive. As corporations once again see opportunities domestically, they will dip into the savings they built up as they recovered from the balance sheet recession. They may even begin to need financing again—and the banks may be tempted to extend it.

As investment demand picks up while savings decline, the day will come when Japan's current account—sometimes called the "widest measure of a country's trade position"—will fall into structural negative territory. Understanding this requires a tiny detour into the laws of accounting that govern trade and investment flows between countries. In a country whose savings are insufficient to finance investment—a situation in which Japan is likely to find itself, sooner or later—the difference will be imported, otherwise the investment could not take place. The laws of accounting—what is known as an accounting identity—dictate that a net inflow of imported capital is identical to the deficit a country runs on the sum of its trade and other "current" financial flows—principally, dividends and interest payments. (A country cannot run a trade-and-other-current-flows deficit unless it can pay for the extra imports, and it does so with the imported capital.) Already, Japan's narrowly defined trade balance (goods and services) is in the red, something exacerbated by the forced shutdown of Japan's nuclear power infrastructure in the wake of the March 2011 earthquake/tsunami at a time of rising global energy prices. The current account does, as noted, include dividend and interest flows as well as trade in goods and services; Japan has over the past decades built up such a pile of claims on other countries that the dividend and interest inflows the country enjoys still exceed the trade deficit, meaning capital imports are not necessary—yet—to cover the trade deficit. But as domestic investment increases while savings fall, those dividend and interest flows coming into Japan will drop off, particularly since such a large chunk of Japan's interest inflows stem from US government securities that now pay historically low rates.

The end of Japan's structural current account surplus has huge implications—politically and economically, in Japan and around the world. (Among other things, from the late 1970s through the early 2000s, Japan's accumulated current account surplus was the primary support for the US dollar.) But for now, we will focus on the fiscal implication.

The coming of a structural current account deficit spells the end of the days when Japan can finance its fiscal deficit entirely from domestic sources—it will have to turn to the imported capital discussed above. The Japanese government is going to have to sell some of its bonds to foreigners. Foreigners will almost surely require higher yields than those currently on offer.

This does not have to be a disaster for Japan—indeed, other things being equal, it will be a good thing. But to ensure it is a good thing, the trends will have to be moving in the right direction: some combination of rising tax revenues and if not absolute reductions in spending, then at least a reduction in the growth of spending.

Some of this will happen automatically in a reviving economy. But ensuring that the economy revives in just the right away—generating enough increased taxes to avoid a fiscal crunch that would derail economic recovery—is going to be a delicate balancing act. Pulling it off requires the right combination of reforms in Japanese business, social changes that promote "animal spirits" without damaging the willingness to pull together, a political mechanism capable of steering the country through the coming shoals, and finally, healthy relationships with other major powers. It is a tall order.

KEYENCE

FIGURE 8. The Logo of Keyence, the Most Profitable Company in Japan During the First Decade of the Twenty-first Century.

8

Business

In March 2011, production lines around the world were thrown into disarray. Manufacturers in industries as diverse as automobiles and electronics suddenly found themselves forced to suspend operations for lack of one or more key components.

The cause was obvious: an earthquake-*cum*-tsunami that had hit the northeast coast of Japan's main island of Honshu. Yet for all the destruction in the disaster's wake, it was not immediately clear why production should be so badly affected. The closest major city, Sendai, had escaped almost unscathed. Most of the horrific scenes that riveted television and Internet viewers around the world showed the devastation of smallish fishing towns, not the ruin of the Japanese economy. The core of Japan's industrial base was hundreds of miles away; only a handful of factories had actually been wrecked by the events of "3/11," as many Japanese came to call the catastrophe. Yet it turned out that these factories made some critical components that could not easily be sourced elsewhere.

That was not the end of supply-chain disruptions that year involving Japanese manufacturers. Some four months after the earthquake, Thailand endured the worst flooding it had faced in a century. Again, production lines around the world ground to a halt for lack of key components. It turned out those components were being made largely by Japanese or Japanese-owned factories in Thailand, factories that had been ruined by the floods.

These two disasters, coming on the heels of each other, forced purchasing agents and analysts to reckon with something many had failed to notice amidst all the talk of Japan's "Lost Decade": Japanese companies had a stranglehold on a range of key upstream components and materials. This seemed to contradict the widely accepted story people had been telling themselves about Japanese business.

That story went something like the following: Japanese companies had at one point dominated the world, but several things had happened to end their reign. The implosion of the bubble economy had weakened Japan's export champions. Countries such as Korea and China had started beating Japan at its own game. The purge imposed on American business by the high dollar/high interest rate regime of the early 1980s had helped spawn a new generation of American champions in the rising IT sector, companies that were now sprinting far ahead of "Japan, Inc." With the emergence of the Internet, distinctions among "manufacturing," "distribution," and "services" had begun to break down worldwide. New players such as Apple and Amazon had made themselves into powerhouses by offering complex bundles of products and services that defied traditional categorization.

Meanwhile, Japanese companies had trouble adapting themselves to a world where the most successful businesses were increasingly providing customers with something that the customer had not realized he or she even wanted until it was offered. Often this "something" was not a single product like a television or a car that Japanese companies could deconstruct and re-engineer for sale at higher quality and lower cost than their competitors abroad could manage; instead it might be a hybrid of product and service, such as an iPod or a Kindle tablet. Even in the one sector—video games—where Japanese companies such as Sega, Nintendo, and Sony had been first out the gate in integrating hardware and software into hit products with global reach, the Japanese were now being passed by foreign rivals that had begun to offer access to games as part of a larger hardware/software/media package.

It seemed that elements of the Japanese system that had once played to Japan's strengths—loyalty and "lifetime" employment, "consensus" management and *nemawashi* (literally, "root-binding" or making sure everyone is on board before a formal decision is made), evergreen debt financing that shielded companies from pressure for short-term earnings—might be turning into liabilities.

The natural disasters of 2011, however, suggested a different story altogether about Japanese business. This story started with reform and unfolded with a newfound emphasis on profitability. It was a tale that featured not just pricing power and quasi-monopolies across a range of industries but also the construction of great offshore industrial platforms in China, Thailand, Vietnam, Malaysia, and the United States—platforms that were ultimately under the control of corporate headquarters in Tokyo, Osaka, and Nagoya.

It turns out that on closer examination both stories are true. Companies such as Sony that once dazzled the world do indeed limp along today without any clear strategy or focus; this firm that invented the portable music player is not even an also-ran in the business any more. Great electronics conglomerates such as Hitachi, Fujitsu, and NEC have been left in the dust by the Korean giant Samsung. Even a Toyota, still the world's most formidable automobile manufacturer, stumbles in ways that would have been unthinkable just a few years ago. Such firms tend to be the names that come to mind when most people think of "Japanese companies."

But the most profitable manufacturers[1] in Japan today are no longer these. An entirely different group now generates the highest profits when measured by operating margins. These companies are barely known outside the business worlds in which they operate. Many deal in upstream components or materials that are largely invisible to end-users. They enjoy technological supremacy and large relative global market shares in their respective businesses. And they have pricing power.

The most profitable company in Japan in the first decade of the twenty-first century was Keyence, making sensors, barcode readers, digital microscopes, and various types of high precision measuring equipment. The second most profitable non-pharma firm was the robotics maker Fanuc specializing in automated systems. The third was Hirose Electric manufacturing a range of connectors used in everything from printers to copy machines to flat-panel displays. Numbers four and five were, respectively, Pacific Metals, Japan's largest ferro-nickel producer, and Union Tool, which specializes in drills, drill-related equipment, and precision rolling machines that produce high quality leadscrews.

---

1. This discussion of profitable Japanese manufacturing companies excludes pharmaceutical firms that owe their position in part to the captive market mandated by national health insurance.

These companies that few have heard of translate into Japanese dominance in many industrial sectors. For example, the combined global market share of Japanese firms in fine chemicals for electronics exceeds 70 percent; for carbon fiber 65 percent. Pry open an iPhone and you will not find many parts with Japanese names on them; the glorious little gizmo was designed and engineered in the United States, manufactured in China, and stuffed with Korean and Taiwanese components. But more than 30 percent of the value-added comes from Japanese companies. Why? Because they supply the critical materials out of which these components are made and the capital equipment on which those components were manufactured. Japanese companies account for a similar percentage of the value-added in the new Boeing Dreamliner. The Boeing/Airbus competition is often presented as a contest between European and American firms, but when the manufacturing and value-added are broken down, it might better be described as a face-off between the Franco-German and US-Japan technostructures.

That Japan's "Hidden Champions"[2] are overwhelmingly manufacturers is no accident. In the wake of the implosion of the bubble economy, the MOF may have been forced into a restructuring of the financial system as it found itself unable to stave off a wave of bankruptcies. But manufacturers were protected, even when financial lifelines were finally cut to establishment companies in the service sector such as Sogo Department Store. As one study put it, it was "essentially impossible to drive manufacturers with elite connections into bankruptcy." R&D spending continued, at over 3 percent of GDP, to be among the highest in the world.

The notion that manufacturing holds the key to economic prosperity is often mocked by orthodox economists. They see it as a relic of the "Fordist" mentality of a century ago that championed great, belching factories as the *sine qua non* of economic power, somehow more valuable than complex services performed by highly trained people. These same economists, however, typically champion the theory of comparative advantage—each

---

2. The term "Hidden Champions," coined by Theodore Levitt and Hermann Simon in 1990, refers to companies that have less then $4 billion in annual sales, enjoy preeminent local and large global market shares in their respective businesses, and are little known either to the general public or the investment community. Japan boasts some 200–250 companies that meet this definition. But unlike the situation in Germany, Switzerland, or the United States, which also boast many "Hidden Champions," more than 95 percent of such companies in Japan are manufacturers.

country should specialize in what it does best, irrespective of what others are doing—as the appropriate guide to a country's optimum industrial structure. But the kind of precision manufacturing in which so many Japanese companies excel is exactly where you would expect Japan's comparative advantage to lie—if, that is, you were willing to concede that comparative advantage derives not simply from quantifiable factor inputs, but from such intangibles as fanatic attention to detail, an emphasis on the appearance and elegance of design, from patience, social cohesion, and teamwork—the explanations for which lie in Japan's cultural, historical, and social inheritance.

To be sure, "Made in Japan" once spelled cheap and shoddy. But even before the Occupation ended, the architects of Japan's postwar industrial policy understood this would have to change. They turned to the work of Edward Deming, a brilliant American statistician who arrived in Japan in 1947 to help GHQ with the census being planned. Deming preached attention to quality at every step of production, quality to be achieved with statistical process control. This message fell like rain on parched soil on the ears of Japanese managers and engineers, pushed as they had earlier been by Occupation officials to churn out cheap throwaways. Deming's methods were adopted with such enthusiasm that the top prize in Japanese business for quality improvement was named the Deming Prize.[3] The quality revolution in Japan was so complete and so thorough that "Made in Japan" became synonymous with the highest standards. This stemmed from conscious decision and implementation on the part of Japan's economic establishment. But the quality revolution also mobilized Japan's greatest social and cultural strengths in the service of economic policy goals.

Today, adverse macroeconomic circumstances and other factors may have dimmed the prospects for some of Japan's most famous companies. But the country's continued supremacy in a wide range of upstream components and materials demonstrates the far-reaching effects of the quality revolution. With industrialization reaching Japan's neighbors—most importantly, China—it has become economically logical to lever cheaper labor there and use Japan's techno/capital strengths in more specialized

3. For decades, Deming was the proverbial prophet without honor in his own country; bewildered by their loss of market share at the hands of the Japanese, American manufacturers finally began listening to Deming. He is credited in particular with helping to turn around prospects for Ford in the 1980s.

areas. The manufacturing prowess perfected during the "miracle" decades facilitated this transition, even if the transition has been obscured by the travails of "name" Japanese firms catering to end-consumers.

THE SERVICE SECTOR

Manufacturing has been the privileged darling of Japan's economic policies and Japan's lagging productivity growth today is often blamed on an inefficient service sector, referring both to the offices, as opposed to the factories, of the major industrial companies, and to service industries themselves such as distribution and retailing. But even in these industries there has been change.

A glance at *Forbes*'s famous list of the wealthiest people in Japan hints at what has been going on. Number one on the list is Yanai Tadashi. His business? Fast Retailing, which under the brand name Uniqlo offers Japanese[4] consumers stylish, quality clothing at reasonable prices. Number three is Son Masayoshi, founder of Softbank, who went head-to-head with Japan's establishment telecommunications industry to push the country into the Internet age. Mikitani Hiroshi, the fourth richest man in Japan, is the country's equivalent of Amazon's Jeff Bezos (Mikitani's company, Rakuten, essentially introduced on-line retailing to Japan), while number 7, Tanaka Yoshikazu, whose company, Gree, is Japan's largest social network, would be Japan's Mark Zuckerberg. Number 12 is Ito Masatoshi, whose company operates a major supermarket chain, owns (or franchises) all the 7-Eleven stores around the world, and revolutionized Japan's shopping habits by blanketing the country with convenience stores. Another man who did not make the *Forbes* list but is thought to be among the wealthiest people in Japan is Yamada Noboru. His company, Yamada Denki, is the biggest discount electronics retailer chain in the country.

These men all demonstrate that it is indeed possible to make money in Japan—and lots of it—by targeting some of the notorious inefficiencies of the Japanese service sector. And for all the talk about these inefficiencies, it bears remembering that standards of service in Japan far exceed what one

---

4. And, increasingly, non-Japanese—a large Uniqlo store opened in 2012 on Fifth Avenue in New York.

encounters in most other countries. Anyone who doubts this should compare the experience of having a home appliance delivered and installed in Japan with that in the United States. The politeness, punctuality, and "customer first" mentality one encounters at even an ordinary restaurant or store in Japan is of the type that can be experienced only in the most expensive such places in most Western countries—all without any expectation of tips.

The ubiquity of the highest standards of service in Japan constitute an immense competitive advantage for the country, even if Japanese companies sometimes do not fully capitalize on those standards. Together with the continued manufacturing prowess evident in the "Hidden Champions," the ingrained tradition of customer service suggests the possibility of a much more positive future for Japanese business than the usual story of decline. But that story of decline is not a fiction. Among other things, the adulation of executives like Son and Mikitani implies that if only other stick-in-the-mud executives would follow their lead, Japan could solve its problems. But it's not that Japan's executives do not understand the need to streamline inefficient practices. It is that they are unwilling to do it.

A conventional analysis of the difficulties faced by Japanese business might conclude that Japan lacks properly functioning mechanisms to allocate human and financial capital away from those sectors of the economy where things have gone wrong to those where things are going right. Such an analysis would be correct. Markets in corporate control, activist shareholders, and investors seeking return do exist in Japan after a fashion, but they are rarely allowed to determine ultimate outcomes. Japan certainly pays a price in forfeited efficiency; to date, that price has been deemed adequate given what it purchases: social stability and economic security for most of the population. The great question confronting Japanese business lies in determining the point at which the price becomes too steep—indeed, whether that point has not already been reached and, if so, what is to be done.

Grappling with this question requires an examination of some aspects of Japanese business that are not easily captured by such common rubrics as return on investment and output statistics. We will start with the nexus of the challenge—employment practices—and the locus of power in the typical Japanese company: the *jinjibu* or personnel/HR department.

CHANGING EMPLOYMENT PRACTICES

The employment practices that emerged out of the early postwar decades continue to serve as a norm for establishment Japanese companies, even if the norm captures less and less of what actually goes on. The "best jobs" are still thought of as those held by permanent employees (*sei-shain*) in well-known, well-connected companies.[5] In such jobs, one joins the firm on graduation from a "name" university, spends two decades in a variety of assignments in which one builds a formidable human network while learning about all aspects of the company's business, and then begins a steady ascent up the corporate ladder accompanied by substantial regular increases in both earnings and social cachet. On topping out—whether that be as General Manager (*buchō*), Division Manager (*jigyō buchō*), Director (*hiratori*), Managing Director (*jōmu*), Senior Managing Director (*senmu*), or President (*shachō*)—one then descends gracefully into economically secure retirement via a series of undemanding but prestigious positions in subsidiaries and affiliates.

Financing this career track has become too expensive for many companies. And many bright younger people do not want the kind of life it entails. This is not simply a matter of devotion to the workplace at the expense of family and other outside interests; that kind of trade-off is faced by ambitious young people in many places. It is also specifically in Japan a growing reluctance to cede all decisions over career development to the *jinjibu* of a large company; to acquiesce in spending the best years of one's life in acquiring an often shallow mix of general management skills rather than the development of real mastery that comes from years of immersion in work which one loves and for which one feels best suited.

Young people in Japan are perfectly aware that companies such as Softbank and Rakuten are openly disdainful of the traditional Japanese career path and do not guarantee lifetime employment. A generation ago, a *meishi* ("business card") with the name of such a firm on it—not to mention that of a foreign company—spelled "also ran" if not "loser," particularly

---

5. Technically, there are two types of *sei-shain*. *Sōgōshoku* ("comprehensive work") are management-track positions typically awarded male university graduates; *sōgōshoku* carries with it a tacit quid-pro-quo involving lifetime economic security in return for complete management discretion over job location and content. *Ippanshoku* ("general work") are more commonly allocated to women and imply clerical duties without much possibility of promotion. Some women are now receiving *sōgōshoku* positions.

when it came to matters such as marrying an attractive, accomplished woman or getting one's children into a prestigious kindergarten. Today, however, high-powered executives at companies like Gree—not to mention Apple and Google—are openly admired. Everyone knows that such firms value expertise and drive, not the go-along, get-along mentality of establishment Japan. And even if many young Japanese would still, if given the choice, opt for the economic security of the "lifetime employment" route in an old-line firm or bureaucracy over the higher risks of a "Hidden Champion" or a foreign firm, many of them know they will not have that choice. For good, secure jobs with predictable increases in pay for people with no particular expertise are increasingly the exception in Japan.

Of course, the decline of good jobs is happening throughout advanced countries, as any glance at the evening news can testify. A world in which both governments and private investors financed too much industrial capacity, in which millions of energetic young Chinese, Indians, and Brazilians are eager and able to do the jobs heretofore done in Japan, Europe, and the United States for a fraction of the pay, in which a predatory financial sector was allowed—even encouraged—to play games that wiped out trillions of dollars in wealth has cumulatively brought on what we see today: tens of thousands of the unemployed young marching in the streets of Athens, Madrid, and Rome while American presidential candidates hurl empty slogans at each other about jobs. It is enough to make one dust off Marxian texts warning that falling profits would ultimately lay bare the contradictions of capitalism.

But what concerns us here is the specifically Japanese corporate response to conditions faced by companies more or less everywhere in the developed world. The "let them eat cake" ethos of American industry with its mass layoffs is—so far—a nonstarter in Japan. Nor does Japan have the explicit social safety net of the European welfare states. Social welfare in Japan has long been tacitly seen as a corporate responsibility, a responsibility backed up by both formal and informal sanctions. It is still extremely difficult in Japan to fire anyone—not only because the courts and the bureaucracy essentially will not allow it but also because letting people go in the Japanese system is an open admission of corporate financial distress. Most Japanese companies will—and can—do it only when survival is in question.[6]

---

6. Companies such as Softbank and Rakuten are exceptions; they have made it clear that people who do not meet corporate expectations will be let go.

Rather than firing people, established Japanese companies generally implement "voluntary" retirement programs in which salaried employees over 40 or so are persuaded to leave their firms with offers of substantial lump-sum payments. And they have come to rely increasingly on temporary workers, often supplied by employment agencies, to fill lower-level positions. Such workers now account for about one-third of the total Japanese workforce, up from 15 percent in 1984. These numbers are approaching levels in countries such as France where legal and social restrictions also make it very difficult to fire full-time, regular employees.

Both "voluntary" retirement and temporary workers bring problems. Voluntary retirement has to be offered to everyone in a given cohort; often it is precisely those men who are most valuable to a company who end up leaving (in many cases, particularly among engineers, for companies in Taiwan, Korea, and China). The ones who stay fear they might not be able to find another job. These fears are valid, the residue of a decades-long stymying of a genuine labor market for mid-career people. The result is what the Japanese call *madogiwazoku* ("window tribe"). The term refers to the universal floor plan of the Japanese office where people with the least to do are relegated to desks the farthest from the command and control posts in the center of the floor. There, under the windows, sit demoralized older men, spending their days shuffling documents and leafing through newspapers, kept on the payroll because the company cannot fire them and they cannot find other jobs.

Meanwhile, the increasing reliance on temporary workers poses a potentially deadly threat both to the social stability and the tacit assumptions about the workplace that have heretofore played such a central role in the success of the modern Japanese economy. We noted in chapter 5 that the constellation of personnel practices labeled "lifetime employment" constituted one of the key institutions of high-speed growth, that among other things, it encouraged long-term strategic thinking on the part of management, since the overriding management aim boiled down to making sure jobs would be there decades hence. That is still true, but it is no longer "everyone's" jobs that are the priority; rather, it is the jobs of the shrinking percentage of employees still governed by lifetime employment protocols—principally, older men and the dwindling numbers of younger counterparts who still get offers of "permanent" positions.

The Japanese system always had an exploitative element to it, but most of that exploitation used to happen among the constellations of suppliers and suppliers' suppliers that served as shock absorbers for the Japanese industrial machine. Subject to relentless pressure to reduce costs, working conditions in such firms could border on the Dickensian—with the one great exception of economic security. Workers might be subject to long hours and almost infinite demands, but even small companies that could barely stagger from quarter to quarter were reluctant to let people go unless they had absolutely no alternative and, as we have noted before, their bigger customers would often throw them lifelines, particularly if they were known to be a member of the bigger company's *keiretsu* or *guruppu* ("business group"). This may have happened for reasons as hard-nosed as they were sentimental; a company that failed to rescue "its" supplier would be suspected by its own customers and bankers of being in financial difficulty. But whatever the reason, the end-result was a degree of economic security.

This is all breaking down. In the first years of the new millennium, many Japanese companies, particularly in the consumer electronics sector, found themselves trapped in a double vise of competition from neighboring countries in the mass-produced end of the market while Silicon Valley waltzed away with hot new fancy gadgetry: mobile phones, portable music players, high-end laptops. Cost reduction became a matter of life and death. Large companies dumped their traditional suppliers in Japan in favor of new facilities opened abroad in places like China and Thailand. But when it came to their own labor practices, major companies could not or would not fire their permanent employees—thus "voluntary retirement." Core employees closed ranks to protect their own, stopped hiring new *sei-shain*, and instead took on "temporary" employees—assigned to do essentially the same work at half the pay (or less than half when one adds the present value of the future earnings stream a Japanese company is committed to pay a *sei-shain*). It is these people who are now increasingly exploited; the shock absorbers of small, nominally independent companies are being replaced by the shock absorbers of poorly paid, overworked temporary staff.

Even worse practices exist. Tales circulate of *burakku kigyō* ("black companies"), firms that pretend to offer permanent positions but have no intention of actually doing so. These firms take in young people, but then subject them to such demanding and grueling work that the young people leave, allowing them to be replaced by new cohorts of workers at entry-level pay.

The result of both the surge in temporary workers and the increasingly naked exploitation of younger workers desperate for the security of "lifetime" employment creates both a macroeconomic and a sociological trap. Lack of demand has hobbled the Japanese economy since the late 1960s when Japan's export-oriented industries began earning more dollars than Japan needed. We saw how the attempts to replace exports with investment as the principal driver of the economy brought on the disaster of the bubble economy and its aftermath. No plausible scenario exists for Japan of long-term economic health that does not include robust domestic demand. Some of Japan's economic policy makers understand this; the government of Abe Shinzo that came to power in November 2012 has, for example, put some pressure on Japan's leading companies to raise wages as a quid-pro-quo for the lower tax rates and cheaper currency the government is intent on delivering. We will have more to say about this in the last chapter, but even if major Japanese companies concede the point and begin raising wages for their *sei-shain*, the increasing reliance on low-paid temps means this may not translate into an economy-wide increase in purchasing power.[7]

Instead, it threatens to undermine the social cohesion that has been so important to postwar Japan. It is difficult to see how this cohesion could survive the emergence of a two-tiered society with a smaller labor aristocracy enjoying secure, good-paying jobs exploiting a larger group of people living from month to month.

For the temporary employee, or *furiita*, as he or she is known in Japan—a compound word coined from the English "free" and the German *arbeiter* or worker, a word that when used by itself in Japanese means part-time job of the type held by a student—still tends to be seen in Japan as someone who stayed or was left on the platform when the train pulled out of the station, even if it was not really his or her fault. Somehow such people are not fully *shakai-jin*, literally "society person"—an adult who has assumed the responsibilities of work and family that go with being a full-fledged member of Japanese society. And that is linked to another problem facing many Japanese companies: globalization.

---

7. As of this writing, average real wages have continued to decline, even as prices for such things as energy and food have begun to rise.

TROUBLES WITH GLOBALIZATION

In cities such as New York, London, and Bangkok, one finds two separate communities of Japanese expatriates. One community consists almost entirely of men assigned to the typical four-year rotation with the local outpost of a major Japanese company, together with their wives and children. Such men are often unhappy with their assignments—they would have had no choice in the matter, simply being ordered by the *jinjibu* (HR department) to relocate—and they fear the "out of sight, out of mind" consequences of being away from headquarters for too long. They may live in larger houses than they did back home. They may find themselves able to sit down when taking the Metro North into Grand Central rather standing in a packed Keihin Tohoku train into Shimbashi. But the essentials of their lives will be what they always have been since they first joined their firms. Their offices will be arranged just as they were back home, and while there may be a fair number of local hires doing lower-grade work, all the key decisions will be made by the Japanese managers. They will socialize with other Japanese just as they would have back in Tokyo or Osaka, wolfing down *yakitori* and sushi in restaurants that cater to an exclusively Japanese clientele, knocking back *shōchū* and whiskey in small hostess bars that differ from the ones back in Shinjuku or Namba only in being a little cheaper and staffed with mostly non-Japanese women, the more successful of whom will have learned to banter in basic Japanese. They will live in suburban neighborhoods where large numbers of other Japanese families cluster: Rye, New York; Finchley, just outside London; the Thong Lor area of Bangkok. Their wives will socialize with each other, and their children will go to Japanese school or attend special Saturday Japanese classes if the city lacks enough Japanese expatriate families to support a full-time school. They do not want to see their children's chances of getting into a top Japanese university compromised, and a youngster who acts "un-Japanese" after spending too many years in an American or British school will not do well in class upon returning to Japan. These families will watch Japanese television in the evenings and on the weekends shop in specialty stores that carry Japanese foodstuffs.

The latter is likely to be the only place where they will run into members of the other Japanese expatriate community: the younger, usually single, often female Japanese who have relocated abroad. These people, probably living in cramped apartments in city centers, perhaps with local boyfriends or girlfriends, will generally have a much better feel for what is going on lo-cally, even in ways that could be of use to business. But establishment Japan has not figured out how to use them—evidence of the broader problem.

Evidence for this broader problem is everywhere. Comparisons of Japan's "hidden champions" with those in countries such as Germany and Switzerland reveal that their great weakness lies not in the quality of their engineering or the dedication of their managers, but in their handicaps when it comes to operating overseas. This is not just a matter of marketing per se but also involves their ability to integrate into the global networks that shape the overall direction of an industry. Mobile phones serve as a good ex-ample. Japanese manufactures captured an early lead in this business, thanks to their superior technology and the challenge of meeting the demanding requirements of Japanese consumers. But they missed out on broader de-velopments, such as the integration of the mobile device with the web, devel-opments that would see first Apple and then Samsung seize global leadership in this business. The Japanese were left with technically sophisticated prod-ucts serving only the Japanese market. The Japanese business press dubbed it the "Galapagos" phenomenon—a Japanese product segment evolving in-dependently from what is going on elsewhere, with sobering implications for such key determinants of ultimate global success as economies of scale.

For explanations, one can look to Silicon Valley, ground zero for the world's IT industries. Japanese managers found themselves missing out on the "buzz" that characterizes the Valley. Why? Sometimes the answer was both simple and opaque: they were not taking their kids on Saturdays to soccer practice with kids from other countries and gabbing with their Indian, Chinese, Korean, and American counterparts. Instead, since their kids attended Japanese schools, they just talked to other Japanese parents. They might have been conscientious and indefatigable salesmen offering first-rate products, but in a hive like the Valley, they missed a crucial trans-mission path of hive intelligence.

GLOBAL BRANDS AND FOREIGN DIRECT INVESTMENT

But it is a mistake to assume that Japanese companies have not "gone global," if that term refers simply to the Japanese presence overseas. A stroll through any developing country urban center, the streets crammed with

Japanese cars and motorcycles, the shops full of durables with Japanese names on them, will give the lie to any notion that Japan, Inc., is surrendering its global reach. Japanese department stores dominate the most fashionable shopping districts in cities such as Bangkok and Singapore; the Japanese Chamber of Commerce in Shanghai dwarfs comparable organizations of American and European businesses. The two-hour drive south from Bangkok's new Suvarnabhumi Airport (itself largely financed by Japanese official loans at concessional rates) to the famous beach resort of Pattaya takes one past scores of Japanese-owned factories; comparable scenes are visible in the industrial areas outside Kuala Lumpur or Shenzhen north of Hong Kong—or, for that matter, around Torrance, California, and Portland, Oregon.

Foreign direct investment ("FDI") has been one of the crucial stories of Japanese business over the last three decades. Here too the success is unimaginable without the manufacturing mastery achieved by Japan's industrial base during the "miracle" years and its determination to control as much of the supply chain as possible. Aside from low-wage assembly operations in Southeast Asia in the 1970s, the first wave of FDI occurred in the 1980s—mostly into the United States and Europe in response to trade friction. But with the rise of the yen in the wake of the 1985 Plaza Accord, cost competitiveness displaced trade friction as the principal motivator for FDI. Japanese FDI accelerated after the mid-1990s and culminated in the "China boom," as it was called in the early years of the 2000s when Japanese companies rushed to open plants in China in response to the double-digit growth rates in that country, the relatively low costs of doing business there, and pressure from the Chinese government.

The result is that by the early years of this century, more than 25 percent of Japan's total plant and equipment investment was being spent outside Japan; by 2004, some one-sixth of the total production of Japanese companies was taking place outside the country. Predictably, this gave rise to fears of what the Japanese labeled *kūdōka*, the hollowing out of Japan's industrial base. Closer examination reveals that these fears are partly exaggerated, particularly when it comes to Japanese control of key upstream technologies. The leakage of Japan's technical know-how to its Korean, Taiwanese, and Chinese rivals is probably due as much to the hundreds of Japanese engineers arm-twisted by their companies into "voluntary retirement" who took jobs with firms in those countries as it is to Japanese FDI; the highest-value–added and most technologically sophisticated manufacturing continues to be done in Japan.

For despite all the moaning about *kūdōka*, the fact of the matter is that Japanese companies really, as we have seen, had no choice when they made their FDI decisions. The pressure to move some functions offshore may actually have strengthened certain sectors of Japanese industry, particularly the manufacturers of materials and precision components that are vital to downstream industries such as automobiles and electronics. Japanese companies have had to learn in the past twenty-five years not just how to export (how to market overseas) but how to cope with all the challenges—legal, financial, political, technological, managerial—that come from operating in cultural and business environments that differ from the ones in which they had been nurtured and achieved their initial successes. Many companies have risen admirably to these challenges; the result, as one business leader has pointed out, is that if one measures the performance of the Japanese economy not with the usual yardsticks of national income and employment statistics but with the total productivity of real assets owned by Japanese entities (i.e., the aggregate sum of domestic holdings plus Japan's FDI), "Japan, Inc." comes out looking much better than it does when the traditional criteria are used.

Yet for all their successes, Japanese business has stumbled in a key aspect of globalization: bringing non-Japanese into significant decision-making roles. This is obvious both at the middle and senior management levels. It is practically a truism that with rare exceptions, if one joins a Japanese company as a non-Japanese, one cannot expect to rise to a position where one will have any real input into corporate strategy or decision-making. It is not that many companies do not try; they understand perfectly well the need for local expertise. But integrating the foreigners is irksome for Japanese managers. It is not just a matter of language, as formidable a barrier as that is.[8] It is also a host of understandings about how to work together to get things done, understandings that are second nature to any half-socialized Japanese adult but have to be spelled out to all but those foreigners with long experience in Japan. Even

---

8. Only a handful of non-Japanese achieve real comprehensive fluency in Japanese; it simply cannot be done without spending long periods of time in Japan and, unless one grew up there and attended Japanese schools, years of concentrated effort that needless to say preclude simultaneously holding down a job with significant responsibilities. Considerably more Japanese achieve real fluency in English than do non-Japanese in Japanese, but the number is still relatively small considering Japan's global presence. And when it comes to third languages—Spanish, Arabic, Russian—the numbers are tiny except for Chinese, where the use of *kanji*, albeit in modified forms, gives native Japanese speakers a bit of an edge; and, perhaps, Korean where the grammar and syntax resemble Japanese.

Japanese people and organizations with the best of globalizing motives tire when having to work with *gaijin* on an intimate, day-to-day basis; it is just so much more comfortable to fall back on dealing quickly and easily with other Japanese.

A preference for one's own is not, of course, limited to Japanese. And for all today's adulation of politically correct "diversity," even a cursory look at business history demonstrates the very real advantages of close-knit networks that can operate with total trust and implicit understandings as givens, for example, the great nineteenth-century German-Jewish merchant banking families or the Overseas Chinese business elites in today's Southeast Asia. But when a real feel for what is going on in a foreign market spells the difference between catching and missing critical trends, the barriers separating Japanese from foreigners can become a terrible handicap, as we have already seen with the relative failure of Japanese companies to decode the buzz coming out of Silicon Valley. These barriers can sometimes seem unbridgeable, particularly when it involves integrating foreigners into Japanese organizations where tacit knowledge about decision-making, about the locus of power, about factions—who is on which side—are sufficiently subtle that a foreigner working in a Japanese company can come across like a rap artist trying to make music with the Amadeus String Quartet.

Meanwhile, the number of foreigners who have made it to the top of major Japanese companies can almost be counted on the fingers of one hand. In two of these cases—Carlos Ghosn at Nissan and Thierry Porté of the Shinsei Bank—they reached their positions only after the companies they were invited to head were in danger of collapse and had been sold to foreign entities (respectively, Renault and Ripplewood Holdings) as a last desperate gamble to keep them alive. Three other prominent cases were Howard Stringer at Sony, Craig Naylor at Nippon Sheet Glass, and Michael Woodford at Olympus.

None of the three had happy experiences. Market scuttlebutt suggested that Stringer, a former CBS executive who had been recruited to head Sony's US operations, had initially been given the CEO nod in 2005 because of despair that any Japanese could be expected to cut through the factionalism that had mushroomed since the passing from the scene of the three great visionaries who had founded and built Sony: Morita Akio, Ibuka Masaru, and Ohga Norio. That factionalism was blamed by many both inside and outside the company for the loss of Sony's pace-setting preeminence in consumer electronics. Whether or not this is the real story for Stringer's assignment, Sony continued to stumble during his tenure and he stepped down from the CEO slot in February 2012, although retaining the chairmanship.[9]

Craig Naylor, a former DuPont executive who had spent some years in Japan with that company, was recruited out of retirement to head Nippon Sheet Glass. He lasted less than two years and, to quote the company's press release at the time of his departure, left due to "fundamental disagreements over corporate strategy".

The most sensational story was that of Michael Woodford at Olympus. This company could almost serve as a miniature scale model of the whole of Japanese business—a magnificent franchise tethered to a whole gamut of poorly performing divisions that had little or no relation to the company's core competency in precision imaging equipment (Olympus makes some 70 percent of the world's endoscopes). The company had engaged in a series of doubtful acquisitions abroad, the purpose of which turned out in many cases not to be strategic but to conceal poor investments the company had made during the bubble economy years of the late 1980s.

Olympus executives had managed to hide those dodgy investments thanks to the usual story in Japan: boards stacked with insiders, collusive bankers, and a pliant business press that, absent signals from the public prosecutor, rarely reports malfeasance on the part of establishment corporations, even when journalists are aware of it. But as the bad numbers continued to fester and grow, it became harder to cover them up. The most straightforward reason for Woodford's surprising appointment as president were expectations along the lines of those that led to the similar appointments at Nissan and Sony: that a *gaijin* would have the freedom to do what a Japanese could not in streamlining and focusing Olympus's business. But Woodford may also have been deliberately set up in order to provide a scapegoat. For it soon appeared that either the original investments or the attempts to cover them up—or both—had attracted the attention of

9. The Japanese media took great glee in reporting that executives like Stringer and Ghosn—the two highest-paid executives in Japan in 2010—earned some ten times what the president of Toyota made, at a time when Sony was losing money and neither Sony nor Nissan were paying much in the way of dividends.

organized crime; that Olympus had become too entangled with criminal elements to extricate itself easily.

It would not be the first time in Japan. Proper capitalist economies are supposed to have institutions that make it difficult to hide bad business decisions, not to mention outright corporate wrongdoing. Those institutions include a disinterested accounting profession, a "watchdog" business press, a functioning legal system that permits outsiders to file suits with some expectation that their complaints will be heard, markets in corporate control that provide a means for ousting managements that have performed poorly, a regulatory apparatus staffed by genuine regulators rather than facilitators, and a constellation of practices that go under the label "corporate governance"—most importantly, activist shareholders and independent boards of directors. Most of these institutions exist—if at all—in only attenuated forms in Japan. To be sure, there have been some attempts to strengthen them in recent years, such as a requirement introduced in 2000 for consolidated accounting or the 2006 Corporation Law that theoretically empowers shareholders. But the historic weakness of these institutions created openings that allowed intimidation to flourish, openings that were exploited in Japan by criminal elements.

The most effective weapon wielded by blackmail artists in Japan is the threat of exposure. While a smoking gun has not yet surfaced in the Olympus case, the circumstantial evidence is overwhelming that some of the dubious payments Olympus had been making for decades to cover up its bad investments had found their way into the pockets of *sōkaiya*, gangsters who specialize in threatening to disrupt shareholder meetings and otherwise reveal embarrassing information if they are not paid off.

Woodford's mistake—if one can call it that—was not to discover these payments; rather, it was to make them an issue. He confronted both the chairman and the auditor of Olympus about the payments. Instead of responding to the allegations, the chairman fired Woodford. Woodford immediately called a reporter at the Tokyo bureau of the *Financial Times* and told him the whole story, a move that might conceivably have saved his life. The *FT* put the incident on its front page the next day, leading not only to a firestorm in the global financial press (the *Wall Street Journal* and the *New York Times* immediately assigned teams of reporters to cover the story) but scrutiny from an FBI that had long been interested in the financial crimes of the Japanese underworld. The

Japanese system has effective means of silencing people who try to stand up to intimidation—up to and including murder.[10] But the instant global brouhaha that followed Woodford's sacking precluded the usual tactics for smothering troublemakers.

One hesitates repeatedly to fall back on cultural shibboleths, but it needs to be emphasized again that for centuries the samurai who formed Japan's ruling class had been inculcated with the notion that absolute, unquestioning loyalty to one's lord was the only ultimate virtue. Most companies on the commanding heights of the Japanese economy are, as noted in chapter 3, in one way or another the direct institutional heirs of the entities set up by the early Meiji government and awarded to former samurai. The cultural inheritance embedded in these arrangements plays out even today, as we see in the Olympus case. A good corporate soldier in Japan never embarrasses his company or his seniors, and the Japanese ruling elite will close ranks to protect its own.

This unwritten code is not something a foreigner can be expected to understand—or, if he does figure it out, to internalize it, particularly when that foreigner has been marinated in very different cultural values, values that stress allegiance to principles held to be transcendent and universal. But the code has an economic dimension that is not often grasped.

WRITING OFF SUNK COSTS

The difficulties Japanese companies have had in giving real decision-making authorities to foreigners form the clearest sign of the way the Japanese business establishment continues to be permeated with this code of loyalty (if one wants to be polite about it) or collusion (if one wants to be critical).

---

10. Two of the most famous cases are the film director Itami Juzo and the lawyer Sakamoto Tsutsumi. Itami, director of the acclaimed *Tampopo*, was beaten by *yakuza* thugs angry at the way the *yakuza* had been portrayed in his film *Minbō no Onna* (The Gangster's Moll). He was working on another film about relations between a specific *yakuza* group and the largest and most powerful of the "new religions"—Soka Gakkai—when he ostensibly committed suicide; a suicide that many suspect was in fact murder. Sakamoto was a lawyer who launched class-action suits against cults such as the Rev. Sung Myung Moon's Unification Church and the Aum Shinrikyo. He, his wife, and his child were murdered in 1989, but the culprits brought to justice only six years later after the Aum Shinrikyo launched a terrorist attack on the Tokyo subways. The television network TBS had taped an interview with Sakamoto and then shown it secretly to Aum operatives.

But the economic costs of that code do not end with the difficulties in attracting and retaining high-quality foreign executives. They are perhaps outweighed by an even bigger problem that can be traced directly to the loyalty/collusion code: recognizing and coping with failure. For the Japanese system lacks institutional means to deal with failure, with the "creative destruction" that the great economist Joseph Schumpeter identified as the *sine qua non* of capitalism.

One can make the argument—and plenty have—that capitalism is in crisis worldwide precisely because "creative destruction" no longer functions properly; that as the indiscriminate bailouts in the wake of the 2008 crisis suggest, what increasingly matters today in determining whether a company survives is not so much quality products, marketing savvy, and cost control, but size and political connections. Whether true or not—and if true, it suggests one more time that the world is becoming more "Japanese" rather than the reverse—Japan has long had particular difficulty in facing up to failure: recognizing it, accounting for it, and writing it off. For the code of loyalty is more than a matter of a willingness to fall on one's sword when necessary to protect one's seniors or one's organization. It also works in the other direction: the CEO resigning to "take responsibility" for corporate misfortune, the company continuing to order from its established supplier even when someone else appears with a better deal. But it is not even enough to call loyalty/collusion a two-way street. It amounts to an entire fabric of relationships that binds both individuals and organizations. To paraphrase E. M. Forester, the good Japanese would prefer, if pressed, to violate some abstract principle—be that "shareholder value" or the "public good"—than betray those to whom he (or his organization) has ties of dependence, of obligation, and, yes, of friendship.

The reluctance to cut off some person or group that is still trying hard but not delivering results has both a sentimental and a practical aspect. In a society in which people and organizations are bound to each other through organic webs of mutual dependence and obligation, the public and humiliating failure of some person or some group inevitably reflects badly on those who are seen as being responsible for that person or that group—on those who had the power to cushion failure and refused to act. Practically speaking, it raises suspicion that they too have been wounded. A company that fires people when it has little for them to do or a bank that calls in loans from a long-standing but troubled customer knowing that will mean the customer's ruin is identifying *itself* as an entity in trouble.

For why would such things by allowed unless those doing the allowing were themselves endangered? Otherwise, such acts—and here is where sentiment enters the picture—are inhuman, or, at the very least, un-Japanese.

To be sure, meritocratic "up or out" employment practices may well, in abstract, induce the greatest efforts from the most able, ambitious, and energetic. Hard-nosed bankers and investors on the prowl for profit may help ensure that money goes to those companies and managers best able to extract high returns from economic assets. Markets in corporate control can and do provide an efficient means of disposing of businesses that are no longer performing well so that capital can be redeployed into more productive sectors. Of course, such practices can also facilitate the systemic looting of the public good for private gain and are inextricably intertwined with the growing and socially dangerous income inequality gaps that have opened up in countries such as the United States and Britain. Opponents in Japan of neo-liberal reforms are quick to point this out. But, even more fundamentally, allowing M&A markets or shareholder value to determine economic and political outcomes in Japan would amount to a social, a political, and a cultural revolution. This is what advocates of root-and-branch reform in Japanese business are, perhaps unwittingly, calling for: a revolution.

Plenty of advocates of just such a revolution can be found inside as well as outside Japan; Japanese business leaders are, after all, perhaps in a better position than anyone else to appreciate what the difficulties with globalization and the lack of adequate economic and political mechanisms to cope with failure—to write off sunk costs—are doing to Japanese business and the Japanese economy. They know that many of the greatest names of Japanese business are losing markets and cachet around the world. In an era when even famous avatars of high technology such as Sharp are publicly admitting they have no choice but to throw themselves open to foreign acquisition, when the president of Toyota is seen weeping on television for slip-ups unimaginable a generation earlier, when choking bureaucracy and all the rituals of Japanese business life bring decision-making to a crawl in an ever-faster paced world, they know that things cannot go on this way. But they do not know what to do. They might, in abstract, agree with the need to short-circuit *nemawashi* (meetings to have meetings to have meetings) or the *ringi* system (a written record of every decision that involves procuring sign-offs from a dozen or more corporate bureaucrats, any one of whom can slow or halt things), but when it comes to acting on these notions, most find themselves trapped by the system that nurtured them.

Back in the early 1990s, advocates for reform were often accused of wanting to turn Japan into some sort of neo-liberal imitation of the United States complete with an abusive financial services industry that busts up decent companies in order to enrich a few predators. But that is no longer a credible charge. Japan's business community now understands that calls for root-and-branch reform are not just code for aping American capitalism (or "Anglo-Saxon capitalism" as the Japanese like to call it). True, in the era of Apple, Google, and Facebook, Japanese talk of American business decline has largely disappeared. Japan's business leaders may still tut-tut at slash-and-burn American practices and note—correctly—how those would never work in socially cohesive Japan. But they are not really looking across the Pacific any more for examples of what to do—or not to do. Instead, they turn their gaze across the Sea of Japan in fear and wonderment at South Korea, a country they long treated contemptuously as a kind of poor relation.

THE KOREAN CHALLENGE

No one would mistake Korea for the United States; its political and economic institutions resemble Japan's far more closely than they do America's (in many cases—e.g., the *chaebol* or business conglomerates—they are actually copies of Japanese originals; the Koreans hate to acknowledge the Japanese roots of so many of their institutions, but the country was, after all, a Japanese colony for thirty-five crucial years). Indeed, no country in the world is more culturally similar to Japan—or perhaps, to be more accurate, is comparatively less dissimilar. Yet Korean companies are cleaning Japan's clocks in everything from consumer electronics to popular entertainment.

Japanese business leaders often cite a strong yen/weak won as the reason. Of course a strong currency can be a handicap for exporters. But complaints about exchange rates too often serve as an excuse for failure to confront deeper problems. The whining by many leading Japanese exporters about the Koreans today is all too reminiscent of what many American business leaders were saying about Japanese competition in the run-up to the 1985 Plaza Accord.[11] The near-halving of the dollar's

11. Japanese often complain that Korea's export champions enjoy what amounts to monopoly profits at home that they use to subsidize their export drives. Again, though, this is reminiscent of what Americans used to say about Japanese competition.

exchange rate in yen terms in the wake of the Accord did little to address the problems faced at the time by the American automobile or consumer electronics industries. Similarly, it is not clear that the recent fall in the yen/won exchange rate will neutralize the Korean competitive challenge. Among other things, Korea's demonstrably superior ability to commercialize its pop culture abroad has nothing to do with a weak currency.

A comprehensive explanation for the emergence of Korean companies as deadly threats to Japanese business, an explanation that goes beyond currency rates, would take another book. But three factors are surely important.

1. There is a more globalized elite. Far from tainting Korean youth with suspicions of being "un-Korean," experience abroad and real competency in English are almost prerequisites for membership in the Korean elite; leaders of Korean business and academia mostly have graduate degrees from top universities in the West. It would only be a slight exaggeration to say that the Ivy League (plus MIT and Stanford) plays the same role in Korean society as a gateway into the ruling elite that the University of Tokyo does in Japanese society.

2. Korean economic and political institutions have much clearer power structures and far more obvious accountability, with the concomitant benefits of quick and decisive decision-making. Witness the difference between Samsung's reaction to the iPhone—vaulting past Apple to become the world's number one smartphone seller—and the stumbling of much of the Japanese IT industry, or the ways in which Hyundai Motors has been nipping at the heels of Japan's automakers in their number one export market, the United States. The Korean *chaebol* may have been criticized in Korea for their oligarchical tendencies, but the identity of the key decision makers in these giant conglomerates is both instantly obvious and a far cry from the groupthink that prevails in most Japanese companies.

3. A final factor surely lies in the way the whole country lives on the edge—on the lack of margin for error. For its entire existence, Seoul has had to cope with an existential threat not thirty miles away in the form of an implacably hostile North Korea intent on its destruction. To top that, in the late 1990s after the Asian financial crisis, the country came so close to economic meltdown that Japanese-style muddling through was not an option. South Korea could not afford the luxury of diddling, vague thinking, and indecision.

This was once true of Japan as well, but has not been for forty years now—and the responsibility for that lies far beyond the business community. What has been happening in Korea demonstrates that a country need not destroy its culture in order to carry out root-and-branch reform. Koreans are as distinctive and prickly about their culture as the most ardent Japanese nationalists are about theirs, although perhaps less self-conscious about it. Among other things, the global successes of companies like Samsung and Hyundai and the slew of Ivy League degrees held by Korean CEOs—not to mention the run-away global mega-hit "Gangnam Style"— have stirred national pride rather than fear that Korea is losing the essence of what makes the country what it is.

THE FUTURE OF JAPANESE BUSINESS AND THE GLOBAL CRISIS OF CAPITALISM

The limited-liability corporation—the institutional form that virtually all Japanese companies have assumed for well over a century now—was imported from the West by the Meiji government. But it was not implanted on the soil of some economic *terra nullius*. Like the institutions of parliamentary government introduced at the same time and for much the same reasons, the outward form of the limited-liability corporation was grafted onto existing arrangements that were, as we saw in chapter 3, both deeply rooted and very sophisticated. It should not, therefore, be a matter for surprise that the institution has never functioned precisely the way it does in those countries where it first took shape: the Netherlands, Britain, and the United States.

In particular, the conceptual pillars on which the limited-liability corporation stands were never internalized in Japan. There is no counterpart in Japanese culture or thought to Lockean notions of contracts, rights, enlightened self-interest, and human beings as atomistic decision makers driven principally by pursuit of personal enrichment. Thus, the primacy of shareholder value and the idea that economic outcomes should be determined by an invisible hand operating in impersonal markets have never been given even lip service in Japan.

But the institution nonetheless served its real purposes in helping to preserve Japan's independence—and arguably far more effectively than did parliamentary government, not to mention other key institutions also imported at roughly the same time such as universities or a military founded on universal male conscription. Japanese businesses equipped their country with the material means to contemplate waging war against the greatest powers on earth. That gift bestowed on the wider society may have been thrown away by the dysfunction of Japan's governing institutions, but Japanese business responded to catastrophe with renewed vigor, rising to the challenge of a postwar world in which a return to national greatness—not to mention the mundane tasks of feeding and clothing the Japanese population—fell disproportionately on its shoulders.

Japanese business is now visibly in crisis. But any attempt to analyze or predict the future for Japanese business in general and the limited-liability corporation in particular requires pulling apart those aspects of the crisis that stem from the institution's embodiment in the specifically Japanese political economy and those that can be traced to the wider problems of the institution itself.

We may not yet be living through the final crisis of capitalism predicted by Marx, but we are quite palpably living through a global crisis of the limited-liability corporation. Legally constituted political authority created this institution in order to accelerate capital formation by providing merchants with an alternative to ruin in the case of failure. But while the limited-liability corporation has its origins in legally constituted politics, it appears to be escaping political control. Neo-feudal corporate aggrandizement has in too many places displaced the original purposes of the limited-liability corporation as an institution, in the process so blurring the connections between wealth and risk that the limited-liability corporation is becoming a key prop in the insulation of the wealthy and powerful from any accountability to the wider society. The decay of cultural, social, and political restraints on corporate behavior not only compromises governments, but like the collapse of resistance to cancerous growths, now threatens the destruction of the natural systems on which human life depends.

But the crisis of the limited-liability corporation plays itself out in different ways in different places. There is no real counterpart in Japan to the way bankers hijacked the organs of the American government after the transformation of Wall Street from partnerships to limited-liability companies. For one thing, despite the legal fictions, Japanese corporations have never seen themselves and never acted as institutions set up for the pursuit of individual private gain. That may be part of the problem in a country that seems persistently to waste capital, but attempts to "reform" Japanese companies so they become more avid profit-seekers—more respectful of capital, if you will—inevitably run up against vaguely defined but real conviction that companies serve social purposes that transcend mere money-grubbing.

This sense in Japan that companies have public obligations—a sense that is both widespread and has been obviously internalized by most Japanese executives—is one of the chief reasons why Japanese companies will so often go the extra mile, even with no quantifiable benefit to themselves. One can point to the behavior of companies such as Ricoh and Renesas Electronics in the days after the disasters of March 2011. They resorted to heroic efforts at great cost to themselves to make up for the damage they had sustained because other companies and industries depended on them. But set against this kind of heroism are the revelations about Tokyo Electric Power's ("TEPCO") shoddy management of the Fukushima nuclear plant it built and ran—the impression it gave that because it was a company ostensibly operating in the public interest, anything it did was therefore, by definition, in the public interest. That included the diversion of corporate funds into PR campaigns propagandizing in favor of a deadly and implacably unforgiving power source in the world's most seismically unstable country, and the deliberate suppression of any research that highlighted the risks of nuclear power. TEPCO is a utility, and admittedly utilities everywhere enjoy quasi-monopolies and state protection from market forces on the grounds of public interest. But TEPCO's behavior points to the way that a presumption that an organization is acting for the wider social good can cloak the most wasteful, self-serving, and ultimately dangerous management practices.

TEPCO itself can almost serve as a template for the wider story of Japanese business. Many of TEPCO's people on the scene in Fukushima acted in heroic and literally self-sacrificial ways during the terrifying days right after the disaster. Yet it is clear that TEPCO's senior management had not been doing its job—a dereliction of duty with catastrophic consequences. Similarly, while we continue to see standards of service and dedication to quality from Japanese companies that many other countries can only dream of, the emergence of such phenomena as *burakku kigyō* ("black companies") and the ruthless exploitation of temporary workers suggests that much of the Japanese managing class is closing ranks to protect their positions and privileges as a group, if not their own individual pockets.

But however the ethos of Japanese business plays out in specific cases, expectations that this or that reform can restore the vitality Japanese business enjoyed during those unique and unrecoverable decades when the Japanese limited-liability corporation did indeed accomplish something of a miracle is expecting too much. For, the problems of Japanese business cannot be disentangled from the wider challenges facing a country that is both culturally and politically adrift. To look to the future of Japanese business, one must look not only to global geopolitical and economic factors, but to the future of the culture and the politics in which it is embedded.

FIGURE 9. The New Female Archetype in Japanese Popular Culture: The *Gyaru* ("gal"). Photograph taken July, 1999, © The Yomiuri Shimbun, Courtesy: The Yomiuri Shimbun.

9

Social and Cultural Change

Japan, once known around the world for cherry blossoms, Mt. Fuji, woodblock prints, and geisha, then for fanaticism and brutality, followed in turn by a stint as a byword for workaholism and quality manufactures, is now likely to be identified by global trendsetters as the home of a great national cuisine, Hello Kitty, *otaku* ("geeks"), and *hentai anime* (animated pornography featuring extreme sexual obsessions).

But that leaves us with a question. What is it that draws all these cultural phenomena together; that links the fashions of Yamamoto Yōji and Kawakubo Rei, the novels of Haruki Murakami, the *manga* of Masamune Shiro, the Zelda game series, animated films such as *Princess Mononoke*—or horror films such as *Ringu* ("Ring")—not to mention Pokémon, Gameboy, and the waves of *anime* and *manga* that have mesmerized Western youth for a generation now? How is it that these things can all be Japanese? How is it that a culture that displays a seemingly limitless appetite for the cute and cloying also brings forth the world's most lavish depictions of sexual perversion? And how can these phenomena stem from the same cultural roots that produced the great ink paintings of the Muromachi period, the Katsura Imperial Villa in Kyoto, and the films of Ozu and Kurosawa?

THE GLOBAL REACH OF JAPANESE CULTURE

One is tempted to ramble on about Japanese creativity—and there is no doubt that by whatever yardstick one chooses to use, the Japanese are an unusually creative and artistic people. But avoiding banal tautologies in explaining this creativity is a tricky matter. Perhaps we can make some progress by trying to understand why Japanese creativity manifests itself in ways that reverberate today around the world—and what it tells us about how society is changing while remaining "Japanese." For that reverberation has happened before.

In the late nineteenth century, Japan's arts dazzled the West, provoking something pretty close to a revolution in everything from painting to architecture. But what fascinated artists like Monet and Van Gogh was not Japan's traditional high culture—it was the throwaway products of the floating world, the *ukiyo-e* (woodblock prints portraying the pleasure quarters) that, as we saw in chapter 2, were at least partly pornographic in origin and in any case were regarded by the Japanese elite as little better than trash. It was when the Japanese were entertaining *themselves* in Edo's Yoshiwara and Kyoto's Shimabara—two of the most famous of the licensed pleasure quarters—that they gave birth to the brilliant culture that would later mesmerize the world.

Similarly, it is not the mainstream products of the Japanese cultural establishment today that can be found everywhere, it is largely the stuff produced by people working at the margins of Japan's official "culture"— and doing it without any thought of appealing to *gaijin* ("foreigners"). At a time when Japanese cuisine enjoys a global cachet as the last word in exquisite, healthful refined dining and any self-respecting foodie anywhere can prattle on about the proper ratio of buckwheat to ordinary flour in *soba* noodles or the difference between tuna sushi made with *chutoro* and that with *ōtoro*, it is still quite common to encounter Japanese who assume that no foreigner could possibly like raw fish or use chopsticks. The guardians of traditional Japanese culture tend to want foreigners to sample Japanese culture in walled-off museums or as part of officially approved exchanges; they do not know how to react when Western children snap up representations of *ninja* and Pokémon or the gold standard for extreme pornographic drawings on the net is set by Japanese artists. Japan's business and bureaucratic establishment has not figured out how to commercialize much of this global surge of interest in contemporary Japanese culture—in and of itself, evidence that it is not under control.

One is tempted to trace the origins of much characteristically Japanese creativity to the Japanese tolerance for contradiction, for ambiguity. Aristotle instructed Westerners not to tolerate contradiction; no such command ever resonated through Japanese thought; as we noted in the discussion of the "Management of Reality" in chapter 5, social and economic success in Japan is often a function of an ability to live with and manage contradictions that would drive Westerners crazy. Japanese may experience discomfort in having to adapt themselves to the different—and mutually contradictory—"realities" of the type we have considered, but training since early childhood in reality management helps people cope with the psychological toll.

So do the arts. The contradictions that abound in Japanese society have long provided an inexhaustible resource for Japanese artists in all genres. Returning the favor as it were, the arts serve—along with alcohol—as *the* critical way of releasing the tension that living with contradictions brings with it.

Many of the best examples come from the treatment of that embodiment of postwar Japanese culture, the salaryman. At the same time that the entire apparatus of Japan's official cultural establishment—baseball, mainstream TV programs—was exalting the virtues that made for the successful salaryman, a rich stream of *manga* ("comics") and other subversive forms portrayed the salaryman as "weak, irresponsible, and interested only in sex—always unsuccessfully—and money." The salaryman was required not only to demonstrate a self-sacrificial enthusiasm for his company and his job, but—and this is the key point—*he was required to believe it* if the act was to be convincing; the Japanese word *makoto* conveys the psychic demands. *Makoto* is typically translated as "sincere," but the sincerity it implies is not the Western sense of guilt at putting on an act in which one does not really believe. Instead, the Japanese word suggests that one must force one's inner feelings into accordance with social expectations. The salaryman had to believe he was a soldier for a cause—his company—that was worth giving his life for. But he also had to live with the knowledge that he was ultimately a replaceable, exploited cog in a faceless, industrial machine. *Manga* helped him do that, as did songs like *Oyoge, Taiyaki-kun!* This runaway hit song of the mid-1970s, originally aimed at children, features the lament of popular small cakes (*Taiyaki* is the Japanese word for the cake; *kun* is the affectionate suffix used for boys and young men in place of the more formal *san*). The batter for these cakes is poured into identical molds in the shape of fish and one of the cakes holds the hopeless dream of swimming free (*Oyoge* means *Swim!*). The tune is both catchy and sad, a bit like the only Japanese pop song ever to make it to the top of the Western pop charts, *Ue o Muite Arukō* ("I'll look up when I walk") which for some inexplicable reason got labeled the *Sukiyaki Song* in the West; the original has nothing to do with food and describes a young jilted lover resolving to gaze at the stars while he walks lest his tears spill on the ground—an almost archetypical Japanese sentiment of putting on a brave front while crying inside. Similarly, the hero of *Oyoge, Taiyaki-kun!* knows there is no chance he can ever escape the mold into which he has been poured and swim free like a real fish, but he still dreams.

Jesus taught the moral equivalence of the thought and the act. This makes little sense in Japan. Westerners are often outraged to see Japanese men openly leafing through pornographic magazines, ogling pictures of naked women and reading *manga* ("comics") that feature the most bizarre and even violent forms of sexual perversion. But crime statistics suggest that the number of Japanese who actually engage in sexually abusive acts is no higher than elsewhere. Westerners who find themselves aroused by sexual thoughts that violate their conscious values tend to feel bad about it; it gives Western pornography its furtive, seedy quality. But for many Japanese, lustful thoughts are just harmless fantasy, one reason, perhaps, why Japanese erotica is so much more exuberant than its Western counter-parts—and, if the truth be told, of so much higher artistic quality.[1]

This kind of thing extends beyond erotica. The overt sentimentality of so much Japanese culture sticks in the Western craw; Westerners can usually swallow sentimentality today only when it is dressed up as camp or coated with irony. But Japanese tend to enjoy sentimentality for its own sake—going gaga over cute children, adorable pets, mawkish love stores, and tales of earnest youngsters struggling against all odds to achieve their dreams. Westerners know that such things are not the real world; that kids are brats, pets messy, and people use each other. The Japanese know that too, but they do not let it bother them much, or at least get in the way of a good cry.

---

1. Making soft core porn films was long the prototypical assignment for a budding film director; once he proved himself with these films, then he would be promoted to more "serious" sub-jects. The coming of the Internet has pretty much destroyed the commercial porn film trade in Japan, however.

Westerners whose only acquaintance with Japanese aesthetics might lie in the exquisite presentation of dishes in a Japanese restaurant or pictures of gardens and temples can be shocked when they arrive in Tokyo for the first time and encounter the sheer chaotic ugliness of much of Japan's urban landscape. How can such an aesthetically inclined people tolerate it? But in Japan there is a kind of unspoken agreement both to notice the ugliness and not notice it. Certain places and things—a garden, the entryway to a traditional restaurant—will be understood as "beautiful." They will indeed be beautiful in a meticulous and almost breathless way. One is not supposed to see the ugly, banal building that abuts the garden or the junky street outside the restaurant lined with electric poles and helter-skelter signs. But because one is also inescapably aware of these things, an artist can call attention to them in arresting ways that lead to a deliberate and delicious moment of disequilibrium, something entirely in keeping with the oldest traditions of Japanese art. It is that disequilibrium that gives Japanese cinema, animation, fashion, and video games a lurid, eye-popping quality that continues to astonish.

This may account for much of the global resonance of Japanese culture. Japan is hardly the only place any more where learning how to cope with contradiction is becoming increasingly essential to preserving a degree of sanity. But Japanese culture's fully realized nightmarish visions juxtaposed with open sentimentality gives it an appeal that quite obviously speaks to people around the world—particularly young people. It also shows us the degree to which the country has indeed been changing.

The Japanese themselves are acutely conscious of the subtle and not-so-subtle changes that have overtaken their country since the end of the immediate postwar period. As evidence one could point to the runaway popularity of the three-part film series *Always: San-chome no Yūhi* ("Always: Sunrise on Third Street"), the first installment of which swept Japan's equivalent of the Academy Awards in 2005. The films depict the intertwined lives of a group of ordinary people in the opening years of the economic miracle, symbolized first by the 1957–58 construction of Tokyo Tower in the background and, in the last of the three films, the coming of the 1964 Tokyo Olympics. Characteristically close attention is paid in these films to period dress and speech, and the first appearances of such symbols of postwar prosperity as refrigerators, television, and electric guitars. But the real subject matter of the films is less rising living standards as such than the social shifts they would bring in their wake.

Of course, as programs such as *Mad Men* or the endless flood of British period dramas demonstrate, the Japanese have no monopoly on fascination with the recent past. If anything distinguishes films like the *Always: San-chome no Yūhi* series from their American and British counterparts, it is less the extreme attention to period detail—the makers of *Mad Men* are just as meticulous about getting it right as Yamazaki Takashi, the director of the *Always* series—than the arguably greater nostalgia, the lack of irony, the sense that something important was irretrievably lost in the tide of modernity.

Mad Men may, as one writer suggested, invite viewers simultaneously to revel in the sexism it depicts while letting themselves off the hook with a notion that it isn't really true: that sexism has disappeared from our world. The *Always* series makes no such attempt to have it both ways; we are expected to understand that the affection and love the principals demonstrate for each other, depicted with characteristically unembarrassed sentimentality, is under deadly threat.

The Japanese have coined a whole vocabulary to cope with some of the most obvious changes of the last few decade; to get a grip on what has been happening, we might start with some of the most widespread neologisms.

THE *GYARU*

Gyaru, a stylized rendition of the English "gal," covers a whole collection of female personae that have emerged over the past two decades: *oyajigyaru, kogyaru, gangurogyaru, himegyaru, ogyaru, onēgyaru*. They may vary widely in styles—the *oyajigyaru*—literally, "old guy gal"—puts on a fake masculine act chugging down beers and using loud, masculine language; the *kogyaru* or "high school gal" hikes her school-uniform skirts up to her crotch and flaunts her fattish bare thighs with heavy, "loose" white socks draped below her knees; and the *gangurogyaru* sports a luridly artificial dark tan, bleached hair, and make-up that looks as if it had been laid on with a trowel. But what characterizes all the *gyaru*—the "gals"—is an in-your-face rejection of the traditional ways in which Japanese females were expected to present themselves.

In the classic paradigm, the Japanese female started life as a cute little girl in pigtails and white knee socks radiating an eager, chirpy cheeriness. Later, she was to hide her budding sexuality in the universal sailor-suit school uniform that with its long skirts, rolled ankle socks, and ample blouse seemed, in the manner of a *hijab* or nun's habit, deliberately designed to blur and suppress any overt signs of the schoolgirl as a sexual creature. No passion was expected of her other than perhaps an innocent crush on an older girl, and certainly she was supposed to respond to any sign of masculine interest with stuttering, blushing befuddlement. On reaching marriageable age, she was, in her kimono or the subdued elegance of a classic French-inspired dress, to convey desirability with soft-spoken, feminine language; meticulous, understated grooming; and an aura of exquisitely polite deference. As wife and mother, she was to be infinitely kind and accommodating, demonstrating with the way she acted and talked that her interests and comforts came well after those of husband, mother-in-law, and children. Finally, when she herself became a mother-in-law and grandmother, she was allowed a tiny bit of arrogance in the way she treated her daughter-in-law, but it was forgivable because, after all, she had the interests of her son and grandchildren at heart. She was expected to be the indulgent *obāchan* ("grandma") to her grandchildren and fuss over and humor her husband, who was now obviously of little use to anyone any more and increasingly unmanageable as he slipped into senility. But no one—least of all her—was to make this clear to him; she was indeed the lead conspirator in hiding from him any overt evidence of his obsolescence.

The various *gyaru* personnae and related phenomena dynamite every one of these stereotypes. The innocent cuteness of the classic little girl became *Rorīta fasshon* ("Lolita fashion," or young women dressed up as supposedly sexless little girls), while uniform skirts hiked up as far as they will go mocked the dowdiness of traditional school wear. Many—even in Japan—confused these fashions with sexual come-ons; when the super-short uniform skirts first appeared, the media worked itself up into a frenzy over *enjo-kōsai* (literally, "compensated dating"). A handful of schoolgirls were, to be sure, accepting money from older men to spend time with them—often sex was not involved; the girls just allowed themselves to be ogled and touched. But the extent of *enjo-kōsai* was grossly exaggerated; as usual, the hysteria said more about parental fear of new technologies (most *enjo-kōsai* was arranged via texting on cellphones) and misreading of coded youth language than it did any actual surge in free-lance prostitution among the young. Indeed a key motive behind the fashions is to provoke misreadings. Teenage girls in *Rorīta fasshon* and absurdly short skirts are not signaling their sexual availability to perverts; they are demonstrating that they have decoded the fear of their sexual power that lay behind the deliberate suppression of "underage" female sexuality in the traditional clothing marked out as suitable for girls.

Meanwhile, by assuming the garish make-up and deliberate sluttiness of the *ogyaru* ("dirty" gal) or *gangurogyaru* personae, their older sisters gave the Japanese equivalent of the raised third finger to received notions of how a woman is to present herself on reaching "marriageable" age. The *burikko* of the 1980s, mentioned in chapter 6, had already demonstrated a knowing scoffing at male expectations for female behavior, but the *gyaru* gave them a savage kick. On the streets or subways of Tokyo or Osaka—or in pubs or cafés—one encounters everywhere today packs of outrageously dressed young women known as *joshi-kai* (literally, "women's meeting," but implying complete liberation from male expectations) shrieking at each other in loud, deliberately vulgar language, forming a portrait that in every last detail is the opposite of traditional Japanese femininity—which, one suspects, is the whole point.

Of course, the *gyaru* personae are an exaggeration, a form of theater. Most *gyaru* do end up settling down. But again neologisms suggest that accommodation to "reality" is only partial. The *onēgyaru* (literally, "older sister gal") may dress in a slightly more subdued fashion than she once did, may get married, and even become a mother. But she retains elements of her *gyaru*-hood; as a mother she may adapt the *yanmama* (originally, "yankee" or "delinquent mother"; now, just young mother) style. Meanwhile, a woman who never married but stayed on as an OL (office lady) long past the mid-twenties when it was traditionally appropriate for an OL to leave the firm may become an *otsubone*. This term is lifted from Japanese history; in its original meaning, it referred to the senior women in the harems kept by the Tokugawa shoguns. The *otsubone* would often be more versed in the intrigues and factionalism at the shogunal court than even the most theoretically powerful of the Shogun's official advisers. Like her Edo period namesake, the modern *otsubune* knows where all the secrets in the firm are buried; she thus renders herself untouchable.

OBATARION, SODAI GOMI, AND "SILVER DIVORCE"

One of the more interesting of the neologisms—traceable back to the 1985 American parody zombie film *Return of the Living Dead* that was a bigger hit in Japan than in the United States—referred to "battalions" of women in late middle age (the film had been released in Japan under the name *Batarion*). Loud, brassy, and vulgar, they were said to descend in packs on chic stores, snapping up brand-name goods on sale, or they traveled in groups overseas with nary a man in sight and picked clean duty-free counters in airports. They bossed their husbands around with impunity, and, as with the various *gyaru* personnae adopted by their daughters, turned a socially sanctioned Japanese female archetype—this time that of the sweet, gentle *obachan* ("auntie")—on its head.

The counterpart of the *obatarion* is the *sodai-gomi*, literally big piece of junk, the term used in Japan for something like an old television or monitor that has to be thrown away but is too large to dispose of through ordinary trash-collecting. But in this case it refers to an older man who has retired and is hanging around the house in his wife's way. Just as special arrangements have to be made to get rid of a defunct washing machine, so there is no easy way to dispose of the retired *sodai-gomi*. The result is often a *jukunen rikon* ("middle-aged divorce") or "silver divorce" as it has come to be known, using the English words.

Most "silver divorce" is initiated by women. Divorce in Japan was historically rare; even when husband and wife could barely stand each other, they usually stayed together. Divorce could damn a man's career prospects and would often leave women penniless. But today, if a woman can hang on until her husband has gotten the lump-sum payment that a *sei-shain* ("permanent employee") receives on reaching retirement age, divorce can be financially feasible for her. She may not have much chance of finding a job, but Japanese courts will typically divide the divorced couple's total holdings in half.

The sharp rise in the divorce rate—it has essentially doubled since 1990—has given rise to a minor literature in Japan seeking to explain it, particularly since divorce rates have risen most dramatically among older people. Starring roles in this literature range from avaricious women ready to toss aside their husbands the moment they can no longer be milked for cash—implicit in the *sodai-gomi* term—to clueless men who ignored their wives for thirty years and now expect to be waited upon hand and foot. Many do blame wider social and economic factors: the HR practices of traditional Japanese companies that left no time for men to be husbands and fathers; the decline of the traditional role for Japanese women discussed in chapter 6 with nothing but an off-stage role in the salaryman's life to take its place; and the reduction in Japanese family size (the ideal family is now regularly depicted as one man, one woman, one boy, and one girl) that leaves the traditional housewife and mother little to do after the children are up in school and, as they say, several decades in which to do it.

"HERBIVORE" MALES

Sōshoku-kei danshi (literally, "males with herbivore tendencies") has gotten a lot of play in the Western press, since this neologism resonates with universal concerns over changes in the traditional male role—the "End of Men" as the American writer Hanna Rosin put it in discussing similar matters in the United States. For like their Western counterparts, many Japanese men are acting in ways that would have been unthinkable even one generation ago. It would not occur to a young Japanese father now that nuzzling his little daughter in public after she had scraped her knee might be shameful. His grandfather would not have done so; before the war, men were never seen in public in the first place in the company of their young children except during ritualized events such as weddings and funerals where even then it would have been completely up to mothers to tend to the children's behavior. Today, however, younger Japanese men are almost as openly affectionate with their girlfriends, wives, and children as their Western counterparts; teenage boys show little of the discomfort around girls that was once considered part of proper masculine behavior, and if Japanese young people do not manage quite the same indifference to gender that characterizes life in American college dormitories, groups of young Japanese of both sexes working and playing together is no longer thought particularly remarkable. Teenage boys now call each other by their given names—something unthinkable to the older generation—and even in the office, younger Japanese men display little of the unease that their fathers would have experienced in working with women as colleagues rather than as "office flowers" serving tea or making photocopies.

The herbivore label suggests, however, that we are dealing with something beyond palpably relaxed mores. Again, neologisms provide a clue. Like the *sodai-gomi* epithet applied to retired men, the flippant terms often used for younger men can border on open contempt. Many young Japanese women today refer to their boyfriends as *Kīppu Kun*. *Kīppu* is the English "keep" while *Kun* is, as noted above, the suffix used instead of the usual

San ("Mr./Ms.") when speaking to or about a boy.[2] The implication is that the boyfriend is kept around because he is useful in some material way to the woman, not because she has any deep feelings for him. Thus *Asshi Kun* (literally, "Young Master Legs") can be relied upon to provide transportation because he has a car, *Meisshi Kun* ("Young Master Food") will take her out to fancy restaurants, and *Mitsugu Kun* ("Young Master Presents") provides her with expensive baubles.

This kind of table-turning in which women now feel free to use the same kind of objectifying language about men that males traditionally used about women is a phenomenon that, of course, can be seen elsewhere in the developed world. But again, what is interesting here is the difference in the underlying assumptions about what has happened to men. In the reflexive misandry that pervades American popular culture today, males—at least straight males—are depicted as clueless losers; as insensitive, boorish louts. In Japan, they are more likely to be depicted as weak, as passive—herbivores at the mercy of *nikushoku onna* (literally, "carnivorous women").

A look at the hit television program *Ore wa Abare Hatchaku* that which ran in the 1979 and 1980 seasons can tell us something about the shifts in Japan since then in expectations for males. The title of the program is almost untranslatable; it suggests a kid who has so much energy and exuberance he cannot be controlled. The show centered on the adventures of an 11-year-old boy and his relationships with his older sister, parents, teacher, best friend, rival, and the classmate of a girl for whom he carried a not-so-secret affection. The actor who played the boy's father died in 2011, provoking a wave of nostalgia for a program that once loomed as large in the Japanese popular imagination as *Leave it to Beaver* or *Dennis the Menace* did in the American.

The central character, Chotaro, is a paradigmatic example of the traditional Japanese ideal of budding masculinity. A macho little number, he wears super-short denim shorts, no matter how cold the weather. The only way he can express emotion is to get into fist-fights and land in one or another scrape. He is no good at schoolwork, but his serious-minded, decent teacher cannot help but like him. His sister, with pretensions of being a proper young lady, thinks he is an insufferable brat, but his good-hearted mother knows how to put up with him. His father wanted to be a carpenter and it is clear that is where his real vocation lies, but to make a

---

2. Men will also use the suffix when speaking to or about other men no matter what their age if the men are their subordinates or were their childhood friends.

respectable living, the man has been forced to take a job in a suburban department store where he sells do-it-yourself home carpentry kits, and—significantly for any discussion of masculinity—spends his days kowtowing to customers and a supercilious boss. *Otōsan* ("Dad") usually ends up letting off steam in the only socially acceptable way—by blowing up at his son's escapades—but the two always make up for they are in essence older and younger versions of each other, and the father's example suggests in a not-so-subtle way what will happen to Chotaro when he grows up and his boyish energy and enthusiasm are tamed and broken by social and economic reality.

For the time being, however, Chotaro's only real vulnerability is his innocent passion for his classmate Hitomi-chan.[3] He does not know how to articulate this passion. She finds him trying and tends to prefer his rival, the suave, mannered Masahiro, who is the son of Chotaro's father's boss. But when confronted by real danger or a genuine ethical conundrum, Chotaro usually proves himself the better boy. Hitomi-chan understands this at some level, despite her irritation at Chotaro's blunt and clumsy ways.

In everything that traditionally mattered in Japan, Chotaro is what a boy should be. As the very title of the show indicates, he overflows with hyper-boyish energy. He is good-looking, but in an all-boy, masculine way that contrasts with the pretty-boy looks of his rival Masahiro. He may not be articulate or good at academics, but his heart is in the right place. He is a true and loyal friend and he senses what other people are feeling, even if he sometimes does not know what to do about it.

The type of persona Chotaro represented has not exactly disappeared in Japan, but when encountered today in the media is likely to be represented as a nostalgic throwback. (Both the leading man and his son in the *Always* films are good examples.) Chotaro may have won the battles with his rival on the TV show, but the Masahiros of the world won the war and got the Hitomis. Androgynous, pretty-boy looks and a suave, mannered sensibility are seen everywhere as the standard to which boys and young men are expected to aspire, particularly if they hope to attract women.

One is tempted to conclude that women now determine how Japanese men should act and present themselves. But this is too simplistic. In some

3. When speaking to or of young girls, the suffix "chan" is used rather than "san." "Chan" is also sometimes informally used by family members of either sex when talking to each other—thus *otōchan* ("Daddy")—and by women when talking to or of close childhood female friends.

fundamental sense, males preen and females choose not only in all cultures and all eras, but throughout the entire animal kingdom. The androgynous dandy is a type that goes as far back into Japanese history as the Heian aristocracy where skill with the brush and poetic sensibility meant a great deal more than martial, masculine accomplishments. During the Edo period, as we have seen, the *onnagata* (Kabuki actors specializing in female roles) were the great trendsetters of fashion and the arts while the *bishōnen* ("beautiful boy") was depicted in ways that made it impossible to tell him from his female counterpart unless the genitals were exposed (as they were in *shunga*—erotic prints). The *bishōnen* as a sexual persona persisted into the modern world, and while his gender became obvious after Meiji, he was still willowy and sensitive. To be sure, a pederastic strain was long visible in Japanese culture, but the *bishōnen* type is one that today usually excites— and is cultivated for—females. One can cite as evidence the contemporary passion for *yaoi* or *boizu rabu* ("Boys' Love")—tales of homoerotic affairs among impossibly beautiful youths, produced by and for women—or the stadiums full of girls screaming at the products of Johnny's Jimusho, the talent agency that has for two generations now brought forth an unending stream of pretty boys to prance about on stage and absorb vicariously female adolescent sexual energy.

The historical and artistic record thus makes it abundantly clear that Japanese women have long held the cultured, sensitive aesthete as a kind of ideal masculine type (i.e., this is not some phenomenon that cropped up in the last twenty years). But in the past, economic and social reality inevitably intervened. Until recent decades, women rarely chose their own husbands; even when they did, what was most important was a young man's prospects for obtaining an economically stable position in society, because that was the only way *she* could look forward to a decent life. For most of the postwar period, that meant his acceptability to powerful economic organizations—corporations/bureaucracies—defined, as we have seen, by his educational background, his drive, and the absence of any scandal or character trait that would prevent him from fitting in to Japanese organizational life. If he had handsome features and a passion for modern jazz or the symphonies of Anton Bruckner, that was nice, but he was not going to have the time to cultivate such outside interests in any case.

Today, many Japanese women no longer need men to achieve either economic independence or the only social status that matters to many of them—their standing among women like themselves. They now enjoy the freedom to apply sexual and romantic criteria as well as economic to their choice of mate. This is pretty much true in every developed country—men everywhere are confronting more demanding women; just being a "good provider" no longer cuts it anywhere in the developed world.

But something possibly peculiar to Japan has also changed in the last generation—the generation since *Ore wa Abare Hatchaku* captured the hearts of the TV viewing public. It is as much the breakdown of the traditional means by which the Japanese male attained emotional fulfillment and achieved self-respect as a man as it is any unique ability by newly empowered Japanese women to demand something their Western sisters are not also asking of potential husbands and boyfriends.

MASCULINE IDENTITY IN JAPAN

Japanese culture and society has long been permeated with the homosocial, particularly among males. Japanese males have for centuries now relied on other males to whom they were not related by blood to forge bonds that were both crucial to achieving emotional intimacy and to economic/political alliances. Of course, family blood-ties and heterosexual pair bonding have always been there as well—no society could survive without them. But what strikes the observer is how relatively more central the male bond was in Japan than in, say, traditional Chinese society where family blood-ties trumped all, or in the West where at least since the introduction of Christianity, erotically grounded heterosexual pairing has enjoyed pride of place as the supreme human relationship. In premodern Japan, loyalty to lord and male group invariably took precedence over family ties, not to mention erotic infatuations. In the immediate postwar decades, it is only a slight exaggeration to say that American and Japanese males viewed home vs. school or workplace in precisely opposite ways. To the American "man in the gray flannel suit," the office was where he had to go and the relationships he forged there were largely impersonal alliances of necessity; it was at home where he relaxed and became himself. To the Japanese salaryman, real intimacy was often to be found more in the company of workmates and old school friends—*nakama*—than in a home that often served as little more than a refueling stop.

It is a mistake to see the Japanese male group through a primarily erotic lens. To be sure, even as late as a century ago, homoerotic feelings were associated with more masculine youths while early interest in females was thought unhealthy and debilitating.[4] But already by the mid-Edo period, the "honorable" pederasty (*shudō*) associated with the samurai class was fading, and with the coming of Meiji and its laws against homosexual activity drawn up in response to Western models, it had disappeared altogether.

The male group was not where the Japanese male went for erotic fulfillment; it is where he went for emotional intimacy. The only real competition when it came to a relaxed, accepting environment where he could be "himself" lay in his childhood relationship with his mother.[5] Fathers, teachers, and other authority figures were distant and demanding, while females other than mothers and, occasionally, older sisters, were sources of anxiety. "Nice" girls were unavailable while courtship and marriage was an ordeal one had to get through to fulfill social expectations (courtship in any case being seen to by parents and other older people in authority). Sexual release was available, to be sure, from prostitutes, but paying for sex was hardly conducive to relaxed emotional intimacy. Being human beings, Japanese men found themselves sometimes swept up into passionate love, but historically, as we noted in chapter 2, any eruption of erotic passion was usually treated as a disruptive tragedy.

Of course, marriages often worked out in even a Western sense, providing a man with intimacy and companionship throughout his life. But for many millions of Japanese men, their most important *emotional* relationships were with their *nakama*, their buddies. And it was invariably men in Japan who determined the circumstances under which boys became men, who set the criteria for adult masculine identity, and decided who had met those criteria and who had not.

Again, there is nothing particularly unique about much of this. In almost every traditional society known to us, boys left the female-dominated realm of the home—or were forcibly removed therefrom—and spent some

---

4. This was largely true in the United States as well, although the homoeroticism was less explicit than in Japan. According to Jeffrey P. Dennis's *We Boys Together: Teenagers in Love before Girl-Craziness*, a study of American popular culture before the Second World War, boys were expected emotionally—if not sexually—to be attracted to each other; precocious interest in girls was seen as threat to masculine development.

5. The traditional intimacy between mother and son in Japan is something that would have been seen as unhealthy, at least in northern Europe and the United States, if not in Mediterranean countries. Japanese boys as old as 6 had access to their mother's breasts and often slept in the same bedding with their mothers throughout childhood.

years in all-male environments, whether those be schools, workshops, hunter/warrior groups, or budding priesthoods. They returned to the female realm as husbands and fathers only after they had been certified as men by other men. This male life-journey is not only well-nigh universal among all human societies outside the modern developed world, it is even visible among other primates and other highly evolved social mammals such as elephants.

As with so much else that we have looked at in this book, what sets the Japanese experience apart from other countries is in part a matter of degree, not of a fundamental qualitative difference. Male groups have played critical social and political roles in almost all societies, but they were disproportionately dominant in Japan. The forces that now buffet the male group—the political and social empowerment of women; new economic realities that favor feminine virtues of empathy and emotional intelligence over male competitiveness, hierarchy, and brawn—are by no means limited to Japan. But the consequences threaten to be more devastating for Japanese men and to play themselves out in different ways from what we see in the West.

CHANGING JAPANESE MALE GROUP DYNAMICS

The unrestrained male group dynamics that played such a key role in both the tactical brilliance and strategic disaster of the war years[6] were redeployed in the immediate postwar years in the service of economic growth. For a generation, Japanese corporations were successful in passing off to Japanese young men a kind of ersatz version of the intimacy and heroism of "bands of brothers" that had characterized the emotional lives of their fathers at the front. Many observers noted the quasi-military aura of the Japanese corporation during the "miracle" years—the instantly visible hierarchy, the stress on sacrifice, on *gaman* ("endurance" or "perseverance"). Japanese HR managers quite deliberately exploited male group dynamics in order to build *esprit de corps* and spur their corporate troops into fever pitches of work and sacrifice. Young corporate recruits typically

---

6. An important new paper suggests that much of the tactical superiority of the Japanese soldier during the Second World War lay not in his "fanaticism" as Western propaganda of the time had it, but rather the "primary group tie or bonding experience that promoted unit cohesion."

spent the first years of their working lives in all-male dormitories; they not only worked together, they played together and lived together—they even, as the packs of young salarymen descending on the *soaplands* and pink cabarets of Shinjuku and Osaka's Namba might suggest, had sex—not with each other, but "together."

In other words, they lived, acted, and thought like soldiers—and that was intentional, to elicit the kind of dedication and spirit that will lead young men to fight and die with and for each other. But there was, of course, one crucial difference. The Japanese salaryman was being asked to give his life not for defense of his home, for his country, for his buddies, or to protect his mother and sisters, but to make and sell more stuff.

In the early decades of the postwar period, this was a sufficiently important goal that the culture could plausibly make psychologically convincing demands on the young businessman that he demonstrate the mentality of a soldier prepared to offer the ultimate sacrifice. The postwar settlement discussed in chapter 4 had left the making and selling of stuff as the only path open for Japan to recover a measure of national greatness. On an individual basis, being a good corporate soldier enabled a young Japanese male to attain both social and self-respect as a man, to be admired by his fellows, and to achieve *entrée* into what had taken the place of the military as Japan's pre-eminent male group. The rewards for membership included not only stable income and status but also emotional intimacy and socially sanctioned sexual release—first, perhaps through the "water trade" ("entertainment" expenses could be and often were written off through corporate expense accounts), and then through marriage.

Today, the culture already treats the salaryman in ways that border on open contempt; fashionable young women refer to the salaryman as *oyaji* ("old guy"). The men who are admired today are not salarymen, but entrepreneurs, designers, the *aidoru* ("idols") churned out by Johnny's Jimusho, and self-made sports stars such as Ichiro, the soccer player Nakata Hidetoshi, and the young golf sensation Ishikawa Ryo.

A fundamental disconnect exists, however, between what the culture portrays as desirable on the one hand, and actual opportunities on the other. A parallel could be drawn with the gap between the message professional sports in the United States beams at young black males and the reality of the choices they face. Few young Japanese men are going to make it as entrepreneurs in a business world that still fundamentally distrusts the type, the good jobs available to designers and graphic artists form a tiny fraction of the numbers who aspire to success in such professions, and the athletic talents of an Ichiro or the sultry looks of the boy *aidoru* pop stars stamped out by Johnny's are not, to put it gently, evenly distributed among Japan's male population.

The old apotheosization of salaryman virtues by managers of reality such as the Yomiuri machine and its baseball team noted in chapter 6 at least had the virtue of guiding Japanese boys and young men onto paths that could lead to plausible outcomes. But as noted in the preceding chapter, the economic traumas of the last two decades have made it much harder for young men to grab the stable positions in corporate and government bureaucracies that still constitute the only sure paths to social status and security in Japan.

The result, among other things, is waves of sexual and social anxiety and a concomitant withdrawal of millions of young Japanese men from engagement with each other or with the opposite sex. Again, neologisms provide a clue. The most famous is *otaku*, a term that like *sushi* or *sayonara* is now pretty much recognized everywhere. But while abroad the word has acquired the sense of someone with a fanatical interest in Japanese pop culture—*anime/manga*—in Japan *otaku* suggests a person (probably a young man) with an obsession so all-consuming that he has given up contact with real humans. The obsession is usually related to technology or pop culture, but it does not have to be. The key to the *otaku* is not the target of the obsession itself but the way it trumps everything else in life.

Other terms are darker. *Moe*, derived from the word for "bud," refers to men who make no attempt to establish relationships with actual females; instead they worship fictional characters, usually fantasy projections of very young girls. *Hikikomori* (literally, "pull-in and retire") is the label applied to the young men who never leave their bedrooms. An obvious overlap exists with *otaku*—one can be both—but the *hikikomori* need not necessarily have an obsession; he just has to loathe and fear the world of obligations and expectations to the point that he withdraws from it. One cannot, of course, be a *hikikomori* unless one has a mother who is prepared to provide food and lives in a house with the necessary bedroom.

The term suggests the underlying problem: unwillingness to grow up, to become a man. Complaints about Peter Pans who will not accept adult responsibilities and commitments have been heard everywhere since the dawn of time. But in the Britain of Evelyn Waugh or the United States of

F. Scott Fitzgerald, life as an eternal boy free of responsibilities and commitments was only possible for upper class males; the alternative was destitution. But no one starves in Japan, the United States, or Britain now.

In the latter two countries, the young men drifting from dead-end job to dead-end job while their sisters swell the ranks of single working mothers are found primarily in the lower-middle and working classes. But Japan's *otaku* and *hikikomori* come mostly from the upper middle class.

The passivity and withdrawal conveyed by these labels would seem the flip side of the various newly defiant female personae we looked at above. But a facile juxtaposition of "herbivore" males and "carnivorous" females fails to consider the crucial element of class. The typical *hikikomori* probably grew up in a financially comfortable household; it is likely that as a child he barely saw his father, a man who had climbed through the hierarchy of a large Japanese corporate or public sector bureaucracy and was almost never at home. His mother had put all her energies into getting the boy into a good school and catering to his every need. Meanwhile, the *gangurogyaru* (the heavily made-up "gal" with the lurid tan) probably had a mother who was out of the house all day working as something like a shop attendant while her father drove a taxi or held down a job as a manual laborer in one of the myriad of small, family-owned companies that served as the subcontracting baseboard of the Japanese industrial machine.

In other words, the *hikikomori* and the *gangurogyaru* are not brother and sister, in either a literal or symbolic sense. And while the economic and social forces that gave rise to both of them may be comparable to those that produced the football lout in Britain or the single American mother who finds men "useless," they do not occupy the same relative positions in society.

THE RE-EMERGENCE OF CLASS

A generation ago, the Japanese saw themselves as overwhelmingly middle class—indeed, as effectively classless. For a society in which hierarchy is woven into every aspect of life up to and including the language itself, this was remarkable. Of course, it was never literally true. Even in the 1950s, no one could possibly have confused a mandarin high up in the ranks of the Ministry of Finance or the Industrial Bank of Japan with a farmer or laborer in the *shita-machi* (Tokyo's traditional working-class neighborhoods).

But the Second World War had effectively wiped out Japan's store of wealth. Occupation reforms abolished all inherited titles save for those of the Imperial Family itself, expropriated rural landlords of their hold-ings, and stripped the *zaibatsu* families of their ownership of Japan's most famous companies. From a strictly economic point of view, Japan in the immediate postwar years had indeed become a largely single-class soci-ety—a very poor one. The rapid economic growth of the postwar years did, in the following decades, lift pretty much all boats while the com-pensation practices of established corporations prevented anything like the emergence of an American-type class of obscenely rich bankers and CEOs lording it over the rest of society from the commanding heights of the economy. Most of the Japanese who got filthy rich during the "miracle" years were real estate brokers or owners of construction companies; they enjoyed local influence and were often linked to the Liberal Democratic Party, but in comparison to the University-of-Tokyo-bred upper ranks of the bureaucracy, the major banks and established corporations, they were seen as *arriviste* vulgarians with little real status. Many of the most influ-ential people in Japan—CEOs, bankers, senior bureaucrats, not to mention university professors or editors of the major newspapers—were quite mod-estly paid. But what contributed to the illusion of a largely middle-class society was less the relatively egalitarian distribution of money than the spread of salaryman culture, the coming of television, and the largely suc-cessful efforts of the great media empires such as Yomiuri and Dentsu to use the new medium to insure that most Japanese internalized salaryman norms.

Writers such as Mickey Kaus and Michael Lind have noted something similar in the United States. Even though the United States emerged from the Second World War wealthier than it had ever been before, Americans in the 1950s (at least white Americans) watched the same television pro-grams, ate the same foods, and had largely similar notions of what was right and wrong. Today, however, the gaps between classes are so wide and so obvious that all one has to do is order a microbrew or a Bud Light or switch on a television set to Fox News, on the one hand, or PBS, on the other, to broadcast one's class.

Class division and class hatred in the United States are now, to be sure, far more visible and pronounced than in Japan; there is no figure in Japan quite comparable to a Rush Limbaugh or Glenn Beck spewing vitriol at learning and the manners and lifestyles of the educated. Nor can one find anything like the disdain for the mores of lower class males that oozes from elite organs of American opinion. But in both countries, one encounters bewilderment and anguish at the disappearance of what seemed in living memory to be if not exactly a classless society, then a society in which most everyone pulled together, where most everyone shared the same tastes and aspirations. Again, neologisms provide a clue—two of the most widely used are *kachigumi* ("winner's group") and *makegumi* ("loser's group"). A generation ago, such terms would have been, if not exactly nonsensical, then largely meaningless. But in today's *kakusa shakai* ("differentiated society"), everyone feels their force. That both the United States and Japan could start from such different points economically yet follow a similar conceptual trajectory with respect to class underscores the contention that far more is involved than money.

In most places and most times, the lower classes are disciplined by the threat of destitution. Adam Smith famously noted that "a single week's. . . dissipation (can) undo a poor workingman forever." But dissipation is now possible for everyone in affluent societies such as the United States and Japan.

The result, in the United States at least, has been a neat reversal of Smith's disquisition on the existence of two systems of morality in most societies: a "loose system. . . adopted by what are called the people of fashion" characterized by "the pursuit of pleasure to some degree of intemperance" and an "austere system. . . admired and revered by the common people" in which excesses are "abhorred" and "detested." Today in the United States it is members of the upper–middle and upper classes who work hard, stay married, and lead lives that in practice are temperate and sober. It is no longer the rich man's son who wastes his substance on riotous living, it is the lower–class male. As the economy shifts away from jobs demanding male brawn and competitiveness to those favoring female empathy and diligence, as the schools come under the control of women flustered by the boisterousness of boys, young American and British lower–class males leave school early, shirk any commitment to job or family, and derive what solace they can in pursuits both the wider culture and the women they might hope to attract hold in contempt. In the meantime, both economic and biological forces have pulled these women into the workforce where concern for their children makes them relatively docile, industrious workers, increasingly unwilling to become involved with a man who does not pull his weight, who is just one more mouth to feed and a big obstreperous one at that.

If the great danger of today's bifurcated societies in the United States and Britain is a lumpenproletariat of males on the one hand, and an exploited group of poor single women on the other—with elites increasingly blind to the plight of both—in Japan the dangers are different. Japan displays little of the lower–class male loutishness that is now par for the course in the United States and Britain. To be sure, a handful of youngsters—*chinpira* as they are known—drop out of school, strut about in obnoxious clothing, drift into motorcycle gangs, and may, unless they are rescued by some battle-scarred older male authority figure (Japanese TV dramas are filled with such tales), end up in the *yakuza*, in prison, or both. But the numbers are tiny. The overwhelming majority of young Japanese men, especially those from modest circumstances, are respectful, hard-working, polite, and with a keen sense of duty—to themselves, their families, their friends, their organizations, and the wider society. It is perhaps the key reason why Japan is such a pleasant place to visit and live and why the place has had a mind-boggling effect on generations of foreigners: because ordinary Japanese people take their responsibilities seriously. They manage the art of being deferential without being obsequious; of conveying self-respect at the same time they display empathy and an eagerness to be as helpful as they can.

This was historically just as true, if not more so, of Japanese women as of men, and, unlike their male counterparts, at all levels of society (Japanese upper–class men can often come across as self-important martinets). The exquisite mix of deference and concern for others that Japanese women were traditionally socialized to project—something that characterized Japanese women from the lowliest chambermaids and prostitutes right up to the very top of the upper crust—helps explain why Japan has had such a seductive as well as a mind-boggling effect on a century and a half of Western males. But the emergence of what in another era would have been called "attitude" among younger lower–class Japanese girls while their upper–class sisters refuse to play the dutiful wife and self-sacrificial mother roles long carved out for them suggests something fundamental to Japanese culture is indeed shifting.

Many would say "it's about time!" We already noted in chapter 6 that the postwar settlement had stripped women of much of their historical support networks without offering any substantive compensation in the form of either autonomy or closer marriages-of-equals along Western lines; even when husbands wanted it, salaryman practices intervened to smother the quality of most such marriages in their cribs. One can, under the circumstances, hardly blame Japanese women for collectively saying they have had enough.

But it creates ticklish challenges. One of Japan's greatest strengths is its social cohesion: the near-universal sense of solidarity, of mutual trust, of responsibility. It is difficult to see how these can survive unscathed if ordinary Japanese males are no longer raised by warm, loving mothers and cannot look forward as a matter of course to marriage and family. The male group will survive; when marriage and family collapse, the male group re-emerges as the pre-eminent social organization. But the male group could possibly turn feral, as it has in much of the West.[7] So far, the various *gyaru* ("gal") personae and the increasingly open misandry of so much Japanese society remains a matter of theater—of poses, fashions, slang. One wonders how long that will be true.

Bright, well-turned-out Japanese women from "good" homes today are getting themselves educated and making it clear that like their Western sisters, they expect to take what they view as their rightful positions in Japan's leadership class—and that does not mean any more serving as mothers to the next generation of elite sons. But they are not yet really integrated into the power structures of core Japanese institutions, as they increasingly are in the West. One can today, to be sure, find women in positions of real responsibility in major corporations, universities, the bureaucracy, and the media. But their numbers are still small.

The result is possibly the worst of both worlds. Japan may be losing the services of history's most devoted wives and mothers without reaping the benefits of an influx of capable, competent educated women into the governing ranks of society's most important institutions. Japan could conceivably be left with what the enemies of feminism have long warned would be the consequences of a society-wide displacement of males: enervated, emasculated upper-class males together with feral male loutishness at the lower levels. But Japan has manifestly failed to reap the social benefits that feminism's advocates have predicted from the full empowerment of women: institutions informed by inclusiveness and empathy with a sense of mission that transcends mere survival and competitive jostling for position.

---

7. A visit to the trading floor of a Wall Street firm will quickly disabuse anyone of the notion that the feral male group can be found only in the ranks of lower-class males.

Feral male loutishness is—so far—largely confined in Japan to the realms of fantasy and to boys' nights out in heavily policed entertainment districts such as Tokyo's Kabukicho. But the country's leadership class not only appears both enervated and emasculated, it shows no sign of getting ready to incorporate inclusiveness, empathy, or anything resembling a sense of mission that goes beyond the sullen, aggrieved nationalism that, as we will see in the final chapter of this book, increasingly hampers Tokyo's attempts to construct healthy, durable foreign relations.

THE DECLINE OF JAPAN'S LEADERSHIP CLASS

Whatever blame rests on shifting gender roles for the failures of Japan's leadership class—and whining about them without policy response is itself indicative of leadership failure, since there is no going back to the "good wife, wise mother" of the prewar era—leadership in Japan is in visible decline. There is no comparison between Japan's political leaders today and men such as Yoshida Shigeru, Ishibashi Tanzan, and Ikeda Hayato who led Japan out of the devastation of the immediate postwar years. Even a morally compromised figure like Kishi Nobusuke, whom we have met several times (munitions minister in the Tojo cabinet and, after the war, the prime minister who rammed through the Diet the legal basis of Japan's subordination to the United States) radiated qualities of intelligence, competence, and worldliness that his grandson Abe Shinzo, the current prime minister, palpably lacks. That one could make similar comparisons between Nicolas Sarkozy and Charles de Gaulle, or George W. Bush and Dwight D. Eisenhower does not make the problem any less severe for Japan. Particularly because the leadership problem is not confined to politics; one can, as we noted in the previous chapter, find Japanese entrepreneurs and executives today with the guts and vision of Honda Soiichiro, Morita Akio, Ohga Norio, Matsushita Konosuke, Inayama Yoshihiro, and Inamori Kazuo. But they are no longer running Japan's great industrial companies. Meanwhile, the contrast between the senior bureaucrats in MITI and MOF in the immediate postwar decades—forced to rebuild a ruined economy with little but their wits to fall back on—and their cautious, demoralized successors today is obvious.

The events that began March 11, 2011, with the destruction of the Fukushima Dai-Ichi nuclear plant exposed the rot at the heart of Japan's leadership class for all the world to see. Great disasters cast searing—if temporary—stabs of light on political arrangements that have been corrupted. Like swarms of cockroaches rushing for cover when the switch is turned on in a filthy apartment, those grown fat feeding on the public interest flee in panic when catastrophes such as Chernobyl, Hurricane Katrina, and the financial collapse of 2008 expose collusion, malfeasance, and sheer incompetence to public view.

So it was with Fukushima. As everyone knows, the events began with a horrific earthquake and the tsunami it unleashed. The tsunami may have destroyed everything in its path, including the nuclear power plant, but it was not unprecedented. There had been an even greater one a thousand years ago along the same coast. But not only had Tokyo Electric Power ("TEPCO") failed to guard against risk factors of one in a thousand, something that given the consequences of nuclear meltdown can reasonably be demanded of those who would build and operate such facilities, it turns out that the first of the towers at the plant was wrecked not by the tsunami but by the earthquake itself. One can eliminate the danger of tsunamis by removing oneself from the coast, but in Japan, there is no getting away from earthquakes.

In the weeks after the disaster, it became evident that in opting to rely so heavily on nuclear power, Japan had made a pact with the devil. TEPCO's senior management all but disintegrated; despite the distortions, prevarications, and outright lies being disseminated at the time by the government through its mouthpieces in the establishment media, Tokyo itself had been at risk. A Chernobyl-type cloud of poisoned gas could easily have forced the evacuation of 30 million people, something that would have meant the end of the modern Japanese state.

There are two versions of what happened. In one, after being told that TEPCO might abandon the plant altogether, the then-prime minister, Kan Naoto, commandeered a helicopter, flew up to Fukushima, and demanded that TEPCO do what was necessary, even though that might involve sacrificing the lives of some of its managers and workers. In the other version, Kan's intervention made worse a situation that was beginning to come under control. One does not know which version to believe, although the first is more credible. Kan had good reason to distrust companies like TEPCO and its protectors and facilitators in the bureaucracy. Kan had first come to national prominence when serving as Health and Welfare Minister in a coalition government sixteen years earlier. He discovered that bureaucrats in his ministry were allowing some Japanese pharmaceutical companies to sell blood derivatives that they had already been informed by the American FDA were infected with the HIV virus. As a result, scores of Japanese hemophiliacs came down with AIDS. Kan had been discouraged from making the scandal public; in official Japan, the reputation of a ministry and the well-being of its clients in industry are usually more important than the lives of ordinary people. But Kan went ahead anyway.

The dynamics of 3/11 were similar, even if the scale of the catastrophe was incomparably larger. General Electric, the original designer of the plant, had warned TEPCO of serious flaws that needed to be remedied, warnings that were ignored. To act on those warnings would have been to admit that nuclear power plants could be risky; it would contradict the message that the "nuclear village" of TEPCO and its apologists in academia, politics, and the bureaucracy had promulgated: that nuclear power was a clean, risk-free technology. To undertake repairs to a functioning plant or to move backup power equipment out of the reach of a tsunami higher than the seawall that had been erected to protect the plant was to admit that, after all, risk had not been eliminated. One is reminded of Japanese banks operating without capital set aside for loan losses. To assume that a certain percentage of loans will go bad is to acknowledge that certain lending decisions might have been flawed.

Japan's is, alas, far from the only case of a leadership class that has become so self-serving and so in thrall to its own propaganda that it risks destroying the country it leads. One need only point to the British high command in the First World War repeatedly throwing the flower of British manhood into the maw of German machine guns, the Soviet *nomenklatura* under Brezhnev, or today's MBA-minted American predator class blowing up the world economy.

But for one final time in this chapter—if not for the last time in this book—what draws our attention is what is peculiar to Japan: in this case, the particular ways in which the Japanese leadership class has become so incompetent and so dangerous. We noted in the previous chapter the difficulties Japanese businesses have in writing off sunk costs, but the problem goes beyond business and beyond money. Japanese institutions have unusual trouble acknowledging and facing up to strategic error. *Individuals* can be blamed and even sacrificed; the world is familiar with the ritual apologies and resignations of the titular leaders of Japanese institutions who have, for one reason or another, gotten entangled in scandals. While many of these exercises are just for show—the people involved being compensated behind the scenes and returning to power once the storm blows over—countless individual Japanese do display an admirable willingness to accept responsibility for mistakes and worse; there is nothing in Japan like the contemptible refusal of so many Americans to step up and admit they were wrong, hiding behind their lawyers to avoid accepting responsibility for a mess that is of their making. But on an *institutional* level in Japan, inability to admit error, to undertake drastic changes of course unless forced to, is something that can be seen not just in the examples from Japanese business that we considered in the previous chapter. It is also visible in everything from the behavior of the Japanese Imperial Army in the Second World War down through the near-impossibility of killing off any public works project that has been formally approved, even if overwhelming evidence surfaces of ruinous cost overruns and horrific collateral damage. Like zombies or vampires, such projects keep rising from the dead—because after all they were signed off on by a powerful ministry or its client and to kill the project once and for all would mean admitting that *the ministry had made a mistake.*

This kind of inability to confess error is probably rooted in the quasi-sacred aura that surrounds institutional arrangements in Japan. We noted in chapter 2 the deliberate efforts by the Tokugawa Shogunate to place the Japanese institutional order beyond questioning, something not simply decreed by a sacred essence (e.g., the divine right of kings) but a manifestation of the sacred itself. As we have seen, this sense of institutional sacredness not only survived the collapse of the Shogunate but was strengthened by the Meiji government in its construction of a nationalism thought essential to rally the Japanese population to the efforts necessary to survive as an independent nation in the Hobbesian global order of the late nineteenth century.

The emperor's formal admission in 1945 that he was not, after all, divine, and a postwar constitution that implanted into the Japanese body politic such notions as the rule of law and the sovereignty of the people tarnished the sacred aura that had, before then, radiated from the core institutions of the Japanese power structure. But the aura had not been eliminated. The decision some forty years ago to embark on an ambitious program of nuclearization is a case in point. Nuclear energy plants can only be run by large, centralized organizations that inevitably by their nature accumulate technical, financial, and political power, making these plants instantly appealing to Japanese bureaucracies that thrive on amassing and hoarding such power.[8] Furthermore, nuclear power held out the prospect of realizing the dream that had tantalized Japan's leadership class since the waning days of the Shogunate: loosening reliance on capricious foreigners. Thus, Japan's largest utilities, backed and supported by a phalanx of elite bureaucrats at MITI and the Ministry of Construction, powerful politicians such as former Prime Minister Nakasone Yasuhiro, and local LDP leaders bewitched by the prospect of an unending stream of lucrative patronage contracts, made the fateful decision to erect scores of nuclear power plants in the world's most seismically unstable country. Eminent "experts" in the scientific and academic communities gave them cover while the Japanese establishment media trumpeted the message that in the hands of skilled, conscientious Japanese engineers, nuclear power was a completely safe technology offering untold benefits to Japan. (The Yomiuri empire was particularly assiduous in spreading this message.) Once the decision had been made, there was no going back—either because of the huge sunk costs or, even more to the point, because there was no institutional means to reverse a decision of that magnitude. To do so would be to acknowledge fundamental error on the part of institutions that are not supposed to be capable of it.

But the effects of exposure to radiation cannot be altered by whatever the Yomiuri newspapers choose to disclose—or not—about the influence-buying of the nuclear village. What *can* be concealed is how widespread that exposure might be. In the days after 3/11, the airways were filled with government spokesmen and paid apologists for the nuclear village urging calm and downplaying risk while more critical voices were deliberately marginalized. This kind of cover-up can, for a while, work with radiation poisoning—as opposed to, say, faulty levees—since the poisoning is invisible and only manifests itself years later. But the cover-up did not really work. When some foreign countries began advising their nationals to leave not just the area around the plant but Tokyo itself, even ordinary people who usually paid little attention to such matters realized they were being lied to.

---

8. It is no surprise that the one major developed country even more reliant on nuclear power than Japan is *dirigiste* France.

People began making comparisons with the waning days of the Second World War. The newspapers of those times continued to be filled with accounts of glorious Japanese victories despite the American bombers filling the skies at night and the mounting numbers of wounded and dead young men. Some sixty-eight years later, the mayor of Minami-Soma, the city nearest the stricken nuclear plant, made a plea on YouTube broadcast around the world for volunteers to help his stranded city. He pointed out that Japan's establishment press had withdrawn all their journalists, so that news was not getting out. The government had ordered people within a thirty-kilometer radius of the plant to stay indoors, meaning that stores and gasoline stations could not replenish their supplies. Residents of a city that had already been badly damaged by the earthquake-cum-tsunami (hundreds had died in a city of some 75,000) could neither leave (no gasoline) nor stay (not enough food in the stores).

As the days and weeks enfolded, it was hard for anyone who loves Japan not to feel outrage at the contrast between the way ordinary Japanese conducted themselves and the behavior of the men who had placed them in this horror and then abandoned them. Throughout the stricken region, good, decent people by the tens of thousands had lost everything they had, up to and including their entire families. Making things even worse, though, if that can be imagined, was the endless uncertainty. Many could not start rebuilding their lives because their homes had not just been wrecked but poisoned. Yet without whining or histrionics, they did what they had to do in a spontaneous flowering of order and mutual compassion that left the world agog. Their example provided a vivid, tear-inducing reminder to many (including me) of just what it was they loved so much about the country.

The sense of duty—doing what had to be done—extended into the ranks of TEPCO's regular employees and lower-level managers on the scene. Plant manager Yoshida Masao, for example, played a critical—even central—role by ignoring TEPCO's head office orders to halt injections of seawater into the plant. Yoshida led a group of TEPCO workers dubbed the "Fukushima Fifty" who at horrendous personal cost may have saved their country from unimaginable catastrophe. The nuclear physicist Dr. Kaku Michio, the founder of string theory, contends that the massive influx of seawater Yoshida ordered was the only thing that prevented the cores from exploding. Yoshida died from esophageal cancer in July 2013, but not before TEPCO had formally reprimanded him for disobeying the order.

It would be unfair to tar all of Japan's leaders with the same brush of incompetence and callousness with which one can indict those who pushed nuclear power on the country. The official reins of government at the time were in the hands of the Democratic Party of Japan ("DPJ"), many of whose leaders, including Kan, had come together to form the party in outrage at the way the Japanese government in 1995 seemed to have washed its hands of responsibility for the citizens of Kobe in the earthquake of that year that had laid waste to much of that city. We have noted how history may conclude that Kan himself helped save the situation with his intervention (among other things, the plant manager Yoshida had succeeded in gaining Kan's trust). At least initially, the daily briefings of Edano Yukio, Chief Cabinet Secretary at the time, seemed in their frank, no-nonsense manner a welcome contrast with the equivocations and prevarications people remembered from 1995. But as evidence seeped in that Edano was actually parroting "information" fed him by the nuclear village, the establishment press turned on the government, taking it to task for the lack of coordination in mounting rescue efforts. While these efforts were indeed poorly coordinated, that was largely a legacy of what the DPJ had inherited. The DPJ had been elected precisely in order to remedy the structural problems that produced the lack of coordination—something the press saw fit to overlook.

Kan would fall from power some six months later, a victim in part of a backlash against the handling of 3/11. As Fukushima went from a critical life-threatening emergency to a sore wound that, festering though it might be, no longer—for the moment—threatened the survival of Japan itself, the problems that had been dogging Japan before 3/11 reclaimed the center of attention: deflation, the sluggish economy, open revolt in Okinawa over the continued presence of US bases, fiscal numbers that could not be squared under any conceivable scenario, a general suffocating malaise that settled back in as foreign companies continued to grab market share in industries that had once been the proud preserves of Japan, Inc. In the meantime, the country managed to drift into the worst confrontation with China since 1945; for the first time in nearly seventy years, there was actual talk of going to war.

The upshot? The very group that had made the fatal decision to turn Japan nuclear, that had presided over a stagnant economy for two decades, that had mucked up relations with China and toadied to every self-serving, ill-thought out initiative blowing out of Washington, would find itself at the end of 2012 back in power. And not just back in power, but "swept back into power" as the foreign media had it, since at first glance it appeared that a landslide electoral victory had propelled them there. It was as if the Russians, after a few years of *glasnost*, had asked the Communist Party to restore Brezhnev's Soviet Union or the Americans had begged Dick Cheney, Donald Rumsfeld, Douglas Feith, and Paul Wolfowitz to resume their control of the US security and foreign policy apparatus while beseeching Michael "heck of a job" Brown of Hurricane Katrina infamy to become Secretary of the Interior.

An old but hard-to-kill falsehood tells us that people get the leaders they deserve. Was this after all true in Japan, despite the virtues and decency of the Japanese people?

No. But to understand that, we need to take a closer look at Japanese politics.

FIGURE 10. Tanaka Kakuei, the Most Formidable Politician of Postwar Japan, as Prime Minister in January, 1974. © Mainichi Shimbunsha; Courtesy the Mainichi Newspapers.

10

Politics

Politics in Japan can strike the observer as almost hopelessly dysfunctional. Core functions of government are performed badly or not performed at all. Japan's relations with its closest neighbors (Taiwan excepted) are in shambles, and while that is not all Japan's fault, countries do not get to choose their neighbors. The more prickly and threatening a country's neighbors, the more the country needs astute diplomacy and credible long-term security arrangements. Japan has neither. Meanwhile, at home, it has been obvious for a generation now that an economic model based on exports, an undervalued currency, and privileged access by corporate behemoths to financial and human capital should be replaced. But whenever underlying chronic economic malaise sharpens into acute crisis—as it does repeatedly and did again late in 2012—political leaders reach for the same worn-out recipe: trash the yen, chew up yet more of a depopulating countryside with white elephants, and hope that the rest of the world will absorb more Japanese stuff. Most damningly, as we saw in the previous chapter, when confronted by the ultimate test of the strength of a country's institutions—natural catastrophe—Japan's politics failed miserably, even if Japan's society came through in ways that earned the world's admiration. It was Japan's political class, not its people, that had locked the country into an energy infrastructure that risked the country's destruction. Yet when that was made clear, the response, after a year's hesitation, was to double down on nuclear power. To be sure, getting rid of nuclear power would be painful, entailing spikes in trade deficits, possible power shortages, and writing off the trillions of yen that have been sunk into the nuclear plants. But visionary government is all about leading a country through hard transitions. Japan sits on a disproportionate percentage of the world's "green energy" patents and is both culturally (a long tradition of thrift) and geographically (abundant solar and hydro power) superbly positioned to act as a vanguard nation in the coming and inevitable global transition to sustainable energy. Leaders comparable in caliber and vision to those of early Meiji could have rallied Japan to energy transformation, in the process revitalizing their nation and restoring a sense of mission to its people. Instead vested interests, intent on turning the switches back on at the nuclear plants, rammed through legislation to shield them from scrutiny or accountability as they prepared to resume their high-stakes poker game with the devil over his energy sources.

This is political failure on a monumental scale. One is inevitably tempted to ask what else could be expected from a country that has had nineteen prime ministers in the last twenty-five years, from a country in which all attempts to construct any lasting alternative to its rickety political infrastructure have been sabotaged by the establishment press, the public prosecutor, and a myopic Washington that manifestly prefers a pliable client state to a genuine ally with a healthy and robust politics of its own.

Yet any attempt to write Japan off as a failed state—implicit in such rhetorical questions—risks depriving the term of all meaning. When one falls gravely ill in Japan, a telephone call to the local fire station will summon an ambulance within minutes. The follow-up care will be excellent, and one will not be presented with a bill that spells economic ruin to oneself or one's family. The streets are safe and clean, and the public transportation a marvel of efficiency. Schools graduate numerate citizens literate in the world's most complicated written language. Japan's money, backed by nothing but trust in its economy and its political institutions, stands behind only the US dollar and the Euro as a global settlements and reserve currency. The collective force of the country's economic activity can move the world's largest financial markets—those for the US dollar and US government securities—and has played pivotal roles for good or evil in the economic destinies of other nations, for example, the direct investment that provided Thailand with a platform for growth, the capital goods that were critical to Chinese industrialization, or the waves of exports that forced a restructuring of the American economy.

It will not do, however, to imagine that Japan provides any sort of demonstration that a society without politics is somehow possible. Japan is about as far as one can get from the neoliberal fantasy of a market society from which politics and power have disappeared. The political is everywhere in Japan, hobbling and constraining markets, permeating all aspects of life. But it can be hard to see.

Part of the problem is conceptual. Westerners—particularly Americans—are so inured to the notion that in a proper political order, the exercise of power is confined to explicit rule-making, rule-enforcement, and security provision that they can find it hard to grasp other ways of organizing societies. Of course, Americans are aware that the totalitarian states of the twentieth century attempted to politicize all aspects of life, to abolish all distinctions between public and private, to destroy any symbol or locus of authority independent of the state. But it was precisely that totalization that made these places seem such nightmare entities. Japan is quite obviously not one of them; it boasts veritable thickets of symbols and loci of authority that manifest no obvious connection to any identifiable center of state power. Furthermore, Japan boasts all the familiar institutions of democratic capitalist societies that mediate between the citizen and the state: courts, limited liability companies, stock markets, private as well as public schools, a plethora of religious sects, a constitution, and seemingly independent media, not to mention political parties that compete for votes in free and open elections. On the surface, Japan appears to differ from its peers among the advanced capitalist countries only in having a central government that is somewhat weaker than the norm— why observers sometimes reach for comparisons with Italy in trying to make sense of Japan.

But most of the mediating institutions listed above were grafted onto existing political arrangements not because of any organic internal development but because Japan needed to create the appearance of a modern state organized along Western lines if it was to be accepted into the "community" of nations. Earlier arrangements were, in many cases, left untouched and they continued in large part to function the way they always had—providing for order and the organization of social and economic life. We saw in chapter 3 how the Meiji leaders had adopted not one but two sets of institutions—constitutional government and direct Imperial rule—to legitimize their seizure of power. We noted in chapter 4 how as a condition of recovering nominal sovereignty after the Occupation, Japan was forced to import yet a third set of legitimizing political institutions, this time imposed on Japan by the United States: a new constitution, popular sovereignty, democratic education, women's rights; that while these institutions had some real effects that Japan's conservative ruling elites have not succeeded in reversing (although they are still trying and are arguably closer to success today than at any point since 1945), they were certainly never accepted as a font of political legitimacy.

The resultant blurring of the actual sources of political power is very much in line with Japan's political history and continues to this day to stymie root-and-branch institutional reform, not to mention precluding any genuine revolution. It is impossible to overthrow a ruling class if you cannot find it. The shoguns pretended they were exercising power at the pleasure of the emperor and as we saw, shortly after the establishment of each of the three Shogunates, power quickly dissipated away from the shoguns themselves to other powerful entities in the ruling setup. The so-called Sat-Cho clique that brought on the Meiji Restoration exercised genuine power and everyone knew it, even if they went through the motions of carrying out the Imperial Will and procuring parliamentary appointments. But when they died off, they left behind them the power vacuum that allowed for the destruction of practically all they had worked for.

The most astute analysts of political power in Japan all, at different times over the course of the last century, reached similar conclusions about its sources. One often encounters the term "feudal" in discussions of Japanese reality—not as a colorful synonym for "backwards" but because in a feudal system, power is fractured among clusters of independent power centers, many of which are subordinate in only the most nominal, ceremonial way to any unified government authority. The lack of coordination between the Imperial Army and the Imperial Navy and the constant hijacking of policy by low-ranking officers in the field made this obvious during the war years. But the dissipation of power continues today; the great ministries still fill most key policy-making positions on their own and are not subject to substantive—as opposed to ceremonial—legislative oversight or judicial review.

Since the passing from the scene of the Meiji leaders, the central reality of Japan's political setup has been the absence of any entity enjoying an unambiguous right to rule and a set of institutional procedures that can settle disputes between competing power centers, procedures that will be accepted as fully legitimate on all sides. Japan's provoking of a war it could not possibly win grew directly out of the absence of open political process.

Policy in Japan is almost entirely rudderless; what coherence it has stems not from initiatives conceived by the formal organs of government but rather from demands made on the Japanese polity by the outside world and from groups inside Japanese society that have accumulated sufficient mass that they cannot be ignored. As we saw in chapter 4, the situation was not corrected after the Second World War, even though the events of the 1930s had demonstrated that a country with no brakes and no compass can and will bring disaster on itself and, if it is sufficiently powerful, on its neighbors. We noted that a more benevolent postwar political order was made possible because the United States assumed for Japan two of the key powers by which a state is identified and which can give rise to the most contentious of political questions: the providing of external security and the conduct of foreign relations. Meanwhile, the third critical state power—economic policy-making, including such matters as taxation and monetary arrangements—required no political discussion at the time since everyone accepted the overriding goal of reconstruction. The conditions of the immediate postwar decade gave policy makers responsible for the economy unprecedented freedom to experiment until they found a recipe that worked. Absent the necessary political infrastructure, however, they could not change that recipe once it had been settled on, even though external conditions would shift radically.

But the emergence of this benevolent postwar order did require politics of a sort—not a politics capable of steering Japan in a new direction when circumstances changed, but a politics that could accommodate and/or neutralize potential claimants to power, a politics that could run interference among the great ministries and between the ministries and other power clusters, and, finally, a politics that could reassure other countries that what they were dealing with in Japan was a familiar setup of parties, elections, prime ministers, and courts.

That politics would be called the 1955 system.

THE 1955 SYSTEM

We first encountered this term back in chapter 4 when we noted how the CIA had provided covert funding that helped pay for the merger of the two leading "conservative" political parties to form the Liberal Democratic Party ("LDP").[1] Kishi Nobusuke, the Tojo lieutenant who had emerged from prison as the great *éminence grise* of Japan's early postwar politics, acted as the key facilitator of the merger. Kishi was responding to the very real threat of a Left takeover of Japan's parliamentary machinery. The Japanese Left had split over issues raised by the 1951 San Francisco Peace Treaty. But the rising tide of labor militancy discussed in chapter 4 and a series of growing electoral pluralities held out the tantalizing possibility of a sweeping electoral victory for the Left if differences could be put aside. In October 1955, the two leading factions of the Japan Socialist Party ("JSP") came together in order to force an election. This was enough to scare Washington, the business community, and other key right-wing leaders with the prospect of a socialist victory if similar hatchet-burying did not take place on the right. The LDP was born a month later and a majority of the existing Diet members in the Lower House joined the new party, forestalling an election that it seemed the JSP would have won easily.

To a casual observer, what happened that year might have appeared like the birth pangs of a two-party system, with the LDP on the right and the JSP on the left. The two did consolidate their respective positions as Japan's largest political parties, positions they would maintain for the next generation. But what took shape was not a two-party system, if by that term one means a politics dominated alternately by a left-leaning and a right-leaning party, both capable of governing, both stepping in and out of power while competing for votes with differing policy visions. The initial purpose of the LDP was not so much to compete with the JSP as to shut the Japanese Left out of any chance of ever getting its hands on any significant lever of power in Japan—why the LDP could rely on secret slush funds from the CIA whenever homegrown money ran short. At the time, a majority of the Japanese electorate favored the implementation of Left policy goals: universal economic security, collective ownership of the means of

---

1. The covert aid systematically channeled to the LDP by the CIA in the 1950s and 1960s had been long suspected, but was finally revealed in an article in the *New York Times* "CIA Spent Millions to Support the Japanese Right in '50's and '60's," October 9, 1994.

production, and an end to the military relationship between the United States and Japan. A credible unified party espousing such goals would likely have won elections organized along British lines until well into the 1970s. But although Japan's was ostensibly a parliamentary system that at first glance resembled its British counterpart, elections were conducted in such a way that the JSP never had a chance.

It was not just a matter of the LDP's ability to tap into funds from the CIA and the Japanese business community—funds that were obviously not available to the JSP. Two key elements of the Japanese setup ensured that the LDP's overwhelming financial advantage translated into absolute control of Japan's parliamentary machinery for the subsequent half-century, even though the LDP rarely could command even 50 percent of Japan's popular vote. First, rural districts were disproportionately represented in the Lower House where legislation theoretically originated, and the disparity between urban and rural votes grew worse over time as people left the countryside for the city. Second, each district sent multiple representatives to the Lower House. Unlike most electoral systems in which constituencies elect one representative to a legislature, Japan's electoral districts sent as many as five of the top vote-getters in a given election to the Diet, even though each voter had only one vote. (US states each elect two senators, but they do not stand in the same elections.) To retain a seat, it was thus not necessary to garner more votes than an opponent. All that was needed was to place. "Winning" an election thus had little to do with demonstrating that one would be a better legislator than the other guy or that one's party had a more compelling vision for Japan's future. It involved ensuring that a minimum number of one's supporters showed up at the polls on election day. The most reliable way to do that was to pay them one way or another.

The LDP maintained its lock on the Diet by targeting enough funding to enough rural districts to ensure that its candidates were repeatedly elected. The setup involved the participation of key ministries, since cash distributed by the LDP itself was not enough to guarantee electoral victories. Ministries would channel spending to districts where they could be assured that sympathetic legislators would approve the necessary budgetary allocations for the ministry.

Three characteristic features of Japanese party politics stemmed from these arrangements. First, most legislators grouped themselves into *zoku* ("tribes") around specific ministries. The most powerful of the *zoku* was that associated with the Ministry of Construction, since this ministry was the source of so much infrastructure spending. Other important *zoku* clustered around the Ministry of Agriculture, the Ministry of Transportation, and the Ministry of Posts and Telecommunications.

The LDP's notorious factionalism formed a second characteristic of Japanese party politics that grew out of the 1955 setup. This factionalism had nothing to do with differing policy views, not to mention ideology; that is, it was not a matter of "liberal," "moderate," or "conservative" wings in the sense those terms would be understood in the West. Most LDP politicians were, to be sure, viscerally anti-Communist, but that was not because of any devotion to classical liberalism; the reasons lay in their hatred of the Soviet Union and of Japan's home-grown leftists. It was precisely the ideological fervor of the leftists that so infuriated the LDP and the Japanese Right; it seemed "un-Japanese." To the extent LDP politicians had any political ideology at all, it was a species of the strong-state corporatism that had been the governing philosophy of the "Reform Bureaucrats" of the 1930s.

Most of the organized Japanese Right may have ended up under the LDP's political umbrella—an umbrella that also provided space for those that might have been called centrists elsewhere—but it was not a Right made up of libertarians and other free-market devotees. Such Japanese did not exist in 1955 and would not emerge in significant numbers for another generation, and even then only in certain academic and business circles. The Japanese Right consists—then and now—of those who seek to restore the overt nationalism and openly authoritarian social hierarchy of the prewar and war years. The Right encompasses people from all kinds of backgrounds—the functionaries who cluster around the Throne in the Imperial Household Agency, scions of the old aristocracy and the prewar bureaucratic and business elite, intellectuals and writers obsessed with defining the "essence" of the Japanese,[2] self-made owners of businesses in fields like construction and "entertainment," and thugs who take time off from their day jobs as loan sharks and blackmail artists to roam central Tokyo in sound trucks blaring ear-splitting renditions of wartime songs. (There is, in fact, no clear line separating the political and cultural Right in

2. A good example of the type is Ishihara Shintaro, who started his career as a kind of iconoclastic Japanese version of Norman Mailer, moved from writing into politics, served as Governor of Tokyo and now heads an explicitly xenophobic rightist party complete with the use of deliberately insulting language for the Chinese and the Koreans.

Japan from the *yakuza*, and factions of the LDP have long used the *yakuza* to intimidate political opponents.)

Whatever their background and class, however, rightists are united by a hatred for the high-minded Left and for Occupation reforms that democratized the school system and, in their view, destroyed Japanese children's love of their country—why the Japan Teacher's Union has, throughout the postwar period, been the single greatest target of the Right's ire. The Japanese Right's worldview serves as a kind of backhanded demonstration of the remark attributed to Chesterton that when people stop believing in God, they don't believe in nothing, they believe in anything. The success of the Meiji government in destroying Japan's traditional Buddhist-saturated popular religion and substituting a spiritually thin gruel of hyper-nationalism and worship of the "national essence" left behind an endemic spiritual crisis. This is evident in the rise of the "new religions" that we encountered in chapter 3. But this spiritual crisis is also at the heart of the inability of Japanese rightists to entertain the notion that their nation is capable of evil. Acknowledging the scope of the Rape of Nanjing, the terror bombing of Chongqing, or the atrocities committed by Unit 731 is literally intolerable, for it threatens to besmirch the only ontologically grounded sense of the sacred to which they have access— "Japaneseness" and their status as members in good standing of a holy race living in a holy land.

Rightist politicians thus naturally gravitated toward the LDP. Fringe leftist parties have been around since the late 1940s, but no fringe counterparts on the right developed until LDP hegemony was temporarily broken in the 1990s. But—and this is the crucial point for understanding how Japanese politics would evolve over the next half-century—LDP factions did not coalesce along lines corresponding to the relative fervor of devotion to the emperor or the Rising Sun flag. Factions were organized through money and patronage.

A brief thought experiment will demonstrate why Japan's multi-seat constituencies made factionalism inevitable. In order to maintain its lock on the Diet, the LDP had to put up several candidates in each district. These people would inevitably end up competing against each other for votes, even though most (or all) would win seats in the Diet. Demonstrating to party elders one's suitability as a candidate meant demonstrating, on the one hand, that one had access to funds and could direct spending toward a district and, on the other, in a mutually reinforcing arrangement, that one had a sufficient number of local supporters to assure the minimum number of votes to place would be garnered. Thus, candidate A would be identified with the construction industry and would have excellent ties with the Ministry of Construction (he might well be a former bureaucrat from the ministry). His network of local supporters (*kōenkai*) would be led by presidents of local construction companies who could look forward to grabbing contracts from infrastructure spending in the district in return for ensuring that their employees all voted for the candidate. The candidate himself would rely on the faction leader—a heavyweight politician in Tokyo who could see to it that, once elected, the man had seats on the right committees and his district got its share of construction spending. Meanwhile, candidate B might be close to the Transport Ministry, and have as the leader of his *kōenkai* the local Japan National Railroads station master, while candidate C would draw his strength from the local branch of *Nōkyō*, the nationwide federation of agricultural cooperatives, and boast of his close ties to the Ministry of Agriculture. The *kōenkai* were as well organized and lovingly maintained as any urban machine from American political history. But while the Daley or Pendergast machines operated without significant local opposition in, respectively, Chicago and Kansas City, each Japanese district would inevitably have several overlapping *kōenkai* and each of their favored sons would cluster in the Diet with representatives sent from similar *kōenkai* in other districts.

The 1955 system may have cemented the LDP's lock hold on the Diet—indeed that it was its purpose—but its third key feature paradoxically made room for smaller parties. The LDP may have had a near-monopoly on representation from rural districts, but the multi-seat system permitted smaller parties that drew votes from urban shopkeepers and workers in other family-owned urban enterprises to capture seats that might otherwise have gone to the Socialists or the Communists. The most important of these smaller parties was the Komeito, the political arm of Soka Gakkai, the largest and most successful of the "new religions" as they were called. The new religions mostly trace their institutional and theological roots to the urban Buddhist sects of the premodern era (Nichiren being the most important). The new religions themselves had sprung up in the spiritual vacuum left behind by the Meiji government's destruction of Japan's traditional religion. This put them to some degree at odds with the "holy Japanism" of the Japanese Right (indeed, the new religions had been persecuted during the 1930s), why they kept institutional distance from the LDP rather than just becoming another LDP faction. But their political arms, particularly the Komeito, nonetheless served a useful role in the 1955 setup. The Komeito not only siphoned off votes from the Left, it also provided a voice, however muted, for those who otherwise would have had none—critical to maintaining the seemingly benevolent character of the political system, despite the exclusion of the organized Left.[3]

Japanese election campaigns became exercises in getting out the vote. Sound trucks roamed the streets of a given district blaring out the candidate's name. Neither expositions of policy nor American-style negative campaigning would be of much use; what counted was reminding people for whom they were supposed to vote. The business community channeled funds to the LDP as a whole (with help from the CIA through the 1950s and 1960s), ensuring that the LDP could run a sufficient number of candidates in each district so that LDP control of the Diet was guaranteed. Key positions in the party and the government—the prime minister, cabinet ministers, chief cabinet secretary—were rotated among faction leaders following negotiations usually conducted after official hours in expensive restaurants and clubs in Akasaka, the upscale nightlife area that adjoins the Tokyo district where one finds most official government buildings.

Japan may have been a one-party state, but the LDP was not equivalent to that party. The LDP's role lay in providing political protection for the entire constellation of power holders that formed the totality of Japan's governing setup. This setup consisted, in addition to the LDP, of the bureaucracy and what the Japanese called *zaikai* or powerful figures in business and finance organized into such groups as the Keidanren. The LDP did not determine policy. To the extent anyone determined policy, it was the administrative vice ministers of the respective ministries, the highest career positions in the Japanese bureaucracy. Key tasks for the LDP included buying off the support of all significant players with the capacity to

---

3. Komeito went to great ends to disavow any formal ties with Soka Gakkai. But it is well understood that the party existed primarily to preserve the tax-exempt status of "religious" institutions and to deflect investigations into the financial affairs of Soka Gakkai and its founder, Ikeda Daisaku, who was treated by the party faithful as a demi-god. On numerous occasions over the past sixty years—up to and including the present government—the Komeito or its institutional successor, New Komeito, has entered into governing coalitions with the LDP to secure these ends.

make trouble (the LDP maintained some sort of link with every important group from the *yakuza* to PTAs and associations of housewives formed to protest inflation), and acting as buffers and negotiators among other constituent parts of the ruling elite.

The closest thing to a political center in the entire setup was not the Diet or a faction-ridden LDP but the Budget Bureau of the Ministry of Finance, the most powerful bureau in the most powerful of the ministries. But while the Budget Bureau might have had the theoretical ability to discipline an errant ministry or cut off funds to the uncooperative, such power was rarely used. "[T]he secret of the MOF's power," as one commentary put it, "lies in the MOF's role as the ultimate guarantor of the bureaucracy's freedom from political interference. The pressure for political discussion over the allocation of money—the very stuff of democratic politics—does not arise in Japan because the MOF acts to maintain the existing financial balance of power among the various ministries." While the MOF may thus have had the ultimate responsibility for keeping the Japanese system going, it did not have the political or conceptual resources to set the country on a different course when that became necessary. But if the MOF lacked such resources, certainly no other entity had them—most particularly, an LDP that had few institutional resources independent of the bureaucracy and the *zaikai* that would permit the party to exercise any kind of centralized control or map out new policy directions. There was no Japanese equivalent of the Brookings Institution or the Heritage Foundation—not to mention large legislative staffs—from which the LDP could seek independent policy advice. The LDP was completely dependent on the bureaucracy for everything that goes into policy formation, from data-gathering to the drafting of legislation.

This was not initially a problem. The 1955 system emerged as it did because of the circumstances of history—the twin legacies of the Occupation and the failure of the Meiji leadership to provide for the legitimate passage of power. Key players in the 1955 system succeeded in seeing to it that the system flourished. They engineered the postwar recovery via the institutions and methods we examined in chapters 4 and 5, and they kept leftists away from any proximity to real power and decision-making, thereby assuring continued protection from Washington.

Forestalling any kind of Left electoral success was not, however, simply a matter of voting arrangements; it also involved draining away the

Left's appeal. We noted above that for at least the first two decades of the 1955 system's existence, a probable majority of Japanese voters favored universal economic security, collective ownership of the means of production, and an end to the military relationship with the United States. The system did, as we have seen, actually end up providing for something close to universal economic security, and while the Left's dream of collective ownership of the means of production would not be realized along doctrinaire socialist lines, neither would the commanding heights of the Japanese economy be seized by men who defined their primary mission as delivering high returns to private investors, not to mention making themselves rich. Those who ran the Japanese economy in both the nominally "public" and "private" sectors generally saw themselves as patriots engaged in a collective effort to restore Japan's industrial might and national greatness.

The only Left demand that was completely flouted was the termination of the military relationship with the United States. Even here, though, it was soon obvious that Japanese establishment leaders had no intention of being dragged into American military adventures. They were happy to profit from the Vietnam War and take shelter under the US nuclear umbrella, but they quickly learned how to deflect American pressure for more extensive rearmament, even if they had to put up with American bases scattered here and there throughout the Japanese archipelago. One might even argue that the Japanese Left served a key, if unwitting, purpose in propping up a system that ultimately depended on American indulgence—the JSP had to be credible enough to serve as a bogeyman to scare off the Americans when Washington pushed rearmament too hard or, later, trade conflicts began to emerge. Anger at American foreign policy would, it is true, serve as one of the principal sparks for the waves of student protests that inundated Japanese universities in the 1960s, but as we saw in chapter 4, these protests never came close to shaking the system.

The 1955 system did, however, have two serious flaws. It had no mechanism that allowed for a significant change of direction. And it was vulnerable to takeover by an ambitious outsider who could master the intricacies of its networks and power balances. It is no accident that such an outsider would appear at just that historical juncture when external circumstances would force on Japan the first significant "course correction" since the end of the Occupation.

TANAKA KAKUEI

Tanaka was the greatest and most influential politician in postwar Japan. This is not to say that Japan did not have other remarkable leaders; we suggested in chapter 5 that Ikeda Hayato may be the most underrated figure of the twentieth century anywhere in the world. But although men such as Ikeda, Yoshida Shigeru, and Kishi all served as prime minister, they were not politicians. They were mandarins who rose through the ranks of Japan's elite institutions. Ikeda had been administrative vice minister in the Ministry of Finance, the pinnacle of the bureaucratic elite. Yoshida, who negotiated the San Francisco Peace Treaty, had been one of Japan's most illustrious diplomats in the prewar period. Kishi had come from MITI's prewar predecessor, the Ministry of Commerce and Industry.

Ikeda's successor as prime minister, Sato Eisaku, was cut from the same cloth; he was in fact Kishi's biological brother,[4] had been educated at Tokyo Imperial University (the name of Tokyo University before 1945), and had had a career as a successful bureaucrat in the Ministry of Railways (folded into the Ministry of Transportation after the war) before "entering politics," as they say, with a safe seat. From there he rotated through key positions (chief cabinet secretary, minister of construction, minister of finance, minister of international trade and industry) before becoming prime minister in 1964. Sato's career trajectory followed what seemed a solidifying pattern: childhood in a well-connected family, graduation from an elite university—preferably *Tōdai* to use the Japanese acronym for Tokyo University, two decades or so at an important ministry, followed, if one was sufficiently able, with a seat in the Diet, a series of key political appointments and, finally, elevation to the prime ministership. Demonstrating one's skill at appealing to and mobilizing voters had very little if anything to do with any of this; Yoshida, Kishi, Ikeda, and Sato were all brilliant, savvy men, but none of them had even a trace of the charisma that is normally thought necessary to succeed in democratic politics. (Yoshida did have a certain stubbornness of style that earned him the sobriquet *wan man*—one man—and far-fetched comparisons to Churchill, but the others came across as almost completely colorless, why de Gaulle would famously dismiss Ikeda as a "transistor salesman.")

---

4. Kishi had been adopted into the Kishi family to assure a male heir, once a common arrangement among elite Japanese households—thus the different surname from his brother Sato.

Tanaka, however, was a born politician, as colorful and charismatic as they come, and he got where he did by deploying quintessentially political skills: the ability to put together electoral and legislative coalitions, a genius for understanding the sources of power in money and in the ambitions of men, a consummate grasp of how to harness and appeal to those ambitions, an intuitive sense of when to cut deals and when to intimidate. In the process, he broke through the defenses that the architects of the 1955 system had, in keeping with long political tradition in Japan, erected against the interference of mere "politics" in the affairs of state. In doing so, he provoked bitter and visceral reactions that continue to reverberate right into the present while shocking the 1955 system into realignments that define Japanese politics today.

The American figure whom Tanaka most closely resembles is Lyndon Johnson. At times the parallels can seem almost uncanny. Both came from desperately poor, backward regions—the Texas hill country and the *ura-Nihon* (Japan's backside), as it was contemptuously known, of the northwest coast of Honshu, a place that due to the local microclimate (icy winds blowing out of Siberia that pick up moisture over the Sea of Japan, and then dump it) gets more snow than any low-elevation place on earth. (Nobel Prize winner Kawabata Yasunari would set his most famous novel, *Snow Country,* in this bleak, wintry land.) Both had dreamers for fathers, men who lost everything they had and were reduced to debt and manual labor; both had mothers with social pretensions who poured all their resentments and dashed hopes into their favored sons; both had childhoods marked by humiliation, and teen years in which they were forced into stints as common laborers. Both were physically weak as youths, yet demonstrated stamina and energy for work that were a marvel to all around them. Neither had much formal schooling—Tanaka had to drop out of school at age 14; Johnson did go to a college, but it was scarcely more than a glorified high school. Yet both had such a capacity to absorb and marshal detail—names, dates, connections, who owes what to whom—that the only appropriate label is genius. Both spoke with accents and mannerisms that instantly set them off from the "Harvards," as Johnson would refer to the men around John F. Kennedy, or the *Tōdai*-bred mandarins of Tokyo's bureaucratic elite (Ikeda would call Tanaka a "man of the rickshaw class") but from early on both had the knack of attracting the notice of well-connected men who would give them crucial breaks and introduce them into circles of power and wealth. Both thus benefited by the support of key establishment figures such as Franklin Roosevelt and Sam Rayburn, or, in Tanaka's case, Yoshida and Viscount Okochi Masatoshi, the prewar nobleman who ran one of the Japanese military's largest subcontractors and had first spotted the teen-aged Tanaka's energy and intelligence. But both Johnson and Tanaka would maintain even more intimate ties with other, far less reputable men. These shadowy figures of vast wealth, such as Herman Brown who built Brown and Root (now KBR, Inc., the hugely controversial military contractor) and the real estate mogul Osano Kenji who died in 1986 as one of Japan's richest men (he owned much of Waikiki), provided their respective political protégés with crucial financial backing. Both Johnson and Tanaka married socially far above them, choosing brides in Lady Bird Taylor and Sakamoto Han who uncomplainingly endured their husbands' frequent infidelities and provided indispensable emotional and financial support not to mention tireless work on their husbands' behalf.

Perhaps most critically, both Johnson and Tanaka deployed money in their quests for political power on a scale that had never been seen before in either the United States or Japan. Much of that money would flow from their absolute mastery of the tactics by which legislators can pry open the public purse. But some of it would come from sources so tainted that Tanaka would land in jail and Johnson probably would have had it not been for the assassination of President Kennedy.

For all their financial corruption, however, both were genuinely outraged about the way despised groups in their respective societies were thought of and treated by their countries' elites, and both saw themselves—correctly—as champions of such groups. Johnson brought electrification and other public works to rural Texas, famously engineered passage of critical civil-rights legislation, launched the War on Poverty, and, with Medicare, lifted the prospect of destitution from America's elderly because of medical bills. Tanaka channeled rivers of public spending at Japan's rural districts (with special consideration for his own Niigata Prefecture), ending for good the millennia-long history of an impoverished countryside squeezed to benefit urban elites.

Tanaka's particular genius lay not in overthrowing the 1955 system but in hijacking it. Tanaka not only built Japan's most formidable local *kōenkai* (network of supporters) in Niigata, he created a nationwide network of legislators who were personally loyal to him: the *Tanaka gundan* ("Tanaka army"). Again, the parallels with the way Lyndon Johnson became the most powerful US senator of modern times are almost eerie.

THE "NIXON SHOCKS" AND TANAKA'S PRIME MINISTERSHIP

Tanaka's techniques only became as effective as they did, however, because of what was happening in the wider world as the 1960s wound down. Tanaka engineered the solution to the temporary crisis in US–Japan relations brought on by the "Nixon shocks" (the closing of the gold window, the surcharge imposed on Japanese imports into the United States, and the diplomacy with Beijing undertaken without informing Tokyo). MITI minister at the time, Tanaka's deal-making and political skills enabled him to pose simultaneously as the great defender of Japanese industry from American pressure, all the while negotiating behind the scenes with both American trade diplomats and Japanese textile companies for a face-saving climbdown for all sides that would see the lifting of the American tariff in return for "voluntary" restraints on the Japanese export surge. The contrast with the hapless Sato, accused of endangering Tokyo's relationship with Washington, would precipitate the latter's resignation. Having accumulated just enough support among LDP legislators, Tanaka edged out for the LDP presidency Sato's anointed successor, the ex-MOF bureaucrat Fukuda Takeo. Tanaka then automatically became prime minister.

Meanwhile, Tanaka had written (or had had written) a best-selling book that contained crucial clues both into the operation of the political machine he built and into the ways in which the Japanese economic model would survive the downfall of Bretton Woods and its system of fixed exchange rates. The public works spending on the scale advocated by the book, entitled *Plan for Remodeling the Japanese Archipelago*, was only possible because Japan had begun to accumulate trade surpluses. But the particular ways in which that spending would happen not only provided the financial gasoline that would fuel Tanaka's political machine for the next generation—in essence, using public spending to lock down electoral districts and thus the Diet—they also allowed for continuation of an economic model built around an objective that had, by the late 1960s, actually become moot: the accumulation of foreign exchange, specifically, US dollars.

Japan had become the world's second largest economy and no longer needed dollars in order to purchase essential imports. But a sharp rise in the exchange value of the yen—seemingly inevitable in the new floating-rate world—would have brought with it unacceptable political consequences as companies in traditional industries failed and market forces increasingly trumped bureaucratic imperatives in determining economic outcomes. Forestalling all this meant preventing the yen from rising—or at least rising too fast.

The full explanation for how this worked is somewhat technical,[5] but the essence involved deliberately wasteful public spending—wasteful both in the sense that far more money was spent than was actually needed to erect a given project, and that the project itself would not result in much if any increase in economic efficiency. (Indeed many of these projects were money losers as their revenues did not even cover operating costs, much less retire the debt that had been taken down to build them.) The spending mopped up the excess demand generated by the earnings pouring into the coffers of Japan's exporters. Money spent to improve living standards in the cities rather than on white elephants in the countryside could have risked upwards pressure on the currency as households with more money in their pockets began buying imports—that is, after all, what happened in countries such as West Germany and Sweden which, like Japan, enjoyed substantial trade surpluses on the strength largely of exports of high-quality manufactured goods. But by "wasting" export earnings on such showpieces as magnificent buildings at small rural stations in Tanaka's district, the process by which a growing trade surplus leads to currency strengthening was cut short.

It is for this reason that the bureaucracy never really opposed Tanaka's methods. He may have boasted—correctly—of his unprecedented ability to squeeze money out of the Ministry of Finance, but he also made it possible for the MOF to continue what it had been doing for the previous three decades without fundamental adjustment—adjustment that would have required political direction over the bureaucracy that Tanaka never attempted. Tanaka treated the bureaucracy as a source of money and patronage, not as an instrument for effecting any kind of policy that went beyond the opening of a spigot. Since that spigot had to be opened in order

5. Interested readers should consult A. Mikuni and R. Murphy, *Japan's Policy Trap* (Brookings, 2002), chapter 3.

to keep the pipes of the Japanese system from bursting after the collapse of the fixed rate regime, Tanaka's political machine and the bureaucracy would inevitably become tacit allies.

In any case, Tanaka's proposals were, for the time being, premature. He started his prime ministership in a blaze of glory, impressing not only the Japanese public, but also such disparate foreign leaders as Richard Nixon, Henry Kissinger, and Zhou Enlai. With Zhou he negotiated the formal establishment of diplomatic relations between Tokyo and Beijing—a tricky matter domestically since there was so much sympathy for Taiwan in the ranks of the LDP. But the coming of the oil crisis with its concomitant quadrupling of oil prices brought with it 25 percent inflation rates that made Tanaka's talk of public spending to revitalize Japan seem totally out of touch. Meanwhile, a disastrous trip to Southeast Asia that saw Tanaka booed in the streets of Jakarta and Bangkok stripped from him the patina of someone who could be trusted with foreign policy. Possibly inspired by the Watergate scandal unfolding at the same time across the Pacific and perhaps by leaks from hostile bureaucrats, teams of investigative journalists began combing over the history of Tanaka's finances.

Tanaka was not employing methods that were qualitatively different from those used by other politicians—he was just better at it, one reason he had long been given a pass by the establishment press. But the noise reached levels that the quality papers could no longer ignore. Exposés of Tanaka's finances began to appear not just in the fringe press but in the respectable magazine *Bungei Shunju*.[6] They were picked up on by *Newsweek*, just before Tanaka appeared as a luncheon speaker at the Foreign Correspondents Club of Japan (most Japanese prime ministers will speak to the Club once during their tenure). The lunch degenerated into a free-for-all as the journalists present, sensing the possibility of a "gotcha" moment, hurled hostile questions at Tanaka. Not only was Tanaka visibly—and uncharacteristically—flustered, the establishment dailies had to respond to this unprecedented treatment of a sitting prime minister. As if a switch had been pulled, the entire Japanese media went into overdrive about Tanaka and his methods. Tanaka's enemies, led by Fukuda Takeo, whom he had shoved

6. Here lies another parallel with LBJ. *Life* magazine had, like *Bungei Shunju*, commissioned teams of its top journalists to dig into LBJ's finances. The journalists had uncovered enough that *Life* had decided to make a cover story on the subject. The editorial meeting to lay out the story was convened on the morning of November 22, 1963.

aside to become prime minister, scheduled hearings on Tanaka's finances in the Diet. Tanaka resigned as prime minister on November 26, 1974.

Worse was to come for Tanaka. He would never again be prime minister and would find himself indicted and then convicted on criminal charges. Yet he had not even begun to reach the peak of his power.

THE LOCKHEED SCANDAL

In a political history dominated by a string of scandals, the one the Japanese labeled "Lockheed" probably had the greatest repercussions of all the scandals in the entire postwar period. Scandals play a crucial role in the Japanese political setup by disciplining those who have accumulated such leverage over other elements of the power structure that they threaten the system itself. The very success of Tanaka's methods gave him that leverage, even if those methods ultimately worked to reinforce rather than undermine the postwar Japanese system. It was thus almost inevitable that a scandal of some sort would emerge around Tanaka, and in due course it did.

But the Lockheed scandal differed from the typical scandal because it started outside Japan. And far from bridling its supposed target, it ended up loosening the restraints on Tanaka.

Japanese politics of the 1970s were dominated by what the press dubbed the "Kaku-Fuku War," referring to Tanaka and Fukuda. (Tanaka is such a common name in Japan that people bearing it are often identified by given rather than family names.) Tanaka may have been forced to resign as prime minister, but in Japan where titular and actual power rarely coincide, Tanaka easily vetoed Fukuda's attempts to succeed him directly. Miki Takeo, the leader of a small LDP faction with a reputation—deserved or not—for "clean" politics, became prime minister.

Everything was going according to script in the wake of the *Bungei Shunju* revelations and Tanaka's resignation. As major figures do in Japan after a hullabaloo of one sort or another forces a stepping down from a public position, Tanaka was continuing to pull strings behind the scenes while the way was being prepared for his re-emergence on the official stage.

But then in February 1976, under questioning from a US Senate subcommittee, A. Carl Kotchian, vice chairman of Lockheed, admitted that his company had bribed a "high" government official in Japan to land an order from All Nippon Airways ("ANA"). The official was Tanaka. The amounts involved were relatively small—500 million yen, then worth some $1.6 million; Tanaka later said he had no recollection of the specifics, an entirely plausible claim. Tanaka may have accepted the bribe—if he did, indeed, accept it—not because he needed the money but as a favor to Lockheed's agent in Japan, the Marubeni Corporation, and to its president who had personally appealed to Tanaka for help with the order. This was the way Tanaka operated—doing favors for people and thereby building up debts to be called on in the future. It is the way most Japanese politicians operated—indeed, it is the way LBJ operated or, for that matter, Richard J. Daley or most American congressmen. What distinguished master politicians like Tanaka, Daley, and LBJ from amateurs is that these men did not limit their favors to the powerful. They did things for just about anybody, understanding that today's two-bit town councilman may be tomorrow's important governor or that the impoverished widow has relatives who will not forget who it was that swept aside bureaucratic nit-picking to secure a pension for her.

This was the secret of Tanaka's power and he deployed it with a skill never equaled before or since in Japanese history. It seemed astonishing to him that doing a favor for a businessman—calling ANA's president to land the order—would get him in trouble, particularly because he was simply doing what everybody else did, just doing a better and more thorough job of it.

But two things made it damning: (1) the very fact that he was so much better at it than his rivals; and (2) because it was not just a matter of one Japanese helping another. This time, the money came from overseas, which made it impossible to maintain the usual polite facades about such matters. (Indeed, there was a lot of private grumbling in Japan about Kotchian specifically and foreigners in general. A good Japanese in Kotchian's place would have protected his employer and its customers and agents. That Kotchian was testifying under oath cut no ice with many Japanese; he should have been prepared to go to prison rather than fingering others.)

The revelations that poured out of the investigations in both Washington and Tokyo were excruciating to many establishment Japanese. It was as if a high-minded Victorian lady were forced to endure explicit discussions of her husband's sex life. She may have known that he kept a mistress and visited prostitutes, but unless she had her face rubbed in it, she could easily pretend not to notice. The Lockheed affair not only dragged into the open the actual operations of Japanese politics in ways that no one could avoid seeing, it threatened to expose the entire history of the CIA's secret funding of the LDP and the role the CIA had played in the party's foundation. (The Ford White House was indeed nervous about the potential damage to the security relationship between the United States and Japan from the scandal fallout.)

Among other things, the scandal shone a spotlight on Kodama Yoshio, a shadowy ultra-rightist "fixer" and underworld figure who had shared a prison cell with Kishi when arrested by the Occupation. Kodama had begun to work for American intelligence on release from prison and had emerged as one of the key operators used by the CIA to channel money to the LDP.

This was not made explicit at the time—the full extent of the ties among Kodama, the *yakuza*, Kishi, the CIA, and the Japanese ultra-right would only become widely understood in the 1990s. But the Lockheed scandal not only inevitably involved exposure of Kodama's name (Lockheed used him as an agent who would tell the company whom to bribe in Tokyo and how much), but also the extent of his influence. That much of a supposedly respectable Japanese government was under the thumb of a thug; that the United States used this thug to throw around money to manipulate Japanese politics as if Japan were some Central American banana republic or tinpot Middle East dictatorship was a concept that the Japanese governing elite—not to mention its intellectuals and journalists—simply could not bring themselves to entertain, even though it was manifestly true. So they turned with primeval fury on the man who had forced them to look in the mirror: Tanaka Kakuei.

The media referred to him in the most insulting way they could, stripping all honorifics from his name. (English lacks the concise means with which one can convey disdain in Japanese simply by dropping an honorific or deliberately using the wrong one.) When arrested and thrown in jail for three weeks before posting a huge bail, he was treated like any common criminal. Following release, he was forced to make a public appearance in court every week for seven years where he was grilled by teams of prosecutors. He would be convicted in January 1983. He never went back to prison—before his appeals ran out, he suffered a debilitating stroke and died. But with first a criminal indictment and then a conviction hanging over him, there was no longer any possibility of his return as prime minister—or, for that matter, to any public position other than that of backbencher for his district. He would, however, become the most powerful person in Japan, so powerful he acquired the informal title *Yami Shogun* ("Shadow Shogun").

TANAKA BECOMES *YAMI SHOGUN*

Possibly because he had been so vilified, Tanaka dispensed with the usual Japanese fictions about power and the motives of those who wield it. Powerful people in Japan are expected either to pretend they have none or else that they exercise it with great reluctance; that they have sacrificed their own happiness in order to serve the people, His Majesty, the nation, the company, or what have you. Tanaka poked fun at this palaver, boasting that prime ministers danced to his tune, evaluating them as if he were a teacher discussing inexperienced but promising pupils, comparing his relationship to Japan's official government with that of a stockholder who owns the majority of a firm's shares to the company's management team, and suggesting that analysts who had trouble grasping his position in the Japanese power structure consider the example of his contemporary, China's paramount leader, Deng Xiaoping. Indeed, when Deng led an official mission to Tokyo in the summer of 1978 (the only time in history that the de facto leader of China has visited Japan), Deng made sure to schedule an "unofficial" visit to Tanaka's residence. Beijing was under no illusions about who ran things in Tokyo.

Tanaka's continued unshakeable hold on his home prefecture of Niigata ensured that he could not be dislodged from the Diet. And the growing ranks of the *Tanaka gundan* meant no one could become prime minister without its support and thus no prime minister could oppose Tanaka openly. He also developed links with the opposition—even into the heart of the JSP—with his characteristic methods, allowing him to command legislative majorities on any existential question.

The first Tanaka disciple to become prime minister, Ohira Masayoshi, had joined hands with arch-Tanaka rival Fukuda to have the LDP dump Miki, the sitting prime minister. Under the terms of the deal they worked out, Fukuda would serve as prime minister for a term, followed by Ohira. Fukuda would be the last Japanese prime minister until Koizumi Junichiro in 2001 to assume the office without the explicit support of either the Tanaka political machine or one of the splinters left from its breakup in the early 1990s.

Ohira died in office in 1979 and Tanaka arranged for the appointment of Suzuki Zenko, who got the job mostly because he seemed to have so few enemies. But Suzuki's manifest failure to do what was minimally expected of a prime minister meant he had to be replaced. Tanaka paid a visit on Kishi—still, in his eighties, a powerful figure who could pull strings over those factions of the LDP that had had to give way to the *Tanaka gundan*. They agreed that Japan needed a prime minister who could be taken seriously by people like Ronald Reagan, Margaret Thatcher, and François Mitterrand, and they settled on a smaller faction leader with openly rightist views, Nakasone Yasuhiro.

Nakasone would go a long way toward erasing the image of the typical Japanese prime minister as a weak, powerless drone. Practically the first thing he did as prime minister was to visit South Korea on his own initiative in order to repair relations with that country; he did not consult, much less seek the approval of the Foreign Ministry bureaucrats, who were taken by surprise. He went on to strike up a plausible friendship with President Reagan and made a convincing case to all and sundry that Japan needed strong, confident leadership centered in the office of the prime minister.

But his debt to Tanaka was so great and his need to bow to Tanaka's wishes so obvious that the press dubbed his government "Tanakasone." Nakasone was a sufficiently gifted politician that when Tanaka's conviction was handed down in October 1983, Nakasone managed to survive the rage whipped up in the media and the opposition in the Diet, even though any withdrawal of the *gundan*'s support would have forced his resignation. But there was no disguising the reality that Nakasone continued to serve at Tanaka's pleasure.

Tanaka was finally destroyed not by his enemies but by his two closest lieutenants and by the man whom Tanaka would describe as his "lost son." Tanaka's 1983 conviction meant that all hope of an official rehabilitation had been lost. Yet he would not step down or aside; that would be to concede his enemies' charges: that he was somehow uniquely corrupt rather than, as he saw it, just better at doing what everybody did and being open about it. But the impasse blocked the paths to power of the most ruthless politicians in Japan. They would conspire in secret against Tanaka. When they had the numbers on their side, they confronted him with a fait accompli: the creation of a new "study group" carved out from the ranks of the *gundan*. It is the kind of story that would require a Mario Puzo—or even a Shakespeare—to do it justice, for it was effectively parricide; Tanaka had a stroke, and while he would linger on for a decade before he finally died, he never recovered. The machine he built would survive intact into the early 1990s in the hands of the two *capo regimes*. But then the son would turn on them too, break the machine, and try several times over the following twenty years to construct something Japan had not had since the dying off of the Meiji leaders: a genuine government rather than just a machine delivering money for votes.

THE CAPO REGIMES: TAKESHITA NOBORU AND KANEMARU SHIN

We have already met Takeshita—he was finance minister under Nakasone and helped negotiate the 1985 Plaza Accord that put an end to the era of the super-weak yen. He would succeed Nakasone as prime minister in 1987. Like Tanaka, the man who had been his mentor and whom he had betrayed, he was brought down by scandal, but continued to control Japanese politics for years after his resignation.

But he did not control things alone. Unlike Tanaka, Takeshita had a kind of co-equal in the political boss Kanemaru Shin. Kanemaru would never be prime minister, but in classic Japanese fashion, he was probably the more powerful of the two. He placed Takeshita in office and after Takeshita's fall, would, with Takeshita's help, designate the next three prime ministers. He too would eventually be brought down by a scandal, arrested, and convicted. In the meantime, though, as much as anyone, he would assume Tanaka's place as *Yami Shogun* of Japanese politics.

The difference between Kanemaru and Tanaka lay in the sheer scale and the blatancy of Kanemaru's approach. This was partly due to Kanemaru's crude, impulsive nature. Tanaka's buffoonery was a calculated act and behind it lay a wily political mind, capable, for example, of threading the way through minefields of history and national passions to negotiate an understanding with Zhou Enlai about how to put aside contentious issues that would otherwise have blocked the establishment of formal ties between Beijing and Tokyo. But Kanemaru was, in fact, a buffoon—rushing off to Pyongyang on his own, for example, to strike deals with North Korea that could not be delivered on, in the process rattling Seoul, Washington, and the Japanese foreign policy establishment.

But what ultimately made the crudity of Kanemaru's methods tolerable and even effective—for a while—were the floods of money gushing through Japan as a result of the bubble economy that we studied in chapter 7. Thanks to the measures taken by the Ministry of Finance and the Bank of Japan in the wake of the Plaza Accord, money was available to throw around in amounts that even Tanaka at the height of his power could not have imagined.

Excess in the Japanese system is a sure prelude to scandal and the scandal that emerged at the height of the bubble economy acquired the label "Recruit" after the name of the company at its center. The mistake made by Recruit's founder and president, Ezoe Hiromasa, was to use all the money flooding through the system to attempt to change its fundamental power alignments. The easy money being made by people in real estate and finance (*zai-tekku*—financial technology—it was called)—not to mention all the businesses springing up to cater to the nouveau riche—began to reduce the allure of the traditional Japanese career path. We have looked at the cultural and demographic implications of that, but there was an important political dimension as well since salaryman culture had played such a central role in diverting and suppressing what might otherwise have been restive political sentiments.

A gifted entrepreneur, Ezoe spotted the need for the infrastructure of a genuine labor market. When he began to build it, however, with magazines that listed job offerings and organizations providing paid career advice to ambitious young people, he raised the hackles of those who were accustomed to policing Japan's employment practices. They made preparations for a bill that would make it illegal to disseminate employment information without going through official channels.

The response in Japan when threats like this begin to emerge to one's business is to cozy up to the relevant bureaucrats with luxurious entertainments and ways to earn money that do not involve open bribery (among other things, Ezoe commissioned bureaucrats to write lavishly compensated articles in his magazines and invited them to give speeches at conferences he organized—very well-paid speeches) and to find politicians who can run interference with the bureaucracy. That costs money, but in the Japan of the late 1980s, money was not a problem—particularly because Ezoe used the Tokyo stock market to spin off subsidiaries, offering politicians the chance to buy shares before they were made available to the public. The shares could be resold into the soaring market at great profit;

if the politicians needed money to make the initial investment, a Recruit subsidiary would lend them the funds.

The combination of the nature of what Ezoe was doing and the scale on which he did it provoked the inevitable reaction and toppled the Takeshita government. Takeshita was followed by Uno Sosuke, who lasted only three months (the first and only time in history that a sex scandal brought down a Japanese prime minister—Uno's mistress accused him of being cheap by trying to buy her off with insultingly low amounts of money);[7] Kaifu Toshiki, who had, almost uniquely among Japanese politicians, been untouched by the Recruit scandal, proved surprisingly popular and was thus allowed to serve for two years; and, finally, Miyazawa Kiichi, a cerebral old-style mandarin and MOF graduate. Miyazawa would become famous in the United States when President George H. W. Bush threw up over him during a state visit to Tokyo. But for all his intelligence, learning, and decades of experience, to get the prime ministerial nod—and to stay in office—he regularly had to humiliate himself in front of a Kanemaru who deliberately assumed the persona of an overgrown hoodlum. The complete ascendancy of Tanaka's way of politics over the old mandarin elite could not have been clearer.

Then in 1992 a yet bigger scandal broke: Sagawa Kyubin. The name came from one of Japan's top delivery companies, a company much like Fed Ex or DHL. Just as Recruit had raised the hackles of those who controlled Japan's traditional career path, Sagawa Kyubin threatened the Japanese post office and its ministerial patron, the Ministry of Posts and Telecommunications. All kinds of permits were needed for the company to carry out its business, and to secure those permits, the company did what it had to do—effectively bribed politicians to run interference.

---

7. The rumors that circulate in Tokyo about the sexual escapades of Japan's prime ministers include bevies of mistresses, parties where the waitresses wear no panties, and kept boys installed in apartments in San Francisco. None of this can be completely substantiated, although one prime minister was almost certainly gay, two were probably bisexual, and strict monogamy among any would be astonishing. Exuberant, overflowing sexuality is thought to be part of the package that makes for a vital, charismatic leader. That Uno kept a mistress was a dog-bites-man story; what made it news was that he was so cheap with her and treated her so shabbily. The Japanese political class could make little sense of the hysteria in the United States over the Monica Lewinsky scandal. If it had been a Japanese scandal, it would have been the oral sex in the Oval Office that brought Clinton down. A politician is expected to have a robust libido, but enough control over it that he can confine his dalliances to unofficial times and places.

But things had changed in the three years since the Recruit scandal. The bubble economy had ended. Financial game-playing no longer delivered such easy money. It was not just the dry-up of funding, however. The onset of bubble deflation in 1990 had brought with it revelation after revelation about the rot at the heart of Japanese finance. What specifically came to light were not just incestuous relations between politicians and financiers, but the pervasive presence of organized crime at the highest reaches of Japanese finance and politics. The revelations that accompanied the scandal about the role of the criminal underworld finally provoked a political crisis, for they tore off the last shreds of legitimacy still clinging to the 1955 system.

Paradoxically, only great politicians have the political skills necessary to transform the straw of anger and revulsion at politicians into the bricks capable of breaking an old order and forging a new one. And the greatest politician in Japan at that point was probably the man Tanaka had once called his "son"—Ozawa Ichiro.

OZAWA ICHIRO

Like Tanaka, Ozawa has roots in a relatively poor, "backwards" part of Japan—in Ozawa's case, the Iwate Prefecture that would become world-famous when so much of its coastline was destroyed by the 2011 tsunami. He came to Tanaka's attention in his very first campaign in 1968 when he stepped in to take over the seat his recently deceased father had held; Tanaka made him the leader of a group of young legislators who would see to it that members of the *gundan* ("army") stayed loyal. The group acquired the title *Shōnen Tantei Dan* ("Boys' Detective Group"), an allusion to a series of popular comics and television shows for children.[8] Ozawa became Tanaka's most trusted confidante, but then, as we have seen, conspired with Takeshita and Kanemaru to overthrow Tanaka and take over his machine (Ozawa is said to have sat up all night weeping the

---

8. The shows were derived from the 1929 German children's novel, *Emil and the Detectives*, that obviously resonated in Japan since it spawned so many spin-offs. In the original, a boy who has been robbed organizes a group of other boys to track down the thief and bring him to justice. In the Japanese spin-offs, groups of grade-school boys—usually with a token girl or two—set about ferreting out bad guys and helping (characteristically clueless) police officers solve crimes.

night before they pulled off their coup). Under the joint reign of Takeshita and Kanemaru, he became more and more powerful, entrusted during Miyazawa's prime ministership with the position of Secretary General of the LDP.

The Sagawa Kyubin scandal culminated in Kanemaru's arrest in March 1993, all covered in gloating and minute detail in the media. Among other things, prosecutors found gold bars and some $50 million in negotiable securities stashed away in Kanemaru's Tokyo home. With Kanemaru out of the picture (like Tanaka, Kanemaru would have a stroke; he died in 1996), a struggle set in for control of the *Tanaka gundan* as former prime minister Takeshita sought to promote his new protégé Hashimoto Ryutaro over Ozawa. Takeshita succeeded, but it was something of a Pyrrhic victory, since Ozawa responded by leading forty-two supporters out of the *gundan* to form his own faction.

Ozawa was convinced that the time for radical reform had arrived and that he was the man to carry it out. Ozawa may have started his political life as Tanaka's hatchet man; he was not only well-schooled in Tanaka's methods but arguably their most adept living practitioner. But he began to reveal something that Tanaka for all his brilliance had lacked: an appreciation for the ends of politics beyond just keeping oneself and one's allies in power and bestowing largesse on dependents. Among other things, Ozawa demonstrated an increasingly nuanced understanding of the fundamental structural flaw in the Japanese political setup, coupled with the outlines of a plan for doing something to correct it.

Two things in the early 1990s helped Ozawa see that even more was at issue than control over a political machine now deeply mired in mud thrown off by the scandals we have discussed. The first was the Gulf War. President George H. W. Bush had put together a global coalition to reverse Saddam Hussein's invasion of Kuwait. But not only did Japan, as Washington saw it, hide behind the notorious Article 9 of its constitution to avoid putting any of its people in harm's way, Tokyo was reluctant to cough up a significant share of the expenses for the war. For a country that was as heavily dependent on Middle East oil as Japan, a country that appeared to spew money everywhere and had been boasting of its emergence as the world's premiere economy (the bubble economy had just ended and few understood at the time that what seemed to be hiccoughs were in fact the onset of a chronic economic disease from which Japan has not yet recovered), the failure even to write a check struck Western capitals as the worst sort of freeloading. Appalled at the inability of Tokyo's political class to grasp the stakes involved, Ozawa banged heads together to squeeze out the necessary funds. Thanks to Ozawa, Japan ended up contributing more than any other country toward the war's expenses. But the delayed, grudging nature of it all seemed too little, too late.[9] Ozawa came to believe that if Japan wanted to be taken seriously by other countries, it had to have a foreign policy that was something other than purely reactive—and that the inability to generate proactive foreign policy stemmed directly from Japanese politics.

The second event that played a key part in Ozawa's road-to-Damascus-like conversion from skilled political infighter to visionary leader was the publication in 1990 of the Japanese translation of Karel van Wolferen's *Enigma of Japanese Power*. Van Wolferen's book was one of a series writings that appeared in the late 1980s that collectively acquired the label "revisionist."[10] What needed "revision," according to these books and articles, was the prevailing understanding of Japan in the West as a garden-variety liberal capitalist democracy. But while the other "revisionist" writers tended to stress the threat the Japanese economic juggernaut posed to the global trade and financial order, van Wolferen diagnosed the central flaw in the Japanese political setup: the absence of what he labeled a center of political accountability.

Enigma provoked spasms of outrage and attempts by official Japanese government spokesmen to smear the author. But the depth of telling detail made it impossible to discredit on specific grounds (Van Wolferen had covered Japanese politics for two decades as the Tokyo correspondent of *NRC Handlesblad*, then the leading quality newspaper in the Netherlands).

Enigma not only struck a chord but summoned up a veritable orchestra. At the same time Japan's official establishment was attempting to portray van Wolferen as "anti-Japanese," he was receiving letters from officials high up in the power structure who asked that their names be kept secret,

---

9. In fact, Japan's contributions played a critical role, something acknowledged by General H. Norman Schwarzkopf in his memoirs. The Japanese embassy in Riyadh quietly funneled millions of dollars to coalition troops, allowing them to bypass the Washington bureaucracy.

10. Other major examples of revisionist writing included a book by former US trade negotiator Clyde Prestowitz and a lead article in the *Atlantic* by the journalist and former presidential speech writer James Fallows. I also contributed to "revisionism" with a lead article in the *Harvard Business Review*, but missed being included in the revisionist canon when the *BusinessWeek* journalist Robert Neff, who coined the term and wrote a cover story about the phenomenon, could not find me—I was on vacation between jobs in the pre-net world.

but urged him to continue to set down his thoughts.[11] Pundits joked of a second era of *rangaku*—literally, "Dutch learning," a reference to Edo period scholarship on the West that relied exclusively on writings in the Dutch language that filtered into Japan from the official Dutch trading outpost in Nagasaki harbor. Van Wolferen received the ultimate accolade in Japan, a widely used neologism: *akauntabiriti*, coined from "accountability."

Ozawa wrote a book of his own with ideas that obviously reflected the buzz *Enigma* generated,[12] as well as what he had learned from the aftermath of the Gulf War. In *Blueprint for a New Japan*, Ozawa argued that Japan needed to become a "normal" nation, normal in the sense that it would have a "normal" politics, a "normal" foreign policy, and a "normal" military under explicit political control. Many in Japan refused to believe Ozawa capable of writing such a book—not to mention that he would take the time to do it himself—but whether or not portions of the book were ghostwritten, there is no doubt that Ozawa had thought long and hard about what was wrong with his country.

Fixing things started, in his mind, with two fundamental reforms: (1) a genuine two-party system that would force parties to compete not by throwing cash around but by articulating clear policy visions; (2) political control over the bureaucracy. Tanaka had demonstrated that a strong politician could bend the bureaucracy to his will. But Ozawa proposed to use Tanaka's methods for more than just largesse. He wanted to use those methods to set political priorities.

Like Martin Luther tacking his theses to the church door, Ozawa issued a series of demands to the LDP leadership: reform of the rules of politics in order to promote real political competition. When the LDP predictably failed to meet Ozawa's June 1993 deadline, he led his faction out of the LDP. Tanaka had taught him to develop strong ties with key figures in opposition parties—particularly in the Japan Socialist Party—and he used those ties to ram a no-confidence motion through the Diet, forcing Miyazawa's resignation and precipitating an election. The results allowed Ozawa to put together a coalition government. Ozawa installed in the prime minister's office a telegenic former provincial governor, Hosokawa

---

11. A follow-up book he wrote for the Japanese market would become the single largest-selling book ever translated into Japanese except for the Bible.

12. Ozawa and van Wolferen later became personally acquainted after van Wolferen wrote a book entitled *The Character Assassination of Ozawa Ichiro*.

Morihiro, who had started a new party that had done startlingly well in the election. The LDP's forty-eight–year lock on Japan's electoral politics had finally been broken.

Things started off on just the right note. The public was enthralled with Hosokawa while US President Bill Clinton convinced himself that the new Japanese prime minister was a sort of soul mate, conveyed into office by the same kind of longing for change that had propelled Clinton into the White House.

Longing for change may have been a factor in the elevation of both men to their positions as nominal heads of their respective governments, but that—and their good looks—are about the extent of the parallels between the two. Hosokawa was, to be sure, the first non-LDP prime minister since 1955, but everyone knew Hosokawa was there because the new *yami shogun* had put him there. While Hosokawa was indeed personally popular, the new *yami shogun* could not make the same boast. While he had his admirers, he was also among the most controversial people in Japan—widely disliked and even hated.

What Ozawa had done had real consequences for LDP politicians who were suddenly deprived of their means of delivering largesse to constituents, means that guaranteed their own livelihoods. So, of course, the LDP hated Ozawa. But the hatred went far beyond the LDP. Part of it was his own fault. He may have been Tanaka's most gifted disciple and he may have developed a grasp of the larger picture that his mentor did not share, but he was sometimes unwilling to do what Tanaka had done so effortlessly—go the extra mile to charm the socks off of practically anyone. He was said to lack Tanaka's skill at *nemawashi*—literally, "root binding" or getting everyone on board behind the scenes; he was also accused of being cheap. Ozawa could be supremely effective in negotiations and deal-making in closed rooms; he could hardly have gotten where he did had he not been. He did not, however, bother to hide his increasing contempt for establishment journalists and many other politicians. They retaliated by portraying him as arrogant and aloof, a portrayal that stuck in the minds of many.

But there was more to it. The hatred Ozawa generated was bound up in his legacy as Tanaka's heir. Anyone who has spent any time in Japan knows there are two sides to the place—a dark side intimately bound to the bright like some sort of evil twin. On one side lies the breathtaking refinement that infuses Japan's arts and design, the exquisite nuance and formality of the Japanese language as spoken by a well-born matron or high official, the elegance of ritual that surrounds everything from a business meeting to a formal dinner to the doings of the Imperial Court. On the other side, one finds the helter-skelter urban craziness of the streets of Tokyo and Osaka, the menacing, calculated rudeness in the swagger and buzz talk of gangsters, the blatant reveling in bawdiness and sleaze at the bars and cabarets of Kabukicho and Namba. Next to the classic Japanese beauty in her kimono or Chanel suit is the hostess or *gyaru* ("gal") we met in the preceding chapter; beside the bright, eager youngster in short pants, pageboy haircut, and necktie stands the *chinpira* (delinquent) with his greased, spiked hair roaring about on a motorcycle with no muffler—or, increasingly these days, the budding *otaku* living in a squalid little room piled high with the detritus of his fetish.

The "evil twin" of the *Tōdai*-bred dedicated public official with his erudite language and professed concern for nothing but policy and the broader good is the crude, deal-making politician consorting with "developers" and corrupt construction bosses, greasing palms everywhere with ill-gotten money. The ascendancy of the Tanaka machine, culminating in his disciple Kanemaru's hold over Japanese politics, had not just been an affront to all who had exalted ideas of the positive potential for politics—it had brought to the fore the Dr. Jekyll/Mr. Hyde aspect of the way power is exercised in Japan in a manner that no fiction—no matter how polite or frequently repeated—could possibly conceal any more. The bureaucracy may have been hijacked by the Tanaka machine, but the series of scandals culminating in Sagawa Kyubin demonstrated that bureaucrats themselves were willingly complicit in their own corruption.

This was all a horror to those responsible for maintaining Japan's "face"—to itself even more than to the rest of the world. Such people included the public prosecutors and judges, editors of the quality newspapers (particularly the *Asahi Shimbun*), academics and intellectuals, not to mention the high-minded political types who had traditionally clustered around the Japan Socialist Party. Ozawa was the most brilliant product of the machine that represented everything they detested about what had happened to their country. No matter how penetrating his diagnosis of Japan's political sickness, no matter how capable he might prove in curing that sickness, they could not forgive him. He managed both to stand as an embodiment of the established, if unspoken features of Japanese political life that embarrassed many Japanese, while simultaneously promising to rid Japan of these features in ways that posed a direct threat to all who benefitted from them, even at the same time they loathed any reminder of just what those features were. To call this hypocrisy misses the point—it is a species of doublethink of the type Orwell analyzed: the ability to act on two contradictory sets of notions and to grasp where a train of thought might lead and cut if off before it became dangerous. Ozawa threatened to make it impossible for Japan's political class to continue this mental dance. He would have to be brought down by the self-appointed guardians of Japan's political order.

GUARDIANS OF POLITICAL ORDER

Two sets of guardians exist working in tandem: the public prosecutor and the editors of the quality newspapers (plus the top producers at NHK, the "public" television network). They follow a standard script. Politics is arranged in such a way that a politician can almost always be charged with violation of one or another statute. The statutes are sufficiently vaguely worded that the public prosecutor has enormous discretion in determining who might be charged and on what grounds. (Japan's legal infrastructure is rooted in continental rather than common law; precedent thus lacks the determinative role played in such countries as the United States and Britain.)

The public prosecutors see themselves as the ultimate defenders of the integrity of Japanese governance. When they determine that a politician has become what they regard as a threat to order, they will select a violation of one sort or another—often quite trivial—and inform the quality press. Scenes for the consumption of television viewers are carefully staged with prosecutors "raiding" the offices of the supposed miscreant. Newspapers like the *Asahi* will work themselves into fever pitches of outrage about the "betrayal" of public trust. If the politicians (or bankers or business executives—the same dynamic is at work in policing economic organizations) behave with the proper degree of contrition, resigning from their positions with deep bows and formal apologies, the whole thing can blow over like an afternoon thunderstorm with the politician in question returning to public life after a period of "reflection." But when the targets refuse to play their assigned roles, they can provoke a reaction that borders on hysteria. (Tanaka and Kanemaru had thumbed their noses at the whole charade, one reason they so enraged the prosecutors and press.)

In wrecking Ozawa's first attempts to construct a genuine two-party system in Japan, the guardians went by the recipe book. In a tactically astute move, they avoided launching a direct attack on Ozawa himself. Instead they found an item that allowed them to smear the very shield Ozawa had adopted: the fresh, clean face of Hosokawa. A blueblood descended from one of Japan's most illustrious families (his ancestors had played a central role in the founding of the Ashikaga Shogunate), Hosokawa was about as unlike a typical *gundan* member as it was possible to get. But it turned out he had nonetheless accepted a loan years earlier from none other than Sagawa Kyubin. He had paid the loan back, but had not paid interest on it. In the climate of the times, this was enough to start a hullabaloo in the press that forced his resignation.

He was succeeded by Hata Tsutomu, a key ally of Ozawa's and, like Ozawa, a former member of the *Tanaka gundan*. But Hata lasted in office only nine weeks. The remnants of the *gundan* that had stayed in the LDP under Hashimoto's leadership had figured out a way to strike back at the Ozawa who had betrayed them and to destroy the coalition he had built: lure the JSP out of it with an offer of the prime ministership.

There was bitter irony in what happened. The LDP had been put together in the first place to prevent the socialists from coming to power. The JSP had, over time, degenerated into little more than a talking shop. The JSP hurled slogans at the LDP and struck poses of probity. But in donning the mantle of an opposition party without actually doing anything that could result in the formation of a genuine government, the JSP served in practice as a useful prop for the existing power structure by preempting the emergence of an actual opposition. Characteristically, Tanaka had understood this very well, forming quiet alliances with key JSP politicians and helping them financially, brushing aside their holier-than-thou poses as something they had to do politically.

In 1994, however, when for the first time in over a century, Japan had the makings of a real opposition taking power and forming a genuine government, the JSP revealed its true colors. The LDP dangled the prospect of the prime ministership in front of the JSP and, like a watchdog seduced by a succulent chunk of meat, it trotted off wagging its tail. What made it particularly ironic was that under the terms of the deal worked out, after the JSP got its prime ministership for a term, it agreed to support not just any LDP candidate, but Hashimoto Ryutaro for the following term. Hashimoto was the man whom former prime minister Takeshita had anointed as the leader of the remnants of the *Tanaka gundan* still in the LDP. With his rightist views and Tanaka-schooled methods, he represented everything the JSP had ostensibly stood against for two generations. It was as if George McGovern had thrown his support to Richard Nixon in return for a ceremonial cabinet post of little actual power.

The first experiment in opposition government was over. For the first—and last—time since 1949, the JSP would get its prime minister: Murayama Tomiichi. It would be a mistake to say Murayama accomplished absolutely nothing—he did make a formal apology for the events of the 1930s and 1940s, something elements in the LDP have been trying to retract ever since. But actual governing was back where it had always had been: fragmented among the various ministries and LDP legislators in the Diet. Hashimoto took over as head of the coalition in January 1996 and with the economy beginning to recover, called an election for October which the LDP won. The JSP essentially disappeared; the meat it had been fed turned out to have been poisoned with complete electoral disillusionment at the party's hypocrisy.

But while the first experiment with a two-party system seemed to have failed, the ten months in which the LDP lost its control over Japan's parliamentary machinery left two changes in its wake—changes that could not be easily reversed. First, the Japanese public had realized that a non-LDP government was not only possible, but that they might have a real say-so in it. Second, the Hosokawa government implemented electoral reforms that made conceivable the vigorous political competition Ozawa had called for.

THE 1994 ELECTORAL REFORMS

The reforms weakened the key feature of the 1955 system: the one vote/multi-candidate electoral system that guaranteed money would play the central role in elections. Under the new system, a Japanese voter in a Lower House election receives two ballots rather than one. On one ballot, the voter chooses a single candidate. The candidate who gets the most votes in the voter's district becomes that district's only representative to the Lower House. Three hundred members of the Lower House are chosen this way.

But the Lower House has 480 members. On the second ballot the voter receives, he or she marks the name of a party, not of a candidate. The reforms divided Japan into eleven "proportional representation" districts that collectively send the remaining 180 legislators to the Diet.

Japan thus has a hybrid system combining elements of the single-seat US/UK method and the proportional method used in continental Europe. (Japan also has an Upper House with limited powers—it can send legislation other than the budget back to the Lower House that can override it only with a 2/3 vote. Half the 242 seats of the Upper House are determined in a given election; like the Lower House, some of these seats are contested in single districts; the rest are allocated according to proportional representation.)

But these reforms did not break the power of the LDP. The ostensible purpose of the proportional seat component had been to allow smaller parties to retain some seats in the Diet. But the proportional seat component also left the LDP—and other parties—with the ability to place legislators in office without their having to appeal directly to voters as candidates. And the reforms did little to rectify the imbalance between the countryside and the city.

The reforms and the brief taste of non-LDP government did, however, lead to a veritable hubbub of activity as political entrepreneurs broke up old parties, merged with other parties, and spun off new parties. The largest of these was the New Frontier Party, headed by Ozawa.

But the party was not large enough to unseat the LDP again. With what appeared to be an economic recovery underway, Hashimoto's LDP won what seemed a decisive victory in the October 1996 elections—the first election held under the new system.

The victory was decisive, however, only in terms of the numbers of seats the LDP captured: 239 of 500.[13] That allowed Hashimoto to form a government by bringing in the small handful of Socialist legislators left over in the wake of the devastation the election had wreaked on their party (they had tried changing their name to the Social Democratic Party of Japan—it did not work). The LDP would end up inducing enough other legislators to join its ranks that it could rule without the Socialists. But for all its control of the Diet, the LDP's share of the popular vote in the election had been below 39 percent. Ozawa's New Frontier Party had picked up

13. At the time, 200 seats were elected using the proportional representation system—later reduced to 180.

28 percent of the popular vote and held 156 seats. The threat Ozawa posed to LDP hegemony had not ended; it had only begun.

Among other things, the members of Hashimoto's second cabinet had barely started to warm their cabinet seats when the Ministry of Finance engineered a hike in the consumption tax. The MOF had begun trying to introduce this tax in the late 1970s, partly in response to the excesses of the Tanaka machine. The MOF succeeded, finally, in 1989, one reason Takeshita, who was then prime minister, saw his poll ratings tumble. The initial tax rate was 3 percent, but the MOF had visions of raising it incrementally until the tax became the primary source of revenue for the Japanese government.

We looked at some of the economic fallout of the 1996 increase in chapter 7, but the hike had political implications as well. As we noted, it turned out to have been one of the worst policy mistakes ever made by Japanese officialdom. It aborted the nascent recovery, precipitating a series of bank failures and forcing the authorities into the hugely unpopular bank bailout package of later that year—all of which was blamed, fairly or not, on the LDP.

The LDP was fortunate that a Lower House election did not have to be held until 2000, but the LDP lost the 1998 Upper House elections. Hashimoto resigned to "take responsibility" and was replaced by his foreign minister, Obuchi Keizo. Obuchi—yet another *gundan* soldier—would serve for less than two years before suffering a stroke and dying soon thereafter. A caretaker prime minister, Mori Yoshiro, was appointed and, taking advantage of some sympathy for the hapless Obuchi (stress had been implicated in his early death), Mori led the LDP to another electoral victory in the June 2000 elections. Memories of the tax hike had begun to fade, the opposition was fragmented, and the LDP still enjoyed disproportionate representation from rural areas.

Although Mori is actually a savvy politician, he put on an act as a buffoon, playing the lightning rod to absorb popular resentment that would create the space for him to resign at just the right moment to allow Hashimoto to return to office. But then something unexpected happened.

With Ozawa in opposition, de facto leadership of what was left of the *Tanaka gundan* had passed to Hashimoto—why it was taken as a given that he would again resume the prime ministership. As a political tactician, however, Hashimoto was not in the same league with his mentors. In response to a media campaign decrying the lack of transparency with

which *yami shogun* such as Takeshita had been designating prime ministers, the LDP had instituted a "primary" vaguely modeled on American
lines. The "mandarin" factions of the LDP—the political descendants of
Fukuda Takeo, the man who had been Tanaka's great rival, and, ultimately,
of Kishi—saw the primary as a chance to recapture what its leaders viewed
as their rightful hold on Japanese politics. But they had learned something
over the preceding generation since Tanaka had shoved them aside: that to
succeed in the Japanese politics of the new millennium, you have to put on
a convincing act as a reformer, even if your real purposes are precisely the
opposite of reform.

KOIZUMI JUNICHIRO

Like most Japanese politicians, Koizumi came from a political family; his
grandfather had been a cabinet minister and his father director general of
the Japan Defense Agency. Koizumi started his own career as secretary to
Fukuda Takeo, Tanaka's great rival and the last man to occupy the prime
minister's office without having been put there by the Tanaka machine or
one of its successors. Koizumi won his own first election in 1972 and rose
through the ranks of the LDP, serving in a number of key positions before
emerging in the 1990s as one of the three key leaders of the non-*gundan*,
mandarin factions of the LDP.[14]

Koizumi's career and political heritage was thus about as orthodox as
it is possible to get for a Japanese politician. But he did not come across as
orthodox. His bouffant hairdo, eclectic musical passions (Elvis Presley to
Wagner and Sibelius), and camera-friendly persona allowed him to strike
a convincing pose as a reformer. On the strength of that, he won the LDP
primary. Although the non-binding primary was held only among party
members, Koizumi's victory was so overwhelming that the LDP leadership simply could not ignore the results, particularly since the election that
mattered—the one for party president among LDP Diet members—was
scheduled for only three days later. Koizumi could not be denied the post,
which automatically made him prime minister.

---

14. The three leaders—Koizumi, Kato Koichi, and Yamasaki Taku—were known by the acronym
    for their family names "YKK"—a play on the famous zipper-maker.

Koizumi was Japan's first politician fully to grasp the political uses to which modern media could be put. Like Ronald Reagan and Tony Blair, who also rose to power because of their skills at employing modern media for political ends, Koizumi succeeded by dressing up a conservative—even reactionary—agenda in genial, reformist, television-friendly clothing.

Much of the world would confuse that agenda with neoliberalism. With the Republicans under President George W. Bush ascendant in Washington and conservative governments coming to power in Paris and Berlin, Tokyo had no reason to disabuse anyone of the notion that Japan had joined a supposed worldwide trend away from state control and toward freer markets.

There is no doubt some of the people around Koizumi—most particularly, his economic minister Takenaka Heizo—were influenced by neoliberal ideas.[15] Koizumi himself was also sympathetic to neoliberal thinking; Koizumi embodied a shift in the conceptual view of the Japanese Right away from the mixture of clientelism and strong-state corporatism that characterized the Right in the early postwar decades to a contemporary mixture of reactionary nationalism with neoliberalism. But neoliberal talk and moving-with-the-times posturing ultimately served less as a cloak for reforms—whether neoliberal or otherwise—than an attempt at a restoration of the situation that had prevailed before Tanaka seized control of Japanese politics: undivided rule by a trained, technocratic elite.

The first step in this restoration involved breaking up the machinery that had provided Tanaka and his successors with the financial fuel for their methods. The legislation for which Koizumi is best remembered was the so-called "privatization" of the Japanese post office. The post office was in fact the world's biggest bank; post offices blanketed the country and with their friendlier service and slightly higher interest rates, collected more money than the largest of Japan's nominally private banks. This money created a giant slush fund at the disposal of the government and was used, among other things, to finance much of the white-elephant spending that Tanaka and his successors had wielded to garner votes.[16]

15. Among other things, Takenaka would loudly claim credit for finally solving the non-performing loan problems of Japanese banks, although as Richard Koo has noted, most of these loans were already written off before Takenaka took office.
16. Financially, the post office is essentially a giant Ponzi scheme since most of the projects it finances do not generate returns sufficient to retire the loans taken down to pay for them. The post office funds deposit withdrawals with new deposits or with money newly created by the Bank of Japan.

Koizumi may have been closely identified with this bill whose real purpose was to drain this pool of money, but he admitted he had not even read it—it had been written inside the Ministry of Finance. Koizumi's obvious political skills were used to get it through the Diet and sell it to the public as a species of "reform."

"Privatizing" the post office was only the first step in depriving the various successors of the Tanaka machine with the money needed to operate. The Koizumi government set about reducing the deficit spending that had become increasingly important to financing public works after the collapse of the bubble, announcing a cap on government bond issuance in September 2001. (This backfired as any good Keynesian could have told them it would; the government backtracked in 2003 in the face of a sharply contracting economy.)

The Koizumi government also set about rewriting the social contract that the mandarins of the 1950s had effectively agreed to as the price for ending the labor militancy of that decade. As we saw in chapter 7, under Koizumi, companies were allowed to rely increasingly on non-permanent employees; Takenaka's much-trumpeted clean-up of bank balance sheets served to staunch the flow of credit to failing companies —"zombies" they were labeled—that had heretofore helped provide for universal economic security. This was all advertised as the final coming of free-market capitalism to Japan, but when some entrepreneurial deal-makers started taking the government at its word, staging raids on companies and busting them up to generate higher returns, the public prosecutors moved in and arrested two of the most prominent: Horie Takafumi and Murakami Yoshiaki. These men had made the mistake of confusing neoliberal posturing with any actual intention by the authorities to cede control over economic outcomes to investment bankers and capital markets; their arrests served as an unmistakable warning to others with similar ideas.[17]

In the foreign policy arena, Koizumi sought to restore the absolute primacy of the relationship with the United States that had been the legacy of the conservative mandarins of the 1950s. Koizumi did everything he could to show his enthusiasm for the American invasion of Iraq. Not that

---

17. To be sure, Horie had countenanced dodgy schemes to boost the share price of his company. But the humiliation and stiff prison term he had to endure formed such a contrast to the kind of wrist-slapping usually meted out to well-connected insiders found guilty of financial crimes (e.g., Olympus executives) that it was obvious the authorities' prime motive was to make an example of him.

there was much in practical terms he could do; true, Tokyo dispatched some "troops," but since they were noncombatants, all they effectively did was serve as targets; the "peacekeepers" that the Dutch had also sent had to spend most of their time guarding the Japanese.[18]

But the symbolism mattered. The Bush White House was desperate to portray the Iraq War as something other than an unprovoked American invasion, and Koizumi's show of support helped them do just that. Koizumi would be rewarded; on the eve of Koizumi's retirement as prime minister in September 2006, Bush personally escorted him to Memphis, Tennessee, for a several-hour tour of Graceland where Koizumi proceeded to belt out several Elvis Presley hits.

Provocative gestures toward Japan's neighbors formed the flip side of the obsequiousness to Washington, although these gestures were also largely symbolic. Among other things, Koizumi began making visits to Yasukuni Shrine for worship, something guaranteed to raise hackles in China and both North and South Korea.

YASUKUNI SHRINE AND FOREIGN RELATIONS UNDER KOIZUMI

Yasukuni Shrine is a large Shinto shrine in central Tokyo that enshrines Japan's war dead as well as others seen as having given their lives for the Japanese Empire. The shrine formed one of the central institutions of the State Shinto we looked at in chapter 3, and had been the spiritual center of the prewar and wartime *kokutai* (national polity/emperor system) ideological apparatus used to justify and legitimize Japanese aggression in the 1930s. Yasukuni continued after the war as the symbolic shrine of the nationalist Japanese Right and the politically powerful Association of War-Bereaved Families, a group whose political clout in Japan had once been compared to that of the National Rifle Association in the United

---

18. Japan also bought a significant chunk of the extra bonds the US Treasury issued to finance the Iraq War. But this was inevitable in a dollar-centered global financial order. By going to war without raising taxes, the United States increased the demand side of its economy without doing anything to increase the supply. The gap was made up by the principal suppliers to the United States—led by China and Japan who were paid for their goods in dollars. So they automatically helped finance the war; China purchased even more additional US Treasury bonds than Japan did and it was not because of any love for the United States in Beijing.

States. Visits to Yasukuni by high-ranking officials of the Japanese government became particularly problematic after 1978 when a new high priest enshrined fourteen indicted Class A war criminals, including Tojo Hideki, at Yasukuni.

The emperor stopped making visits to Yasukuni; two of the fourteen had been pro-Axis cabinet ministers whom Emperor Hirohito partly blamed for the war, a matter that would come to light in 2006 with the disclosure of some internal documents of the Imperial Household Agency. Even more to the point, with the enshrinement of the indicted war criminals, official visits to Yasukuni by Japanese government ministers began to provoke strong protests from Japan's neighbors. Nakasone nonetheless went to Yasukuni twice while he was prime minister to pay his respects, but after he stepped down in 1987, prime ministers stayed away—until Koizumi.

Koizumi's annual visits to Yasukuni may have seemed perverse; what conceivable practical purpose was served in provoking the anger of neighboring countries? But such a question could only be asked by those who failed to grasp the importance of symbolism, of theater in Japanese politics.

Japan's neighbors tend to see Yasukuni visits as coded messages that the Japanese Right is in ascendance and is thumbing its nose at global opinion, but there is something more at work. Early in this chapter, we noted how the Meiji government's destruction of Japan's traditional Buddhist-infused popular religion had left behind a spiritual vacuum. For many Japanese, Yasukuni serves as the physical embodiment of the only cause that has filled that vacuum, a cause that gives them something to grasp that is larger than themselves. Yasukuni enshrines the millions who gave their lives for this cause, including most particularly the kamikaze pilots who are regarded by many as almost Christ-like figures, martyring themselves for their country and their people. To fail to pay homage to the kamikaze pilots and the others who died for Japan simply because doing so might disrupt trade agreements or the sensibilities of neighbors strikes many as an assault on everything that matters. Even the enshrinement of the "war criminals" did not change the views of many Japanese; as we saw in chapter 3, the Tokyo War Crimes trials had been almost completely discredited as arbitrary exercises in "victors' justice." Most Japanese believe— and with good reason—that who got indicted as a war criminal and who did not was as much a matter of luck and relative skill at bureaucratic infighting as actual, measurable culpability.

Nationalism may be the most virulent and destructive of the monsters Nietzsche foresaw crawling out of the abyss opened up by the death of God, but it is the only cause that gives untold millions a reason for living. The world wonders why the Japanese cannot act like the Germans in their stance toward what happened in the 1930s, but to many Japanese, requests that they do so seem like suggestions that they commit spiritual suicide. The war and its aftermath did not kill love of country and its past in Japan as it largely did in Germany; it only wounded it. Among other things, the Japanese still take uncomplicated pleasure and pride in their cultural heritage. No director in Germany today, for example, can mount a straightforward production of any of Richard Wagner's operas. These may be the crowning glory of German music theater and among the most magnificent and influential achievements in world cultural history, but the use to which the Nazis put these works makes it impossible for German directors to stage them in accordance with their author's copious and specific instructions. No such problems dog producers of *Kanadehon Chushingura*, the greatest of the Kabuki plays.

Of course, many right-wing politicians in Japan—as elsewhere—are utterly cynical about the way they exploit national longings and the spiritual crisis of modernity in order to amass power. But many others—Koizumi and the current prime minister, Abe Shinzo among them—do genuinely believe not only that Japan's contemporary malaise is a spiritual crisis dressed up in economic and social clothing, but that they are offering the only leadership that could show their fellow countrymen a way out of this crisis. The Yasukini visits only make complete sense in this light.

As, indeed, does Japan's stance vis-à-vis the United States on the one hand, and Japan's neighbors on the other. As we saw in chapter 4, the conservative mandarinate of the 1950s represented that element of the Japanese power structure that had survived the aftermath of the war and the Occupation. We traced the steps by which they had wrested control of their country back from the American authorities and from the liberal, democratic elements in Japan to whom the Americans had, before the Reverse Course of the late 1940s, initially intended to hand over power. The mandarins had made the crucial decision, symbolized in Kishi's ramrodding of the Security Treaty through the Diet, that for the foreseeable future Japan would cast its lot with the United States and seek shelter under the American military umbrella rather than attempt to build independent security and foreign policy arrangements in East Asia. At the time, this seemed the only course open to them that preserved their control over domestic political outcomes while keeping at bay those would destroy what, in their view, made Japan, even if the price involved surrender of key elements of sovereignty to Washington.

For their part, Tanaka and Kanemaru had been much more relaxed about things, quite open to working out live-and-let-live arrangements with Beijing and Pyongyang. And although Ozawa was no leftist, he nonetheless believed Tokyo should negotiate new arrangements with both Washington and Beijing—that the subordinate relationship with the United States should be replaced with something closer to a genuine alliance of equals, that Japan should do everything it could to portray itself as sympathetic to China's return to great power status, and that Tokyo should work to be seen as a potential partner by Beijing.

But the conservative mandarinate which Koizumi represented would have none of it. At least in the near term, they saw any change in the existing relationship with Washington as threatening to put Japan on a road to becoming a Tibet of the Pacific, with Japan's culture and essence overwhelmed by a newly ascendant China. Better to continue to humor American whims and mollify the occasional American tantrum than to be under the thumb of a Beijing that could not be manipulated and sweet-talked like Washington could. Tokyo had had sixty years of experience in catering to the Americans in ways that allowed Japan to preserve something of what the Right viewed as Japan's national essence; the Right did not see any comparable act as being possible with Beijing—and not just because Beijing is a lot closer to Tokyo than Washington is.

Making it all a bit ironic was the boost Koizumi's popularity received from an economic recovery due in considerable measure to orders for capital equipment pouring in to Japanese companies from China. The balance sheet recession was finally over. The banks had been cleaned up and corporate profits were surging, thanks in large part to all those orders. The recovery in corporate profits had not yet translated into rising employment levels, not to mention wage and salary hikes, but surely that was only a matter of time, wasn't it? In the meantime, cheap imports from China helped reduce the cost of living.

Surging corporate profits were not the only reason Koizumi was so popular. In the 2003 election, Koizumi and the LDP had gotten something of a scare. Ozawa had taken his New Frontier Party of Japan into the Democratic Party of Japan that had been formed back in 1996 and was, in 2003, under the nominal leadership of the popular Kan Naoto, whom we met in the preceding chapter. The Democratic Party made significant gains in its share both of the popular vote and of the seats captured in the Lower House of the Diet. But 2005 was a different story. A master political tactician, Koizumi seized what seemed to be a defeat—the failure of the postal privatization bill in the Diet—and converted it into a landslide electoral victory. When the bill failed, he used his prerogative as prime minister to dissolve the Diet and call for a new election. He cast the election as one between the forces of reform led by himself on the one hand, and, on the other, the coalition that had blocked the bill—opposition legislators, yes, but also LDP members who had voted against it. Much of the public lapped up Koizumi's ability to pin a dinosaur label on his opponents—both in and out of the LDP—and gave Koizumi one of the most commanding electoral victories in Japanese political history. It appeared that the Tanaka machine had finally been completely broken. The 2005 election devastated that part of the *Tanaka gundan* that had remained in the LDP, while delivering what seemed at the time a possibly fatal setback to Kan's and Ozawa's Democrats.

Koizumi was rewarded with the ultimate accolade in Japanese politics: a third term as prime minister, something previously achieved since 1970 only by Nakasone. The postal reform bill was resubmitted to the Diet where it passed. Koizumi had done what he was supposed to do in paving the way for the return of pre-Tanaka LDP hegemony. He stepped down in 2006, turning over the prime ministership to none other than Kishi's grandson, Abe Shinzo.

THE LDP AFTER KOIZUMI

Koizumi engineered the promotion of his protégé Abe as LDP president and thus automatically prime minister. No clearer sign could be sent that the descendants of the conservative mandarinate of the 1950s believed the restoration of conservative hegemony was complete. Abe's mother had been Kishi's daughter; his father, Abe Shintaro, had started his political life as an aide to Kishi and had effectively been the leader of that part of the LDP outside the *Tanaka gundan*. Japan's longest-serving foreign minister, Shintaro had been closely identified with pro-American, anti-Communist views and was for decades seen as almost certain to become prime minister.

He had been blocked by the *Tanaka gundan*, however, and died comparatively young just before Ozawa led much of the *gundan* out of the LDP in 1993. Now the son would step into the position that the father had viewed as something akin to an inheritance.

But Abe's ascension demonstrated overreaching on the part of the Right. Giddy with Koizumi's success, the Right had not fully absorbed the key lesson of the Koizumi years: that the wolf of rightist hegemony had to be dressed up in the sheep's clothing of reform. For no sooner was Abe in office then he set out to enact what Koizumi had only hinted at: replacement of the postwar constitution; a robust, unapologetic military; an affirmation of the central place of the Imperial House in the sovereign edifice of the Japanese state; and the promotion of an understanding of the events of the 1930s that would portray them as a legitimate response to Western colonialism and the threats of alien ideologies—Communism, liberalism—imposed on East Asia by the force of arms.

But this agenda went nowhere. Much of the Japanese population was simply bewildered by it all; it seemed irrelevant to their lives and concerns. They were worried about their livelihoods, financing their retirements, whether their kids could find decent jobs, and how to take care of their aging parents. Meanwhile, the Social Insurance Agency inside the health ministry admitted it had mixed up or lost pension records of up to 50 million people. While this could not be pinned directly on Abe, all his rightist talk had the effect of making him come across as particularly tone deaf or *k.y.* (an acronym for *kūki yomenai*, literally, "cannot read the air"—the slang acronym actually uses the Roman letters).

The media began to poke fun at Abe, accusing him of being out of touch, labeling him an *obotchan*—the Japanese term for a spoiled rich kid who, to use the equivalent Americanism, was born on third base and thinks he hit a triple. Abe lasted barely a year, pleading health problems as an excuse for resigning. He was succeeded by Fukuda Yasuo, whose elevation in September 2007 to LDP president—and thus prime minister—seemed proof that the party had run out of any ideas or plans beyond cycling the ineffectual descendants of yesterday's leaders into and out of office. Fukuda was the son of Fukuda Takeo, who had been Tanaka's great enemy. Fukuda *Takeo* may have been an old school MOF-graduate-turned-politician, but he did come across as someone with an agile mind and sharp elbows. His son *Yasuo*, however, seemed like a tired salaryman; he had indeed started his career as a salaryman—the only thing unusual about him since most politician's sons with political ambitions go either into the bureaucracy or right into politics as young men. When Yasuo did finally move into politics, he inherited his father's network of relationships and supporters—but not his father's drive and wits.

Yasuo had been a reasonably effective LDP Secretary General under Koizumi, but as prime minister, he proved a failure both as a politician and as a statesman. He had promised to undo some of the damage Koizumi and Abe had wreaked on relations with Beijing, offering the prospect of some way out of the Yasukuni Shrine question that would satisfy Beijing while mollifying the Japanese Right. But this was a circle that could not be squared; a Tanaka might have pulled it off, but not someone with Fukuda Yasuo's rather meager political talents. He made noises about requiring people over 75 to pay more toward their health care; the Upper House—by then, thanks to the pension debacle, under the secure control of Ozawa's Democratic Party—responded by censuring Fukuda, the first time this ever happened to a Japanese prime minister under the postwar constitution.

Fukuda resigned almost exactly one year after he had taken office, obviously overwhelmed by all that was pressing in on him. The external environment had deteriorated rapidly. The greatest financial crisis in eighty years was unfolding in the United States, one that would send the Japanese economy into free fall. While this could not be blamed directly on the LDP, it made the party seem even more out of touch, particularly when it became clear the party had no real ideas about what to do in response. Ozawa's DPJ had massacred the LDP in the 2007 election for the Upper House. Ozawa was in the process of building a nationwide network of candidates for the Lower House election—an election that could not be postponed beyond 2009. That network looked set to become the most formidable political force assembled in Japan since the high-water days of the *Tanaka gundan*.

In response, all the LDP could do was manage to find one more descendent of a 1950s leader to captain the ship as it went down: Aso Taro, the grandson of Yoshida Shigeru, who had negotiated the San Francisco Peace Treaty. In his defense, Aso inherited an almost impossible situation when he took over in September 2008. He gamely appointed some fresh faces to his cabinet, and when the media tried to make an issue of his penchant for heading to a famous bar in the Imperial Hotel for drinks after work, he thumbed his nose at them, saying he was not going to change his habits and that anyway he picked up his own bills. With his sense of style and appreciation for pop culture (he was known as a *manga* fan) he came across as bit of throwback to Koizumi.

But there was no hiding the desperation of the party. The people around Aso took a leaf from Tanaka's playbook, throwing money around (*baramaki* is the Japanese term) in an attempt to buy votes, but it was too little too late. With demand for Japanese exports collapsing in the face of the onset of global depression, Japanese households understood that the institutions they had relied on to provide for economic security were crumbling. What is more, they were hearing about plans for an explicit welfare safety net that would replace these institutions—and the source of those plans was an increasingly credible Democratic Party of Japan.

An electoral tsunami was coming and everyone knew it. The dream that had inspired Ozawa for twenty years seemed close to fulfillment. An era of real politics—vigorously contested elections and competing policy visions—might be at hand. Would Japan finally have a genuine leader? A leader who could and would relegate bureaucrats to their proper sphere? A leader who was capable of negotiating with the President of the United States as an equal? A leader who could forge a political relationship with a rising China that would complement and undergird increasing economic ties?

Alas, the answer would turn out to be "no." And those who would see to it that Ozawa's dream turned to ashes would not be confined to the ranks of his legions of enemies in Japan. They would extend into the halls of the Pentagon, the State Department, and the West Wing of the White House.

FIGURE 11. Prime Minister Kishi Nobusuke signs the US–Japan Treaty while
President Dwight D. Eisenhower Looks on. Courtesy of Associated Press.

11

Japan and the World

On April 11, 2010, Prime Minister Hatoyama Yukio arrived in Washington for a global conference on nuclear security. He led the government of what was said to be America's closest ally in all of Asia-Pacific. His country served as the lynchpin of the American military presence in East Asia, and its support would be critical in any future confrontation—cold or hot—with a China that much of the American foreign policy establishment had identified as the only power on earth with the potential to pose an existential threat to the United States.

The importance of Prime Minister Hatoyama's country was not limited to the realm of security. His country's economy was the world's second largest. It was one of America's biggest trading partners. Its industrial and technological infrastructure was so interwoven with that of the United States that it would be difficult to say where one stopped and the other started; none of America's critical manufactures—computers, mobile devices, commercial aircraft, automobiles, armaments—could be made without the myriads of components and materials that companies from Prime Minister Hatoyama's country supplied. His country's banks and brokerages had for more than thirty years been the largest and most important external funders of the American government, trade, and current account deficits. His country's financial regulators had, as far back as 1978, repeatedly and proactively intervened in global foreign exchange markets to help ensure the dollar's continued role as the world's premiere settlements and reserve currency.

As for Prime Minister Hatoyama himself, he stood as a living, breathing embodiment of the ideals that were said to legitimize the global reach of American power. Americans prided themselves on having remade Prime Minister Hatoyama's country into a liberal, capitalist democracy—and what better proof of their success could they point to than Prime Minister Hatoyama? For he had been propelled into office not by a *coup d'état* of disaffected soldiers or the machinations of standing committees and politburos, but by that ultimate test of a democracy: a peaceable transfer of power from one party to another after a free, fair, and transparent election—one that Prime Minister Hatoyama's party had won in a landslide only seven months earlier.

One might suppose, therefore, that Prime Minister Hatoyama would have been treated as the first among his nominal equals when the leaders of forty-seven countries gathered for that important conference on nuclear security. Of course, diplomatic protocol required that pro-forma courtesies be extended to the representatives of all the countries in attendance, including one whose military sheltered and protected elements that plotted with terrorists and another that had made it clear that its ultimate foreign policy goal was to drive the United States out of Asia. But before President Obama met with these people, which he would have to do, wouldn't President Obama want to sit down with Prime Minister Hatoyama for several hours of searching discussions on just how good allies could work together to promote the goals of the conference? After all, Prime Minister Hatoyama was the duly elected, democratic leader of the only country that had ever suffered nuclear bombing and could thus be expected to have an unusually keen appreciation of the need for nuclear security. Perhaps after the formal part of the conference was over and the other leaders had returned home, President Obama and Prime Minister Hatoyama would spend the weekend at Camp David, going over the results of the conference, comparing notes on what less friendly countries might be doing. In the process, would they seize the opportunity to bring up other challenges both men had had to face? One might have hoped so; each was almost uniquely situated to offer the other confidential pointers on such matters as propping up an imploding financial system or coping with political opposition that would sooner see a nation in ruins than its elected leaders succeed. Interpreters would not have been needed; Prime Minister Hatoyama had a graduate degree from Stanford and spoke good English.

Whatever they actually ended up talking about, however, perhaps the most important outcome would have been the fact of the conversation itself. For surely President Obama would not have passed up the opportunity to forge the kind of friendship Ronald Reagan had made with Margaret Thatcher or Lyndon Johnson had cemented with Ludwig Erhard—particularly because Prime Minister Hatoyama's country was so much more important to the United States in 2010 than even Great Britain or West Germany had been, respectively, in 1981 and 1964.

Of course, this is all a fantasy. Prime Minister Hatoyama did attend the conference. But he was not granted time for even a short courtesy call on the president; the most he could get was a ten-minute aside during a large and noisy dinner. Meanwhile, leaders of China, Germany, Pakistan, and India all had face-to-face private meetings with Obama.

It was a deliberate snub. And it was not the first. Four months earlier, Prime Minister Hatoyama had sought to schedule a one-on-one meeting with President Obama when both leaders were in Copenhagen for a global climate conference. White House Press Secretary Robert Gibbs had specifically announced that there would be no meeting, offering the patently transparent excuse that the two leaders had just met the previous month in Tokyo. Instead, Hatoyama talked with Secretary of State Hillary Clinton during a dinner. When, afterwards, he gave Japanese reporters the usual boilerplate descriptions of their discussion, complete with references to "understanding" and "cooperation," Clinton took the highly unusual step of calling Japan's ambassador in Washington, to register her displeasure. Three weeks before the Copenhagen meetings, Defense Secretary Robert M. Gates had turned down an invitation by his Japanese counterpart to a welcoming ceremony and dinner during Gates's visit to Tokyo—an act of calculated rudeness on a par with John Foster Dulles's refusal to shake the hand of Zhou Enlai at the 1954 Geneva conference convened to settle the division of Vietnam.

The reasons for the shabby treatment Hatoyama received were obvious: he had won the election that put him into office partly by promising to renegotiate a treaty the Japanese government had recently signed with the United States, a treaty that involved the relocation of one of the largest American military bases in East Asia.

But there was more to it than this one treaty. To understand what happened, we need to start with the people who now determine Japan policy in Washington, the people who decided that Hatoyama should be treated as an enemy rather than a friend. Let's call them the "New Japan Hands."

THE "NEW JAPAN HANDS"

They form a floating, semi-permanent Japan policy establishment in Washington. They go back and forth from the State Department, the Pentagon, the National Security Council, and the American Embassy in Tokyo to think tanks such as the Center for Strategic and International Studies and the Center for a New American Security. Many hold concurrent appointments at the Walsh School of Foreign Service at Georgetown or the Nitze School of Advanced International Studies at Johns Hopkins. Prominent among them are men such as Michael Green, Torkel Patterson, David Asher, and Kurt Campbell. Most of these people know a lot about Japan—they have almost certainly lived in the country and probably speak its language.

A typical New Japan Hand had first come to Japan as a student, soldier, or a Mormon missionary, where he had acquired fluency in Japanese and a tacit feel for the way Japan works. If he were intelligent, articulate, ambitious, and demonstrated an interest in security matters and other issues critical to the US–Japan relationship, he (the New Japan Hands are all men) would discover doors opening to the top reaches of the Japanese policy establishment. Internships with key LDP legislators and well-funded sinecures at Japanese universities or foundations would then follow.[1]

At every step along the way, however, his continued access to funding and to key decision makers in Tokyo required that the budding New Japan

---

1. The role of foundations funded by the late Sasakawa Ryoichi in shaping global opinion of Japan is particularly critical. An ardent fascist and indicted war criminal, Sasakawa made a fortune in the postwar years from his effective monopoly of boat racing, one of the few legal avenues for gambling in Japan. His fortune allowed him to become an important political player in rightist circles in Japan; a parallel could be drawn with American billionaires such as Richard Mellon Scaife and the Koch brothers. But while these wealthy American rightists worked primarily to influence American domestic opinion, much of the efforts of the Sasakawa foundations—the Nippon Foundation, the Sasakawa Peace Foundation—aim at influencing foreign views of Japan. It is essentially impossible for a budding American analyst of critical issues in the US–Japan relationship to avoid entanglement with Sasakawa money.

Hand put forward arguments along the following lines: the military relationship between Japan and the United States has been essential to keeping the peace in East Asia. It is, if anything, likely to become ever more important given the rise of China and the unpredictability of a rogue North Korea intent on acquiring nuclear arms. Thus, no other issue—whether trade, finance, unresolved history, or what have you—should ever be allowed to cloud the primacy of the security relationship. This relationship has functioned well, but there is one area that needs improvement: the Japanese military should assume a more active role in providing for Japan's defense and helping the American military project force ("interoperability" is the favorite term of the New Japan Hands).

Effective arguments along these lines translated into ever-greater access to the corridors of power in Tokyo that in turn led to growing influence in Washington. If someone in the White House or the Pentagon needing to know Japanese establishment opinion on a given issue called a New Japan Hand and got an accurate and useful reading, he or she was more likely to call that person again. Senior bureaucrats in Tokyo at the Defense Agency or the Foreign Ministry—or in the Japanese Embassy in Washington—understood this and would see to it that the New Japan Hands got the information they needed. In good time, they would also turn to a New Japan Hand to get a message across to a key decision maker in Washington.

But there is something more at work in what amounts to the monopoly the New Japan Hands have achieved in the last two decades over what official Washington says and does about Japan. The New Japan Hand label is, of course, a deliberate play on the term used for the small group of State Department officials and other establishment figure of the 1920s and 1930s who helped determine Japan policy back in those days: the "Old Japan Hands"[2] as they came to be known after the war. The Old Japan Hands had had close links to the cosmopolitan, Anglo-philic elements of Tokyo's conservative elite. Unable to derail the train rushing toward war—and thus partly discredited in Washington—the Old Japan Hands had nonetheless retained enough influence to persuade the Occupation not to insist on the abdication of the emperor. But they had then, as we saw in chapter 4, lost

---

2. The most important "Old Japan Hand" was probably Joseph Grew, US ambassador to Japan from 1932 to 1941.

influence to the "China Crowd" at the State Department and been shut out of any further voice in the Occupation.

No such problems dogged the New Japan Hands. They were nurtured and protected by two of the most powerful people in the American foreign policy establishment: Richard Armitage, Deputy Secretary of State in the George W. Bush administration, and Joseph Nye, chairman of the National Intelligence Council under Bill Clinton and former dean of the Kennedy School at Harvard. With this kind of potent, bipartisan support and with no rivals for influence over Japan policy, the New Japan Hands found themselves with the kind of power wielded by the one-eyed man in the kingdom of the blind.

There had been a time when Japan had loomed large in the American imagination. Back in the era of trade conflicts, of fears that Japan would overtake the United States in the race for global economic hegemony, of fascination with Japan's economic methods and its social cohesion, students had crowded into Japanese language programs in American universities. American newspapers had sent their top reporters to Tokyo, and editors had encouraged searching pieces on what made Japan tick. American business may have chafed under what many saw as "unfair" Japanese competition, but Tokyo was the place where rising young executives could prove their mettle—to paraphrase the song, if you could make it there, you could make it anywhere. And, of course, in the halcyon days of the bubble economy, bankers had flocked to Tokyo, the world's monetary honeypot. Even after the bubble's implosion, Japan had continued to command the attention of the leaders of the world's financial establishment—they all knew what would happen to everyone if the Japanese banking system melted down.

But by April 2010, US–Japan trade conflicts were largely a thing of the past. No one was predicting any longer a global economy run out of Tokyo and while Japan might still be trapped in a vise of stagnation and debt, it was no longer worries over Japan's banking system that kept treasury secretaries, finance ministers, and central bank governors up at night. Students aiming at business careers wanted to study Chinese, not Japanese,[3] and aspiring business leaders were earning their spurs in Shanghai and Singapore, not in Tokyo. Top journals stationed only one

---

3. Japanese language programs in American universities now primarily attract students interested in contemporary Japanese culture.

reporter in Tokyo—or closed their bureaus altogether—and editors made it clear that what they wanted out of Japan was "human interest" puff pieces, not detailed analysis of politics or business. The Japanese themselves coined a term for the whole phenomenon: "Japan passing," a play on the "Japan bashing" of the 1980s.

Penetrating analysis today of Japanese reality in English is still out there, but you have to know where to look. The financial press, true, still sometimes runs comprehensive stories on Japanese economics and finance, but a harried White House, State Department, or Pentagon official is not going to trawl the web for the kinds of in-depth discussions of Japanese politics and society that can still be found at places like *Asia Pacific Journal: Japan Focus*[4] or the NBR Japan Forum. Instead, he or she gets a quick rundown from someone he or she knows and trusts—and has probably worked with—among the New Japan Hands.

So when the Obama White House was confronted in 2009 by a new government in Tokyo saying specifically that it needed to reopen the issue of the base removal and, more generally, that it hoped to renegotiate the foundations of the US–Japan alliance, the New Japan Hands instructed the White House on how to act: the new government was not to be trusted, and until it earned some trust, it should be treated in as pointedly rude and dismissive a way as diplomatic propriety would permit. Lacking either the ability or the inclination to test what they were being told, administration officials fell into line.

The New Japan Hands were not lying. Tokyo had signed a treaty that the new government did want to reopen. The United States did help provide for Japan's security, and if the American soldiers on the ground there were not exactly in harm's way, they would inevitably be involved in any full-scale conflagration in East Asia—one reason they were supposedly there was to make that less likely to happen. Hatoyama had indeed campaigned on promises to reduce the overt American military presence in Japan and had called for a renegotiation of the basis of the US–Japan alliance.

But there was even more involved. Within weeks of the September 2009 election that had put Hatoyama in office, the architect of that victory,

---

4. Full disclosure: I have been a coordinator of this web-based clearing house for scholarly and serious investigative articles on Japan and Asia that bills itself as offering "in-depth analysis of the forces shaping the Asia-Pacific. . . and the world."

Ozawa Ichiro, had begun a series of visits to Beijing that culminated in his leading a delegation of some 600 of Japan's top political, business, and cultural luminaries to China on December 12–13. Ozawa told the Chinese leadership that the new government in Tokyo was planning to overhaul Japan's security and foreign policy arrangements. Nothing was more calculated to make the New Japan Hands see red. For they believed that Ozawa was corrupt, untrustworthy, and anti-American—and that Hatoyama was an incompetent flake. Among other things, it is what they read in the establishment Japanese press, and it is what they had heard from their most trusted sources in Tokyo—people they had done business with for decades, people who were either LDP politicians themselves or senior bureaucrats who had long relied on the LDP for political protection.

To understand how they arrived at these conclusions, let's start with the base issue itself.

OKINAWA AND THE FUTENMA MARINE BASE

Futenma is one of two large training and air support bases in Japan operated by the US Marines. The treaty that Hatoyama sought to renegotiate involved an agreement to relocate this base. But Futenma is not just anywhere in Japan. Of the twenty-some Marine bases around the world involved in air support and air training, only Futenma is located right in the midst of a crowded urban area. Even more importantly, it is on Okinawa.

Okinawa is the largest of the Ryukyu islands that stretch from the Japanese mainland practically to Taiwan. These islands once formed an independent kingdom that had had tributary relations with both China and Japan.[5] Although ethnically closer to Japan than to China—the languages spoken in the Ryukyus were, for example, related to Japanese rather than Chinese—the Ryukyus were culturally and politically distinct and were not formally incorporated into Japan proper until 1879.

---

5. When the islands were invaded in the early seventeenth century by the Satsuma *han* of Kyushu, the Ryukyu capitulated without resistance. But to avoid provoking the Qing, the Tokugawa Shogunate had the Ryukyu continue to maintain the traditional tributary relationship with China while simultaneously sending annual delegations to Edo.

With the growing emphasis in the Meiji period and on into the twentieth century of the "purity" and "uniqueness" of the Japanese "race," Okinawans presented an uncomfortable anomaly. They were not foreigners but they were not really full-blooded Japanese either. Okinawans thus endured both discrimination for not being fully Japanese and coercive attempts to make them precisely that. Those attempts included assaults on the institutions and practices—religion, languages, arts—that had served to mark the Okinawans as different.

The tale of much of modern Okinawan history would thus seem all too familiar to Bretons, Basques, Corsicans, Native Hawaiians, Inuit, Navajos, Uighers, Ibo, Kurds, Chechens, Mayans, or any of the hundreds of other ethnicities and cultures that failed to get states of their own when the world was carved up in accordance with Wilsonian self-determination and Westphalian notions that each "nation" ought to have—and be—its own "state." But few of these other ethnicities have had to endure quite what the Okinawans have: first, deliberate designation as cannon fodder, then enforced mass suicide, and, finally, de facto military occupation in perpetuity not by the conquering nation but by a third country. Tibetans may accuse Han Chinese of cultural genocide and Palestinians may be outraged at Israeli settlements on the West Bank, but the Chinese are not inviting thousands of *Russian* soldiers to occupy Tibet forever, nor does the Israeli government collaborate with *German* immigrants to displace Palestinians and seize their land.

In the waning days of the Second World War, the Japanese government turned Okinawa into a sacrificial offering to forestall what seemed the inevitable American invasion of the Japanese mainland. The resultant Battle of Okinawa counts as one of history's greatest military atrocities; up to one-third of the population died, many in massed forced suicides that were deliberately staged to give the United States a supposed taste of what an invasion of the mainland would entail.

The Japanese military had already turned Okinawa into what amounted to a garrison state before the Americans arrived; following the battle, the United States rebuilt the Japanese installations, added some new ones by expropriating farm land,[6] and proceeded to convert them all into the logistical center of the American military presence in East Asia.

6. The farmers whose land was seized were eventually compensated by the Japanese government rather than the American.

While Tokyo recovered nominal sovereignty over the Japanese mainland in 1952, Okinawa remained under formal US military jurisdiction for another twenty years. But the so-called reversion of Okinawa in 1972 was a polite legal fig leaf over the reality that Okinawa remained occupied land, honeycombed with American military installations and crawling with American soldiers.

The situation suited both Washington and Tokyo well enough. The United States got a major offshore staging ground for its prosecution of the Korean and Vietnam wars—a staging ground largely paid for by the Japanese. Perhaps even more important in the eyes of American strategists was the role Okinawa played in the bluff-and-feint of great power politics, a role thought to involve such things as discouraging North Korean adventures or giving Beijing pause before it launched an invasion of Taiwan.

Meanwhile, Okinawa allowed the rest of Japan to pretend to be a fully sovereign country in control of its own security and its own foreign policy when it fact it was not—and is not. Countries that—voluntarily or not—turn control over their destinies to others typically pay a price that involves such things as large and intrusive bases on one's own land that are under some other country's control, bases that see whorehouses and seedy bars spring up on their perimeters with the same inevitability that weeds grow in untended soil. But what sticks in the craw when the bases are not your own is the knowledge that local girls are selling their virtues to foreigners rather to one's own boys. Meanwhile, one has to endure foreign soldiers in foreign uniforms sauntering down one's streets as if they owned the place, endless petty—and not so petty—crimes committed by these soldiers, military vehicles bearing the insignia of another country barreling down one's roads, and—in the modern world—foreign military jets screaming overhead. One rarely encounters any of this in mainland Japan, and where one does—in Yokosuka on a peninsula some thirty miles south of Tokyo, for example, that is the home base of the US 7th Fleet, or in Iwakuni near the western tip of Honshu where the Marines have another major air station—it happens in faraway corners, out of sight and out of mind to most Japanese.

But not in Okinawa. On mainland Japan, it is very easy not to notice that in some crucial ways the Occupation never ended. No such dissembling is possible in Okinawa, where one acre in eight is under the control of the US military, where some 90,000 Americans (38,000 troops, 43,000 dependents, and 5,000 civilian Defense Department employees) share space on a crowded little island with 1.1 million locals, where sonic booms fill the air night and day.

Naturally, many Okinawans seethed about what had been and was being done to them. But for some two decades after the so-called reversion, most of the rest of Japan managed to forget about them. The bureaucracy and the LDP used its usual methods to keep the situation in Okinawa under control: strategic *baramaki* ("throwing money") for local construction executives; rightist thugs to intimidate leftists and other agitators organizing demonstrations against the bases.

These methods worked less well in Okinawa than they did in other places; so much of the population had been radicalized and the American presence was so overwhelming. But they were enough to keep things on a manageable boil until September 4, 1995. That night, two American marines and an American navy seaman abducted a 12-year-old schoolgirl, bound her, took her in a rental car to a deserted beach, and proceeded to gang-rape her. The island exploded in rage; over 80,000 people (more than 7 percent of the entire population) marched in protest near the gates of Futenma—the largest demonstration in the history of Okinawa. The symbolism of the rape could scarcely have been more powerful. With echoes of one of the most gut-wrenching episodes of the Battle of Okinawa—the deliberate sacrifice of 219 schoolgirl-*cum*-student nurses ordered by the Japanese military to the front where most of them died—the victim almost overnight came to symbolize Okinawa itself: raped by Washington and abandoned by Tokyo.

Even the most obtuse recognized that the situation had become untenable. Tokyo saw that using money and thugs to sweep things under the rug might not work much longer; the Pentagon, still smarting from the loss of its prize bases in the Philippines not four years earlier due to strident local opposition, feared being turned out of Okinawa altogether.

There was a seemingly obvious solution: closing Futenma and transferring its operations to the nearby Kadena American Air Force base, the largest American base in East Asia. But the overwhelming logic of this solution derived from premises of strategy, logistics, and deterrence value. Other premises turned out to be more important, chief among them inter-service rivalry and Okinawan desires to be wholly rid of the American military presence altogether. The Marines would stonewall any attempt to share command with one of their two permanent installations overseas with the Air Force, and no one in Washington was prepared to endure the scorched-earth tactics the Marines would use to keep this from happening. Meanwhile, Okinawan activists feared that any consolidation of the American military presence on the island at Kadena would make it less rather than more likely that the United States could be forced to leave Okinawa for good.

Instead, the American and Japanese governments entered into negotiations to move Futenma's operations in ways that would keep them wholly under the control of the Marines. The two sides agreed to transfer some of Futenma's functions to Guam while building a new heliport for the rest. But even though Tokyo agreed to bear most of the costs, costs that the US Government Accounting Office itself conceded had been inflated, the agreement went nowhere. For the planned new facilities involved the devastation of one of Okinawa's last pristine areas, Cape Henoko on Oura Bay, the destruction of irreplaceable coral reefs, and the probable loss of several protected and endangered species. In any case, it was implacably opposed by the local inhabitants.

In the last days of Koizumi's prime ministership, Japanese government officials nonetheless went ahead and enacted the treaty. Donald Rumsfeld, then Secretary of Defense, had threatened to pull US troops out of Japan if the treaty were not signed, shouting: "We don't stay where we're not wanted. We'll just pack up and leave." The LDP trusted to vague notions that over time they could somehow put their hands on a fire hose that would spew out enough money and threats that it could inundate the local opposition and allow the relocation to proceed.

But no such hose was immediately at hand. Despite promises that construction of the new facility would begin promptly and the move away from Futenma completed by 2014, there was simply no way politically that any government in Tokyo was prepared to do what had become necessary actually to start that process.

For the events surrounding Futenma and the plans for Henoko laid bare the contradiction between all the happy-talk in Washington and Tokyo on the strength of the alliance and the reality that this so-called "alliance" between the United States and Japan depended on the acquiescence of a conquered population that was no longer willing to acquiesce.

When a conquered population rises up—when it is no longer possible to co-opt local elites with bribes, when behind-the-scenes intimidation no longer works—occupying governments are faced with two choices. They can gun people down in the streets, as the British did in India in 1857 or the Soviets did in Hungary in 1956. Or they can acknowledge their own unwillingness to bear the continued moral and military costs of imposing hated rule on a conquered people—as the British did in India in 1949 and the Russians did in Poland and East Germany in 1989—and prepare to accommodate to new realities.

The new realities of the Okinawan uprising left Japan with two choices. The first was an open acknowledgment in Tokyo that the US–Japan "alliance" is not an alliance at all. Japan is not an ally of the United States and never has been. Instead, it is more of a protectorate—allowed a certain freedom to manage its own domestic affairs, but required on all significant foreign policy and security questions (as well as economic policy issues with system-transformative implications) to defer to the will of Washington. That open acknowledgment would entail, among other things, moving most of the US military establishment on Okinawa to the Japanese mainland so that the costs of occupation—costs in national pride, in infringements of sovereignty, in the corruption that an occupying army always brings with it, not to mention the noise and disruption of large bases—be distributed throughout Japan rather than shunted off onto one sliver.

The other choice involved a restoration of Japan's control over its own destiny and its own affairs—a recovery, in other words, of the sovereignty that had been thrown away in the 1930s by the country's unwillingness to face fundamental political questions and to bridle that most dangerous element in any political setup: ambitious, hotheaded young men with the means of physical coercion at their disposal. If that restoration were successful, if Japan really did become a fully sovereign state again, it might well end up as an ally of the United States. Indeed, it probably would; given Japan's sheer physical proximity to the world's rising new superpower, a China that is having problems curbing its own hotheaded young men, realist political theory—not to mention common sense—would suggest that the United States is Japan's logical ally. But Japan cannot be an ally of the United States—or anyone else—until it is first a sovereign state.

This is what the DPJ in general and Ozawa in particular recognized; it is what lay behind Hatoyama's call for a renegotiation of the US–Japan alliance. But the Pentagon and the New Japan Hands in Washington reacted by effectively plugging their ears and screaming with rage. Meanwhile, in Tokyo, the guardians and principal beneficiaries of the 1955 system—the LDP and the bureaucracy—simply refused to accept the reality of what the Okinawan uprising entailed; they somehow believed they could put

Humpty Dumpty back together again. So they all tacitly joined hands to destroy the new government. And they received help from three unexpected places: Beijing, Pyongyang, and the tectonic plates under the Pacific Ocean.

THE DESTRUCTION OF THE HATOYAMA GOVERNMENT

The DPJ's enemies landed their first blow five months before the September 2009 election. As the party looked set to ride an unstoppable electoral steamroller into power, the public prosecutor and the establishment press reached for their usual recipe in dealing with ambitious politicians who threaten to overturn the established order: tripping up the politician in question for violating one or another obscure campaign statute while trumpeting the "news" of the investigation in the press. As leader of the DPJ, Ozawa surely knew something like this was coming, and presumably thought he had prepared himself. But the prosecutors went ahead anyway, even though they had little to go on, launching an investigation into supposed false reporting on a land purchase.

The prosecutors would soon drop their investigation for lack of evidence, but others among Ozawa's enemies resorted to an ingenious tactic to keep the "news" of his "shady" dealings in front of the public. In reaction to widespread concern that Japan's prosecutors had become effectively a law unto themselves (the conviction rate in Japan is in excess of 99 percent), Japan had just upgraded court-appointed citizens' panels to something like US grand juries, supposedly to restrain prosecutorial zealotry. These panels had been a leftover from Occupation reforms and had historically become involved mostly in cases of minor offenses such as traffic violations. But the newly empowered panels were turned inside out from their ostensible purpose of reining in hyperactive prosecutors for something entirely different: a useful tool to smear reputations in the absence of evidence against the target that would stand up in a court of law. The citizens' panel overseeing the Ozawa investigations "required" the prosecutors to "reopen" the case; it would stay conveniently open until it was clear Ozawa's ambitions had been thwarted and the government he had put in place had been broken; it would then be quietly dropped.

But we are getting ahead of our story. The opening of the investigation—accompanied by the usual hysterical finger-wagging over "betrayal" of the "public trust" in places like the *Asahi Shimbun's* editorial page—convinced Ozawa that he had no choice but to step down as the leader of the DPJ. Having lived through a generation of scandals, including the trumped-up scandal of 1993 that had brought down his first attempt to create a genuine opposition government, Ozawa knew exactly what happens when a Japanese political scandal is allowed to unfold according to script—how it would shunt to the sidelines for the time being every other critical issue, including examinations of the way power is actually exercised in Japan and the prospect of the first peaceful transfer of real power in modern Japanese history. He figured he needed to get this latest scandal out of view and the quickest way to do that was to remove his name from the limelight by resigning the party presidency. To ensure that he continued to have a major say-so in events behind the scene, he engineered the selection of Hatoyama as his successor over the arguably more popular Okada Katsuya.

The example of Ozawa's mentor Tanaka Kakuei may have influenced his thinking, for as we saw in the preceding chapter, Tanaka had been at his most powerful *after* he had left office. Ozawa presumably believed that the marriage of his matchless political skills with Hatoyama's spotless reputation and sterling name would be enough to enable him to carry out his vision, even if he were not prime minister.

Ozawa's short-term political tactics worked. By resigning his position as party president, he deprived the DPJ's enemies of the last remaining hope of derailing the DPJ freight train. September would see one of the greatest landslides in the history of Japanese elections. The DPJ's margin of victory was so overwhelming it appeared the LDP-bureaucrat nexus that had controlled Japanese politics and governance since 1955 had been broken for good.

But while Ozawa's short-term tactics may have been unimpeachable—in a manner that would have done Tanaka proud, he had nurtured a new "army" of politicians throughout Japan that played a key role in the DPJ landslide—in the long run the tactics failed. Ozawa had made it clear that he wanted to impose genuine political leadership on the bureaucracy and to renegotiate the basis of the US–Japan relationship. Even had he been prime minister, it is not clear in retrospect that he could have carried out these monumental tasks. True, Tanaka had demonstrated how powerful politicians could bend the bureaucracy to their will, but as we saw in the previous chapter, Tanaka did not ultimately challenge bureaucratic prerogatives in policy formation.

What Ozawa intended, however, went much farther than Tanaka's inimitable tactics of squeezing money out of the bureaucracy for allies and dependents. Much of the bureaucracy's power lay in its control of the panoply of institutions and methods that provided economic security for most Japanese. We have encountered examples in earlier chapters: bank oversight that provides all kinds of incentives to keep credit flowing to companies that might otherwise go bankrupt, employment protocols that make it difficult or impossible to fire anyone, myriads of licensing and other practices that allow inefficient businesses to stay afloat.

Arguments have been heard ever since the collapse of the bubble that vibrant economic growth will not return until the Japanese economy is unshackled from all these inefficiencies and practices. This may be true, but Ozawa and the DPJ understood it was not enough just to get rid of them. For modern history—in both Japan and elsewhere—demonstrates that once a population realizes that economic security is possible, it will punish any government that does not provide for it. Indeed, the LDP had lost its hold on Tokyo's parliamentary infrastructure precisely because the electorate believed—correctly—that with "lifetime" employment shrinking and the erosion of life support that had kept less competitive businesses afloat, economic security could no longer be taken for granted.

Ozawa sought to replace these practices with explicit, legally enforceable means of delivering economic security. In place of norms that made it difficult to fire people or spending on white elephants to boost "employment" in depressed areas, welfare and unemployment compensation would be beefed up. The DPJ largely accepted the argument that Japanese society had become too risk-averse; but if entrepreneurs, managers, and young workers were going to be encouraged to take risks, they had be reassured that failure did not translate into a lifelong sentence of poverty and social death. It is one reason why DPJ policy makers were so fascinated with countries such as Denmark where a robust social safety net underpins an economy buzzing with vitality and entrepreneurial verve. The DPJ's most memorable slogans *kokumin no seikatsu dai-ichi* ("the people's livelihood comes first") and "from concrete to people" were meant to convey the essence of their plans to redeploy spending away from white elephants to welfare; to evaluate economic policies on the basis of what they actually did to improve people's lives.

But such plans posed a deadly threat to the way power had historically been exercised in Japan. It was not simply a matter of politicians fearing they would be blocked from trading pork for political support; the DPJ's plans would deprive bureaucrats of much of their often arbitrary latitude in dispensing political and economic protection.

It should not be a matter of surprise, therefore, that the bureaucracy reacted with visceral loathing to the new government. They could not express that loathing in so many explicit words without exploding the *tatemae* (cover for reality to which everyone gives lip service) of bureaucrats as servants of Japan's elected government. But as masters of passive-aggression, they could sabotage in all kinds of subtle ways anything the new government tried to do—and ensure the new government took the heat; that it would be seen as "incompetent."

It is just possible that Ozawa might have checked them. But he had been hobbled by the ersatz "investigation"—hobbled in ways that he had perhaps not fully foreseen. That left it up to Hatoyama.

Hatoyama was never the flake that he was portrayed. He had politics and modern Japanese history in his blood; in the grand tradition of Japanese politics, he hails from one of Japan's oldest political families; his grandfather Ichiro had actually been prime minister back in 1955 when the LDP was first formed. Slightly diffident and almost too empathetic, if he has a weakness, it is a distaste for the bare-knuckle side of politics. If Tanaka resembles Lyndon Johnson, Hatoyama comes across as an Adlai Stevenson or a Jimmy Carter.

Rumbling about Hatoyama's finances constituted the first of the wholly predictable attempts to discredit him. But these accusations were even more palpably threadbare than the charges being leveled at Ozawa—Hatoyama's mother had written him a series of checks that his secretary had reported as coming from other supporters—and they failed to get much traction.

But then the DPJ's enemies hit pay dirt with Futenma. As we have seen, under Rumsfeld's pressure, the LDP government under Koizumi had signed the treaty to move Futenma, knowing full well that it could not be implemented. The LDP had been stalling ever since. But the moment Hatoyama took office, starting the relocation suddenly became the top priority in the US–Japan relationship. Hatoyama at first attempted to brush aside all the pressure being generated in both Washington and

Tokyo, asking—quite reasonably—why the issue had overnight assumed such overwhelming urgency and suggesting maybe it should be shelved.

JAPAN'S "AGENTS OF INFLUENCE"

To understand what subsequently happened, one has to start with the apparatus that Tokyo has built over the past sixty-five years to influence both American opinion and American policy. Every country that wants and needs something out of Washington nurtures something like this, but with the notable exception of Israel, no country has built as robust and effective an apparatus as Japan has. The obvious reasons come down to the high stakes for Tokyo and the skill with which the Japanese do this kind of thing: flattering the powerful by using Japan's incomparable mastery of *amae* (inducing indulgence by pretending to push boundaries).

As we have seen, Japan has never been able to extricate itself from what John Dower in his history of the Occupation memorably called the American embrace—and since the late 1980s it has effectively stopped trying. Most ordinary Japanese now tend to admire and like the United States, even if they are not particularly curious about it anymore; certainly, there is very little left (outside Okinawa) of the often virulent anti-American feelings of the 1960s and early 1970s, driven as they were by imposition of the Security Treaty in 1959 and then the Vietnam War. Nor, in the era of iPads and Google, does one hear in Japan today the contempt for American society and business that one often encountered in the 1980s. Meanwhile, much of the elite—particularly in the bureaucracy, the LDP, and established *zaikai* (business and finance) circles—has long reconciled itself to the surrender of key elements of sovereignty to Washington as a reasonable price to pay for continued control of outcomes in Japan itself.

But the comfort of this embrace depends on American benevolence, and with a country as mercurial as the United States, such benevolence cannot be assumed. Tokyo has accordingly constructed over the decades its formidable apparatus of foundations, journalists, government officials, and academics all charged with monitoring and shaping US opinion on Japan, aided by the large Japanese business community in the United States that tends to act as branches of "Japan, Inc." For Tokyo cannot count on any natural allies in the United States when it comes to influencing Japan policy. There is nothing comparable to the Christian Zionists of the American religious Right and their close links to Israel's Likud Party, and while Japanese-Americans number in the hundreds of thousands, most of them have few connections any more to Japan itself and little sentiment for their ancestral homeland beyond nostalgia.[7] American presidents have palpably hesitated to implement policies that could affect Israel, Cuba, or Northern Ireland for fear of retaliation from, respectively, Jewish, Cuban-American, or Irish-American constituencies. No such considerations vis-à-vis Japanese-American voters influence Japan policy. Tokyo has to rely on its own ability to flatter, soothe, and, when necessary, mollify Washington.

But while a lack of natural allies in the United States may on the surface seem like a disadvantage, it also keeps Japan out of the American media spotlight, allowing for the shaping of American opinion to take place with very little scrutiny. Whatever one may think or say about Israel's efforts to influence American policy, they do not go unnoticed. The same had once been true of Japan's efforts as well. The fear back in the late 1970s and 1980s that the Japanese industrial juggernaut would turn the United States into an economic colony of Japan had given rise to a spate of indignant books and articles describing how Japan's "Agents of Influence," to use the title of one of the most explosive, had extended their tendrils right into the heart of American economic and business policy-making.

Such days are long gone. While the formidable institutional apparatus Tokyo built to monitor and influence US opinion is still very much in place, as the new millennium dawned, there was little to get excited about. US–Japan trade conflicts were largely a thing of the past and policy elites in Washington and Tokyo tended to have similar views of such matters as the threat China might pose to global order or how to cope with the latest bellicose blustering from Pyongyang. If the Japanese thought Washington had gotten too entangled in the Middle East, they kept their thoughts to themselves and were, in any case, pleased that a byproduct of heavy US involvement in the region was protection of the shipping lanes through which Japan imported much of its petroleum. The one area where Washington still put pressure on Tokyo—beefing up Japan's defense capability (i.e.,

---

7. The relative lack of concern among Japanese-Americans for American policy toward Japan— particularly in contrast to that of American Jews over the Middle East, Irish-Americans over Northern Ireland, and Cuban-Americans over Cuba—may have something to do with the internment of tens of thousands of Japanese-Americans during the Second World War and the determination on the part of the rest of them to demonstrate what "good Americans" they had become.

"interoperability")—was something most elite Japanese policy makers also wanted to see; they found this pressure useful in achieving what at least the more right-leaning among them saw as their ultimate goal: the repeal of the second clause of Article 9 of the Constitution that theoretically prohibited Japan from maintaining "war-making potential."

As the decade proceeded, Japan's agents of influence in the United States thus had an increasingly easy task, particularly given the warm glow surrounding the relationship between Koizumi and George W. Bush. The agents of influence still monitored American opinion closely and were now and again deployed for such matters as eliciting US help in Japan's attempts to secure the return of some of its citizens abducted decades earlier by North Korea; Tokyo did not want to be cut out of any deal with Pyongyang that did not address this issue. And, of course, they had to reassure the Pentagon that the Futenma realignment would be proceeding soon, even when there were no concrete plans to set it in motion. But the agents of influence kept their ties with the New Japan Hands in good working order and could rely on those ties to ensure that the Pentagon, the White House, and the State Department heard only what they wanted them to hear. With the George W. Bush administration collapsing in the wake of Katrina, the debacle in Iraq, and, finally, the onset of the subprime crisis and the greatest economic implosion since the 1930s, there was, in any case, little danger that the American media spotlight was suddenly going to switch focus from Afghanistan, Iraq, and the banking crisis to the impasse in Okinawa.

But with the DPJ victory, suddenly the agents of influence were confronted with a new and unprecedented task. Heretofore, they had been charged with carrying out the agenda of the Japanese ruling elites in the LDP, the bureaucracy, and the *zaikai*. Now, they were charged with precisely the reverse: to undermine and discredit an elected Japanese government.

The agents of influence rose to the challenge, spreading the same story everywhere: Hatoyama's was an incompetent, anti-American government, one that threatened the peace and stability of East Asia. This was a message that resonated particularly with the New Japan Hands and the Pentagon. The New Japan Hands were not ignorant of Japan; they knew perfectly well that Ozawa had been the architect of the DPJ's victory. They were aware of how powerful he was—many of them remembered that it was he who had pushed Tokyo into bearing a major share of the cost of the first Gulf War; they knew he had almost brought down the LDP-bureaucrat nexus in 1993 and understood that he stood a good chance of success this time, success that would curtail the power of their friends and counterparts in Tokyo, success that could, among other things, end their effective monopoly of Japan policy in Washington and threaten disruption of the comfortable quasi-colonial security relationship between the United States and Japan.

Even before the DPJ victory, the New Japan Hands had already reacted with fear and loathing to Ozawa's talk of reforming the relationship. Back in February 2009, on her first trip abroad as Secretary of State in the incoming Obama administration, Hillary Clinton had flown to Tokyo to secure a new agreement updating the 2006 pact on the Futenma relocation. Washington had begun to notice that despite all the talk, absolutely nothing was being done in Japan to implement that agreement. The new administration intended to put Tokyo on notice that it should not mistake Obama's campaign rhetoric for any intention to change American policy vis-à-vis East Asia. Obama retained Robert Gates, Bush's Secretary of Defense, and dispatched Clinton with the message that it was high time the Japanese started acting on their promises.

By that point it was becoming increasingly clear that Washington could do little to halt the LDP's impending defeat. To ensure Ozawa got the message that the United States would not tolerate any reneging on the 2006 agreement, she insisted on a meeting with him that he initially tried to dodge. Then she pointedly remarked at a press conference that "a responsible nation follows the agreements that have been entered into, and the agreement that I signed today with Foreign Minister Nakasone is one between our two nations, regardless of who's in power."

Ozawa had been making comments to the effect that what really mattered in cold military terms to the security of East Asia was not Okinawa, but the US 7th Fleet headquartered at Yokosuka. The bases in Okinawa were mostly training and back-up facilities. In any credible scenario of actual conflict—the resumption of war on the Korean peninsula, a military confrontation between Taiwan and China—the US forces that would see immediate action would be those on the ground in Korea or, as Ozawa had pointed out, sailors in the 7th Fleet, not the Marines on Okinawa.[8]

---

8. On November 22, 2011, I heard the late Sam Jameson, the former Tokyo correspondent for the *Los Angeles Times* and long the de facto dean of the American journalist community in Japan, ask eminent New Japan Hand William L. Brooks at a talk Brooks gave in Tokyo to justify the strategic significance of the Marine presence on Okinawa. Jameson added that in three decades of covering the issue, he had "never understood" this. Brooks essentially conceded Jameson's point, saying that it was part of the "package" that provided for the security of Japan and East Asia.

Ozawa's comments were infuriating enough to the Pentagon and the New Japan Hands given all the effort that had been expended on negotiating the solution-that-was-no-solution (the negotiations with Tokyo and, even more importantly, whatever had been done to persuade the Marines to accept Futenma's replacement). But what really made them see red was Ozawa's suggestion that Japan's security arrangements should be "UN centered" rather than "US centered." Nothing Ozawa said could have provoked more rage in official Washington, something Ozawa may not have fully understood. At the hastily convened meeting between Ozawa and Clinton that Ozawa had initially refused, Ozawa had given voice to some of his thoughts about collective security, leading to an "icy" reception from Clinton.

Some Japanese commentators have insinuated that the public prosecutor's investigation into Ozawa's finances began shortly after this meeting on orders from Washington. There is no smoking-gun evidence of this, but Ozawa had certainly by this point been fingered by the New Japan Hands and their powerful backers—particularly Richard Armitage—as an enemy of "the relationship." Ozawa's stepping aside in the wake of the prosecutorial inquiry did little to mollify the New Japan Hands; understanding the way Japan worked, they knew that Ozawa might well end up a powerful puppet-master the way his mentor Tanaka had been. Their rage grew when Ozawa led the delegation to China in December 2009. Ozawa was received with a warmth that formed such an obvious and striking contrast to the way he had been treated by Hillary Clinton (or Hatoyama had been insulted by Robert Gates) that both the American and Japanese media began speculating on a fundamental shift in the alignments among the three countries.[9]

So the agents of influence had an easy sell when they began spreading the message that Hatoyama was the incompetent head of an anti-American

9. A speech by Armitage at what amounted to a public conclave of agents of influence and New Japan Hands at the Pac Forum of the CSIS on January 20, 2010, is particularly revealing. Although Armitage natters on with the usual polite fictions about "our Japanese friends" and noninterference in Japanese affairs, he cannot avoid flashes of bewilderment at the DPJ and fear at what it means for Futenma. The mask of politeness and diplomatic propriety slips about halfway into the speech when he cannot bring himself to refer to Ozawa by name; Armitage makes a snide reference to Ozawa's Beijing trip, calling it "the specter of the Japanese liberation army descending on Beijing," complaining that Ozawa "had not been to Washington for ten years," as if Ozawa were a renegade lieutenant who had failed to report for orders. As of this writing, the speech can be seen on YouTube at http://www.youtube.com/watch?v=AbqO2GU1khQ. The remarks on Ozawa start at 5'39".

government. The Obama White House fell right into the trap; its treatment of Hatoyama gave the major Japanese newspapers the evidence they needed to begin insinuating that Hatoyama "threatened" Japan's most important foreign policy relationship. In most countries, the kind of rudeness and contempt with which Washington treated a national leader would have led to an outpouring of resentment as people rallied around their government. But not in Japan. The establishment press was far more exercised by its hatred of Ozawa, its determination to rid Japanese politics of Tanaka's legacy, and its nostalgia for cozy relationships with LDP politicians than the spectacle of its prime minister being treated like an errant schoolboy by the leadership of what was supposed to be Japan's "ally."

The pressure on Hatoyama grew overwhelming. What he then did points to the fundamental problem facing all elected Japanese governments, a problem that can be traced as far back as the legacy of the Meiji leaders: the difficulty of imposing political control on bureaucrats who believe themselves "above" politics.

This is not a situation unique to Japan. It is not possible to govern without experts, without knowledgeable bureaucrats. The great trap of highly complex modern societies is the resultant arrogance these bureaucrats develop and the contempt they begin to feel for all attempts to "interfere" in the way they do things. Americans should have an increasing sympathy for the Japanese predicament when they contemplate what has happened since the end of the Cold War to the national security bureaucracies: the Pentagon, the FBI, the CIA, and the NSA. President Obama was elected in part to tear open the thick cloaks of secrecy that had been draped over these bureaucracies by his predecessor's administration. But he has not only been unable to call a halt to their institutional aggrandizement, he has quite obviously become their agent. Why? Because he discovers that they are no longer under effective political control.

The problem is even more acute in Japan where democratic politics has never fully attained the function it performs in countries like the United States and France: legitimizing the exercise of power. Japan's senior policy makers in the bureaucracy still tend to view themselves the way their prewar predecessors did—as "servants of the emperor," or, today, of "Japan," rather than of voters, not to mention the grubby, grasping politicians elected to represent them. When it came to matters such as relations with Washington, Hatoyama had no place to turn but his experts, his technocrats—the people who had spent decades immersed in the minutiae of American opinion and policy-making, the people who were on a first-name basis with Richard Armitage, Joseph Nye, and the New Japan Hands. These men did not view themselves as Hatoyama's staff, charged with carrying out policies determined by their nominal superiors in the office of the prime minister. They saw Hatoyama and everything he repre-sented as a threat to "Japan." So they sold him a bill of goods: that "some-how" the Futenma imbroglio with Washington could be put behind them.

Hatoyama then made what he later conceded in private conversations was the worst mistake of his career. Desperate to end the pressure being placed on him by the media and the bureaucracy, fearful that everything the DPJ hoped to accomplish had been placed at risk, he took the advice of his Foreign Ministry bureaucrats at face value and announced that he would "stake his political career" on settling the Futenma issue by May 2010.

This is a fairly common ploy by Japanese politicians in tight spots—Koizumi had, for example, said he would "stake his political career" on getting the postal privatization bill through Diet. Sometimes it works, as it did for Koizumi when he exercised his prerogative as prime minister to dissolve the Diet and call for an election after the bill failed, an election he won. But in Hatoyama's case it backfired. Okinawa erupted with outrage at what appeared to be the DPJ's betrayal of the promise it had made the island's voters to end the de facto American occupation. The Obama ad-ministration refused to give Hatoyama any kind of lifeline, *vide* the way Hatoyama was received at the nuclear security conference. The White House indicated it would wait to see concrete signs that construction of the new base had begun before it would deign to treat Hatoyama with the kind of courtesy or recognition extended as a matter of course to most foreign heads of government, particularly those from democratic "allies."

But despite what the bureaucrats had told Hatoyama, there was no possibility that implementation of the Futenma relocation agreement could begin by May. If the LDP had been unable or unwilling to deploy the brute force that would have been necessary to carry out its provisions, certainly the DPJ was not.

Then on March 26, a South Korean Navy vessel exploded, killing 46 seamen. An official investigation by South Korea and the United States (with representatives from three other countries) would conclude the cause had been a North Korean torpedo. Many accused the investiga-tion of being a rush job or even a cover-up of what might actually have happened. Among other things, the Swedish delegation distanced itself from the conclusion that the explosion was an act of sabotage by the North Koreans, while some prominent South Koreans went public with their doubts.[10] But whether the incident was a deliberate exercise by North Korea's dying leader, Kim Jong-Il, to ratchet up tensions in an attempt provide cover for the impending passage of power to his son—and no conclusive evidence has ever come to light of this—or an opportunistic response by Seoul and/or Washington to an accident, it reinforced the fear of North Korea felt in Japan. This fear was often linked to a vague sense that it was the US security umbrella that kept North Korean lunatics at bay—and that Hatoyama's "incompetence" was somehow tearing holes in this umbrella, leaving Japan vulnerable to Pyongyang's warmongers.

Even a cursory analysis demonstrates that these feelings were misplaced. North Korea's leaders may run one of the world's most loathsome and tyrannical police states, but they are not suicidal maniacs and, given recent history in Iraq, Afghanistan, Libya, Iran, Syria, Bosnia, and—going farther back—Grenada, Guatemala, Indonesia, Nicaragua, Panama, Cuba, and the Dominican Republic, it should not be a cause for wonder that they feel threatened nor that they play a weak hand as best they can. That play involves demonstrating how expensive it will be to take them down.

If they should miscalculate—and the risk certainly exists—if they should accidentally precipitate a war with bellicose language and staged outrages that in reality are closer to the snarls and bristling of a small cat in the presence of a large dog than an actual invitation to go at it, the US forces on Okinawa will have very little to do with what would happen. Action will be seen by the two million South Korean soldiers and 40,000 US troops in South Korea. And while it is possible that Pyongyang will use its missiles to hold Osaka as well as Seoul hostage, it is not clear new training facilities on Okinawa for the Marines would affect this one way or another, other than perhaps to make Pyongyang feel yet more threatened.

But little of this made it into the mindset of typical Japanese voters, not to mention what they saw on television or read in the newspaper. Instead, what they were led to believe was that this government they had elected to fix the economy and replace a fraying safety net with a new and better

10. Chief among them were Lee Seung-Hun, a physicist at the University of Virginia who called the official investigations conclusions "absurd," and J. J. Suh, director of Korea Studies at Johns Hopkins's Nitze School.

one was instead somehow mucking up Japan's security arrangements and leaving their country vulnerable to North Korean attack.

The pressure on Hatoyama grew intolerable. Pilloried in the press and with his poll numbers plummeting, fearing the ruin of all that he and Ozawa had worked and planned for, he persuaded Ozawa that the two of them should jointly submit their resignations from their respective positions as prime minister and secretary general of the DPJ. Perhaps their successor could accomplish what they had failed to do. For their successor was one of the most attractive men in Japanese politics: Kan Naoto.

3/11 AND THE FATE OF THE KAN GOVERNMENT

It is here that we rejoin the story left off at the end of chapter 9 when we first met Kan, the fresh-faced politician with roots in the student protest movement who had demonstrated back in 1996 that he had the bureaucrats' number and was not afraid to stand up to them. He had founded the DPJ with Hatoyama, and when the latter resigned, Kan immediately ran for and won the party presidency, which automatically made him prime minister. Kan had faced only token opposition in the party election from a candidate known for his close ties to Ozawa. At the time, some speculated that even the staging of the opposition candidacy might have been nothing more than a bluff-and-feint move by Ozawa and Kan for media consumption. Establishment commentators with memories of their impotence at the backstage puppet-mastering of Tanaka and Kanemaru were hyper-alert to any sign that Ozawa might still be calling any shots despite his resignation as the DPJ's Secretary General and were prepared to give Kan the same kind of grief they had given Hatoyama if they suspected that were true.

But it was no bluff—Kan really did distance himself from Ozawa. He had barely been in office two weeks when he began to talk about doubling the consumption tax, directly contradicting not only the DPJ's campaign platform, but one of Ozawa's most passionate beliefs. Taxes were one of the few real checks that Japan's elected government had on the bureaucracy; as we noted in chapters 7 and 10, the MOF had for a generation been trying to turn this tax into the principal revenue source for the Japanese government, not simply in order to resolve Japan's fiscal dilemmas but also to take taxation out of the realm of political discussion. Ozawa understood that realization of the MOF's dream would amount to the end of any leverage politicians had over the bureaucracy—why he was so adamantly opposed to a hike in the tax. Much of the electorate agreed with him.

Kan had made a terrible blunder. Coming, as it did, with memories of Hatoyama's vow to settle the Futenma relocation issue all too fresh, it reinforced the view that the DPJ did not really stand behind its campaign promises. Kan quickly backtracked, but the damage had been done and the party lost its majority in the Upper House in the July election. Ozawa publicly rebuked Kan and challenged him in the September election for the party leadership, an election which Kan barely won. Kan then proceeded to purge the cabinet of Ozawa's supporters, possibly because he hoped the establishment press might give him the pass they had denied Hatoyama.

Many of the replacements—his Finance Minister Noda Yoshihiko; the Foreign Minister Maehara Seiji; Edano Yukio, who would later become Chief Cabinet Secretary and the public face of the government during the aftermath of 3/11—were graduates of the *Matsushita Seikei Juku* (Matsushita Institute of Government and Management), a kind of elite finishing school for would-be politicians established by Matsushita Konosuke, the founder of Panasonic. The Matsushita school and its graduates represent a Japanese variation on a meme that had spread worldwide before the 2008 financial crisis: the notion that the endemic problems of politics and government can be solved if only countries could be turned over to the kinds of people who manage the best-run corporations, people who talk the language of efficiency, technology, prioritization, core competencies, and win-win scenarios, who display a crisp, no-nonsense, leadership style, complete with PowerPoint slides and data-mining. This powerful construct with its vision of an end to the messiness, the horse-trading, the palpable sleaze of democratic politics was visible everywhere from the George W. Bush White House to Nicolas Sarkozy's Élysée Palace, from Thaksin Sinawatra's Bangkok to Stephen Harper's Ottawa. It resonated in a Japan with a business elite that was increasingly on the defensive and blamed their country's plight on the failings of its governing class. They probably were right about that; they understood that there was something wrong with Japan's politics; that among other things, bureaucrats cannot ultimately run countries.

But neither can business executives—nor can politicians who confuse what it takes to run companies with what it takes to run countries. The graduates of the Matsushita school looked and talked the part; men like Maehara and Genba Koichiro who would succeed him as foreign minister are handsome, dapper, and well-spoken. They fit perfectly into board rooms and can schmooze as equals with the kinds of people who throng to Davos for the annual World Economic Forum. But they had a harder time coping with the demands of rural construction executives who wanted to know when shovels could be pulled out for the next government project so they could pay their staff, with small farmers uneasy over talk of trade liberalization, with scared older salarymen hearing about "meritocratic" reforms in Japan's employment practices, with college kids facing a dry-up of the kinds of jobs they had been told were their only paths to security and respectability. And these Matsushita graduates certainly had little idea of how to calm thousands of enraged Okinawans or bridle hundreds of wily bureaucrats accustomed to outlasting one "reformist" politician after another with bureaucrats' prerogatives and turf boundaries intact.

By cutting Ozawa out of the picture, Kan and the people around him were ultimately attempting their own version of a politics without politicians, or least the kinds of deal-making, back-scratching politicians who had been schooled by Tanaka. Might it have worked had it not been for 3/11? It is very unlikely. True, Washington had decided for the time being to cut Kan a bit of slack. In his first telephone conversation with Japan's new prime minister, Obama had elicited a commitment out of Kan to continue to work on the Futenma relocation, but this time no deadlines were set.

Beijing, however, was not cooperating. The Chinese had noticed what had happened; they saw that Washington had systematically set about gelding a Japanese government that had dared to hint at reordering its foreign relations and its security arrangements. A Chinese trawler sailed into waters off some remote islets that were administered by Japan but also claimed by China. The trawler appears deliberately to have rammed a Japanese coast guard vessel. A Japanese coast guard officer leaked a video of the encounter; the man was distraught at what he saw as the pusillanimous stance of the Japanese government toward Chinese provocations, but the result was the first in a series of confrontations that would escalate into arguably the greatest foreign policy challenge faced by Japan since 1945. Beijing had set out to demonstrate—deliberately or not—that while it may possible for Tokyo to be a subservient vassal of Washington and it may be possible for Japan to have good relations with China, it was no longer going to be possible to be and to have both. Squaring that takes the kind of political genius exhibited by men like Tanaka Kakuei who had, some four decades earlier, succeeded in shelving this very issue with Zhou Enlai when it had threatened to derail the establishment of formal diplomatic relations between Tokyo and the People's Republic of China. The skills necessary for this sort of diplomatic *tour de force* are not acquired from classroom lectures on zero-based budgeting but long experience in the bluffing and deal-cutting of actual politics—experience that Tanaka and Ozawa had had but in which Kan and his foreign minister Maehara demonstrably fell short.

We will come back shortly to the imbroglio over these islets; it would return with a vengeance some months after 3/11. In the meantime, we turn again briefly to that tragedy. We saw what happened in chapter 9—how Kan had personally taken charge after it appeared that the operator of the stricken nuclear plant, Tokyo Electric Power, was on the verge of abandoning the facility.

One might assume Kan would have been thought a hero, and it is still possible that if and when the definitive history of those terrible weeks is finally written, Kan will have emerged as the savior of his country. But that was not the way he was regarded at the time. True, in the first few days after the tragedy, one could find positive comparisons with the government's response to the Kobe earthquake of 1995 together with an understanding of the far greater challenges posed by the 2011 catastrophe. But as news of the earthquake and tsunami was gradually superseded by the open-ended disaster of the nuclear plant, what the public saw—and the media reported—was incompetence and paralysis at the highest levels of both Tokyo Electric Power and the Japanese government.

Washington behaved in exemplary fashion. Perhaps because of unease at the way the Marines had been allowed to endanger one of America's most critical relationships, perhaps because of genuine sympathy, but most probably to save the security relationship with Japan that had been put in serious jeopardy by the events in Okinawa, the United States gave unstinting and genuinely helpful aid. Particularly important was the reconstruction of the Sendai airport. The US military is accomplished at getting a facility in shape in record time so aircraft can land. Sendai, the largest city on Honshu north of Tokyo, had had its transportation links effectively cut off by the combined effect of the earthquake and the radiation from the stricken nuclear plant. The reopening of the airport eased the city's sense of desperate isolation; it also, of course, demonstrated how good the US military was at this kind of thing—and the efficiency and competence with which the rebuilding was carried out formed an obvious contrast with what was going on around the Fukushima plant.

Two months later, three members of the Senate Armed Services Committee, John McCain, Carl Levin, and former Marine Jim Webb, voiced the truth: that the Futenma relocation treaty was a nonstarter. They were perhaps the only people in Washington who could have pulled it off, who could actually stand up and say that the emperor had no clothes. As Rodney Armstrong, formerly Second Secretary at the US Embassy in Tokyo put it,

> The Henoko project is a problem created for themselves by the American military's failure to recognize that Okinawa not only cannot accommodate Futenma, it cannot accommodate any new substitute for Futenma. The only solution is joint basing with the Air Force at Kadena. This was the conclusion of all neutral observers from the beginning of the issue seventeen years ago, and it was accepted by Senators Levin, Webb, and McCain in their 2010 report. If inter-service rivalries prevent this solution, then the Marines must leave Okinawa.

But all this was too late to save Kan. Shortly before the catastrophe, conventional wisdom had it that he would not last more than a few weeks. The rally-around-authority effect noticeable after many catastrophes worked in the case of 3/11 just long enough to throw him a temporary lifeline. He used it to announce his determination to stay in office at least until a reconstruction bill could be shepherded through the Diet. Once he had succeeded in this goal, however, exhausted and with the pressures around him again reaching overwhelming levels, he resigned with a parting blast at the "nuclear village"—bureaucrats, power companies, and the LDP—that he saw as principally culpable for the disaster.

The subsequent struggle for the DPJ leadership revealed the fatal fault line in the party between the Ozawa faction and its opponents. The most important of Ozawa's opponents consisted, on the one hand, of the Matsushita graduates with their visions of efficient, technocratic governance, and, on the other, refugees from the defunct Japan Socialist Party accustomed to political posturing rather than governing. The Matsushita graduates and the former socialists agreed on little else, but they both saw Ozawa and his followers as representatives of the corrupt old politics of Tanaka's era. Ozawa's candidate, Kaieda Banri, had initially been favored to win, but then his opponents coalesced around perhaps the most un-likely figure imaginable given the party's history: Kan's erstwhile finance minister, Noda Yoshihiko.

Noda's victory came across to many as a return to precisely the kind of politics that the DPJ had been elected to replace. He got the nod because he had fewer enemies than any of the others; his colorlessness paradoxi-cally made him palatable to the party's various factions and to the bureau-crats, if not to the voters. Noda conceded the point, comparing himself to a tasteless, bottom-dwelling river fish, while commentators recalled the "cold pizza" label affixed to Obuchi Keizo, who had died in office in 2000.

Indeed, Noda seemed a throw-back to an old-style LDP hack, rising to the top mostly because of skill in surviving factional infighting and read-iness to do the bureaucrats' bidding. But if voters were going to get the equivalent of an LDP politician, why not go for the real thing?

THE IMMOLATION OF NODA'S GOVERNMENT

Noda's government was destroyed by two things: the consumption tax hike and the growing imbroglio with China over the Senkaku Islands.

Let's start with the tax. Noda seems genuinely to have believed that the tax hike was essential to avoiding a fiscal catastrophe. One possible explanation for what happened lies in a bargain Noda may have struck with the MOF to finance reconstruction in the wake of the earthquake. As Kan's finance minister, Noda was inevitably the public face for the funding of disaster relief, and it appears he agreed with MOF bureau-crats to spearhead a doubling of the tax as the price for release of the necessary reconstruction funds. A contributing factor in his support of the tax hike may have been his known admiration for Margaret Thatcher and her reputation for doing what she thought necessary for her country, irrespective of public opinion polls (which, in Japan's case, showed over-whelming opposition to the tax hike). Many also suspect pressure from Washington.

Whatever the ultimate explanation, Noda proceeded with a kind of willful stubbornness to do what savvy political observers knew would be fatal to his party's prospects. Taking a leaf from a style book noted above, Noda announced he would "stake his political career" on getting the tax hike through the Diet.

He could not do so, however, with the DPJ alone. As Noda insisted on proceeding with the tax hike, Ozawa threatened to repeat what he had done back in 1993 when the LDP refused to agree to electoral reform: walk out with his followers and form a new party. That forced Noda to cut a deal with the LDP, and the LDP exacted a very high price. The law did not require a new lower house election until the fall of 2013, but the LDP price tag for their support of the consumption tax hike turned out to be a promise from Noda to dissolve the Diet and call a new election by the end of 2012.

It is conceivable—barely—that had it not been for what happened over the Senkaku that Noda and the DPJ might have hung on, even without Ozawa's political skills, the skills that had put them in power in the first place. But Noda fumbled everything about the Senkaku—the response to the rightist mischief-making in Japan that helped put the issue back on the front-burner, the diplomacy with Beijing, even the coordination with Washington. The "incompetent" label that the DPJ's enemies had been attempting to pin on the party began to seem all too valid to an increasingly fearful Japanese public reading reports of anti-Japanese riots in China and Chinese warships steaming toward Japanese waters. For the issue at hand was not just taxes and the economy; it was the actual prospect of war.

THE SENKAKU ISLANDS AND JAPAN'S TERRITORIAL DISPUTES

As a *casus belli*, the Senkaku are no more plausible than the assassination of an Austrian archduke by a young Serbian rabble-rouser. A group of five uninhabited islets and three rock outcroppings, the Senkaku are located some 110 miles from the southernmost point of the Ryuku island chain and 92 miles from an islet of Taiwan's. No one paid them much attention until the late nineteenth century, although earlier cartographers— not to mention fishermen and other mariners—were aware of them. A Tokugawa era geographer had labeled them Chinese islands, and they were mentioned in some Ming and Qing writings. The Chinese call them the Diaoyu Islands.

The Senkaku form one of the three territorial disputes Japan has, respectively, with its neighbors: China, Korea, and Russia. Each of the three disputes has its own independent story, but they are nonetheless closely

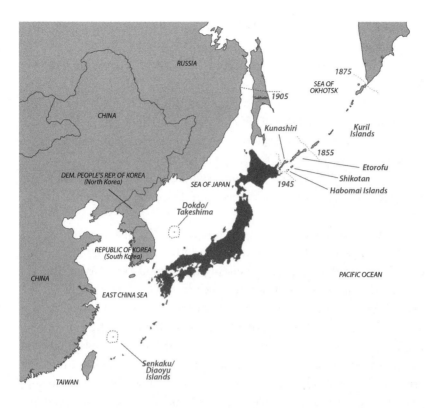

MAP 2. Japan and its Neighbors: Disputed Territories. Courtesy Nicholas A. Perdue, Drawn from the Economist.com.

linked—not least for fear in Tokyo that a concession on any one of the disputes would lead to loss of the others.

The least important—and the one probably easiest to settle—is that with South Korea over what the Koreans call Dokdo and the Japanese call Takeshima. These are a group of rock outcroppings (known to Westerners as the Liancourt Rocks) about halfway between Japan and Korea that are under South Korean control but also claimed by Japan. As with most such disputes, there are blustery narratives on both sides about national rights and the perfidy of the other side. The fishing grounds around the rocks have some value, and there is methane hydrate in the sea floors nearby. But the real obstacle to a solution seems to be the precedent a Japanese concession would set for the other two territorial disputes: that over the Senkaku Islands and the one with Russia over what the Japanese call their

Northern Territories—three islands and a small group of islets that form the southern end of the Kurile island chain.

The entire Kurile chain had been awarded to Japan after the 1905 Russo-Japanese War; the more southerly of the islands, granted to Japan by treaty in 1875, had long been thickly settled by Japanese. Unlike the Senkaku—not to mention Dokdo/Takeshima—these are real islands. Etorofu, the largest, is over 3,000 square kilometers, while number two Kunashiri is nearly 1,500 (O'ahu, by comparison, is just over 1,500), and they have both military and economic significance. They sit astride access to the open ocean by the Russian navy and abut some of the richest fishing grounds on earth.

In violation of its nonaggression pact with Japan, Soviet troops attacked and seized the southern Kuriles in the days right after Japan accepted the Potsdam declaration ending the Second World War. This act of naked conquest as most Japanese saw it is one of the reasons for the decades-long hostility between Japan and, successively, the Soviet Union and the Russian Federation. (After the collapse of the Soviet Union, Russia reaffirmed the Soviet claim to the southern Kuriles.) The displaced inhabitants of these islands and their relatives formed an important pressure group in Japan; it was long political suicide in Japan for anyone to suggest that there was any possible resolution other than the Russians simply leaving these islands.

But as with the other disputes, there is more to it. Under the terms of the San Francisco Treaty, the status of the Kuriles had been left undecided; under some interpretations, Japan had given up its claim, but the treaty nonetheless did not recognize the USSR's occupation. Shikotan (225 square kilometers) and the Habomai islets were in any case considered part of Hokkaido rather than the Kuriles. For these reasons, Moscow refused to sign the treaty. But since then, Moscow has several times offered to negotiate over the dispute, offers that Tokyo invariably spurned. The most significant of these offers occurred in 1956 when Moscow sent a feeler indicating it would return Shikotan and Habomai if Japan would renounce its claim to the two larger islands. The United States, seeking in the early days of the Cold War to stoke anti-Soviet feeling in Japan, put pressure on Tokyo not to respond to the overtures, linking the American demand to Japan's hopes to recover Okinawa.

There the situation has remained for well on sixty years. Moscow may be prepared to cut a deal—one that would involve not only return of

Shikotan and Habomai but also some sort of joint development of the two larger islands. Russia needs Japanese markets, investment, and technology and has shown signs that it is prepared to be flexible in order to get access to those.

But Tokyo would have none of it. The Russians took those islands illegally, displacing tens of thousands of Japanese and in the face of mountains of historical evidence of Japanese settlement that goes back centuries. To enter into negotiations over what many Japanese see as theirs by right and by inheritance would be an outrage. The refusal to compromise on what seems a point of principle helps explain the stance that Tokyo has taken toward the Senkaku: that "there is no dispute." In the case of the Senkaku, the Japanese have the upper hand since they occupy these islets; to start negotiating with Beijing over the Senkaku might, it is feared, undermine Tokyo's stance toward Russia: that Moscow seized the southern Kuriles illegally and should leave them.

The Japanese maintain that they took possession of the Senkaku as *terra nullius* in 1895 without challenge. But it is not quite so simple. Japanese entrepreneurs had already started a dried bonito-flakes and bird feathers business on one of the islands and had petitioned Tokyo to incorporate the islands into the Japanese empire, a petition that Yamagata Aritomo, to whom we were introduced in chapter 3 as the father of Japanese imperialism, did not deem fit to grant until a few months before the onset of the Sino-Japanese War. The Chinese argue that the islands were, along with Taiwan, the spoils of that war that they see as unjustified imperialist land-grab. Perhaps as a result, the United States did not recognize the Senkaku as part of the package when Okinawa and the rest of the Ryukyu chain were nominally returned to Japanese sovereignty in 1972. But that was not because of opposition from Beijing; it was because of opposition from Taipei. The Republic of China on Taiwan, which at that point still claimed to be the legitimate government of all of China, had been much more vociferous in its assertion of its claims to the Senkaku than Beijing had been. The Nixon administration was already preparing the groundwork for the resumption of relations with Beijing and did not want to provoke Taipei any further than it already had with outright support of Japan's position on ownership of the islands. Since Washington passed on the ownership question, Taipei did not press its claim, accepting, without ceding the claim, that for the time being the Senkaku would revert to nominal Japanese control with the return of Okinawa.

The issue is widely reported to have come up during the 1972 negotiations between Tanaka Kakuei and Zhou Enlai that led to the establishment of formal diplomatic relations between Japan and the People's
Republic of China. The two leaders agreed to shelve the dispute, an informal agreement that was reinforced later in the decade by Deng Xiaoping
and the LDP Secretary General of the time, Ohira Masayoshi, who would
shortly become prime minister.

There the matter lay until a few years ago—Japan controlled the islands
and the waters around them, but they were also claimed by both Beijing
and Taipei (of course, Beijing did not recognize the legal authority of the
government in Taipei).

What happened? An increase since 2010 in the number of confrontations between Japanese coast guard vessels and both mainland and
Taiwanese fishing ships might suggest that economic reasons lay behind
the return of the dispute; the islands are thought to sit astride beds of
methane hydrate; recent technological developments have rendered these
a potentially valuable energy resource.

But the politics are more important. Sudden Chinese assertiveness in the
last few years is not confined to the Senkaku; Beijing is renewing old claims to
vast swathes of the South China Sea, in the process provoking confrontations,
diplomatic and otherwise, with the Philippines, Malaysia, Indonesia, and
Vietnam. There have been incursions along disputed borders with India. It is
at least plausible that hard-line factions within Chinese military and governing circles have decided to settle old scores. Deng had laid down the notion
of "peaceful rise": that China should concentrate on building up its economy
while maintaining a pliant and non-threatening face to other countries. But
with China's emergence as the world's second largest economy and among its
largest net creditors, China's hotheads believe their country need no longer
fear provoking others. With its vast manufacturing infrastructure and a
modernized military, the time has come, they say, for China to reassert its
rightful place as "the central country" (what the country's name in Chinese
means), if not in the world as a whole, then at least in Asia.

Thus we see the picking of fights with Japan, with Vietnam, with the
Philippines, with India, and with the United States. But domestic politics
also plays a crucial role. The Chinese Communist Party ("CCP") has jettisoned Leninist dogma on the "leading role of the party" as the basis for its
claim to legitimacy. Instead, it increasingly resorts to a species of aggrieved
nationalism. Among other things, this helps deflect popular anger over

the widening gap between rich and poor and the overwhelming evidence of structural corruption in high places. It is no accident, according to this line of thought, that the confrontations over the Senkaku and in the South China Sea occurred in the wake of the downfall of Bo Xilai, the powerful party boss of the major city of Chongqing who had effectively attempted to buy his way onto the Standing Committee of the Politburo. The resulting scandal, complete with charges of murder brought against his wife and accounts of riotous living abroad by his son, arguably represented the greatest crisis of legitimacy for the CCP since the Tiananmen demonstrations of 1989. The CCP needed to change the subject.

Whatever the balance of power at any given moment in Beijing, however, there is little doubt of the dominant worldview in China's ruling circles: that a benevolent order had long existed in Asia, an order that saw China at its center, radiating peaceful civilization to the surrounding lands, until this order was disrupted by a rapacious, imperialist West. According to this line of thinking, Japan played a particularly destructive and nefarious role in wrecking the peace of Asia, betraying its Asian heritage by joining the Western imperialists and then outdoing them in the looting and raping of China. Peace and the natural order of things—a benevolent China at the center of Asian civilization—will not be restored until the United States leaves Asia. Japan, now depicted by the Chinese as a contemptible American vassal, represents perhaps the greatest challenge to the realization of this dream.

There is also no doubt but that the CCP has, in recent years, rewritten the defining sagas of modern Chinese history, sagas used to cement the image of the party and to mold patriotism. These sagas once featured class struggle, the tale of the Long March, and civil war against Chiang Kai-shek's Kuomintang culminating in the 1949 revolution. Now the sagas tend to begin with the humiliation of China in the Opium Wars and move quickly into a long tale of heroic fighting against the Japanese from the 1895 conflict through the rejection of the Twenty One Demands in 1915 to the 1937–45 war in China itself. There are obvious rationales for the emphasis on this new way of presenting modern Chinese history. The earlier accounts featured Chinese fighting Chinese; now all patriotic Chinese—Communist or Kuomintang—are seen fighting foreigners. Given the ambitions of the CCP to reincorporate Taiwan into China proper, emphasizing the role of all Chinese in anti-Japanese struggles helps put the Kuomintang—still the ruling party in Taiwan—on the CCP's side against the "separatists" there.

These new sagas of modern Chinese history also work well in channeling popular outrage onto an external target—sometimes, all too well, even for the CCP's comfort. Any new account of Japanese outrages—manufactured or not, historical or contemporary—is almost guaranteed to produce some sort of reaction in China: demonstrations, vandalism against Japanese-owned properties, nationalist fervor. Things can end up out of control; in a repressive society, it is no easy task to keep steam-letting confined to approved channels of anti-Japanese sentiment. But the regime sees that as preferable to allowing no outlet at all; with the Cultural Revolution and the Tiananmen incident forming its institutional memory, it understands that stifling all venues for expressing anger is not a safe option.

Much analysis of the Senkaku imbroglio in Japan—including much thoughtful analysis—runs along the lines above. The essence: China is attempting to restore the tributary relationships with its neighbors that prevailed in dynastic times, with these countries reduced to the status of supplicants and vassals or, like Tibet and the historical Uighur lands in Xinjiang, forfeiting their independence altogether. The CCP cynically foments hatred of Japan and exploits it to deflect popular rage at its own failings.

Of course, there is some truth to this analysis—quite a lot of it. (Among other things, it appears some people in China were paid to participate in anti-Japanese demonstrations.) But there is another way of looking at things, one we have already noted. Beijing saw what happened in the wake of Ozawa's comments to Hillary Clinton on her February 2009 visit to Japan, not to mention the coincidence of the ersatz "investigation" into Ozawa's finances that destroyed his chances of becoming prime minister. Chinese leaders noted the spasms of hysteria that shook the American foreign policy establishment after Ozawa led his 600-person delegation to their country. They understood how the Hatoyama administration had been deliberately sabotaged by a de facto alliance of Pentagon functionaries, the establishment press in Japan, and Japanese spokesmen in the United States committing what amounted to treason against their own government. And they decided to call Tokyo's—and Washington's—bluff.

More and more "fishing vessels" and other Chinese ships began showing up in the waters around the Senkaku. Ishihara Shintaro, the long-serving governor of Tokyo and a hero in right-wing circles for his blunt language, announced his intention to have the Tokyo Metropolitan Government buy the Senkaku from their owner, a real estate investor and descendent of the entrepreneur who had first established a business there in the late nineteenth century.[11] Ishihara began soliciting contributions for the purchase of the islands. Ishihara appears deliberately to have been attempting to make a diplomatic resolution of the imbroglio impossible by stirring up nationalist and anti-Chinese sentiment in Japan.

The Noda government panicked, demonstrating yet one more time how the DPJ had effectively committed suicide when it drove Ozawa out of the party. Ozawa might have coped with a rabble-rouser like Ishihara; Noda hadn't a clue. Against the advice of a Washington that was finally beginning to wake up to the consequences of its cavalier destruction of an elected Japanese government, Noda arranged for the outright nationalization of the Senkaku, putting them under direct ownership of the Japanese government itself. Noda claimed he had been "sure" the Chinese would understand what he was about: taking off the table an issue that xenophobes like Ishihara had been exploiting. But he badly miscalculated. As long the islands had been in nominally private hands, shelving the issue had been possible without loss of face on either side. Once they had been nationalized, however, there was no resolution without a humiliating public retreat by one side or the other. Noda had blundered his way into committing the cardinal sin of politics and policy in East Asia: backing two parties to a dispute into a situation where neither party can retreat without loss of face.

In the midst of it all, the Japan policy establishment in Washington issued a marvel of a document. The document, entitled "The US–Japan Alliance: Anchoring Stability in Asia," was authored by none other than Richard Armitage and Joseph Nye, and the document was countersigned by a whole roster of New Japan Hands: David Asher, Michael Green, Torkel Patterson, and Robin Sakoda chief among them. In the manner of a parent demanding of a toddler who has not yet mastered the potty whether he is really ready for *big boy pants* rather than *diapers*, the document asks whether Japan wants to be a *first-tier nation*. It turns out, on close reading, that being a first-tier nation involves "cautious resumption of nuclear power," signing a free trade agreement with the United States, importing lots of American liquid natural gas, working with the United States to develop methane hydrates, getting along with Seoul (i.e., find a way to muzzle

11. There were rumors reported in the Japanese press that both Mainland Chinese and Taiwanese had approached the owner with offers of astronomical amounts of money.

rightist loony tunes), and—here is the heart of it—"interoperability" (i.e., beefing up the Japanese military and folding it into the Pentagon). The document conveniently skips over the way Futenma had been used to bludgeon the Hatoyama government to death, calling Futenma a "third-order issue."

Whatever ambitions Noda might have had of leading a first-tier nation, though, it was too late. The rift with Ozawa, the consumption tax, the bungling over the Senkaku had left the Japanese public demoralized and fearful, convinced now that the DPJ was indeed hopelessly incompetent and—what is more—lacked either the gumption or the skills to defend their country against what was depicted as the rising menace in the east. Night after night the television screens were filled with scenes of vandalism against Japanese-owned properties in China, of Chinese warships steaming toward Japanese waters, of crowds of people in the streets of Chinese cities shouting for the death and destruction of Japanese. All this largely drowned out more cautious voices suggesting that much of it was for show.

Noda found himself facing an election against someone who was very definitely committed to making Japan a first-tier nation, who promised to do what it took finally to get the economy moving and to defend Japan. But it was not quite the first-tier nation that the New Japan Hands had in mind.

THE RETURN OF ABE SHINZO

As we saw in the previous chapter, Abe's first stint as prime minister back in 2006 had been a failure. Taking office in the wake of the popular Koizumi, Abe had figured that his predecessor had done enough spadework in straightening out the Japanese economy and squaring things with Washington to allow him to turn from these matters to what was really important to him: the Japanese Right's long-cherished agenda of tearing up the postwar settlement and restoring the *kokutai* ("national polity"— i.e., the prewar emperor system). The "American" constitution with its "un-Japanese" talk of rights and freedom was to be jettisoned, the history of the 1930s and 1940s was to be rewritten, Japan's military was to be set loose from postwar restraints, Japan's public officials were publicly to mourn at Yasukuni Shrine for those who had given their lives for their country, schoolchildren were to be inculcated with proper Japanese virtues, and a degree of sovereign political power restored to the Throne. Alas for Abe, the Japanese public greeted the whole shebang with a long yawn. Pilloried in the press for being out of touch, he resigned after less than a year in office.

But things had changed in six years. The Japanese economy turned out not to have been straightened out at all; in fact, it had nearly skidded into a ditch after the onset of the 2008 global crisis. That is what had created the opening in the first place for the DPJ to come to power. But once in power, the DPJ had, in the eyes of the public, done nothing about Japan's economic troubles other than conspire to raise taxes. Plans to build a real social safety net, to substitute "people" for "concrete" in the words of the party's campaign slogan, had gone nowhere. Meanwhile, the media had succeeded in convincing many voters that the DPJ had almost wrecked the security relationship with the United States and then cravenly and incompetently backed the country into a confrontation with China. And when faced with the greatest test of a government—natural catastrophe—the DPJ had been seen to fail, substituting PR and lies for action.

That the fault for what happened around Fukushima can be blamed directly on the structural pathologies of the Japanese postwar political setup of which the LDP was the embodiment, that the DPJ had been sabotaged by the bureaucracy and what amounted to treasonous conduct by Japan's operatives in the United States—all this counted for little. Political memories are short, particularly in a country like Japan where the press sees itself as a force for maintaining order and confuses the manufacture of hullabaloos over the failings of individual politicians with disciplined, disinterested coverage of the way power is exercised.[12]

Meanwhile, Abe and the people around him had learned their lesson—or rather, relearned what they had forgotten after Koizumi's relative success as prime minister: that no matter how reactionary an agenda might be, it has to be sold as a species of reform. And that if a government appears unresponsive to people's economic fears and aspirations, little else can be accomplished. Abe brought into his inner circle Koizumi's Chief Secretary, Iijima Isao, a man whose political skills have been compared to those of Karl Rove. Just as Rove was instrumental in selling George W. Bush to

---

12. Not that such coverage is to be found much anymore in the United States, but the idea that this is what they should be providing still lurks in the mental background of better American journalists—if not among the people they work for—which is why many of them display unease and outright shame at what has happened to American journalism since the days of Watergate and the Pentagon Papers.

the American public as a "compassionate conservative," so Iijima has been credited with inventing the persona Koizumi assumed as a "reformer."

Iijima set about pulling the same trick with Abe. He persuaded Abe that he needed to talk about the economy and the bold plans he had to rev it up again, not natter on about a "beautiful Japan" (the title of a campaign manifesto Abe had published back in 2006). The Right's game plan to destroy constitutional government and restore the authoritarian "family state" of the prewar years must be kept under wraps until the LDP had the numbers to ram the shredding of the constitution through the Diet. That could only happen if voters could be convinced the LDP would take care of the economy so the party could sweep the two elections needed for commanding majorities in both houses of the Diet. On December 16, 2012, the LDP won the first of the elections, the one for the Lower House. That put Abe again in the prime minister's seat, but this time he was determined not to make the mistakes he had six years earlier. The LDP needed to win the second election—the one for Japan's Upper House, to be held in July 2013—and to do that, Abe had to make the Japanese public believe that they finally had a leader who would do what it took to restore their confidence in the economy.

THE ECONOMIC REVIVAL?

Japan has been suffering a decades-long hangover from the binge of the late 1980s. Alcoholics understand that the jittery nerves of a bad hangover—not to mention the dry, clammy mouth and the thudding headache—can all be made to go away with a nice, stiff drink, or two, or three. Of course the drinks do not solve the underlying problem; in fact, they make it worse. But for the moment, they sure feel good. This hangover "cure" does, however, depend on access to a liquor cabinet.

Fortunately, for Abe and the LDP, they had one in the form of the Bank of Japan. But the key to the liquor cabinet was held by BOJ governor Shirakawa Masaaki and while Shirakawa was hardly the central banking equivalent of a teetotaler—BOJ assets had expanded by over 50 percent during the four-and-a-half years he had held his job—Shirakawa had always been clear that while he was prepared to supply enough liquidity to get a nice cocktail party going, he was not going to empty the cabinet so his hosts could stage a drunken blowout.

But a blowout was what Abe and the LDP wanted. As soon as they seized control of the prime ministership and the Lower House, they began to pressure Shirakawa to resign so they could put their own man in charge of the liquor cabinet. Bowing to the inevitable, Shirakawa did step down and was replaced by Kuroda Haruhiko.

Kuroda was a savvy choice. He had held all the top posts on the international side of the MOF—he had been responsible, among other things, for exchange rate policy—and from there had gone on to the great plum position reserved only for the most illustrious of MOF bureaucrats: presidency of the Asian Development Bank.[13] He was thus well known not only to finance ministers and central bankers throughout Asia but also to the movers and shakers in Washington, London, Paris, Frankfurt, Basel, and New York charged with stamping out the financial fires that have been popping up with such alarming frequency over the past three decades. Being a seemingly sober, buttoned-up member of this club gave Kuroda a certain freedom of action that would not have been available to a wild-eyed populist unknown in Western policy-making circles. Conflagrations in global foreign exchange and bond markets—not to mention countervailing moves by his counterparts abroad—would have defeated much of what Kuroda wanted to accomplish; as it was, while he faced some grumbling about the sudden weakening of the yen in the wake of his appointment, that was about all he had to contend with from overseas. (Ben Bernanke, for example, had little but cautious praise for what Kuroda set about doing.)

For while Kuroda's demeanor and résumé may have been orthodox, there was nothing orthodox about his thinking. An intellectual disciple of Irving Fischer, who had argued in the 1930s that depressions and deflation call for radical measures by monetary authorities, Kuroda set about using monetary policy to shake Japan out of its deflation. The plan was to announce an inflation target and flood the country with money until the target had been achieved. The BOJ had always been reluctant to announce an inflation target, fearing that it would not be able to reach it and would then have its credibility destroyed. These fears were rational. In the United States the Federal Reserve has historically been able to use the bond market to push money into the economy—"open market operations"

---

13. Just as the top positions in the World Bank and the IMF are held, respectively, by an American and a European, the presidency of the ADB is reserved for a Japanese—and, in practice, the MOF decides who gets the nod.

as they are known whereby the Fed buys US government bonds from investors with newly created money. But this works much less well in Japan, where most bonds are held not by end-investors, but by deposit-taking institutions (e.g., banks). Open-market operations in Japan often just end up swelling the balance sheets of banks who simply use the new money to buy more government paper rather than lending the money to businesses.[14]

Kuroda short-circuited this problem by having the BOJ buy newly issued bonds directly from the government itself. This kind of monetary creation is technically illegal in most countries—including Japan—since it allows a government to finance deficits without any kind of accountability; this was the mechanism used in such places as Zimbabwe and Weimar Germany to create hyperinflation. But steps were taken to make the BOJ's actions legal and—at least for the time being—Japan was in no danger of hyperinflation.

Kuroda's actions brought on swoons from liberal Keynesians in the West such as Paul Krugman and Adam Posen. Here, finally, was a central banker willing to try bold policy equal to the challenges all developed countries face today. And unlike Bernanke, who had also been willing to experiment with unorthodox tactics, Kuroda's monetary policy was reinforced by his government's equally bold fiscal policy. Obama had been unable to push more than a single inadequate fiscal stimulus package through a hostile Congress, leaving Bernanke's Fed to shoulder virtually all the burden of restarting the engines of American economic growth. But Abe had campaigned on a slogan of "three arrows" to fix the economy: monetary policy, fiscal stimulus, and widespread deregulation-*cum*-structural reform. Abe could resort to the *baramaki* (throwing money around) of fiscal stimulus with impunity, since the financial fuel would be provided by Kuroda's money machine at the BOJ.

People with a firmer grasp of Japanese political and institutional realities than Kuroda's cheerleaders in the West were, however, more worried—and some of them were ardent Keynesians themselves. Richard Koo argued that Kuroda had "altered the market structure of the past two decades" bringing on the danger of the "beginning of the end for the

14. These problems have begun cropping up in the United States after 2008; Bernanke's quantitative easing has been less effective than textbooks say it should; in the absence of adequate fiscal stimulus, much of it has ended up as stagnant pools of liquidity rather than sparking economy activity, suggesting one more time that much of Japan's experience over the past two decades served as bellwether for what has begun to happen in other places.

Japanese economy." Keynesian stimulus works only if it can be financed. Until now, Japan has had no difficulty financing its gaping government deficits—no difficulty at all. As we saw in chapter 7, that is what permitted Japan to recover from one of the worst balance sheet recessions in history without plunging into depression. It had been possible because interest rates had been kept low, another way of saying the deficits had been made easy to finance. But by deliberately provoking inflation, Kuroda would, if he were successful, inevitably drive up interest rates. Meanwhile widening the gaps between the Japanese government's revenues and expenses into canyons threatened the possibility of a panic in the market for Japanese government bonds ("JGBs").

It is true that most JGBs are held by financial institutions, and as long as they can fund their holdings with deposits (and with Kuroda's money-spinning)—and as long as impenetrable accounting can allow them to maintain the illusion that the bonds are worth what their reported balance sheets say they are—a panic can be avoided and interest rates suppressed. But that, in turn, ignores the possibility that foreign hedge funds, trading derivatives linked to JGBs, will not force broader recognition of the actual worth of the instruments. For more than twenty years, foreigners trading derivatives linked to Japanese financial instruments have periodically destroyed the ability of the Japanese authorities to control the prices of those instruments.[15] It was too much to expect that hedge funds overseas, possessing not a shred of sentiment toward Japan and seeing monetary debauchery on such a scale, would not be working feverishly to devise methods of shorting the JGB market—and with it, potentially, the entire structure of Japanese interest rates.

The other great danger in what Kuroda and Abe were doing lay in what it did to confidence in the yen. Driving down the yen had been a major objective and one could not argue with Kuroda's success in this narrowly defined aim. The yen dropped fast and hard against the dollar—a dramatic contrast with the tepid response of the markets to efforts the Noda administration had made. Japan's old-style export behemoths were ecstatic, but as we saw in chapter 8, these were no longer the dynamos of the Japanese

---

15. One of the best examples occurred in the early 1990s when the Japanese authorities discovered that trading on the American Stock Exchange and the Singapore Futures Exchange of derivatives linked to the Nikkei index of Japanese equity prices was hampering their ability to engineer a halt to the plunging Tokyo stock market. Efforts made to pressure the two exchanges to halt the trading went nowhere.

economy and one could argue that a cheap currency was just a temporary fix that would allow them to do no more than postpone painful reforms. Meanwhile, that cheap currency made things worse for many of the most profitable firms in Japan: the upstream suppliers that enjoyed dominant market shares and pricing power since all it did was increase the costs of their imported materials. And it certainly made things worse for households when prices started rising and wages did not.

A strong yen had effectively saved Japan in the wake of 3/11, allowing utilities to import the fossil fuels the country suddenly had to have, not to mention pay for all the supplies needed for reconstruction, at something other than ruinous prices. The strong yen had for two decades helped Japanese households cope with a relatively stagnant economy; falling prices for daily essentials, for housing, for the occasional luxury or the quick getaway to Thailand or Guam had made the shrinking of economic horizons tolerable. Confidence in the yen was a key reason why most people left their savings in the banking system; in turn, those savings funded JGBs.

Now all this had been put at risk. Abe and the LDP countered that once the back of deflation had been broken, wage rates would start to rise, and to ensure that that happened, they promised to deploy the so-called third arrow of Abenomics. The arrows of monetary and fiscal stimulus were supposed to secure the macroeconomic conditions that would allow institutional reform—the third arrow—to bring on the long-awaited revival of the Japanese economy and a return to the glorious days of the postwar booms when everyone's income doubled once a decade.

On closer inspection, most of these third arrow reforms turned out to be versions of ideas that had been trotted out before. They were either much too modest to bring on any real revolution in Japanese economic arrangements, or—like measures to encourage structural overhaul of the farm sector—they sounded nice in theory but would be devilishly hard to implement in practice. For they undermined key elements of the postwar settlement that had emerged after the struggles of the 1950s: the employment protocols and the "compensation" in the forms of implicit subsidies to those groups in Japanese society—farmers, small-scale distributors, and retailers—that had effectively been agreed to as the price of securing cooperation in bringing on the economic miracle.

This points to what many concluded was the real purpose of the monetary/fiscal double whammy that Abe and Kuroda brought to Japan: a "sugar high" that would create enough enthusiasm so that the LDP could sweep the July 21, 2013, elections for the Upper House. Once that election had been won, the LDP would have the commanding majorities in the two houses needed to tear up the constitution and establish an authoritarian government that would have the legal and coercive powers necessary to roll over all opposition to whatever needed to be done to re-establish Japan as a first-tier nation—including, if need be, economic reforms.

It was a gamble—or "hail-Mary pass" as some American commentators put it—but the stakes were not ultimately economic. They were political. The people around Abe wanted, finally, to stamp out forever the ghost of Tanaka Kakuei. It appeared they had succeeded. They had taken Tanaka's methods and turned them against the very groups that Tanaka had sought to liberate from the tyranny of Tokyo's elites: the farmers, the up-country developers and small-time construction bosses with their hick accents and down-to-earth manners, the urban shopkeepers and small shock-absorbing firms that stood at the bottom of the Japanese economic hierarchy. Their champion Tanaka was gone and his followers had been driven into the political wilderness. Tanaka's greatest disciple, Ozawa Ichiro, had been destroyed as a political force; the party he had built into a once-potent political machine and had then betrayed him had been turned into a laughingstock.

The useful fools, to use Lenin's label for Western liberals, at places like the *Asahi Shimbun* and the *Matsushita Seikei Juku* who had for a generation waged trench warfare against Tanaka and Ozawa would wake up to discover, however, that the Japan they had helped bring about was not one of high-minded technocrats, free of the taint of money and deal-doing, devoting their lives to devising and implementing fair and efficient policies for their country. It was rather one where vampires from the darkest chapters of Japan's past would again rise and walk among the living. Washington had long deluded itself that it had driven stakes through their hearts in the 1940s; Japanese liberals knew better, but they had allowed their disdain for the methods and mannerisms of men like Tanaka, Kanemaru, and Ozawa to blind them to where the real threat to Japanese democracy was coming from.

For Abe and the people around him were not content simply to restore things to the way they had been before Tanaka had seized control of the machinery of Japan's electoral politics in the early 1970s, to return to the world that Abe's grandfather, Kishi Nobusuke, had, more than any other single person, brought into being and had overseen until Tanaka's insurrection.

Because for the Japanese Right, the arrangements of the 1950s—most particularly, the subordination to the foreign policy of the United States, but also the draining of the Left's appeal by the whole apparatus of lifetime employment, company unions, and salaryman culture—had been stop-gap, emergency measures made inevitable by the loss of the war and leftist upheaval in Japan. These measures were to be jettisoned the moment the day arrived when they were longer needed—and it seemed that day had finally arrived.

Abe was able to muster enough self-control to keep this agenda largely under wraps during the run-up to the Upper House election in July 2013. The mask slipped several times—he made Clintonesque equivocations about the meaning of "invasion" in discussing history, dispatched his finance minister, Aso Taro (the same man who had been prime minister in 2008/9 under the last LDP government) to worship at Yasukuni while sending offerings himself, and just generally gave off an impression of impatience with the political posturing required of him. But Abe was helped by the emergence of candidates on his right. The popular Osaka mayor Hashimoto Toru had led his Japan Restoration Party into a merger with a political grouping around Tokyo's xenophobic rabble–rouser, the former governor Ishihara Shintaro; Hashimoto's ill-conceived remarks on sexual issues[16] lit a firestorm in the global media allowing Abe to seem less far to the right than he actually is. Meanwhile, the first two of Abe's arrows had delivered a cheaper yen, a soaring stock market, and rising prices. They had not yet brought on rising wages and there was no assurance they ever would. But the sense that "something," finally, was being done about the economy plus a conviction that Abe would stand up to what much of the public saw as a bullying and hectoring China gave Abe and the LDP what they wanted: victory in the election.

16. Hashimoto had pointed out that while it was incumbent on Japan to apologize for the wartime forced recruitment of women—many of them Korean—into prostitution, Japan was hardly the only country in history to attempt to cope with testosterone-soaked soldiers by organizing prostitution rather than turning a blind eye to what soldiers were doing on their own, that that kind of thing had gone on in the Korean War as well as in the Second World War, and that if the United States had some sort of coherent policy to address the reality of what happens when packs of soldiers are let loose that incidents such as those that led to the Futenma imbroglio would be less common. He was portrayed in the global press, however, as trying to whitewash the past and to advocate for organized prostitution on Okinawa. If one reads his remarks carefully, that is not what he was saying—as most Japanese recognized. But he was nonetheless pilloried for blurting out politically tone-deaf comments. A comparison could be drawn with Todd Akin's comments about rape in the 2012 Missouri senatorial election.

The victory was not quite on the scale of what they had hoped for. The party did not capture the two-thirds majority in the Upper House that would have allowed it to start tearing up the postwar constitution on its own. In the immediate aftermath of the election, Abe and the people around him continued to display the caution they had in the run-up. Hard-right voices began to grumble, but there was no arguing with the broad base of support Abe and his government seemed to command, support given a boost in September by the designation of Tokyo as the site for the 2020 Olympics. With the promise of stimulus to Japan's well-being—both financial and otherwise—and the echo of the 1964 Tokyo Olympics, the award to Tokyo of the 2020 Games led to a surge of precisely the "animal spirits" that Abe and his advisers were counting on to revive the economy.

TPP, THE OFFICIAL SECRETS ACT, AND THE PRIORITIES OF THE ABE ADMINISTRATION

As the end of 2013 approached, however, Abe and his advisers revealed their hand. A government can hide its real aims for a while through dissembling and propaganda. But no government can accomplish everything it wants; at some point, priorities must be set and finite political capital allocated to those matters a government deems most important. Thanks to the two decisive electoral victories plus the palpable relief in bureaucratic and old-line "Japan, Inc." business circles at the destruction of the DPJ and the restoration of the old order—not to mention the offstage cheering from the New Japan Hands[17]—Abe had more political capital at his disposal than any Japanese prime minister since Koizumi in the wake of the latter's landslide electoral victory back in 2005.

How would Abe spend his? On the long-heralded reforms that could bring real changes in employment and compensation practices, corporate control, services, financial markets, agriculture, land use, distribution channels, education, women's empowerment and the whole laundry list that had been preached for a generation by those both in and out of Japan

---

17. A good example of this cheerleading can be found in a paper written in December 2013 by leading New Japan Hand Michael Green and posted on the web at http://m.lowyinstitute.org/files/green_japan_is_back_web_0.pdf.

who had argued that Japan needed root-and-branch microeconomic overhaul?

It was soon obvious that Abe had no intention of using much political capital on such matters, despite all the talk of the "third arrow." Washington—again, perhaps unwittingly—provided convenient cover for Abe's stalling in the form of the widely touted Trans Pacific Partnership, or TPP. At first glance, TPP seemed just one more in the string of "free trade" or "market opening" initiatives that have been blowing out of Washington off and on for some fifty years now. Seen from Japan, these phenomena are something like summer thunderstorms, arising unpredictably out of the clear blue sky. Everyone is going about their business in Japan the way they always have when the winds of American demands suddenly start to pick up. As rain pours down in the form of delegations from Washington brandishing the initiative *du jour*, thunderbolts of bluster from American businessmen, politicians, and trade officials rattle windows in central Tokyo. The Japanese policy establishment huddles like pagan priests of yore to consider what sacrifices might propitiate the angry deities. Women's blouses, auto parts, semiconductors, cigarettes, oranges, construction contracting, insurance, satellites, paper, the yen, licenses for lawyers, sheet glass, pork, beef, cherries, vehicle inspection, financial instruments of one sort or another, steel bars—the product or service varies from year to year, decade to decade, but the trajectory is generally the same. When the storm gets severe enough, some particular nexus of businesses, politicians, bureaucrats, and workers/farmers/contractors that feeds off the targeted arrangements or products have to be cajoled into giving up enough to persuade the Americans to go away. Some sort of agreement is signed that an American president can wave on national television. The rain tapers off, the winds settle, and the thunder diminishes into distant rumbles of doubt from across the Pacific over Japan's commitment to free trade in the abstract. Japan's trade negotiators and diplomats will have done their very best to minimize the sacrifice needed to bring the particular storm in question to an end, while politicians and bureaucrats will quietly have provided some compensation for whatever nexus had to bear the brunt of the burden. (Tanaka Kakuei's genius at managing this kind of thing formed a key reason for his ascent to the pinnacle of Japanese politics.)

Most Japanese, if they thought about it at all, figured that something similar would happen with TPP—that with the old LDP/bureaucrat/*zaikai* (business and financial elite) circles back running the show, arrangements would soon be forthcoming for some group somewhere to make enough concessions to mollify those mercurial Americans sufficiently so they would keep the 7th Fleet around to protect Japan from the mad dogs in Pyongyang and the hateful bullies in Beijing. Farmers, fearing their heads were targeted for the chopping block this time around, began organizing noisy demonstrations.

But on closer inspection, TPP turned out to be not quite your father's free trade initiative, or at least not Abe's father's free trade initiative. (Abe's father Abe Shintaro had served in most of the cabinet positions that feature coping with American free trade hectoring as part of the job description, positions that included Agriculture, Foreign Affairs, and International Trade and Industry. His skill at doing what was required and the resultant high regard he was held in Washington led many to assume he would almost certainly be prime minister, but, as noted in chapter 10, he died too young.) For one thing, TPP had not begun in the United States at all, instead it had started with some smaller Pacific Rim countries—Chile, Singapore, New Zealand, Brunei. But it had then been seized on by American corporate interests, mostly on Wall Street and in the pharmaceuticals, entertainment, agribusiness, and IT sectors, as a means of expanding their hold on copyrights and other intellectual property while placing dispute-settlement beyond the reach of the political process. To be sure, TPP had some old-style "market-opening" provisions for food products, but critics charged that it was far more about providing companies such as Monsanto with the legal and institutional means to dominate global agriculture or to allow American media companies to extend copyrights into perpetuity than it was about giving American business a crack at this or that walled-off market segment in Japan.

Japan's trade and agricultural officials had grown up in a world where they were charged with such things as figuring out how to accommodate American demands that Washington State farmers be allowed to sell their cherries in Japan without destroying growers in Yamagata Prefecture. (They succeeded; high-end American cherries are now available in season in Japan at three to four times what one pays for them in the United States; they are marketed as a separate product from Japanese cherries—to be sure, the varietals are different—and are mostly gone from supermarket shelves before the Japanese cherries appear; the latter are positioned as luxury fruits suitable for gifts.) Coping with a phalanx of Monsanto lawyers and lobbyists[18] intent on securing a lock hold on Japan's seed supply or challenging Japan's food safety laws in secret tribunals would be a very different challenge—one for which Japanese officialdom was much less well prepared.

The small numbers of Japanese officials, journalists, and politically active citizens who had actually grappled with the details of TPP were not the only ones disturbed by its implications. In November 2013, Wikileaks released secret transcripts of the TPP negotiations, charging "wide-ranging effects on medicines, publishers, internet services, civil liberties, and biological patents." Paul Krugman, in a *New York Times* column devoted to TPP, wrote "What's good for Big Pharma is by no means always good for America." Early in 2014, Senate Majority Leader Harry Reid announced his opposition to renewing the "fast track" authority needed for negotiating TPP.[19]

Such widely publicized misgivings about TPP and the cloudy prospects for Congressional approval were a gift to Abe. They allowed him to deflect questions about the "third arrow" of Abenomics with talk of TPP while hoarding his political capital on what he really cared about. And what Abe cared about was not economic reform. Abe's capital went into ramming through the Diet late in 2013 an act governing the treatment of confidential information. This Official Secrets Act, as it was called, gave the government the power to label anything it wanted "classified" and to prosecute anyone who even unwittingly attempted to find out what might actually be going on. Fifty-four years earlier, Abe's grandfather Kishi had made a similar attempt to restore the unlimited police powers the government had enjoyed before the Occupation; Kishi had had to abandon the plan, however, because of the intensity of the opposition.

Kishi's grandson finally succeeded where Kishi had failed. True, the passage of the Act provoked more open revolt than anything a Japanese government had had to contend with for a long time. Abe had to use high-handed tactics to secure passage of the bill; his poll numbers dropped below 50 percent for the first time since the Lower House election and there were actual demonstrations in central Tokyo. But the opposition

18. The chief American agricultural negotiator for TPP through end-2013, Islam Siddiqui, is a former Monsanto lobbyist and prominent champion of genetically modified foods who argued against Japan's labeling of such foods.

19. "Fast track" authorizes presidents to submit trade deals to Congress for a simple up-or-down vote.

was nothing like what Kishi had had to endure when upwards of a million people poured into the streets to protest his blatant attempts to restore the police state of the 1930s. Back in 1959, the demonstrators still had vivid memories of living in a country where anyone could be arrested on any pretext. By 2013, few had any real notion any more of what it would mean to see the reconsolidation and re-empowerment of a bureaucracy of social control, a bureaucracy equipped with the coercive tools to extend intimidation and self-censorship beyond the establishment press into every nook and cranny of Japanese life. Most of the demonstrators against the new act were people who if not old enough themselves to have experienced the Thought Police, mass arrests of left-wing sympathizers, militarist hysteria, and *tenkō* (public recanting of Marxian and Christian beliefs), had grown up in households where these had still been vivid memories. But younger people, glad that the economy might finally be moving and fearful of China, tended to brush off the warnings of older intellectuals and journalists of the implications of Abe spending his political capital not on economic reform but on the dismantling of the infrastructure of democracy and the rule of law.

Abe and the LDP thus ended up paying only a modest political price for the bill, and even much of this was self-inflicted when Ishiba Shigeru, the LDP Secretary General, compared the demonstrators against the bill to terrorists. It was a stupid thing to say, revealing for a moment the real intentions behind the bill, but even that was not enough to engender anything like the mass outrage that had stopped the attempts a half-century earlier to restore the institutional framework of a lawless, authoritarian state.

Abe had used purported concerns from Washington about Japan's security leaks as an excuse for the bill, as if in the wake of the revelations by former NSA contractor Edward Snowden the United States had any credibility left when it came to controls on sensitive information—or, for that matter, on imposing any form of accountability on a national security bureaucracy. Washington no longer bothered even giving lip service to concerns over the fate of Japanese democracy under Abe, instead making it clear in every way that mattered that all the American establishment cared about from Tokyo was "interoperability" (i.e., folding the Japanese defense establishment into the Pentagon infrastructure) and damping down inter-service rivalries inside the Pentagon, which meant giving the Marines the payoff they insisted upon for leaving Futenma. Abe delivered what Washington demanded: the Official Secrets Act, plus a wheelbarrow so loaded with cash that Okinawa's governor, Nakaima Hirokaza, finally cracked and indicated on December 26 he would not stand in the way of breaking ground for the new Marine base on Okinawa.

On the very same day Abe gave the Pentagon what he understood it wanted, he did what *he* wanted: worshipped at Yasukuni. Beijing and Seoul howled with outrage while Washington expressed "disappointment." Since the American policy establishment was directly responsible for the events that had led to Abe's return as prime minister, there was not much more for the moment that could be done or said. But the events revealed that both sides might have miscalculated. The Pentagon and the New Japan Hands, having briskly disposed of a Hatoyama government that had dared to hint at an independent course for Japan, had assumed that Abe, like his grandfather, would do what he was told when it came to issues of security and foreign relations. That, after all, was the long-standing quid-pro-quo that men like Kishi and Yoshida Shigeru had negotiated as the bedrock of Japan's subordination to the United States: Japanese elites get a free hand to do what they want domestically with covert support from the American national security establishment as long as they fall in line with American foreign policy and pay for American bases in Japan. Abe, for his part, having delivered what the Americans had been demanding, seemed to think he could throw whatever birdies he wished at Beijing, secure in the knowledge that he had the unquestioned backing of the world's most formidable military. But he found that Washington was not about to write Tokyo the kind of blank check that Berlin had sent to Vienna in the wake of Archduke Ferdinand's assassination. Washington had, to be sure, already made it clear it would not allow Tokyo to cut its own deals with Beijing, as Ozawa had wanted to do. But nor would it cede to Japan the right to choose the terms and timing of any eyeball-to-eyeball confrontation with China.

COPING WITH CHINA

Realist political theory suggests that the political and geographical setup in East Asia has led in the modern world to the very worst possible configuration of national power when considered from the standpoint of peace and stability. Japan and China may not be doomed to be perpetual enemies as the more gloomy realists would have it. But avoiding that fate starts, among other things, with awareness.

Realists maintain that rough military and economic parity among major nations—the "balance of power"—is conducive to a relatively stable order. A different kind of stability occurs when one country enjoys such overwhelming economic, military, and technological superiority over potential rivals that it is effectively absolute; other countries may whine about it, but they do not mount serious challenges.

The realist recipe for instability and war lies between these two poles: when one country is more powerful than its potential rivals, but not overwhelmingly so. That country will tend to see other powers as threats and act accordingly; other countries will do what they can to prevent their loss of effective independence to the greater power by forming alliances with other second-tier powers and/or by bringing in outsiders who will help "balance" the power of the nearby would-be hegemon. These very moves, however, are seen as threatening by the larger power and can increase the chances of war as well as creating potential for situations where confrontations and miscalculations spiral into broader trouble. Historical examples go back as far as ancient Athens (Thucydides concluded that Athens's fear of a rising Sparta was the ultimate cause of the Peloponnesian war that ended Athenian hegemony); the most pertinent recent case is that of the emergence of a united Germany in the mid-nineteenth century destroying the European balance of power that had kept the peace for the preceding fifty years. As Germany became more powerful than its neighbors, these countries entered alliances with each other, provoking a threatened Berlin to launch three increasingly destructive wars. The wars brought on the end of European hegemony over global affairs and the division of effective political control of Europe not between France and Germany but between the two new outside superpowers: the United States and the Soviet Union.

East Asia holds all the makings of a similar tragedy. China is the greatest power in the region; it always has been and always will be. Yes, there were periods in the past when its internal weaknesses allowed outsiders—the Mongols, the Manchus—to capture the machinery of the Chinese state, although they ruled through Chinese institutions. The latest of these periods of weakness—and the longest—began with the Opium Wars. But just as the other periods ended, so has this latest one. There is simply no plausible way in which China's re-emergence as the preeminent power in Asia can be derailed.

For most of history, China was so overwhelmingly powerful by every conceivable measure of national greatness that most of its neighbors inevitably fell into its political and cultural orbit. The barriers formed by the East China Sea and the Sea of Japan, however, allowed Japan to develop along independent political lines, and even though it based many of its institutions on Chinese models, its cultural trajectory was also distinct. As we saw in chapter 1, Japanese piracy was a constant source of fear and concern along the China coast for upward of a millennium, and invaders from the mainland did, in the thirteenth century, threaten Japan. But these invasions excepted (and significantly, the invaders were Mongols who had conquered China, not Chinese themselves), Japan and China were never existential threats to each other—or even viewed as such. (Hideyoshi's sixteenth-century invasion of Korea is another possible exception—he had designs on China, which is why the Chinese aided the Koreans—but that was one case in some 1,500 years of history.)

That all changed with the coming of the Westerners and the advent of modern, distance-shrinking transport and communication technologies. The weakness of the Qing dynasty appalled and frightened the leaders of Meiji Japan; Japan's foreign policy from the 1860s on would essentially be dominated by one consideration: preventing the re-emergence of a single great power on the Asian mainland. At first, Japan was more fearful that that power might be Russia. But following Sun Yat-sen's 1911 revolution, Japan's military and foreign policy on the continent was increasingly directed at forestalling the re-emergence of an independent, unified Chinese state. As we saw in chapter 3, the Japanese attempted to buttress first this warlord and then that in their attempts to keep China divided, but were finally drawn into a vicious and protracted war against Nationalist China itself. The Japanese army actually succeeded in its aim of defeating Nationalist China; the Ichigo military offensive of 1944 did ultimately destroy any realistic hope that Chiang Kai-shek had of emerging as the head of a unified Chinese state. But moving into the resultant power vacuum was not Japan, it was Mao Zedong's Communists. The strategic blindness of Japan's wartime leaders brought on the very result they feared the most: the emergence of a powerful, unified Leninist state on the continent.

It is ever thus with those who confuse tactical superiority on the battlefield with achieving the aims of war. In 1939, the Japanese military subjected Chongqing to wave after wave of terrorist, saturation bombing. The bombs blew up lots of buildings, to be sure, and killed thousands of people, but they accomplished nothing strategically other than make the Chinese hate the Japanese and create a long-term nightmare that to this day entangles Japan's policy makers.

It is for reasons like this that it is said war is far too important to be left to generals. But it should be no consolation that Japan has plenty of company in committing monumental blunders, in allowing nationalist hotheads with the strategic sense of 10-year-old boys to hijack a country's foreign relations and its security establishment. Japan's defeat in war and its occupation by the United States left it no choice in the way it would cope with the rise of a powerful, threatening neighbor: "balancing" that power with the outsider. Sometime over the last generation, however, things slowly segued from a situation about which Japan had no say to one in which it acquiesces voluntarily.

Some on the Japanese right fantasize that the day will come when Japan can throw off the American alliance and be a sufficiently menacing power that China will have to deal with Japan on Tokyo's terms—or at least that Japan can construct a series of encircling alliances with countries such as Vietnam and the Philippines. This might have been conceivable a century ago; today it is little more than a recipe for a repeat of Europe's suicide in 1914.

Japan has only two realistic choices. One is to work out an accommodation with Beijing. The other is to embed itself ever more tightly into the American embrace.

It is understandable why Japan feels more comfortable with the latter. But in the long run, it may be the more dangerous option.

THE UNSUSTAINABLE CONFIGURATION OF THE US–JAPAN "ALLIANCE"

It is painful to have to write this, but the United States does not fundamentally care about Japan. That does not mean to say that many Americans do not have some sort of personal tie with the country and thus regard it with affection. Devotees of Japanese cuisine, of the novels of Murakami, of the films of Kurosawa and Ozu number in the hundreds of thousands while millions of Americans grew up on *anime*, on Hello Kitty, on Pokémon, and thus have a generalized, vague sense of goodwill toward Japan. But

American elites rarely see Japan as anything other than a military asset, as a tool to realize a dream that is even more dangerous and foolhardy than the LDP's dream of escaping having to deal with China as it is. That dream is that the United States can somehow achieve globally a situation comparable to that which it historically enjoyed in North America: a world where it faces no potential threat, no potential challenge—"full spectrum dominance" to use the language of America's deluded military planners.

How the United States ended up in the grip of this tragic and foolhardy illusion is beyond the scope of this book. But there are a few points that need to be emphasized. First, much of what has happened in the United States in recent decades will seem familiar to any student of modern Japanese history and Japanese political arrangements. The national security bureaucracy put in place to win the Second World War and then to wage the Cold War has slipped out of political control for reasons that resemble those that permitted the Imperial Army to hijack Japan in the 1930s. It is no surprise that some of the most acute analysis of American military overreach—the forces behind it and its consequences—came from the late Chalmers Johnson, who had devoted much of his life to the study of the Japanese bureaucracy. Once a powerful bureaucracy or network of bureaucracies achieves a certain critical mass, its sway over political life can become so great it can be impossible to bring it under political control, particularly when it has the means of physical coercion at its disposal. President Eisenhower warned that this would happen—of the emergence of a military-industrial complex, as he put it, that would destroy American democracy unless brought to heel. His warnings were ignored.

There is only one clear example in modern history of a statesman able to force a change of course on an entrenched and powerful bureaucracy that has the means of physical coercion at its disposal and enjoys wide popular support as the defender of the nation. That example is Charles de Gaulle. It is a tantalizing dream to imagine what the world would be like today if de Gaulle had been a Japanese leader extricating his country from China in the 1930s rather than a French leader extricating his country from Algeria in the 1960s.

Alas, there is no de Gaulle on the American political horizon. A well-run, clear thinking Pentagon—not to mention a president of de Gaulle's stature—would never have allowed the Futenma issue to develop the way it did. The Marines may not equal the Kwantung Army in sheer destructiveness, but when it comes to hijacking their respective countries' long-term strategic interests for narrow organizational imperatives, they are all too similar.

The American Empire is doomed to failure because it is structurally and institutionally ignorant of the wider world. Only a demolition of the national security state can remedy this ignorance. This is not a comment on ordinary Americans' lack of interest in foreign countries, the low numbers studying foreign languages and geography, or the near total dearth of anything but puff pieces on the wider world to be found in the American mass media. There are enough Americans who have spent time abroad, speak foreign languages, and are knowledgeable about conditions in one or another part of the world to staff with competent people the agencies of the American government charged with security policy and the conduct of foreign relations. The problem, as we saw with the New Japan Hands, is that the criteria by which such people are sourced, hired, trained, and promoted serves to winnow out anyone who is disposed to challenge conventional wisdom, even when that wisdom is manifestly absurd—a phenomenon that any student of Japan's bureaucracy-dominated policy-making would find instantly familiar.[20] It leads to the most blinkered kinds of groupthink on any particular issue. The politically aware would have understood that Ozawa's outreach to Beijing, far from being a threat to the United States, was in America's long-term interest. But all that Richard Armitage and the people around him could grasp was what it did to their proprietary hold on the US–Japan "alliance."

That the American Empire continues to stagger on despite the manifest incompetence of its leaders and managers is due in large part to the operations of the dollar-centered monetary and financial order that Japan, as we have seen, played such a central role in bringing about. To note simply that this order helped foster the Japanese economic miracle and its imitators in Korea, China, and elsewhere is to underestimate the degree to which the East Asian growth model is a part of this order, as inseparable from it as the words of a book are from the book itself. Its

---

20. The bureaucratic dynamics that kept the obvious from influencing decision-making have been fully revealed by the debacle of the Iraq invasion. On the eve of the invasion, *The Atlantic* ran a cover story that predicted what would happen to a level of detail that, in retrospect, astonishes with its prescience ("The Fifty-First State?" Nov. 1, 2002). The author, James Fallows, had not needed any special access to classified documents to write the article.

very structure requires the United States to run large trade- and current account-deficits, and it requires Japan, China, and South Korea to maintain large holdings of American dollars—there is no alternative as long as these countries maintain (or are trapped by) export- and investment-led growth strategies.

But those holdings allow the United States to escape the normal financial burdens of empire: the need to support an economically unproductive military establishment out of taxes. This does not mean that there are no costs to the United States of supporting that establishment, but rather that those costs do not lie primarily with the interest payments on the borrowing needed to finance it.

The costs in supporting the military-industrial complex rather are in the disproportionate burdens that fall on the American working and middle classes. The machinery of the dollar-based global monetary order and the financing of the American empire have resulted in secular upward pressure on the dollar and the concomitant and systematic transfer of manufacturing capacity—and now services capacity—out of the United States to its Asian partners. To be sure, it is not Japan that has emerged as the world's headquarters economy, it is the United States. The shape of financing and the architecture of technology in today's world are determined on Wall Street, in Silicon Valley, in America's great research universities, in the laboratories of the national security state. But the actual job of manufacturing and assembling the products themselves is largely done abroad.

The resulting inequality is the direct cause of the political and class hatreds that now threaten the smooth functioning of the machinery of empire. The American public shows itself less and less willing to support the wars that this or that faction of the American imperial elite deems necessary, whether those wars be in Syria, Iraq, Iran, Afghanistan—or the East China Sea. Beijing understands this. China's military capacity does not begin to match that of the United States, not to mention that of some "interoperable" US–Japan joint command. But then neither did North Vietnam's. China wants the United States out of Asia far more badly than the United States wants to stay in the region; Beijing has embarked on a long and high-stakes game to see it happen. The stakes may be equally high for Tokyo, but they are not for most Americans, and when that becomes clear, the US–Japan "alliance" will crumble, leaving Japan alone and friendless.

REJOINING ASIA

It is not an enviable situation in which Japan finds itself. The Beijing government is, like Tokyo's, spooked by its own historical demons and is manifestly hysterical about the slightest challenge to its legitimacy. Fearful, threatened governments are dangerous—particularly when they control large and powerful countries. China's critics are right that Beijing has cynically whipped up hatred for Japan and uses it as a crutch. Beijing responded in the very worst way to the American gelding of the Hatoyama government and by Noda's ham-fisted reaction to the rightist rabble-rousing of Ishihara; it was almost as if Beijing were going out of its way to push Japan into the arms of the United States and to serve as Abe's and the LDP's campaign advisers. But the menace China poses makes it more, not less, urgent that Japan deploy astute diplomacy—that it become capable of assuming a stance somewhere between bluster, on the one hand, and a sullen, thumb-sucking sense of victimhood on the other.

Japan's original sin lies in its attempts to separate itself from Asia. The sin is understandable but the repercussions have been horrendous. When Japan was shaken awake from its self-imposed *sakoku* ("isolation") in the mid-nineteenth century, it discovered a world that had been turned upside down. The China that had always loomed as the origin of power, culture, and technology in the Japanese conceptual universe had been reduced to a stuck pig being butchered by barbarians from distant lands who turned out not to be barbarians at all but the avatars of modernity. As we saw in chapter 3, Japan frantically tried to distance itself from its erstwhile cultural and national kin in order to establish its credentials for membership in this so-called "advanced" club of nations. In the process, Tokyo imported some of the most noxious ideologies emanating from those nations—ideologies that purported to find the roots of culture, nation, and identity in blood and soil. Again, Japan's motives are understandable; the Meiji elite sought to demonstrate—to itself as well as to the West—that it was wholly distinct from weak, pathetic countries like China and Korea. The ideologies harnessed in the service of this goal may have been largely discredited in the West,[21] but they linger on in Japan where their origins have been forgotten.

---

21. To be sure, while fascist thought may have disappeared from polite circles in much of the West, there are elements woven into the political fabric of Russia, the United States, and much of Europe, spores ready to spring forth, like mushrooms after rain, in the right political conditions. Avatars of the politics of austerity seem determined to produce just those conditions.

Among the results is the almost ubiquitous sense of Japan as a country apart. In everyday speech, *Ajia* ("Asia") means Asia-ex Japan; the Western visitor to Japan can be startled when a Japanese acquaintance announces he or she has never been to *Ajia*. Even liberal, well-meaning Japanese will jump to point out how different they are from Chinese and Koreans if any Westerner draws parallels. But perhaps no question is more critical to Japan's future than whether it can find its way to rejoining Asia, not just in the sense of economic ties, which are already extensive, but in seeing itself and its fate as intertwined with that of the broader region.

For it seems safe to predict the coming close of the 500-year ascendancy of the West and the return of the fulcrum of human history to East Asia. Japan has potentially a central role to play in this, but only as an Asian country accepted by its neighbors as such.

That requires dealing with its history. We have discussed why it is so difficult for Japan to face up to its past: the spiritual crisis of modernity that left many Japanese without anything sacred to hang onto other than "Japan" itself; the flaw in Japan's post-Meiji governing setup that allowed the Imperial Army to hijack the Japanese state—a flaw that has not been corrected; the reality that many power holders in Japan today—most obviously, Abe and the people around him—are the direct descendants (genetically and otherwise) of the men who led Japan into disaster.

Japan's apologists are quick to point out that other countries have committed great wrongs with which they have not reckoned; that no matter what Japan does or says, its neighbors will never be satisfied, that they will continue to use the past as a stick with which to beat Japan. This is all true, but it is beside the point. It is not for the sake of the Koreans or the Chinese that a real reckoning with what happened in the 1930s needs to occur; it is for the sake of Japan. Many Japanese will say that a country whose currency features portraits of history's greatest mass murderer and whose governing party has the blood of tens millions of people on its hands lacks the moral standing to demand anything of Japan. But reckoning with the Great Leap Forward, the Great Proletarian Cultural Revolution, and the Tiananmen massacres can ultimately only take place among the Chinese themselves. Similarly, it is the Japanese who will have to confront what put their country in the hands of those who destroyed its independence and made it a byword abroad for brutal, inhuman fanaticism. Trying to bury accounts of what actually happened with fables of a pure and virtuous land, as Abe seeks to do, is simply a way of making it more likely that something similar will happen again soon.

Abe and people like his education minister, Shimomura Hakubun, seem particularly exercised about the effect on children of any actual grappling with the past. They may be right that a collapse of patriotism lies at the root of Japan's problems and that working out any durable arrangements that permit Japan to live with the rest of the world requires first that Japanese recover love of country. But a patriotism that cannot withstand any actual confrontation with the human capacity for error and evil, a patriotism that must be shielded like a hothouse flower from genuine debate, works indeed only for children. Men like Abe and Shimomura probably do regard most Japanese as children and they give every impression of seeking to rule a country of infantilized people. But such a polity will not be well-equipped to cope with its biggest challenge: a rising, pugnacious superpower that has adopted hatred for Japan as its national mantra and devotes enormous energies itself to myth-spinning with the obvious aim of fostering its own malleable, uninformed citizenry.

Meanwhile, many Japanese assume that the South Koreans have no choice but to cooperate with Japan; the North Korean threat and China's support of North Korea preclude other options. But this is to take a static and blinkered view of history. The current power alignments in the region are not fixed forever or even for much longer. Both Beijing and Pyongyang understand that the North Korean regime can only survive as long as China tolerates it. The Chinese have tolerated it to date, but there are signs Beijing is aiming for the greater prize of a *modus vivendi* with Seoul that would lead to reunification of the Korean peninsula under terms that both China and the Koreans would find acceptable. China will not permit a close American ally garrisoned with American troops right on its border, but a unified Korea that has been "Finlandized"—to adopt the term used for the way the Soviet Union allowed Finland to manage its own affairs provided it stayed out of NATO—would be preferable for most Koreans, North and South, to current arrangements. Something would, of course, have to be done about the grip of North Korea's ruling Kim family and the elite circles around it, but to imagine this is beyond Beijing's power is to indulge in wishful thinking.

A far-seeing Japanese government would seek to forestall such an eventuality by building as close a relationship with Seoul as it could manage. When the time inevitably arrives for the American military departure from East Asia and the final reassertion of Asian control over Asian affairs, Japan will be in a far stronger position if it is closely allied with South Korea than if it is seen as the one remaining outpost of a declining American empire.

Standing in the way of good relations with Seoul are two issues. One we have already looked at: Japan's continuing claim on the Liancourt Rocks (aka Takeshima/Dokdo). It casts a dark shadow over Tokyo's relationship with Seoul. The other is outrage in Japan that the Korean pot has the effrontery to call the Japanese kettle black on issues of history in general and, specifically, on the recruiting—much of it forced—of Korean "comfort women" during the war years to serve the sexual needs of Japan's soldiers.

One enters a minefield when writing about such things, but for many Japanese men—particularly the kinds of men who support the LDP and write for nationalist publications—the Koreans are violating a tacit understanding among privileged East Asian males that certain things are not discussed publicly. They are angry about this violation, albeit tongue-tied in the way they express their anger. For the fact of the matter is that the conservative elements of the South Korean elite gelled under Japanese colonialism, were often active collaborators with their occupiers, and everyone knows it, even if few will discuss it. (Among other things, the current president of South Korea, Park Geun-hye, is the daughter of Park Chung-hee who, more than any other single person, can be credited with Korea's own economic miracle. His socialization and thinking about issues of power and development were almost entirely Japanese; he was educated in colonial Manchuria, studied at Japan's top military academy, served in the Japanese army, adopted a Japanese name, and, when he seized power in 1960, proceeded to force-march his country into the ranks of the world's industrialized nations with a rule book that could have been written by Japan's *kakushin kanryō* ["Reform Bureaucrats"]—the men we met back in Part One who put the Japanese economy on a war footing in the 1930s, administered Manchuria and would, in the postwar world, form the nucleus of MITI.) Japan may have postponed any real reckoning with the events of the 1930s, but much the same could be said of many of the most powerful people in South Korea. Yes, the Japanese military organized and administered a system of sexual slavery that threatened every young woman in Korea, but the brokers were often Koreans who had built an infrastructure of sexual "services" that both predated Japanese colonization and would outlive it. In the 1950s and 1960s, when South Korea was still a desperately poor country, the place was practically a standing joke among many Japanese men as a byword for sex tours; every Japanese man of a certain age knows what a *kisaeng* house is. For the Korean government now to insist on official apologies from Tokyo for exploiting Korean women seems to many Japanese another case of a Captain Renault in the film *Casablanca* demanding that gambling cease while pocketing his winnings.

But they can't say so. In today's sexually correct world, "You too!" hardly qualifies as an excuse. So instead, they retreat into an inarticulate pout—into a sense, hard as it may be for outsiders to understand, of being bullied on all sides, fleeing like a picked-on child to Mother's skirts behind whose voluminous folds they pull faces at Seoul and Beijing with their visits to Yasukuni shrine and rewriting of high school history textbooks. But the American national security establishment is not Mother. It has no affection for Japan—maternal or otherwise—and sees Japan as simply one more military vassal, expected to do as it is told and not make trouble.

ABE'S OVERREACH AND THE FUTURE

As the winter of 2014 turned into spring, signs of overreach by Abe and his Hard Right cronies were everywhere. By visiting Yasukuni, Abe had thumbed his nose not only at Beijing and Seoul, but at Secretary of State John Kerry, Secretary of Defense Chuck Hagel, and Vice President Joe Biden. On their October 2013 visit to Tokyo, the two American cabinet secretaries had made a point of laying wreathes not at Yasukuni but at Chidorigafuchi, the cemetery near Yasukuni for the unidentifiable war dead. Then, in December, Biden had spent an hour on the phone trying to persuade Abe to call off his Yasukuni plans. But none of it registered. Abe needed to demonstrate both to himself and to his political base that Japan was something more than an American patsy; visiting Yasukuni in the face of American demands was the most effective way of doing that. Tension between official Washington and Tokyo spiked up to levels not seen since the trade conflicts of the 1980s. For its part, China went ahead with an exhibition in honor of Ahn Jung-geun, a young Korean nationalist who had had assassinated Ito Hirobumi in 1909 at the Manchurian city of Harbin. Arguably the greatest of the Meiji leaders, Ito's portrait had once graced the ¥1,000 note. The Koreans had long asked for such a tribute, seeing Ahn as a hero in the struggle against the Japanese occupation of their country, but many in Japan reacted as Americans might if Venezuela were to respond to Cuban requests and erect a memorial statue of Lee Harvey Oswald in retaliation for the Bay of Pigs. It was for precisely that reason—a wish not to inflame Japanese opinion—that Beijing had long demurred in proceeding with the exhibit, but in the wake of Abe's Yasukuni visit, the Chinese changed their minds, underscoring both the Seoul/Beijing rapprochement and Japan's growing isolation. Commentators in both China and Korea were quick to note that Harbin had not only been one of the centers of Japan's colonial rule of Manchuria, but had been the site of the infamous medical experiments conducted on hundreds of living Chinese and Russians by the notorious Unit 731.

Meanwhile, across the Pacific, the Virginia state legislature passed a bill decreeing that textbooks in Virginia schools should teach that the Sea of Japan is also called the East Sea, its preferred name in Korea, while the US House of Representatives called for Tokyo to acknowledge responsibility for the past, educate Japanese children about what had actually happened in the 1930s, and take steps to implement a 2007 resolution urging on Japan an appropriate apology-cum-restitution for the comfort women.[22] Korean-American communities all over the United States began pushing for memorials to the comfort women.

Back in Tokyo, in a transparent ploy to influence the first real referendum on Abenomics, the February 2014 Tokyo gubernatorial elections, Abe stacked the NHK board of governors with rightist dinosaurs. A favorable electoral outcome for Abe required short-circuiting unfavorable coverage of the Official Secrets Act, of ongoing problems at the Fukushima Dai-Ichi nuclear plant, and of the continuing attempts by the "nuclear village"—the nexus of bureaucrats, power company officials, and politicians who feed off nuclear power—to restart the nuclear plants. Control of NHK is one of the most effective means to influence what gets covered as news and what does not. NHK is said to be Japan's BBC, theoretically above politics, with a role in determining what constitutes news in Japan vaguely comparable to that once played by CBS in the United States in the era of Walter Cronkite. NHK's news programming can come across as bland, but the

22. The sponsor of the 2007 resolution had, interestingly enough, been Congressman Mike Honda, a Japanese-American representing a district in the heart of Silicon Valley. There is little push-back from Japanese-Americans at pressure from Korean-Americans for memorials to the comfort women.

network did attempt to maintain at least the appearance of objectivity and nonpartisanship. No more. One of Abe's new appointees was on record denying that the Nanjing massacre had ever occurred, another had praised a Far Right terrorist who had committed ritual suicide at the offices of the *Asahi Shimbun* in the name of the emperor, while the new chairman, Momii Katsuo, effectively acknowledged that NHK's raison d'être would from henceforth be to act as a propaganda arm of the government. In reaction, a popular announcer resigned from the network; NHK's new leadership had pilloried him for a documentary he had produced on accidents in American nuclear plants. Another commentator said he would no longer appear on NHK's radio shows since he had been pressured to say nothing critical of nuclear power. For his part, Momii managed to provoke additional outrage in Seoul and Washington first by denying there had been any organized forced recruiting of the comfort women and then by asserting that all countries, including the United States, had run such operations during the war.

Control of NHK had become critical because Abe's overreach had stirred two of the great old war horses of Japanese politics to emerge from retirement in desperate attempts to halt the prime minister's agenda and that of the Hard Right circles around him. Their opening lay in the resignation of Tokyo's governor, Inose Naoki. Inose had made himself something of a hero by winning for Tokyo the 2020 Olympics, but found himself tripped up by a run-of-the-mill Japanese political scandal—he had accepted a large chunk of money from a hospital operator.[23] The leading candidate to replace him, Masuzoe Yoichi, also carried a good deal of baggage. Masuzoe had once written that menstrual cycles made women unsuitable for high office, his personal life—three marriages, three children born out of wedlock, and ugly disputes over child support—was something of a mess, and he had been Health and Welfare Minister during Abe's first term, presiding over the pension debacle that had helped drive Abe from office. Seeing opportunity in Masuzoe's flaws, Hosokawa Morihiro declared his candidacy for the governorship and announced his intention to turn the campaign into a referendum on Abe's rule. The handsome, aristocratic Hosokawa is the man who had captivated the country back in 1993 when he had served as the first non-LDP prime minister since 1955 but, as we saw in the previous

---

23. Scuttlebutt in Japan had it that his real mistake was to claim too much credit in landing the Olympics for Tokyo.

chapter, had soon been forced to resign, a victim of the usual Japanese recipe for dealing with ambitious politicians who threaten established ways: a trumped-up hullabaloo over financial irregularities. Hosokawa had stayed out of the limelight since then, devoting himself to pottery, but few had forgotten him or the brief winds of hope he had stirred.

Even more remarkably, Koizumi Junichiro announced his support for Hosokawa's candidacy. Koizumi had not only been one of Abe's key mentors, he had essentially arranged for Abe to succeed him when he stepped down as prime minister in 2006 after one of the most politically successful administrations in modern Japanese history. But like Daedalus watching his son Icarus fly too high with the wings he had made for the boy, Koizumi was becoming increasingly troubled at the use to which Abe was putting the conservative/mandarin renaissance he had bequeathed him. In particular, Koizumi had become convinced that Japan had to end any reliance on nuclear power—among other things, because no arrangements had been worked out to dispose of nuclear waste. Koizumi liked to say that turning the nuclear plants back on was akin to moving into an apartment without a toilet.

The alliance of these two former political enemies created a sensation in the press. They often campaigned jointly and attracted huge crowds wherever they went. It was as if Ronald Reagan had announced his disgust with the policies of George W. Bush and begun stumping for Howard Dean. But ultimately the campaign fizzled out. The worst snowstorm in decades kept turnout low, and many voters resented what they saw as the hijacking of a local election by an attempt to turn it into a referendum on a national issue. Masuzoe, for all his faults, was an experienced politician; he had been a successful television news commentator, and he knew how to mount a careful, well-run campaign that conveyed sobriety and competence. But the biggest problem, again, was the failure of the opposition to come together. Hosokawa split the anti-Abe, anti-nuclear vote with the Communist Party candidate Utsunomiya Kenji, who actually outpolled him. Masuzoe benefited from a candidate to his right, the former general Tamogami Toshio, who had been fired for giving voice to his nutty views on history (among other things, Tamogami had asserted that Franklin Roosevelt had been set up by the Comintern to trick Japan into war).[24]

24. Tamogami may have been recirculating evidence that has recently come to light of the role of Harry Dexter White in stiffening Washington demands on Tokyo in the run-up to Pearl Harbor, demands that found their way into the ultimatum presented to Tokyo known as the Hull note on November 26, 1941. White, who was an aide to the Treasury Secretary, was not

Tamogami performed the same service for Masuzoe that Ishihara Shintaro and Hashimoto Toru had for Abe: making him seem like a moderate. Abe actually hinted at sympathy for Tamogami, while Masuzoe was on record as having criticized Abe. Voters could thus tell themselves that by casting ballots for Masuzoe they were not tying themselves to Abe.

Writ large, the election confirmed that organization and political discipline will defeat a rabble every time, even if the hearts of the rabble are in the right place. Every leader who has actually succeeded in imposing a change of course on his or her nation understands this, whether that leader hails from the Left or the Right, is a force for good or evil, or employs guns and bombs or the loudspeaker and the ballot box as the means to seize and hold power. The one trait that Hitler and Franklin Roosevelt, Lenin and de Gaulle, Mao and Mandela, Lyndon Johnson and Margaret Thatcher all shared was a visceral understanding that goals—whether high-minded or otherwise—are not enough. In the absence of well thought through strategy and hard-nosed tactics, goals are just hot air.

This had also been grasped by men like Kishi and Tanaka. But for a half-century, it had been ignored by a Japanese opposition—Left and otherwise—that has acted as if high-mindedness was enough, an opposition that recoiled like a sheltered, snooty Victorian maiden when confronted with what it takes to succeed at electoral politics and then actually to govern. Ozawa Ichiro, the one opposition politician who did understand these things and could plausibly have imposed a new direction on his country, had been fatally weakened by the people who should have been his supporters, even before the public prosecutor, the establishment press, and the New Japan Hands had tacitly joined forces to destroy what he had built. And no one has emerged in his wake who displays a comparable vision together with such a sure command of the dirty, nitty-gritty of politics and governing.

But this does not change the reality that tens of millions of Japanese are distraught at what is happening to their country. In the weeks before the Tokyo election, Yamazaki Takashi, the director of the runaway hit film trilogy *Always: San-chome no Yūhi* ("Always: Sunrise on Third Street") that we looked at in chapter 9, came out with a new blockbuster that told the tale of a typical contemporary young man—comfortable lifestyle;

exactly a Soviet spy but he was sympathetic to the USSR and may have responded to covert Soviet efforts to provoke a confrontation between the United States and Japan.

repeatedly fails the bar exam—who begins digging into the story of his kamikaze pilot of a grandfather. While the *Always* series used the gumption and humanity displayed two generations ago by people of the type we are to understand built the economic miracle to implicitly rebuke present mores, in the new film, *Eien no zēro* ("Eternal Zero"), it is the pilot's decision to sacrifice his life for something bigger than himself that serves to shame the shallowness and selfishness of the present. Yamazaki based *Eien no zēro* on a novel by one of the rightist figures Abe had appointed to NHK. Yamazaki wisely did not try to portray his pilot hero as some sort of typical cardboard cutout figure of wartime propaganda all eager to die for the emperor. The pilot instead comes off at first more like his grandson: cynical, individualistic, and determined to survive. But he is gradually brought to see that there are things worth dying for—most particularly, one's country and one's kind.

A runaway hit in Japan—Abe publicly said he was "deeply moved"—the film was predictably criticized in China and Korea (by people who had not seen it) as one more piece of evidence that Japan was turning back toward fascism. That isn't really the case. Miyazaki Hayao, the great Japanese *manga* and *anime* artist who had made his own film about the Zero fighter used by the kamikaze, got closer to the heart of the matter when he was quoted in the press saying of *Eien* "They're trying to make a Zero fighter story based on a fictional war account that is a pack of lies. . . they's just continuing a phony myth."

In other words, the real problem is Japan's ongoing failure to digest its past. This not only allows for myth-spinning directed at people desperate for myths that can give their lives meaning. But it also makes the hectoring and recriminations directed at Japanese from across the Sea of Japan and the East China Sea appear a form of free-floating malevolence against which they feel defenseless. It is this more than anything that has allowed Abe and the hard Right circles around him to mount such a successful attack against the entire postwar legacy, aided and abetted—if sometimes unwittingly—by a Washington in thrall to the delusions of empire.

But the vast majority of Japanese—including most of those queuing for tickets to *Eien no zēro* and those who voted for Abe and Masuzoe—do not want war. They would prefer to get along with their neighbors. They only get exercised about small rock outcroppings in distant seas when they are made to feel that their identities as Japanese are somehow wrapped up in such places. They are not interested in marching about chanting rightist slogans and do not wish to subject their children to "patriotic" education complete with uniformed martinets masquerading as teachers who bellow out orders enforced with beatings. They want what people everywhere do: enough money to live in some comfort and dignity, meaningful work that gives a sense of purpose, family and friends, assurance they will not be abandoned when they are old or sick, reasonable safeguards against catastrophe—whether that catastrophe be war or clouds of poisoned gas released by stricken nuclear power plants built in the face of the implacable reality that the Japanese archipelago sits at the juncture of the most unstable fault lines on earth.

If truth be told, Abe and his ilk do not really want war either. But they hanker after what war brings in its train: enthusiasm, sense of purpose, clarity, hierarchy, deference, the sweeping away of doubts and qualms and second-guessing. It is a fantasy. In the era of the *gyaru*, the herbivore male, and the *otaku*—not to mention a rapidly aging society—there is no going back to the 1930s and millions of young men thirsting to die for the emperor. Abe seems to think that unless he can restore something of the spirit of those days that Japan will be unable to stand up to a strident, belligerent China—and, of course, Beijing is doing nothing to disabuse him of this notion with the vast machinery of Chinese state propaganda ceaselessly drumming into the heads of ordinary Chinese the notion that Japan is and always has been the source of all evil. The worst elements in both countries are using each other to stoke the fear and hysteria that like oxygen for life forms, permit demagoguery and repression to thrive.

At the start of this book, we noted that Japan's political culture has long been permeated by a tolerance for contradiction that would be largely unthinkable elsewhere.[25] From time to time, this tolerance permits a coincidence of dreamy, unrealizable goals with the most hard-nosed, hard-boiled tactics. Abe's vision of restoring the *esprit* of the Japanese Imperial Army so that Japan can stand up to China may be difficult to take seriously, but his administration is hardly the first time we have seen Japan run off on some ludicrous tangent in pursuit of absurd goals. One

25. To be sure, as the United States with its drones, data-vacuuming, prison-industrial complex, hordes of zealous prosecutors, multiple overlapping police forces, and global network of bases amasses the machinery of the most formidable repressive apparatus ever at the command of a sitting government all the while prattling on about democracy, freedom, and human rights, one feels a growing reluctance to single Japan out as a political culture with a high tolerance for contradiction.

need only cite *Sonno Jōi* (Revere the Emperor, Expel the Barbarians), Eight Corners of the World under One Roof, and Greater East Asia Co-Prosperity Sphere—not to mention the attack on Pearl Harbor with its implied goal of knocking out an enemy with an industrial base ten times larger than Japan's. One could also cite the complacent expectation encountered in the late 1980s that the shape of global markets, technology, and finance would be set going forward in Tokyo. Any serious reflection would have made it clear that no plausible scenario could have led to the achievement of any of these goals; yet that did not prevent the deploying of superior tactics in an effort to bring them about. One could even argue that those tactics made things worse. Among other things, if the Japanese had not been so tenacious in overwhelming opposition throughout Asia to their vision of a Co-Prosperity sphere, they would have had less opportunity and incentive to commit the atrocities whose legacies continue to poison relations with their neighbors. If the Japanese military had not fought at the ground level with a tactical brilliance unrivaled in the history of warfare, Washington might not have concluded that total war followed by unconditional surrender was the only way to deal with Tokyo. If Japanese manufacturing and cost control had been less good than it was, many in Japan would not have bought into the idea that the global economy would inevitably come to revolve around Japan, a notion that helped lead directly to the bubble economy and its aftermath.

But there has been another thread weaving its way through this tapestry of unrealizable goals married to supreme tactical competence. That thread becomes visible when manifest reality breaks through the delusions of Japan's leadership class, forcing it to confront that reality. Whenever that has actually happened, Japan's tactical competence and social cohesion work together to bring about marvels that can indeed seem miraculous. Once it became clear there was no expelling the barbarian or return to seclusion, Japan remade itself, avoided the colonization that swallowed up the rest of practically the entire non-Western world, and became a formidable power in its own right. Once the war to bring the Eight Corners of the World under One Roof had been irrevocably lost and the Americans had demonstrated they were not going to go away, Japan turned on a dime and figured out not only how to live in the shadow of an overweening, hectoring American presence while preserving its "Japaneseness," but thrived, becoming an indispensable pillar of the American world order. Once OPEC had hijacked global energy prices and driven them to permanent new plateaus, Japan overhauled its economy and energy use so fast and so thoroughly that it came storming out of the 1973–75 global recession more quickly than any other developed country. Once the bubble of the late 1980s economy had deflated for good and it had become obvious there was no blowing it back up, Japan performed an unprecedented feat in global financial history: staving off depression amidst the wreckage of a ruined financial system.

One can only hope that again reality will break through in a way that will see a Japanese leader emerge who can do for his country what Charles de Gaulle did for France—politely but firmly telling Washington that the postwar era is over and that from henceforth his country will be in charge of providing for its own security. Such a leader would insist that within a reasonable time frame, the last American base in Japan be closed and the last American soldier, marine, pilot, and sailor depart. The repeal of clause 2, Article 9, of the constitution that prohibits Japan from maintaining "land, sea and air forces as well as other war-making potential" would indeed be a prerequisite for this scenario. But the replacement must not be some vague document that grants government the power to do what it wants, but rather a set of institutions so robust that they make it clear to everyone from Beijing to Seoul to the typical Japanese family that never again can a lawless bureaucracy hijack the Japanese state; that all elements of the bureaucracy—including both those with the powers of physical coercion at their disposal and those without—have been brought for good under firm legal and political control.

With a security establishment under such control, a Japanese de Gaulle could then offer Washington a genuine alliance, which by definition is an arrangement between equals—not equals when measured by economic size or even military power, but equals in terms of mutual respect for the other's sovereignty and independence. The two countries might even contemplate some steps toward interoperability, with some American military personnel returning to Japan, not as occupiers, but seconded to Japanese bases under Japanese command. Meanwhile, this leader could turn toward China, Korea, and Russia offering negotiations without conditions on the outstanding territorial disputes, acknowledging that while Japan continues to believe it is on the right side of all three, that others have different views and that some sort of settlement that aims at enduring arrangements acceptable and beneficial to all parties is Tokyo's goal. This leader might signal China that he (or, conceivably, she) recognizes and supports

China's return to its historically preeminent position in Asia, but that Japan rightfully requires that China respect the autonomy of its neighbors—that going forward Japan hopes to play postwar France to China's postwar Germany. To those who might say there is no Chinese Adenauer to respond to a Japanese de Gaulle, one can only respond that peace and goodwill have to start somewhere.

A Japanese leader who made it clear not through pro-forma, half-hearted apologies but genuine soul-searching permeating the nation's schools and media that the country really understood what had happened in the 1930s and that it could not happen again would be in a position to shame China for the way in which it dangerously and cynically foments and exploits hatred for Japan. This in turn would require the kind of leadership that could help people in both places see that love of country and kind is not incompatible with recognition of the capacity for error and evil; indeed, that clear-eyed patriotism by politically aware citizens rather than infantilized subjects requires such recognition.

A great Japanese leader would understand and articulate the insecurity that lies beneath the country's economic malaise. Yes, this is a risk-averse society and in today's world that is a problem. But the solution is not to dynamite those institutions that once provided economic security and are no longer able to do so, not to mention replacing those institutions with an aristocracy of entitled workers and managers in well-connected companies while throwing everyone else to the mercy of harsh and unforgiving markets in temporary labor. Rather, the key to restoring entrepreneurial verve is a robust safety net that does indeed allow people to take risks without the prospect of poverty and social opprobrium if the risks end up going bad. Anyone who seriously believes that most people here would settle for life on welfare as opposed to meaningful, productive work if they had any choice in the matter demonstrates contempt for and ignorance of the Japanese people. Cries that such a network is unaffordable are not convincing from those who continue to lavish spending on the kinds of white elephant projects in declining rural areas that the Abe administration has deployed as the so-called second arrow of Abenomics.[26]

---

26. In February 2014, the Abe administration rammed a ¥5.5 trillion ($55 billion) supplementary budget through Diet stuffed with wasteful pork.

Finally, the kind of leader Japan needs would recognize that it is not enough, as Abe has done, to call for the tapping of what many label Japan's greatest underutilized resource: its women. Large numbers of women will not become more economically productive until something is done to alleviate the burdens of elder and child care that fall disproportionately on their shoulders. If Japan wants a birthrate closer to that of France than that of Italy, not to mention an economic boost from millions of working women, an infrastructure of day care comparable to that French families enjoy is critical. In the meantime, a good Japanese leader would encourage some carefully controlled immigration to relieve labor shortages in fields such as construction and nursing.

For the moment, no such leader is anywhere in sight. On July 1, 2014, the Cabinet announced in direct violation of the Constitution and without Diet approval that Japan would henceforth engage in "collective self-defense." It was tantamount to a declaration that Japan had become a lawless state, governed by executive decree. Meanwhile, some companies began raising base wages, but not by enough to offset the 3% hike in the consumption tax that had gone into effect on April 1. The stock market continued on something of a roll and the profits - if not the export volumes - of Japan's old-style export behemoths increased, but there was still no real sign of any self-sustaining pick-up in domestic demand.

But nothing is fore-ordained. In the midst of a growing climate of fear and even hysteria, the hearts of millions were captured for a moment by a modest Japanese boy who won the gold medal in the men's figure skating competition at the Sochi Olympics. The triumph of 19-year-old Hanyu Yuzuru was more than just a classic Japanese story of grit in the face of terribly high odds. For Hanyu had grown up in Sendai, the major city closest to the terrible events of March 2011; he had actually been working out when the earthquake struck. His rink had been wrecked and he had to hobble out to the street on his skates. He had almost given up skating; with his practice venue in ruins, his home badly damaged, and having few resources at his command, he seemed to have nowhere to turn. But then thanks both to his own determination and to the support of people in Sendai—including most crucially that of Arakawa Shizuka, the 2006 women's gold medalist who had also grown up there—he picked up the pieces of his shattered life and went on to the pinnacle of his sport.

Hanyu's victory served as something of a rebuke to the direction his country has taken since Abe's government came to power. Among other things, Hanyu helped turn attention back to Tohoku and the reality that tens of thousands of people still languish in temporary quarters, that only 10 percent of the promised home reconstruction had begun, that the Fukushima plant remains a festering wound. A government that boasted of the resources—financial and otherwise—to mount an Olympics of its own, not to mention bring on the long-heralded economic revival while "standing up" to China, could not seem to manage the mundane, tortoise-like task of rebuilding the ruined towns along the coastline hit by the tsunami. There was talk of bottlenecks and hints at the usual collusion of politics, organized crime, and the construction industry that made gaudy projects more alluring than the straightforward task of erecting thousands of simple houses.

Hanyu's manner also served as something of a contrast to the ugly xenophobia that has emerged in the wake of Abe's ascendancy. While the bookstores are filled with new genres dubbed "dislike China/hate Korea," and the Internet has become so full of *Neto-uyo* ("Internet ultra-rightist") that a major Japanese magazine has coined a new term for all the housewives now flocking to such sites, Hanyu came across as grateful and aware of the debt he owed to others, including others who were not Japanese. He was generous in his expressions of admiration for the great Russian skater Evgeni Plushenko and his regret that Plushenko had had to withdraw from the competition.

One would like to think that Hanyu's story and style writ large could become the story of Japan in the twenty-first century, loosening history's shackles and turning tragedy into triumph—not the hectoring, sneering triumph of those who would rewrite the past, but the unassuming triumph of someone who works hard, who does not give up, who does not show off—of a nice, decent, lovable human being who exemplifies what is most admirable about this country. For it had happened before—to individual people like Hanyu Yuzuru, to his friends and supporters in his hometown, to his country as a whole. One can only hope it will happen again and that it is Hanyu Yuzuru's own personal trajectory—not the sullen, aggrieved nationalism that Abe has brought in his wake—that ends up providing a taste of Japan's future.

Appendix A: The Meiji Leaders

Fukuzawa Yukichi (1835–1901). Osaka. Most important intellectual of the era. Member of first Japanese delegation to the United States. Founder of Keio University and key conduit of Western thought into Japan.

Inoue Kaoru (1836–1915). Choshu. First official foreign minister. Played central role in reorganizing Japan's finances, ending samurai stipends, and replacing land-tax system with modern taxation. Helped oversee construction of the national railways.

Itagaki Taisuke (1837–1919). Tosa. Played key military role in the overthrow of the Shogunate; later fell out with the Meiji government and became the leader of Freedom and People's Rights movement. Considered the founder of Japan's first political party and an early advocate of representative democracy.

Ito Hirobumi (1841–1909). Choshu. Prime minister four times. First governor-general of colonized Korea (assassinated by Korean nationalist). Often regarded by the Japanese as a "George Washington" of the entire group.

Iwakura Tomomi (1825–1883). Nobility. Led first Meiji mission to the West; established institutional foundations for the modern Imperial system and the Diet (Parliament).

Iwasaki Yataro (1835–1885). Tosa. Founder of Mitsubishi and Japan's first great industrialist.

Katsura Taro (1848–1913). Choshu. Key general in the Sino-Japanese War. Governor-general of Taiwan. Prime minister three times.

Kido Koin (1833–1877). Choshu. Yet another key figure in the events leading to the Restoration; architect of the Satsuma-Choshu alliance and, with Okubo Toshimichi and Saigo Takamori, formed the first Meiji government. Played pivotal role in the abolition of the *han* system.

Kuroda Kiyotaka (1840–1900). Satsuma. Prime minister. Helped suppressed Saigo's rebellion. Oversaw development of Hokkaido.

Matsukata Masayoshi (1835–1924). Satsuma. Finance minister in the 1880s, reorganizing and modernizing Japanese finance; later prime minister. Architect of capitalization of Japanese industry.

Mori Arinori (1847–1889). Satsuma. Japan's first ambassador to the United States; seen as the father of the modern Japanese educational system. Advocate of liberal democracy; assassinated by an ultra-nationalist.

Nogi Maresuke (1849–1912). Choshu. Leading general in the Russo-Japanese War and regarded with Admiral Togo as one of the two architects of Japan's victory. Tutor and mentor to Emperor Hirohito when the latter was a boy.

Okubo Toshimichi (1830–1878). Satsuma. Another key figure in the Restoration itself. Finance minister overseeing first efforts at industrial development. Helped to suppress Saigo's rebellion, leading to Okubo's assassination.

Okuma Shigenobu (1838–1922). Hizen (modern-day Saga Prefecture). Placed in charge of foreign affairs at the beginning of Meiji. Founder of the Ministry of Industry and the National Mint. Prime minister twice. Founder of Waseda University.

Oyama Iwao (1842–1916). Satsuma. One of the fathers of the Japanese Imperial Army; key figure in Japanese victories in Sino-Japanese and Russo-Japanese Wars.

Saigo Takamori (1828–1877). Satsuma. Key military figure in the events of the Restoration itself and the mopping up of remaining opposition.

Fell out with his erstwhile colleagues; led the last serious rebellion against Meiji rule in 1877 (loosely dramatized in the film *The Last Samurai*).

Saionji Kinmochi (1849–1940). Nobility. Boyhood friend of the Meiji Emperor. Prime minister three times. Led Japanese delegation to the 1919 Paris Peace Conference. Known as liberal opponent of the militarists near the end of his life.

Shibusawa Eiichi (1840–1931). Tokugawa lands near Edo (modern Saitama Prefecture). Known as father of the Japanese banking system; finance minister.

Togo Heihachiro (1848–1934). Satsuma. Labeled the "Nelson of the East" for leading Japan to its greatest naval victory—the sinking of the Russian fleet at the Battle of Tsushima in 1905.

Yamagata Aritomo (1838–1922). Choshu. Seen as the father of the Japanese military and universal male conscription. Worked to insulate the military from political oversight. Twice prime minister and considered the forerunner of the fascists of the 1930s.

Appendix B: Important Political Figures of Postwar Japan

Abe Shintaro (1924–1991). Japan's longest–serving foreign minister and leader for many years of the mandarin/conservative wing of the Liberal Democratic Party ("LDP"). Thought almost certain to become prime minister, but blocked by heirs of the Tanaka political machine. Known for his close ties to Washington. Son-in-law of Kishi Nobusuke and father of current prime minister Abe Shinzo.

Abe Shinzo (born 1954). Prime Minister for one year in 2006/7 and again beginning December 2012. Long known for his nationalist, right-wing views; attempts to rehabilitate the image of his grandfather, Kishi Nobusuke, and to cast the events of the 1930s in a light more favorable to Japan.

Asanuma Inejiro (1898–1960). Hard-line leftist leader of the Japan Socialist Party ("JSP") in the 1950s during the high-water years of the JSP's electoral influence, he was assassinated by a knife-wielding right-wing nationalist schoolboy on live television in 1960.

Ashida Hitoshi (1887–1959). Prime minister in 1948 in a coalition government that included socialists for the last time until 1994.

Ashida was forced to resign in the wake of the so-called Showa Denko scandal involving accusations of bribery by this major chemical company, setting the pattern for the scandals that regularly sweep over the Japanese political landscape, scandals that serve to bridle ambitious politicians.

Aso Taro (born 1940). Prime minister for less than one year in 2008/9 and deputy prime minister and finance minister in the second Abe Shinzo cabinet. Known for his outspoken, rightist views, embrace of pop culture, and love of fine dining and drinking. His family controls the Aso Mining Company that has been accused of using forced labor from POWs and Korean conscripts during the war years. His mother was the daughter of Yoshida Shigeru; Aso is the son-in-law of Suzuki Zenko.

Doi Takako (born 1928). As the leader of the JSP, she became the first woman ever to head a major Japanese political party. Popular for a while among voters—particularly women—she was instrumental in moving the JSP away from doctrinaire leftism. She resigned as party leader in 1991, served as speaker of the Lower House in the short-lived coalition government of Hosokawa Morihiro, and returned as party leader in the renamed Social Democratic Party after the party had been reduced to a shadow of its former self by voter anger at what seemed a betrayal of the party's roots when it entered into a coalition with the LDP in 1994.

Edano Yukio (born 1964). The public face of the Japanese government in the immediate aftermath of the 2011 earthquake when he served as chief cabinet secretary. Later, minister of economy, trade and industry under Noda Yoshihiko.

Fukuda Takeo (1905–1995). Prime minister 1976–78, emerging out of the Ministry of Finance. Leader of the "mandarins" of the LDP after the emergence of Tanaka Kakuei and the fall of Sato Eisaku. His rivalry with Tanaka, dubbed the "Kaku-Fuku War" by the media, was considered one of the great political battles of mid-twentieth-century Japanese politics.

Fukuda Yasuo (born 1936). Son of Fukuda Takeo; served as chief cabinet secretary under Mori Yoshiro and Koizumi Junichiro and then briefly—and unhappily—as prime minister for a year in 2007/8.

Gotoda Masaharu (1914–2005). Key aide of Tanaka Kakuei, serving as director general of the National Police Agency under Tanaka. The experience gave him a visceral tactical understanding of how to cope with Japan's permanent bureaucracy. Gotoda went on to serve in the cabinets of Ohira Masayoshi, Nakasone Yasuhiro, and Miyzawa Kiichi; as chief cabinet secretary under Nakasone, Gotoda was often credited for much of the success of the latter's administration.

Hashimoto Ryutaro (1937–2006). Disciple of Takeshita Noboru; inherited the remnants of the Tanaka faction after Ozawa Ichiro led much of the faction out of the LDP. Hashimoto served as prime minister from 1996 to 1998 after stints in several other key cabinet posts. Known in the United States for crossing swords with Mickey Kantor in 1994 over trade issues when he was MITI minister.

Hashimoto Toru (born 1969). Popular—albeit controversial—mayor of Osaka and co-founder with Ishihara Shintaro of the Japan Restoration Party that combined rightist views with a decentralization platform, doing very well in the 2012 Lower House elections before imploding. Pilloried in the global media for remarks on the forced recruitment of Korean women to provide sexual services to Japanese soldiers during the war years.

Hata Tsutomu (born 1935). Key ally of Ozawa Ichiro who helped bring about the first non-LDP government since 1955, he briefly served as prime minister in 1994.

Hatoyama Ichiro (1883–1959). Prominent member of the prewar conservative elite that was pushed aside by the militarists, he was about to become prime minister in 1946 when banned from politics by the Occupation. Rehabilitated in 1951, he engineered the resignation of Yoshida Shigeru in 1954, became prime minister (1954–55) and, to secure his position in office, helped in bringing his Democratic Party into the newly formed LDP. Grandfather of Hatoyama Yukio.

Hatoyama Yukio (born 1947). Grandson of Hatoyama Ichiro, co-founder and key leader of the Democratic Party of Japan ("DPJ") that controlled the machinery of Japan's parliamentary government between 2009 and 2012. He served as the first DPJ prime minister.

Hosokawa Morihiro (born 1938). Served as the first non-LDP prime minister since 1955 for eight months in 1993–94 after founding a new party that enjoyed electoral success in the aftermath of one of the largest of the postwar scandals; forced to resign in the aftermath of the very same scandal. Re-emerged to challenge the government of Abe Shinzo by announcing his candidacy in the 2014 Tokyo mayoral election. Scion of one of the oldest aristocratic families in Japan.

Iijima Isao (born 1946). Long-serving secretary of Koizumi Junichiro who is often credited with much of the political success of Koizumi's administration, he became special advisor to Abe Shinzo, convincing Abe he needed to backpedal his rightist agenda, positioning himself instead as an advocate of economic reform. Known as something of a maverick, Iijima has been compared to Karl Rove.

Ikeda Daisaku (born 1928). Widely credited with building the Soka Gakkai into the largest and most formidable of the "new religions," this immensely wealthy and powerful man is also the founder of what started as the sect's political arm: the *Kōmeitō* (Clean Government Party), traditionally seen as the "third party" of modern Japanese politics. While Ikeda formally separated the Komeito from Soka Gakkai in 1964, the sect and the party were intertwined in the public eye. Despite an ostensible centrist orientation (particularly on foreign policy/security issues) the Komeito and its successor, New Komeito, have generally acted as props for conservative rule, forming coalitions with the LDP on a number of key occasions.

Ikeda Hayato (1899–1965). Emerging out of the Ministry of Finance, and sometimes known as the father of the economic miracle, Ikeda took over as prime minister in 1960 following the riots precipitated by Kishi's ramming of the security treaty through the Diet. He is associated with his famous "income-doubling" plan and for leading Japan away from the social conflicts of the 1950s to a focus on economic growth.

Inose Naoki (born 1946). Famous journalist and author who became governor of Tokyo after the resignation of Ishihara Shintaro, first serving as acting governor and then winning a landslide election in 2012 in his own right. Widely credited with securing for Tokyo the nod from the International Olympic Committee for the 2020 Games, he was forced to resign late in 2013 when news surfaced that he had received a large campaign contribution that he had not properly reported. His resignation set the stage for what was seen as the first real referendum on the Abe administration following Abe's consolidation of control of the Japanese government.

Ishiba Shigeru (born 1957). Prominent LDP politician who accepted the position of Secretary General of the party after narrowly losing the party presidential election—and thus the prime ministership—to Abe Shinzo in 2012. Famous (among other things) for comparing demonstrators against the Official Secrets Act (rammed through the Diet late in 2013) to terrorists. Known for his stridently hawkish views.

Ishibashi Tanzan (1884–1973). Served as prime minister for less than two months in 1956–57 before suffering a stroke and giving way to Kishi Nobusuke whom he had previously defeated in the party election. Ishibashi was a prominent journalist and editor of *Tōyō Keizai*, Japan's preeminent economics/business weekly. He formed a key link between prewar liberals such as the famous proto-Keynesian finance minister Takahashi Korekiyo and moderate elements in Japan's postwar political setup who, without being leftists, nonetheless favored a foreign policy less tightly linked with Washington's.

Ishihara Shintaro (born 1932). Starting adult life as a flamboyant young novelist, he served as governor of Tokyo from 1999 to 2012. Famous for his rightist views and blunt, xenophobic language, his Japan Renewal Party, formed with Osaka mayor Hashimoto Toru, briefly—and for the only time in modern Japanese history—represented a challenge to the LDP from the Right.

Kaieda Banri (born 1949). Ally of Ozawa Ichiro, he served as minister of economy, trade and industry under Kan Naoto, then ran for the presidency of the DPJ with Ozawa's backing after Kan's resignation, but was defeated by Noda Yoshihiko, who automatically became prime minister. Following the DPJ's crushing defeat in the 2012 Lower House election, Kaieda replaced Noda as party president.

Kaifu Toshiki (born 1931). Served as a prime minister after the downfall of Takeshita Noboru in 1989 in the wake of one of the largest scandals in postwar Japanese political history and the brief prime ministership of Uno Sosuke. Kaifu had been placed in office as a stop-gap mostly because he had so few enemies, but he turned out to be much more popular—and independent minded—than had been anticipated. Party elders pushed him aside in 1991; he then joined forces with Ozawa Ichiro to help bring on, in 1993, the first non-LDP government since 1955.

Kamei Shizuka (born 1936). Popular "old-style" loose cannonball of a politician who attracted opprobrium from Koizumi Junichiro for opposition to Koizumi's privatization of the post office; won re-election despite Koizumi's attempts to unseat him. Left the LDP and served in the Hatoyama cabinet.

Kan Naoto (born 1946). Co-founder of the DPJ and prime minister during the Great Tohoku earthquake of 2011. Kan's roots were in the student protest movement; he first came to national prominence while serving as health and welfare minister in Hashimoto Ryutaro's coalition government when he uncovered and exposed evidence that blood derivatives with HIV had been knowingly administered to Japanese hemophiliacs.

Kanemaru Shin (1914–1996). Alternately styled "kingmaker," "godfather," and "shadow shogun" of Japanese politics, he emerged as the most important behind-the-scenes political figure in the Japan of the late 1980s. A disciple of Tanaka Kakuei, he was a close ally of Takeshita Noboru and finally brought down in characteristic fashion by the so-called Sagawa Kyubin scandal of the early 1990s.

Katayama Tetsu (1887–1978). Prime minister in 1947/48 from the Socialist Party elected at the high-water postwar tide of leftist sympathies. Responsible for some of the key institutions protecting the rights of workers.

Kato Koichi (born 1939). Prominent LDP politician in the 1990s; secretary general of the party in 1992; direct heir of Miyazawa Kiichi and crucial ally of Koizumi Junichiro.

Kishi Nobusuke (1886–1987). Arguably the most important Japanese political leader of the early postwar decades. The economic czar of Japan's prewar Manchurian colony and minister of munitions in the wartime cabinet of Tojo Hideki, the Occupation arrested and imprisoned him, but he was released without indictment. Played key role in the formation of the LDP in 1955 as conduit of CIA money and, after being defeated in the 1956 party election by the more centrist Ishibashi Tanzan, took over as prime minister after the latter fell ill. Rammed the US–Japan Security Treaty through the Diet in 1959; the subsequent outpouring of rage forced his resignation, but he continued to reign into the 1980s as a powerful *éminence grise*. Brother of Sato Eisaku, father-in-law of Abe Shintaro, and grandfather of Abe Shinzo.

Kodama Yoshio (1911–1984). One of the most important behind-the-scenes power brokers in the early postwar decades. Far Right agitator in the prewar years involved in assassination plots against liberal and moderate Japanese politicians, he amassed a huge fortune in China. He was imprisoned as a suspected war criminal by the Occupation, but never convicted. On release from prison, he became a key link among Far Right circles, the *yakuza*, and the nascent LDP and was a major conduit of secret CIA funding of the LDP. Closely linked to Kishi Nobusuke, he also served as Lockheed's agent in Japan. The 1976–77 Lockheed scandal that brought on the banishment of Tanaka Kakuei from any official Japanese government post (other than Dietman) shone a spotlight on Kodama.

Koga Makoto (born 1940). Prominent LDP politician who served as secretary general of the party under Mori Yoshiro, he was the leader of the politically powerful *Nippon Izokukai* (Japan Association of the Bereaved Families of the War Dead), a group whose clout has been compared to that of the National Rifle Association in the United States. Koga has emerged as something of a critic of Abe Shinzo, however, arguing that the impasse over Yasukuni Shrine should be solved by reversing the 1978 enshrinement of indicted war criminals at the shrine. He has also argued for retaining at least the first clause of Article 9 of the Constitution that renounces war as a "sovereign right."

Koizumi Junichiro (born 1942). Maverick politician who unexpectedly became prime minister in 2001 after winning a newly instituted party primary, he was the first prime minister since the 1970s to have served without the political backing of the machine built by Tanaka Kakuei or one of its institutional descendants. Among the most popular postwar prime ministers, he was the only prime minister since 1987 to hold office for more than three years, stepping down in 2006. He was known for his reformist pose, conservative—even hawkish—foreign policy, close relationship with George W. Bush, and pushing the "privatization" of the Japanese post office through the Diet. He anointed Abe Shinzo as his successor in carrying out his conservative agenda, but would later publicly denounce Abe after the latter's return to office for his pro-nuclear stance.

Koizumi Shinjiro (born 1981). Handsome and charismatic son of Koizumi Junichiro, Shinjiro is an elected member of the Diet and considered one of the most important rising stars of the LDP.

Komoto Toshio (1912–2001). Former president of a major shipping company, he used his wealth to try to buy his way into the prime ministership in the early 1980s, managing to alienate so many establishment figures that his company was allowed to go bankrupt in 1985.

Kono Yohei (born 1937). Prominent LDP politician who served as foreign minister under Mori Yoshiro, chief cabinet secretary under Miyazawa Kiichi, deputy prime minister in the coalition government headed by Socialist Murayama Tomiichi, and speaker of the House of Representatives from 2003 to 2009. Has recently re-emerged in the news because of calls to revisit the 1993 statement issued in his name acknowledging that the Japanese Imperial Army had, in the 1940s, coerced women from Korea and other countries to serve the sexual needs of Japanese soldiers.

Maehara Seiji (born 1962). First elected to the Diet in 1992 in the party formed by Hosokawa Morihiro, he became a prominent member of the DPJ and served briefly as party president. Held a number of cabinet positions during the 2009–12 period when the DPJ controlled Japan's parliamentary machinery, including foreign minister under Kan Nato. Opposed to raising the consumption tax, he was defeated by Noda Yoshihiko in the internal DPJ election to succeed Kan.

Masuzoe Yoichi (born 1948). Popular politician with an early career as a commentator with particular expertise on welfare and "aging society" issues, he was elected to the Upper House, going on to become minister of health, labor, and welfare in the first cabinet of Abe Shinzo and was frequently mentioned as a potential prime minister. After the 2009 LDP defeat, he left the LDP to form a new party and was courted by both the LDP and the DPJ. In the 2014 Tokyo gubernatorial election, he ran and won as an independent with LDP backing, defeating former prime minister Hosokawa Morihiro.

Miki Takeo (1907–1988). Became prime minister in the wake of the resignation of Tanaka Kakuei in 1974, mostly because he was one of the few politicians untainted by rumors of financial shenanigans (he was independently wealthy). When his attempts to "clean up" Japanese politics alienated powerful faction leaders in the LDP, he was summarily dumped in favor of Fukuda Takeo.

Miyamoto Kenji (1908–2007). Leader of the Japan Communist Party ("JCP") briefly in the late 1940s and again between 1958 and 1977, he is credited with mainstreaming the JCP, abandoning calls for violent revolution, criticizing (at different times) both China and the Soviet Union, and recasting the JCP as a voice for the urban working class and small shopkeepers.

Miyazawa Kiichi (1919–2007). Although a cerebral, worldly old-style "mandarin" politician who emerged from the Ministry of Finance, he was politically linked to remnants of Tanaka Kakuei's machine that helped make him prime minister in 1991 (he became famous in the United States when President George H. W. Bush threw up next to him at a state dinner in Tokyo). He was forced to resign when Ozawa Ichiro led his first rebellion against the LDP. Miyazawa probably made a greater impact as finance minister, a position he held in the late 1980s and again in the late 1990s; he was present or a principal in every important international negotiation over financial matters involving Tokyo from the breakup of the Bretton Woods system in the early 1970s until he retired in 2003.

Mori Yoshiro (born 1937). Placed in the prime minister's office as a caretaker following the death of Obuchi Keizo in 2000, Mori acquired a public image as something of a buffoon and resigned after a year. At the time of this writing, served as head of the committee organizing the 2020 Tokyo Olympics.

Murayama Tomiichi (born 1924). The only prime minister from the Japan Socialist Party since 1948, Murayama got the nod in 1994 for helping to bring down the first non-LDP government since 1955 and entering a coalition with the LDP. The voters punished the JSP by abandoning the party in droves. Serving as prime minister for eighteen months, Murayama accomplished little other than finally to pronounce a formal official apology for the events of the 1930s.

Nakasone Hirofumi (born 1945). Son of Nakasone Yasuhiro and one of the most prominent current LDP politicians. He has served as Minister of Education (1999–2000) and Minister of Foreign Affairs (2008–9).

Nakasone Yasuhiro (born 1918). Prime minister of Japan from 1982 to 1987, he was arguably among the most politically successful Japanese prime ministers, forming a close friendship with Ronald Reagan and privatizing Japan National Railroads; the media nonetheless succeeded in pinning the label "Tanakasone" on his government because of his close links to Tanaka Kakuei. Nakasone became a kind of elder statesman of Japanese politics but he is also closely identified with the "nuclear village" that fatally committed Japan to nuclear power.

Nishio Suehiro (1891–1981). Socialist politician who served in the cabinets of Katayama Tetsu and Ashida Hitoshi, he was a casualty of the first of Japan's major postwar scandals. After being acquitted, he re-emerged as a politician to lead the more moderate wing of the Japan Socialist Party out of the JSP in 1960 to form the Democratic Socialist Party of Japan, a party whose institutional descendants are generally to be found in the DPJ.

Noda Yoshihiko (born 1957). The last of the three DPJ prime ministers, Noda assumed office after the resignation of Kan Naoto in September 2011. He is widely blamed for having destroyed the DPJ's electoral prospects and setting the stage for the return of conservative rule in 2012 by his insistence on ramming a hike in the consumption tax through the Diet and his mishandling of the confrontation with China over the Senkaku Islands.

Nonaka Hiromu (born 1925). Prominent member of the LDP who held several key posts in the 1990s and was thought of as a potential prime minister. Recently in the news when he said he had been told by Tanaka Kakuei that Tanaka and Zhou En Lai had specifically agreed to shelve the Senkaku Island issue, contradicting the official Japanese government line that no record of such conversation and thus "no dispute" exists.

Nosaka Sanzo (1892–1993). One of the founders of the Japan Communist Party, he was one of its important leaders in the early postwar decades, playing a key role in organizing the series of strikes that swept Japan in the 1950s as well as the 1960 riots that led to the downfall of the government of Kishi Nobusuke. Nosaka had links to both the Soviet and Chinese Communist parties; near the end of his life, the release of KGB documents revealed not only that Nosaka had at one point been an agent of the Comintern, he had also helped betray a colleague who was murdered by Stalin's secret police; he was expelled from the party.

Obuchi Keizo (1937–2000). Stepped in as prime minister after the LDP's loss of the Upper House elections in 1998 and the resignation of Hashimoto Ryutaro to take responsibility. Clearly overwhelmed by the stress of office, Obuchi had a stroke in April 2000, resigned, and died a few weeks later.

Ohira Masayoshi (1910–1980). First post-Tanaka Kakuei prime minister to owe his position to Tanaka, succeeding Fukuda Takeo in office in 1978 as part of deal worked out between the two major factions of the LDP. Ohira had a reputation as a successful negotiator; he had been foreign minister under both Ikeda Hayato and Tanaka and had helped negotiate the establishment of diplomatic relations with both South Korea and China. Ohira died in office; his death is sometimes blamed on stress resulting from his efforts to introduce the consumption tax at the behest of the Ministry of Finance.

Okada Katsuya (born 1953). Key figure in the DPJ. He joined Ozawa Ichiro in the mass defection from the LDP in 1993 and ended up in the DPJ in 1998. Lost to Hatoyama Yukio in the election for party presidency after the resignation of Ozawa Ichiro in 2009, then served as foreign minister under Hatoyama, failing to achieve some sort of settlement of the Futenma Marine base relocation issue. Served as deputy prime minister under Noda Yoshihiko.

Ozawa Ichiro (born 1942). Arguably the most important disciple of Tanaka Kakuei, Ozawa rose to the position of secretary general of the LDP in the prime ministership of Miyazawa Kiichi, pushing Tokyo to cough up a major contribution to the first Gulf War. Convinced that the greatest obstacle to Japan's becoming a "normal nation" was the lack of real political competition, Ozawa led much of the remnants of the Tanaka political machine out of the LDP in 1993, bringing on the first hiatus to LDP rule since the party's founding in 1955. Stymied in his first attempt to create a lasting opposition government, Ozawa spent the next fifteen years laying the institutional foundations for a real two-party system, serving as the architect of the rise to power of the DPJ in 2009. Widely expected to become prime minister, Ozawa was derailed by the usual Japanese recipe for bridling ambitious politicians: a trumped-up hullabaloo over financing irregularities. Disliked and even hated by much of the Japanese establishment and distrusted in Washington because of his calls for re-negotiating the basis of the US-Japan relationship, Ozawa lost control of the party machinery and was frozen out of power after his disciple, Hatoyama Yukio, was forced from office in 2010 by a tacit alliance of the Japanese bureaucracy, the quality press, and the Japan policy establishment in Washington.

Saito Jiro (born 1936). Ministry of Finance bureaucrat who rose to the highest position in the official Japanese bureaucracy: *jimu jikan* or administrative vice minister of Finance. Saito's predecessors were not well-known to the wider public, but Saito assumed his position in 1993 in the aftermath of the bubble economy and just at the time that Ozawa Ichiro brought on the first hiatus in LDP rule since 1955. Saito thus became unusually prominent as the public face of the bureaucracy. He went on to hold the politically prominent post of president of Japan Post Holdings.

Sakakibara Eisuke (born 1941). Former international vice minister in the Ministry of Finance, the press dubbed him "Mr. Yen" in the mid-1990s because his remarks moved currency markets. Negotiated joint market interventions with the US Treasury in 1995 that reversed the politically dangerous soaring of the yen in the wake of Mexico's so-called "tequila crisis." Maverick intellectual famous for his controversial opinions, he has recently re-emerged as a critic of "Abenomics," arguing that achieving the stated 2 percent inflation target will be difficult.

Sato Eisaku (1901–1975). Japan's longest–serving prime minister (1964–1972), he was the younger brother of Kishi Nobusuke. He negotiated the return of Okinawa to nominal Japanese rule, but angered the Nixon White House when he failed to deliver a respite in Japanese textile exports to the United States, which Nixon had understood was a quid-pro-quo. He was nonetheless awarded the Nobel Peace Prize in 1974 for his efforts.

Suga Yoshihide (born 1948). Key ally of Abe Shinzo, serving in Abe's first administration as minister of internal affairs and communications, and becoming chief cabinet secretary after Abe returned to office in 2012.

Suzuki Muneo (born 1948). In the mold of Tanaka Kakuei and Ozawa Ichiro, he built a formidable local political machine in Japan's northern island of Hokkaido, rising to become deputy cabinet secretary under Obuchi Keizo. He was arrested on accusations of taking bribes from construction companies in 2002; many suspect his real "crime" was his circumvention of Japan's official bureaucracy in an attempt to achieve a settlement of the territorial dispute with Russia (see discussion in chapter 11); many of his constituents are relatives of those who were forced to leave the southern Kurile islands when they were seized by Russia in the final days of the Second World War.

Suzuki Zenko (1911–2004). Placed in the prime minister's office after the sudden death of Ohira Masayoshi in 1980, Suzuki became almost a figure of ridicule for his self-effacement and practice of reciting answers written for him by bureaucrats at press conferences and meetings with foreign leaders. The situation became sufficiently embarrassing that the two great godfathers of Japanese politics at the time—Tanaka Kakuei and Kishi Nobusuke—cooperated in engineering Suzuki's resignation and replacement by Nakasone Yasuhiro.

Takenaka Heizo (born 1951). Prominent neoliberal economist who became a member of the cabinet of Koizumi Junichiro. As an advocate of privatization and restructuring the Japanese economy along neoliberal lines, Takenaka's outspoken comments helped the Koizumi administration maintain a neoliberal pose that was particularly well accepted in Washington. Takenaka claimed credit for a final resolution of the banking crisis inherited from the aftermath of the late 1980s bubble economy, but that claim has been disputed.

Takeshita Noboru (1924–2000). Key disciple of Tanaka Kakuei who led the palace coup against Tanaka in 1983, becoming finance minister (1982–86 in which capacity he helped negotiate the Plaza Accord of 1985) and prime minister (1987–89). Although forced to resign as prime minister in the wake of the so-called Recruit scandal, he continued to be a powerful force behind the scenes through the 1990s.

Tanaka Kakuei (1918–1993). Arguably the most important politician in postwar Japan, he transformed electoral politics by deploying money and patronage on a scale never before witnessed in Japan, in the process shocking the Japanese electoral system into realignments that are still visible today. Served as prime minister from 1972 to 1974; he was forced to relinquish all official titles after being indicted in the wake of the so-called Lockheed scandal. Reigned behind the scenes for the next decade as the "shadow shogun" of Japanese politics, until his most important disciples—Kanemaru Shin, Ozawa Ichiro, and Takeshita Noboru turned on him in 1983; he suffered a stroke soon thereafter.

Tanaka Makiko (born 1944). Controversial and outspoken daughter of Tanaka Kakuei, she inherited much of her father's political machine but not his incomparable skill at building coalitions. Brought into the cabinet of Koizumi Junichiro as foreign minister, she became involved in the imbroglio surrounding Suzuki Muneo's attempt to cut a deal with Russia over the Northern Territories and was forced to resign after openly criticizing Koizumi. She left the LDP, later joined the DPJ, and served in the cabinet of Noda Yoshihiko as education minister.

Uno Sosuke (1922–1998). Served briefly as prime minister in 1989 after the downfall of the government of Takeshita Noboru in the wake of the so-called "Recruit" scandal. Uno was forced to resign after news surfaced about complaints from his mistress that he had treated her shabbily—the one time in modern history that a Japanese politician has had his career ended by a sex scandal.

Watanabe Michio (1923–1995). Important and ambitious gaffe-prone LDP politician in the late twentieth century, serving in a number of cabinet positions between 1978 and 1993, he was long considered a leading candidate for the prime ministership. Known in the West for unthinkingly racist comments about American blacks and Koreans.

Yamasaki Taku (born 1936). Key ally along with Kato Koichi of Koizumi Junichiro, he served as secretary general of the LDP under Koizumi, losing the 2006 intra-party election to succeed him to Abe Shinzo.

Yoshida Shigeru (1878–1967). The most important Japanese political leader in the immediate postwar years, he had had a career as a diplomat, serving as Japan's ambassador in London in the 1930s. He was briefly imprisoned by the Occupation; on release from prison in 1946 he became prime minister, returning to that post in 1948 after the brief socialist interregnum of Katayama Tetsu and the coalition government of Ashida Hitoshi. He negotiated the San Francisco Peace Treaty that ended the Occupation, and continued to serve as prime minister until defeated late in 1954 by Hatoyama Ichiro's Democratic Party. With the 1955 merger of Yoshida's Liberal (later Democratic Liberal) and Hatoyama's Democratic Party to form the LDP, Yoshida continued to be an important power broker into the early 1960s. Grandfather of Aso Taro.

Notes and Suggestions for Further Reading

This book started out as a quick-and-dirty general survey and while it grew, with the support of Oxford University Press, into more than that, the lack of a bibliography betrays its origins. In any case, a comprehensive bibliography that would do justice to the scope of what the book covers would require a book of its own.

Instead, I have provided specific citations for those passages that require them. Then, for each chapter, I have added references to writing in English that both helped to crystallize my own thinking on the specific issues covered in that chapter and would, I thought, interest readers who wish to delve more deeply into those issues.

I start by bringing the reader's attention to the books that have most influenced my own thinking about Japan. The following six works that have been central in my efforts to construct a fully rounded view of Japan's tragic trajectory since the last days of the Shogunate.

1. Karel van Wolferen, *The Enigma of Japanese Power* (Knopf, 1990). The preeminent study in English of Japan's power relations in the late twentieth century.
2. E. H. Norman, "Japan's Emergence as a Modern State," in *Origins of the Japanese Modern State: Selected Writings of*

E. H. Norman, ed. John Dower (Pantheon, 1975). Norman's work—much of it written in the 1930s—was challenged by the first generation of American Cold War scholars, who took issue with the Marxist flavor of some of Norman's analysis of elements in the Tokugawa setup that helped bring on the Restoration (see, in particular, Albert M. Craig, *Choshu in the Meiji Restoration* [Harvard, 1961]). Norman's writing nonetheless continues to serve as a keystone of both Western and Japanese scholarship on the Restoration, while Dower's hundred-page introduction constitutes a superb analysis of the politicization of American Japan studies in the early postwar decades.

3. Ian Buruma, *Inventing Japan: 1853–1964* (Modern Library, 2003). Buruma's little masterpiece demonstrates that "Japan" is essentially a modern construction—and how the construct was accomplished.

4. Masao Maruyama, *Thought and Behavior in Modern Japanese Politics*, ed. Ivan Morris (Oxford, 1963). This anthology of essays by Japan's preeminent modern political thinker, translated and selected by one of the West's greatest Japan scholars, is indispensable to understanding the arc of Japanese political history in the twentieth century.

5. John Dower, *Embracing Defeat* (W. W. Norton, 1999). In this *tour de force* of historical writing, Dower portrays the origins of the overarching reality of postwar Japan: the seemingly inextricable entanglement with the United States.

6. Chalmers Johnson, *MITI and the Japanese Miracle* (Stanford, 1982). This ground-breaking book remains the most serious and comprehensive attempt to analyze the institutional origins of the export-led Japanese growth model.

Ivan Morris's *The World of the Shining Prince: Court Life in Ancient Japan* (Alfred A. Knopf, 1964) and *The Nobility of Failure: Tragic Heroes in the History of Japan* (Holt, Rinehart and Winston, 1975) have long been two of my favorite works on early Japan. Chapters 1–10 of Marius Jansen, *The Making of Modern Japan* (Belknap/Harvard, 2000) form the best introduction to the history of the Tokugawa Shogunate that I know of. Timon Screech, *Sex and the Floating World: Erotic Images in Japan 1700–1820*, 2nd edition (Reaktion Books, 2009) serves as an, um, eye-opener to the motive power behind most of the enduring art of the period—and its sexuality. Edward Seidensticker, *Low City, High City* (Knopf, 1983) portrays the transformation of the shogun's Edo into modern Tokyo—and by extension the transformation of Japan. Andrew Gordon, *A Modern History of Japan: From Tokugawa Times to the Present* (Oxford, 2003) is as close to an ideal textbook as I can imagine. Ezra F. Vogel, *Japan's New Middle Class: The Salary Man and his Family in a Tokyo Suburb* (University of California, 1963) remains the preeminent study in English of the salaryman culture of the early postwar decades. Kent Calder, *Crisis and Compensation: Public Policy and Political Stability in Japan* (Princeton, 1988) shows us how the architects of the "economic miracle" purchased the political stability necessary to make it happen. John C. Campbell, *Contemporary Japanese Budget Politics* (University of California, 1977) describes the engine room of Japan's political setup in the early postwar decades, while Alex Kerr, *Dogs and Demons: Tales from the Dark Side of Japan* (Farrar, Strauss, and Giroux, 2001) conveys with aching poignancy the aesthetic and cultural costs of Japan's lunge for high growth. Edwin Reischauer, *My Life between Japan and America* (Harper & Row, 1986) is an entertaining and revealing autobiography by one of the key architects of the US–Japan relationship. Gavan McCormack, *Client State: Japan in the American Embrace* (Verso, 2007) captures the pathologies of that relationship, while my own book *The Weight of the Yen* (Norton, 1996) sets out to show that while Japan may depend on the United States, the reverse is also true, at least in financial terms. Jacob M. Schlesinger, *Shadow Shoguns: The Rise and Fall of Japan's Postwar Political Machine* (Simon and Schuster, 1997) portrays Tanaka Kakuei and his impact on Japanese politics in the late twentieth century. Richard Katz, *The System that Soured the Rise and Fall of the Japanese Economic Miracle* (M. E. Sharpe, 1998) writes convincingly of what happened to economic arrangements that once worked so well they were called a miracle, while Akio Mikuni and I analyzed the intersection of monetary, political, and balance of payments factors that blocked an easy solution to Japan's macroeconomic problems in *Japan's Policy Trap* (Brookings, 2002). Richard Koo's *Balance Sheet Recession: Japan's Struggle with Uncharted Economics and its Global Implications* (John Wiley & Sons, 2003) and *The Holy Grail of Macroeconomics: Lessons from Japan's Great Recession* (John Wiley & Sons, 2009) point not only to what happened to Japan in the aftermath of the bubble economy, but to the lessons for the wider world, while Ulrike Schaede, *Choose and Focus: Japanese Business Strategies for the 21st Century* (Cornell, 2008) is the best book I have read on the transformation of Japanese business in recent decades.

As I was finishing the manuscript, the New Left Review devoted an entire issue (September/October 2013) to Perry Anderson's "American Foreign Policy and its Thinkers." Together with Robert Brenner, *The Economics of Global Turbulence* (Verso, 2006) and the long update Brenner wrote in the wake of the events of 2008 in "What is Good for Goldman Sachs is Good for America: The Origins of the Present Crisis" (Center for Social and Comparative History, UCLA), these magisterial overviews form an almost ideal framework in which to set the tragic trajectory of Japan's modern history.

INTRODUCTION

"Steven Rattner": "The Lessons of Japan's Economy," *New York Times*, October 13, 2013.
Lafcadio Hearn, *Gleanings in Buddha Fields* (Cosmo Classics, 2004).
Kurt Singer, *Mirror, Sword and Jewel* (Routledge, 1997).
Ian Buruma, *A Japanese Mirror: Heroes and Villains of Japanese Culture* (Penguin, 1984).
Donald Richie, *The Inland Sea*, 2nd edition (Stonebridge Press, 2002). Probably the best book ever on the effect Japan has on foreigners. Everything the late Richie wrote is worth reading; best known for his landmark studies on the Japanese cinema, Richie had good claim to being the preeminent observer among foreigners of life among ordinary Japanese in the latter half of the twentieth century.
"recently encountered": http://www.youtube.com/watch?v=qpZbu7J7UL4&feature =c4-overview-vl&list=PLDbSvEZka6GHk_nwovY6rmXawLcota_AD.
Masao Maruyama, *Thought and Behavior in Modern Japanese Politics*, ed. Ivan Morris (Oxford, 1963), pp. 90–92.
"political aims. . .": Karel van Wolferen, *The Enigma of Japanese Power* (Knopf, 1990).

CHAPTER 1

". . . the land surface. . .": Alexander Murphy, "The Sovereign State System as Political-Territorial Ideal: Historical and Contemporary Considerations," in Thomas J. Biersteker and Cynthia Weber, eds., *State Sovereignty as a Social Construct* (Cambridge, 1996).
". . . Versailles or the Mughal courts. . .": Ivan Morris, *The World of the Shining Prince: Court Life in Ancient Japan* (Alfred A. Knopf, 1964), from which much of the discussion of Heian culture and its literature is drawn, contains the original observation.
"One of the hoariest. . .": Ivan Morris, *The Nobility of Failure: Tragic Heroes in the History of Japan* (Holt, Rinehart and Winston, 1975).
". . . another enduring. . .": Buruma, *A Japanese Mirror*, pp. 132–135, discusses the Yoshitsune/Benkei legends. The entire book is a wonderful introduction to Japanese cultural archetypes.
"Rival Schools. . .": Germain A. Hoston, *Marxism and the Crisis of Development in Prewar Japan* (Princeton, 1986).

Other Recommended Books on Japan's Premodern Era

George B. Sansom, *Japan: A Short Cultural History* (Cresset Press, 1931).
Marius B. Jansen, ed., *Warrior Rule in Japan* (Cambridge, 1995).

CHAPTER 2

". . . almost continuous change": Drawn from Marius Jansen, *The Making of Modern Japan* (Belknap/Harvard, 2000).
"Every tree. . .": Jared Diamond, *Collapse: How Societies Choose to Fail* (Penguin Books, 2005), chapter 9.
"Timon Screech. . .": *Sex and the Floating World: Erotic Images in Japan 1700–1820*, 2nd edition (Reaktion Books, 2009).
"While samurai youths. . .": Gary P. Leupp, *Male Colors: The Construction of Homosexuality in Tokugawa Japan* (University of California Press, 1995).
"But rather than attempt to interfere directly. . .": Karel van Wolferen discusses this at some length in his Japanese language book *Okore! Nihon no Chūryū Kaikyū (Bourgeoisie: The Missing Element in Japanese Political Culture)* (Mainichi Shinbunsha, 1999). I am grateful to him for bringing these examples to my attention.
". . . the merchants were tacit allies. . .": E. H. Norman, "Japan's Emergence as a Modern State," in *Origins of the Japanese Modern State: Selected Writings of E. H. Norman*, ed. John Dower (Pantheon, 1975).
"A paradigmatic. . .": Marius Jansen, *Sakamoto Ryoma and the Meiji Restoration* (Princeton, 1961).

Other Recommended Reading

Herman Ooms, *Tokugawa Ideology: Early Constructs, 1570–1680* (Princeton, 1985).
Masao Maruyama, *Studies in the Intellectual History of Tokugawa Japan*, translated by Hane Mikiso (University of Tokyo, 1974).
Robert Bellah, *Tokugawa Religion: The Cultural Roots of Modern Japan* (Free Press, 1957).
Thomas C. Smith, *The Agrarian Origins of Modern Japan* (Stanford, 1959).
Gregory M. Pflugfelder, *Cartographies of Desire: Male-Male Sexuality in Japanese Discourse, 1600–1950* (University of California, 1999).
Leslie Downer, *Geisha: The Remarkable Truth behind the Fiction* (Headline, 2001).
Liza Dalby, *Geisha* (University of California, 1983).
Donald Keene, *World Within Walls: Japanese Literature of the Pre-Modern Era, 1600–1867* (Henry Holt, 1976).
Timothy Clark, C. Andrew Gerstle, Aki Ishigami, and Akiko Yano, eds., *Shunga: Sex and Pleasure in Japanese Art* (British Museum, 2013).

CHAPTER 3

"between a country": Quoted in Jansen, *The Making of Modern Japan*, p. 434.
". . . could hardly refrain. . ." and ". . .an anxious housewife. . .": Both quoted in Ian Buruma, *Inventing Japan: 1853–1964* (Modern Library, 2003), p. 50.

"E. H. Norman described. . .": Dower, ed., *Selected Writings of E. H. Norman*, p. 436.
"Karel van Wolferen": *The Enigma of Japanese Power*.
". . . Maruyama Maso wrote. . .": *Thought and Behavior* p. 85.

Other Recommended Reading

Roger W. Bowen, *Rebellion and Democracy in Meiji Japan* (University of California, 1980).

W. J. Macpherson, *The Economic Development of Japan 1868–1941* (Cambridge, 1987).

Hane Mikiso, *Peasants, Rebels, and Outcasts: The Underside of Modern Japan* (Pantheon, 1982).

Arthur Herman, *The Idea of Decline in Western History* (Free Press, 1997), chapter 2, "Arthur de Gobineau and Racial Wreckage" on the racial theories picked up on by the Meiji elite.

Takashi Fujitani, *Splendid Monarchy: Power and Pageantry in Modern Japan* (University of California, 1998).

Liaquat Ahamed, *Lords of Finance: The Bankers Who Broke the World* (Penguin, 2009). Excellent introduction to the financial history of the 1920s that formed the backdrop/cause of the rise of fascism in Japan and elsewhere.

Andrew Gordon, *Labor and Imperial Democracy in Prewar Japan* (University of California, 1991).

Sheldon Garon, *The State and Labor in Modern Japan* (University of California, 1987).

Walter LaFeber, *The Clash: U.S.–Japanese Relations throughout History* (W. W. Norton, 1997).

Mark Peattie, Edward Drea, and Hans Van de Ven, eds., *The Battle for China: Essays on the Military History of the Sino-Japanese War of 1937–1945* (Stanford, 2011).

Akira Iriye, *The Origins of the Second World War in Asia and the Pacific* (Longman, 1987).

Saburo Ienaga, *The Pacific War 1931–1945*, translated by Frank Baldwin (Pantheon, 1978).

John Dower, *War Without Mercy: Race and Power in the Pacific War* (Pantheon, 1986).

Herbert P. Bix, *Hirohito and the Making of Modern Japan* (Harper Collins, 2000).

CHAPTER 4

"Chalmers Johnson wrote. . .": *MITI and the Japanese Miracle* (Stanford, 1982), p. 3.

"From top to bottom. . .": John Dower, *Embracing Defeat* (W. W. Norton, 1999), pp. 223–224. I am indebted to Dower for much of the discussion in this chapter.

"As John Dower. . .": ibid., p. 212.

"As Dower. . .": ibid., p. 467.

"Kent Calder . . .": *Crisis and Compensation: Public Policy and Political Stability in Japan* (Princeton, 1988).

". . . dubbed 'total war'. . .": Andrew Gordon, *A Modern History of Japan: From Tokugawa Times to the Present* (Oxford, 2003), p. 277.

"Emerging. . .": Herman Kahn, *The Emerging Japanese Superstate* (Prentice Hall, 1971).

Other Recommended Reading

John Dower, *Empire and Aftermath: Yoshida Shigeru and the Japanese Experience, 1878–1954* (Harvard, 1979).

Takeo Doi, *The Anatomy of Dependence* (Kodansha USA, 2002), classic work discussing *amae*.

Dennis J. Encarnation, *Rivals Beyond Trade: America Versus Japan in Global Competition* (Cornell, 1992), for the origins of policies excluding direct foreign investment in Japan.

Robert Scalapino, *The Japanese Communist Movement 1920–1966* (University of California, 1967).

Andrew Gordon, *The Evolution of Labor Relations in Japan, 1853–1955* (Harvard, 1988).

Akio Mikuni and R. Taggart Murphy, *Japan's Policy Trap* (Brookings, 2002). Chapter 3 discusses Ikeda Hayato's central role in meshing monetary and bank oversight policies to lay the foundations for the "economic miracle."

Byong Chul Koh, *Japan's Administrative Elite* (University of California, 1989).

Edwin Reischauer, *My Life between Japan and America* (Harper & Row, 1986) discusses the "Broken Dialogue" (pp. 151–160) between Washington and Tokyo that led to his appointment as ambassador in 1961.

John G. Roberts, *Mitsui: Three Centuries of Japanese Business* (Weatherhill, 1973).

CHAPTER 5

Recommended Reading

Frank Upham, *Law and Social Change in Postwar Japan* (Harvard, 1987) describes how informal practices that lacked the force of law often governed what could and could not be done.

Andrew Gordon, *The Wages of Affluence: Labor and Management in Postwar Japan* (Harvard, 1998).

Chalmers Johnson, *Japan's Public Policy Companies* (American Enterprise Institute, 1978).

Rodney Clark, *The Japanese Company* (Yale, 1979).

Shigeo Tsuru, *Japan's Capitalism: Creative Defeat and Beyond* (Cambridge, 1993).

Thomas P. Rohlen, *Japan's High Schools* (University of California, 1983).

Ezra Vogel, ed., *Modern Japanese Organization and Decision-Making* (University of California, 1975).

William M. Tsutsui, *Banking Policy in Japan: American Efforts at Reform during the Occupation* (Routledge, 1988).

Yoshio Suzuki, *Money and Banking in Contemporary Japan*, translated by John G. Greenwood (Yale, 1980).

Aaron Viner, *Inside Japan's Financial Markets* (The Economist Publications, 1987).

Yoshio Suzuki, ed., *The Japanese Financial System* (Oxford, 1987).

James Horne, *Japan's Financial Markets: Conflict and Consensus in Policy Making* (George Allen & Unwin, 1985).

Daniel L. Okimoto and Thomas P. Rohlen, eds., *Inside the Japanese System: Readings on Contemporary Society and Political Economy* (Stanford, 1988).

T. F. M. Adam and Iwao Hoshii, *A Financial History of the New Japan* (Kodansha International, 1972).

Hugh Patrick and Henry Roskovsky, eds., *Asia's New Giant* (Brookings, 1976).

Robert J. Ballon and Iwao Tomita, *The Financial Behavior of Japanese Corporations* (Kodansha International, 1988).

Michael L. Gerlach, *Alliance Capitalism: The Social Organization of Japanese Business* (University of California, 1992).

CHAPTER 6

"The assault on nature. . .": Alex Kerr, *Dogs and Demons: Tales from the Dark Side of Japan* (Farrar, Strauss and Giroux, 2001).

"Nixon thought. . .": See account in I. M. Destler, Haruhiro Fukui, and Hideo Sato, *The Textile Wrangle: Conflict in Japanese-American Relations, 1969–1971* (Cornell, 1979).

"Tokyo played its hand. . .": See account of the negotiations in Paul Volcker and Toyō Gyōten, *Changing Fortunes: The World's Money and the Threat to American Leadership* (Times Books, 1992), pp. 88–106. The entire book is a superb introduction to the events surrounding the collapse of the Bretton Woods system and the coming of today's floating rate regime.

". . . The proper value. . .": Then Undersecretary for Monetary Affairs Beryl Sprinkel, quoted in R. Taggart Murphy, *The Weight of the Yen* (W. W. Norton, 1996).

Other Recommended Reading

Satoshi Kamata, *Japan in the Passing Lane: An Insider's Account of Life in a Japanese Auto Factory*, translated by Akimoto, Tatsuru (Pantheon, 1982).

Robert Whiting, *The Chrysanthemum and the Bat* (Dodd, Mead, 1977), *You Gotta Have Wa* (MacMillan, 1989), and *The Meaning of Ichiro: The New Wave from Japan and the Transformation of Our National Pastime* (Grand Central Publishing, 2009) has provided marvelous, thorough introductions to Japanese baseball for American readers.

Yuko Ogasawara, *Office Ladies and Salaried Men* (University of California, 1998).

Robert C. Angel, *Explaining Economic Policy Failure: Japan in the 1969–1971 International Monetary Crisis* (Columbia, 1991).

Edward J. Lincoln, *Japan's Unequal Trade* (Brookings, 1990).

I. M. Destler and C. Randall Henning, *Dollar Politics: Exchange Rate Policymaking in the United States* (Institute for International Economics, 1989).

Ryutaro Komiya and Miyako Suda, *Japan's Foreign Exchange Policy 1971–1982* translated by Colin McKenzie (Allen and Unwin, 1991).

Kozo Yamamura and Yasukichi Yasuba, eds., *The Political Economy of Japan*: Vol. 1, *The Domestic Transformation* (Stanford, 1987).

Takashi Inoguchi and Daniel Okimoto, eds., *The Political Economy of Japan*: Vol. 2, *The Changing International Context* (Stanford, 1988).

Shumpei Kumon and Henry Rosovsky, eds., *The Political Economy of Japan*: Vol. 3, *Cultural and Social Dynamics* (Stanford, 1992).

CHAPTER 7

". . . this time. . .": Carmen M. Reinhart and Kenneth S. Rogoff, *This Time is Different: Eight Centuries of Financial Folly* (Princeton, 2009).

"manias. . .": Charles P. Kindleberger and Robert Z. Aliber, *Manias, Panics and Crashes: A History of Financial Crises*, 6th edition (Palgrave Macmillan, 2011).

". . . balance sheet recession. . .": Richard Koo, *Balance Sheet Recession: Japan's Struggle with Uncharted Economics and its Global Implications* (John Wiley & Sons, 2003).

". . . percentage of household debt": I am grateful to Jesper Koll for this observation.

Other Recommended Reading

Christopher Wood, *The Bubble Economy: The Japanese Economic Collapse* (Sidgwick and Jackson, 1992).

Richard Koo, *The Holy Grail of Macroeconomics: Lessons from Japan's Great Recession* (John Wiley & Sons, 2009).

Richard Katz, *Japanese Phoenix: The Long Road to Economic Revival* (M. E. Sharpe, 2003).

Roger Lowenstein, *When Genius Failed: The Rise and Fall of Long-Term Capital Management* (Random House, 2000)

CHAPTER 8

". . . most profitable": Draws heavily on Ulrike Schaede, "Show Me the Money: Japan's Most Profitable Companies in the 2000s," School of International Relations and Pacific Studies, University of California, San Diego, Working Paper, February 2011, http://irps.ucsd.edu/assets/001/500973.pdf.

"exceeds 70 percent": ibid., p. 6.

"Japan boasts some. . .": These numbers come from Stefan Lippert, who has researched Japan's "Hidden Champions" and published the results widely. See http://www.ohmae.ac.jp/gmba/faculty/faculty/lippert.html.

". . . essentially impossible. . .": Mikuni, *Japan's Policy Trap*, p. 67.

"Such workers": Jonathan Adams, "Temp Nation, the Decline of Life Time Employment in Japan" (Global Post), http://www.globalpost.com/dispatch/commerce/100510/japan-economy-temporary-workers.

"Sometimes the answer. . .": I am grateful to Edward W. Desmond for this observation. Desmond was a *Time* correspondent in Tokyo; his next assignment involved covering the Silicon Valley for *Fortune*.

"Some one-sixth. . .": Ulrike Schaede, *Choose and Focus: Japanese Business Strategies for the 21st Century* (Cornell, 2008), pp. 142–143.

". . . one business leader. . .": The reference is to Richard J. Dyck, chairman of Alphana Technologies, K.K., and board member of the Japan External Trade Organization.

". . . fundamental disagreements. . .": *Wall Street Journal*, April 18, 2012.

Other Recommended Reading

Michael Porter, Hirotaka Takeuchi, and Mariko Sakakibara, *Can Japan Compete?* (Perseus, 2000).

Gillian Tett, *Saving the Sun: Shinsei and the Battle for Japan's Future* (Random House, 2004).

Steven K. Vogel, *Japan Remodeled: How Government and Industry are Reforming Japanese Capitalism* (Cornell, 2006).

Marie Anchordoguy, *Reprogramming Japan: The High Tech Crisis under Communitarian Capitalism* (Cornell, 2005).

Emi Osono, Norihiko Shimizu, and Hirotaka Takeuchi, *Extreme Toyota: Radical Contradictions that Drive Success at the World's Best Manufacturer* (John Wiley & Sons, 2008).

Tim Clark and Carl Kay, *Saying Yes to Japan: How Outsiders are Reviving a Trillion Dollar Services Market* (Vertical, Inc., 2005).

Michael Woodford, *Exposure: Inside the Olympus Scandal; How I Went from CEO to Whistleblower* (Portfolio Hardcover, 2012).

CHAPTER 9

". . . weak, irresponsible. . .": Buruma, *A Japanese Mirror*, p. 203.

". . . as one writer suggested. . .": Sady Doyle at http://www.theatlantic.com/entertainment/archive/2010/08/mad-mens-very-modern-sexism-problem/60788/.

". . . End of Men. . .": Hanna Rosin, *The End of Men and the Rise of Women* (Riverhead, 2012).

". . . An important new paper. . .": Hitoshi Kawano, "Japanese Combat Morale: A Case Study of the Thirty Seventh Division," in *The Battle for China*, pp. 328–353.

"Mickey Kaus. . .": *The End of Equality* (Basic Books, 1995).

". . . Michael Lind. . .": *Next American Nation: The New Nationalism and the Fourth American Revolution* (Free Press, 1996).

Other Recommended Reading

Joseph J. Tobin, ed., *Re-made in Japan: Everyday Life and Consumer Taste in a Changing Society* (Yale, 1992).

Michael Zielenziger, *Shutting Out the Sun: How Japan Created its Own Lost Generation* (Random House, 2006).

Sabine Frühstück and Anne Walthall, eds., *Recreating Japanese Men* (University of California, 2011).

Lucy Birmingham and David McNeill, *Strong in the Rain: Surviving Japan's Earthquake, Tsunami, and Fukushima Nuclear Disaster* (Palgrave Macmillan, 2012).

CHAPTER 10

"Japan sits. . .": Andrew DeWit, "Distributed Power and Incentives in Post-Fukushima Japan," *The Asia-Pacific Journal*, Vol. 10, Issue 49(2), December 3, 2012. DeWit is arguably the leading authority writing in English on Japan's energy future.

"... analysts of power...": E. H. Norman, Masao Maruyama, Karel van Wolferen.

"... JSP on the left": Richard J. Samuels, "Kishi and Corruption: An Anatomy of the 1955 System," Japan Policy Research Institute Working Paper 83, December 2001, http://www.jpri.org/publications/workingpapers/wp83.html.

"... the secret...": Mikuni, *Japan's Policy Trap*, p. 52.

"Ikeda would call Tanaka...": Jacob M. Schlesinger, *Shadow Shoguns: The Rise and Fall of Japan's Postwar Political Machine* (Simon and Schuster, 1997), p. 57.

"The Ford White House...": ibid., p. 87.

"Schwarzkopf...": *It Doesn't Take a Hero: The Autobiography of General H. Norman Schwarzkopf* (Bantam, 1993).

"... as Richard Koo...": *The Holy Grail*, p. 283.

"Hirohito quit Yasukuni visits over concerns about war criminals": *New York Times*, April 26, 2007.

"reactionary nationalism with neoliberalism": I am grateful to Koichi Nakano for this formulation.

Other Recommended Reading

Jake Adelstein, *Tokyo Vice* (Constable & Robinson, 2009) on the Japanese underground, the *yakuza*.

Gerald L. Curtis, *The Japanese Way of Politics* (Columbia, 1988).

John Creighton Campbell, *How Policies Change: The Japanese Government and the Aging Society* (Princeton, 1992).

Gavan McCormack, *The Emptiness of Japanese Affluence* (M. E. Sharpe, 1996).

Mark Selden, "Japan, the United States and Yasukuni Nationalism: War, Historical Memory and the Future of the Asia Pacific," *Asia Pacific Journal: Japan Focus*, September 10, 2008, http://www.japanfocus.org/-Mark-Selden/2892.

Takashi Oka, *Policy Entrepreneurship and Elections in Japan: A Political Biography of Ozawa Ichiro* (Routledge, 2011).

CHAPTER 11

"Clinton took the highly unusual step...": "U.S. Concerned about New Japanese Premier Hatoyama," *Washington Post*, December 29, 2009.

"no such dissembling": http://www.fas.org/sgp/crs/natsec/R42645.pdf.

"regardless of who": See more at http://www.japanfocus.org/-Gavan-McCormack/3059#sthash.nwukkoM2.dpuf.

"Richard Koo argued": Quoted in Ambrose Evans-Pritchard, "The Bank of Japan Must Crush all Resistance," *The Telegraph*, May 24, 2013.

"Chief among them" (note): Mark Thompson, "South Korean Probe Won't Settle Warship Dispute," *Time*, August 18, 2010.

"Critics charged...": For example, Barbara Chicerio, "Trans Pacific Partnership and Monsanto," *Nation of Change*, June 24, 2013.

"Wikileaks released...": "Secret Trans-Pacific Partnership Agreement (TPP)—IP Chapter," http://wikileaks.org/tpp/.

"Paul Krugman...": "No Big Deal," *New York Times*, February 27, 2014.

"Its very structure. . .": Michael Pettis, *The Great Rebalancing: Trade, Conflict, and the Perilous Road Ahead for the Global Economy* (Princeton, 2013) provides a comprehensive demonstration.

"The Japanese maintain. . .": See http://pendientedemigracion.ucm.es/info/unisci/revistas/UNISCIDP32-1DRIFTE.pdf.

"would outlive it": See David Scofield, "Sex and Denial in South Korea," *Asia Times*, May 26, 2004.

"Tamogami may have. . ." (note): Benn Stell, *The Battle of Bretton Woods: John Maynard Keynes, Harry Dexter White, and the Making of a New World Order* (Princeton University Press, 2013).

"Miyazaki. . .": Mark Schilling, "Debate Still Rages over Abe-endorsed WWII Drama" *Japan Times*, February 20, 2014.

"In February 2014. . .": "Pork Filled Supplementary Budget," *Japan Times*, February 13, 2013.

"major Japanese magazine": The magazine in question is *Shukan Gendai*. Michael Hoffman, "Japan's Future May Be Stunted by Its Past," *Japan Times*, March 16, 2014.

Other Recommended Reading

Mayumi Itoh, *The Hatoyama Dynasty: Japanese Political Leadership Through the Generations* (Palgrave Macmillan, 2003).

Laura Hein and Mark Selden, eds., *Islands of Discontent: Okinawan Responses to Japanese and American Power* (Rowman & Littlefield, 2003).

Paul Morris, Naoko Shimazu, Edward Vickers, eds., *Imagining Japan in Postwar East Asia: Identity Politics, Schooling, and Popular Culture* (Routledge, 2013).

John J. Mearsheimer, *The Tragedy of Great Power Politics* (Norton, 2001).

Richard J. Samuels, *Securing Japan: Tokyo's Grand Strategy and the Future of East Asia* (Cornell, 2008).

Richard J. Samuels, *3.11: Disaster and Change in Japan* (Cornell, 2013).

Index

3/11, xii, 199, 203–4, 229, 256–58, 340–45, 360, 390
Abe Shintaro, 310–11, 365, 395
Abe Shinzo
  about, 395
  apologist for wartime actions, 88*n*11
  China and, 312
  deflation and, 199
  economic revival and, 356–63, 358*n*14, 359*n*15
  grappling with the past, 377
  Koizumi stepping down and, 310
  overreach of, 379–86
  political lineage of, 310
  priorities of, 363–68
  return of, 354–56
  Right and, 311
  spiritual crisis in Japan, 308
  wage and tax policy of, 214
Adams, Will, 36–37
aesthetics
  in Heian period literature, 13–15
  Muromachi period, 24
  ugliness and, 237
  warriors and, 24
  Zen Buddhism and, 24–26
Africa, Belgium and, 69
agriculture, 64, 365
Ahn Jung-geun, 379
Ainu peoples, 18–19

Airbus, 206
Akechi Mitsuhide, 28–29
Akihito, Emperor, 108
All Nippon Airways (ANA) and the Lockheed Scandal, 284–85
Always: San-chome no Yūhi, 237, 244, 383–84
Amazing Japan (Odorokubeki Nihon) (*The Economist*), 97
Amazon, 204, 208
American Embassy in Tokyo, 318
ANA and the Lockheed Scandal, 284–85
Anglo-Japanese Alliance of 1902, 70
anime, 233
Antaku, Emperor, 16
anti-nuclear activists, 119
Apple, 173, 204, 211, 216
Arakawa Shizuka, 389
architecture, Heian, 11
architecture, medieval, 23
Argentina, 96
Aristotle, 235
Armitage, Richard, 320, 336, 338
Armstrong, Rodney, 344
Army, Imperial Japanese
  brutality of the, 84–85
  in China, 90
  disbanding the, 100, 112
  Navy, Imperial Japanese and the, 268

Army, Imperial Japanese (*cont.*)
    post-Meiji hijacking of state by, 376
    in Russo-Japanese War, 71
    veto power in government, 86
Army, Kwantung, 85, 87–88, 91
Asahi Shimbun, 297, 329, 361, 381
Asano of Hiroshima, 39
Asanuma Inejiro, 94f, 122, 395
Asher, David, 318, 353
Ashida Hitoshi, about, 395–96
Ashikaga or Muromachi Shogunate, 21,
    23, 27, 299
Ashikaga Takauchi, 21
Ashikaga Yoshimitsu, 24–25
Asia, Japan's separation from, 375–79
Asian Development Bank, 357
Asian financial crisis, 193–95
Aso Taro, 312–13, 362, 396
Association of War-Bereaved Families, 306
atomic bombs, 84, 91, 109
Aum Shinrikyo, 222n10
Aztec empire, 35

Bagehot, Walter, 188–89
bailout of financial system, 188–90
Bali, 166
Bank of Japan (BOJ)
    bubble and raised interest rates by
        the, 179
    credit provided by, 139
    economic revival and the, 356–58
    gold exchange, 169
    interventions to maintain currency
        rate, 172
    Kanemaru and the, 290
bankruptcy
    assets with collapsed values, 179–80
    assumption regarding Japanese
        companies and, 191
    bureaucracy and, 141
    financial system, 189
    industrial organizations and, 131
    manufacturers, 206
    Sogo Department Store, 191
banks
    assumptions of, 191
    bubble economy and, 177–79, 186, 188
    lending decisions, 258

long-term, 139n6
Meiji period, 64–65, 66
panics and, 189, 189–90
post office and, 304–5
shortage of funds, 138–39
baseball and salaryman culture, 152–57,
    156n1, 249–50
Beck, Glenn, 252
Belgium, 69
Bernanke, Ben, 357, 358, 358n14
Bezos, Jeff, 208
Biden, Joe, 379
birth rate, 161, 164, 166, 168
Bismarck, Otto von, 67, 69
Blair, Tony, 304
Blueprint for a New Japan (Ozawa), 295
Boeing, 206
BOJ. *See* Bank of Japan
Boxer Rebellion, 70
Bo Xilai, 351
Bretton Woods system, 169, 171, 172, 183, 281
Brezhnev, Leonid, 258, 263
Britain
    class division in, 253, 254
    dollar/yen rates and, 183
    end of empire, 92
    importance to U.S, 317
    India and, 326, 327
    Japan's appropriation of knowledge
        from, 64
    men in, 250–51
    monarchy in, 80
Brooks, William L., 335n8
Brown, Herman, 280
Brown, Michael, 263
Brunei, 365
Buddhism
    aesthetics and Zen, 24–26, 25n8
    cremation and, 6
    education at temples, 74–75
    eighth century, 9–10
    forgetting of the Law (mappō), 15
    Nichiren, 25, 25n8, 122
    Oda Nobunaga and, 28
    on sexual desire, 48
    Shinto and, 7, 75
    temples, 13n5, 19, 74–75
    Tokugawa period, 74

Budget Bureau of the Ministry of
    Finance, 276
Bungei Shunju, 283, 284
bureaucracy
    as above politics, 337
    decision making and the obvious, 373,
        373*n*20
    DPJ and, 355
    high-speed growth and, 140–42
    rule by, 111
    Tanaka and, 329–30
    taxes and, 340–41
    and the US military, 372
Burma, 90
Buruma, Ian, xxii
Bush, George H. W., 187, 291, 293
Bush, George W., 189, 256, 304, 306, 320,
    334, 341, 355–56
business/corporations
    bureaucracy, 140–42, 142*n*7
    China and Japanese recovery, 309
    entrepreneurship, 144–45
    free-market capitalism and, 305
    free money and, 177, 185–86
    global brands and foreign direct
        investment, 216–22, 218*n*8, 220*n*9
    global crisis of capitalism, 227–30
    globalization, 215, 215–16
    government run like, 341–42
    high-speed growth and, 128–30
    Japan, Inc., 141, 142, 332, 363
    Korean challenge, 225–27, 225*n*11
    LDP and, 271, 275–76
    limited-liability, 128, 227–29
    monopolies, 40, 142*n*7, 205, 229
    overview, 203–8
    service sector, 208–9, 208*n*4
    socializing private *zaibatsu*, 112
    on sovereignty surrender to the US, 332
    temporary workers, 212, 213–14, 305
    Tokugawa period and modern, 44
    writing off sunk costs, 222–25
    See also employment practices

Calder, Kent, 117
Campbell, Kurt, 318
capital accumulation and first constitutional
    government, 67–68, 68*n*3

capitalism
    American, 225
    contradictions of, 211
    creative destruction and, 222–23
    free-market, 305
    global crisis of, 227–30
    Great Depression and, 88
    Japan's feudalism and, 22
    WW II and, 111
capo regimes (Kanemaru and Takeshita),
    289–92, 291*n*7
Carter, Jimmy, 172, 331
Casio, 173
Catholicism, 26–27, 75, 76*n*5
CCP (Chinese Communist Party), 351–53
census taking, 43
Center for a New American Security, 318
Center for Strategic and International
    Studies, 318
Chang'An (now Xi'an), 9, 10
Cheney, Dick, 263
Chernobyl, 257
Chiang Kai-shek, 89, 170, 351, 370
Chidorigafuchi cemetery, 379
Chikamatsu Monzaemon, 50
children
    birth rate, 161, 164, 166, 168
    care of, 159–61, 164
    grappling with the past and, 377, 380
    television shows for, 292, 292*n*8
    See also education
Chile, 365
China
    Abe and, 312, 362, 379–80
    Ashikaga shoguns relations with, 24–25
    balance of power and, 368–71
    Chongqing bombing, 84
    Diaoyu/Senkaku Islands, 345, 346–54,
        347*f*, 353*n*11
    diplomatic relations with Japan, 283
    family-blood ties in, 246
    FDI and, 217
    foreign investment in, 137
    Fukuzawa Yukichi and, 77
    Greater East Asia War, 86–88
    Hideyoshi and, 29–30
    high-speed growth institutions, 98
    industrialization of, 207

China (*cont.*)
  iPhones and, 206
  Japanese assurance regarding WW II
    and, 110
  Japanese companies in, 205
  Japanese culture in relation to, 76
  Japanese engineers in, 212, 217
  Japan's economic recovery and, 309
  Japan's premodern borrowings from,
    4–6, 9, 11, 12–13
  Kamakura and Muromachi
    shogunates and, 23
  Kublai Khan and, 20
  Manchuria, 87–88, 88*n*11, 91
  Marco Polo and Nomonhan incidents,
    89–90
  Nanjing massacre, 84
  Obama and, 317
  occupied Japan and, 100, 101, 113
  Okinawa and, 322–23, 322*n*5
  Ozawa and, 309, 322, 336
  Philippines and, 350
  premodern Japan and, 3, 35
  Pure Land sects, 25
  Senkaku/Diaoyu Islands, 345, 346–54,
    347*f*, 353*n*11
  Sino-Japanese War of 1895, 69–70, 70*n*4
  Taiwan and, 324
  Tanaka and, 287, 289, 309
  Tibet and, 323
  US and, 170, 350, 351
  US/Japan relationship and, 319,
    342–43, 368–74
  Vietnam and, 5, 350
  Western occupation of ports in, 53–54
  Yasukuni Shrine and, 312, 379–80
Chinese Communist Party (CCP), 351–53
Chinese language, 5, 12
Choshu, 39, 59, 63
Christianity
  Christian weddings, 7
  during Meiji period, 75–76, 76*n*5
  during Tokugawa Shogunate, 36–38
  Nagasaki bombings and, 38
  Oda Nobunaga and, 28
Christian weddings, 7
Christmas, 162, 162*n*2
Churchill, Winston, 92, 278

CIA (Central Intelligence Agency), 113,
  116, 270, 270*n*1, 271, 286
Cisco, 173
class
  based revolution, 55
  Christianity and peasants, 37
  craftsmen, 38
  leadership class decline, 256–63, 260*n*8
  lower, 25, 253
  lower-middle, 143
  merchant, 25, 38, 74
  middle, 251–52
  mixing of classes in the Tokugawa
    period, 45
  nationalism and, 74
  overview of class division in Japan,
    38–39, 38*n*1
  re-emergence of, 251–56
  rigidity of distinctions, 58*n*5
  untouchables, 38*n*1
  in the US, 374
  See also peasants; *samurai*
Clean Government Party (Komeito), 122
Clinton, Bill, 190, 193, 296, 320
Clinton, Hillary, 317, 335, 336, 352
Cold War, 22, 101
comfort women, 380, 380*n*22
Communism, 88, 101, 102, 106, 122, 272, 311
Communist Party, 101
competition, control of, 130–31, 131*n*1
conscription, 72–73
Constitution
  capital accumulation and the first,
    67–68, 68*n*3
  GHQ writing the, 104, 104*n*1
  Meiji period, 80–81, 104
  on war-making potential, 334
contradiction
  of capitalism, 211
  creativity and, 235
  doublethink, 298
  learning to cope with, 237
  Meiji political fictions, 110
  reality management, 143–47, 145*n*8
  realized goals and, 385
  religious practices, 7
  Tokugawa period and, 44–45, 51, 53
  in US, 385*n*25

US/Japan relations, 326
vocabulary to describe, 44–45
copyright, 365
Corporation Law of 2006, 221
corporations. *See* business/corporations
creative destruction, 222–23
Cronkite, Walter, 380
Cuba, 333, 380
culture
    artistic legacy of the Heian period, 11–12
    cheapening and coarsening of, 150–52
    foundations for high-speed growth,
        114–16
    high, 23–26, 25n8, 45
    Meiji period changing, 71–79, 77n6
    the noble loser, 16–17
    predictability, 115–16, 127
    race and, 78–79
    seductive tactics, 101–2
    Tokugawa period and modern, 44–45
    Tokugawa Shogunate, 43, 45
    under feudalism, 23–26
    See also aesthetics; contradiction;
        popular/mass culture; salaryman
        culture; social and cultural change
Curley, James Michael, 116
Czechoslovakia, 104

daimyō (lords)
    allegiance and "fiefs (han)" of, 22–23,
        24, 27, 29
    as bureaucrats, 43
    peasantry and the, 71–72
    pederasty and, 37
    requirement to spend time in Edo, 42
    samurai fealty to their, 39
    use of force by, 34
Daley, Richard J., 116, 274, 285
Date Masamune, 27
Date of Sendai, 39
Dean, Howard, 382
Defense Agency, 319
deficits, fiscal
    accountability and, 358
    Japan, 188, 191–93, 196n4
    stimulus and, 196n4
    US, 150, 173, 196n4
de Gaulle, Charles, 256, 372–73, 383

Deming, Edward, 207
Democratic Party (US), 171n7, 174, 187, 193
Democratic Party of Japan (DPJ)
    "agents of influence" and the, 334–35
    destruction of the, 363
    founding of, 340
    Fukushima and the, 355
    gains of 2003 election, 309–10
    Hatoyama government destruction,
        328–32
    nuclear power and the, 262
    Ozawa opponents and, 344–45
    sovereignty of Japan and the, 327
    taxes and campaign promises, 340–41
Deng Xiaoping, 137, 287, 350
Denmark, 330
Dentsu, 146–47
Diamond, Jared, 43
Diaoyu/Senkaku Islands, 345, 346–54,
    347f, 353n11
Diet (parliament)
    bank bailout, 190
    debates in the, 144
    Democratic Party and the, 310
    election system for the,
        300–303, 301n13
    electoral districts, 271
    establishment of the, 68
    LDP and the, 270, 275, 300, 303
    legislative authority of the, 105
    Meiji leaders' decision-making and
        the, 81
    Ozawa and the, 295
    Tanaka and the, 287
    taxation and the, 196, 198
divorce, 48, 241–42
Dodge, Joseph, 106, 112–13
Doi Takako, about, 396
Dominicans, 36
dot.com bubble, 181
Dower, John, 103, 107, 109, 111, 332
DPJ. *See* Democratic Party of Japan
Dulles, John Foster, 114n3, 317
Dutch East India Company (VOC), 40
Dutch East Indies, 90, 92

earthquake of 1923 (Tokyo), 83, 84
earthquake of 1995 (Kobe), 262

earthquake/tsunami of March 2011, xii, 199,
　203–4, 229, 256–58, 340–45, 360, 390
East Asia
　balance of power in, 368–71
　disputes and loss of face, 353
　growth model, 98, 114, 373–74
　Japan's place in, 376
　nationalism and xenophobia in, 86
　US military presence in, 150, 170, 308,
　　319, 321, 335n8, 365
Easter Island, 43
East Germany, 327
"East Sea" (Korea's preferred name for
　the Sea of Japan), 380
economy and finance
　Asian financial crisis, 193–95
　assumptions of bankers and fiscal
　　deficit, 191–93
　bailout of financial system, 188–90
　balance sheet recession, 179–80
　bubble economy of late 1980s, 177–79
　capital accumulation, 67–68
　Germany as model, 64–65
　government spending, 195–200, 196n4
　high-speed growth and global
　　economic framework, 168–74,
　　171n7, 172n8
　mania-panic-crash-balance sheet
　　recession, Japanese experience,
　　181–88, 184n2, 185n3
　rice and, 15
　savings, 138
　state power and economic activity, 112
　Tokugawa Shogunate, 40–45
　See also postwar miracle
Edano Yukio, 262, 341, 396
Edo (city), 24, 31, 39, 45
Edo period. See Tokugawa (Edo) period
education
　high-speed growth and, 133–36, 134n3,
　　136n4
　indoctrination of the peasantry, 73
　Japanese children in other countries, 215
　literacy, 45, 55, 133, 134, 134n3, 150
　lower-class males, 253
　occupation reforms and the political
　　Right, 273
　PTAs, 160–61

US public, 64
　on WW II, 110
　See also children
Eien no zero (Eternal Zero), 384
Eisenhower, Dwight D., 120, 121, 256,
　314f, 372
elections, 95, 107, 267, 271
　See also politics
electoral reforms of 1994, 300–303, 301n13
Embracing Defeat (Dower), 103
Emishi peoples, 18–19
emperors
　divinity of, 259
　GHQ's treatment of, 107
　imperial institution, 6–8
　Tenno Heika (heavenly sovereign), 7–8
　tombs of, 2f, 6
employment practices
　changing, 210–14, 210n5, 211n6, 214n7
　debt and employment levels, 196
　firing, 129, 143–44, 212
　high-speed growth and, 131–33, 133n2
　labor militancy, 106
　lifetime employment, 131, 191, 204,
　　210, 211, 214, 330
　retirement, 212
　women, 164–65, 167–68
　See also salaryman culture
Enigma of Japanese Power (van
　Wolferen), 294–95
Enryaku-ji (temple network), 10
entrepreneurship, 144–45, 249
environmental damage in high growth
　years, 151–52
Erhard, Ludwig, 317
Ethiopia, 33
Eurasia, Japan's relation to, 3
Europe
　airline manufacturing and, 206
　balance of power in, 369
　early European travels to Japan, 26–27
　FDI and, 217
　feudalism in, 22
　imperialism of, 33
　Iron Curtain, 104
　Tokugawa Shogunate and, 35–36
exchange rates, 170, 172–73, 183–84, 193–94
Ezoe Hiromasa, 187, 290–91

family, company as, 128–29
family, in television, 145
farmers
    LDP and, 117, 123
    taxation and, 197–98
    trade and, 364, 365
Fast Retailing, 208, 208n4
FBI (Federal Bureau of Investigation), 221
FDA (Food and Drug Administration), 258
FDI. *See* foreign direct investment (FDI)
    and global brands
Federation of Economic Organizations
    (*Keidanren*), 140
Feith, Douglas, 263
feudalism, 21–27, 21n7, 25n8, 268
finance. *See* economy and finance
financial system, high speed growth and,
    136–40, 138n5, 139n6
Financial Times, 221
Finland, 377
firearms, 26, 27, 28, 35, 40
firebombing, 109
Fischer, Irving, 357
Fitzgerald, F. Scott, 251
flower arrangement, 161
Forbes's list of the wealthiest people, 208
Ford, Gerald R., 286
Foreign Correspondents Club of Japan, 283
foreign direct investment (FDI) and
    global brands, 216–22, 218n8,
    220n9, 222n10
Foreign Ministry, 319
France
    conservative government in, 304
    dollar/yen rates and, 183
    gold exchange, 170
    Indochina and, 92
    Japan's appropriation of knowledge
        from, 64
    Southeast Asian colonies, 89–90
    temporary workers in, 212
    WW I and, 84
Francis Xavier, Saint, 26, 36
Freedom and People's Rights movement,
    68
French Indochina, 90, 92
Friedman, Milton, 172
Fuji film, 173

Fujitsu, 173, 205
Fujiwara family, 8–10, 15–16, 90
Fukuda Takeo, 284, 287, 303, 311, 396
Fukuda Yasuo, 311–12, 396
Fukuoka, 20
Fukushima nuclear plant, 229, 256–58,
    260–62, 390
Fukuzawa Yukichi, 77, 391
Futenma Marine Base
    3/11 earthquake and the, 343–44
    Abe and the, 367–68
    about, 322–24, 322n5, 323n6
    Japan's "Agents of Influence" and, 332–40
    Kadena Air Base and, 325–26, 344
    Kan and the, 342
    negotiations and agreements
        regarding, 326–32, 338
    Okinawa, 322–23, 322n5
    Okinawan opinion on the, 262, 324–26
    rape of Okinawan girl, 325, 362n16
    strategic significance of, 335n8
    US Senators on relocation of, 344
future for Japan, 385–90
futures market in Osaka, 42

gambling, 143
Gameboy, 233
gangurogyaru, 251
Gates, Robert M., 317, 335
GDP, 96, 182, 195, 196n4
geisha, 46–47, 162–63
Gempei War, 16
Genba Koichiro, 341
gender. *See* men, Japanese; women,
    Japanese
General Electric, 258
Genroku era, 53
geography of Japan, 3
Gephardt, Richard, 187
Germany
    balance of power in Europe and, 369
    conservative government in, 304
    dollar/yen rates and, 183
    East, 327
    economy of, 90, 149
    examining the past, 108, 110
    Hidden Champions in, 206n2
    importance to US, 317

Germany (*cont.*)
 Japanese education modeled on, 134
 Meiji banks modeled on, 64–65, 66
 Nazis, 87, 88, 89, 90, 110, 112, 308
 Obama and, 317
 recovery from WW II, 99
 Sino-Japanese War and, 69
 treatment of the 1930s in, 308
 Tripartite Pact, 90
 US dollar and, 170
 war-time actions of, 84
 WW I and, 84
Ghosn, Carlos, 219
GHQ. *See* occupation of Japan
Gibbs, Robert, 317
global brands and foreign direct
  investment, 216–22, 220*n*9, 222*n*10
global crisis of capitalism, 227–30
globalization, 215–16
Gobineau, Count, 78
Go-Daigo, Emperor, 21
Gojung, King, 71
gold-backed financial instruments, 66–67
gold to dollar rates, 169–70, 172
Google, 211, 332
Gotoda Masaharu, 396–97
government spending, 195–200, 196*n*4
Great Depression, 88, 96, 101, 180, 181
Great Leap Forward, 376
Great Proletarian Cultural Revolution, 376
Great Recession, 180
Gree, 208, 211
Green, Michael, 318, 353
Grew, Joseph, 319*n*2
Guam, 326
Gulf War, 293–94, 294*n*9, 334
guruppu gaisha, 140
Gyaru (gal), 232*f*, 238–40, 255

Hagel, Chuck, 379
haiku, 43
Hakata Bay, 20
han (fiefs or domains), 23

Hanshin Tigers, 156
Hanyu Yuzuru, 389–90
Hasekura Tsunenaga, 27
Hashimoto Ryutaro, 190, 293, 299, 301–2, 397

Hashimoto Toru, 362, 362*n*16, 397
Hata Tsutomu, 299, 397
Hatoyama Ichiro, about, 397
Hatoyama Yukio
 about, 397
 destruction of the government of,
  328–32, 352
 DPJ and, 340
 foreign policy/Futenma change and,
  321–22, 337, 338, 339
 Obama and, 315–18
Hawaii, 69, 71
health care/insurance, 95, 150, 205*n*1, 312
Hearn, Lafcadio, xxii
Heian-kyo. See Kyoto
Heian period, 10–18, 24, 245
Henderson, Bruce, 114–15
hentai (animated features of sexual
  perversions), 44
herbivore males, 242–46, 243*n*2, 244*n*3, 251
Hidden Champions, 206, 206*n*2, 209, 216
Hideyoshi, 29–31
high-speed growth consequences
 baseball and the salaryman culture,
  152–57, 156*n*1
 costs, 150–52
 global economic framework, 168–74,
  171*n*7, 172*n*8
 overview, 149–50
 women, 158–68, 162*n*2, 163*n*3, 164*n*4,
  165*n*5, 167*n*6
high-speed growth institutions
 bureaucracy, 140–42, 142*n*7
 corporations, 128–30
 economic theory and, 97–98
 education, 133–36, 134*n*3, 136*n*4
 employment practices, 131–33, 133*n*2
 financial system, 136–40, 138*n*5, 139*n*6
 industrial associations and the control
  of competition, 130–31, 131*n*1
 management of reality, 142–47, 145*n*8,
  146*n*9
 overview, 127–28
 See also postwar miracle
hikikomori, 250–51
Hirohito, Emperor, 79, 81, 85, 108, 307
Hirose Electric, 205
Hiroshima, 84, 91, 109

Hitachi, 112, 129, 173, 205
Hitler, Adolf, 89, 90, 383
HIV/AIDS, 258
Hojo family, 21
Hojo Masako, 19
Hokkaido, 18, 103
Hollywood, 187
homosexuality, 14, 77, 245, 246–47
Honda, 130, 131, 140, 141, 173
Honda, Mike, 380n22
Honda Soiichiro, 256
Honma Masaharu, 109
Honshu, 279
Hosokawa Morihiro, 295–96, 300,
    381–82, 397–98
Hume, David, 67–68, 68n3
Hungary, 327
Hurricane Katrina, 257, 263, 334
Hussein, Saddam, 293
Hyundai, 66

IBJ (Industrial Bank of Japan), 130, 138, 191
IBM, 142, 164n4
Ibuka Masaru, 219
Iemitsu, 46
Iijima Isao, 355–56, 398
Ikeda Daisaku, about, 398
Ikeda Hayato, 97, 121, 126f, 137, 140, 142,
    256, 278, 398
Iki Island, 20
IMF (International Monetary Fund), 193,
    357n13
Imperial Household Agency, 307
Imperial Institution, 6–8, 105, 108, 111, 252
Imperial Palace, 177
Inamori Kazuo, 256
Inayama Yoshihiro, 256
Incan empire, 36
Income Doubling Plan, 97
India, 96, 317, 350
Indochina, 90, 92, 350
industrial associations, 130–31, 131n1, 140
Industrial Bank of Japan (IBJ), 130, 138, 191
industrial organization
    birth of modern, 65–67
    father of the modern, 62f
    Germany as model, 64–65
    group companies, 66

zaibatsu, 66, 112
inflation, 149, 180, 184
ink paintings, 23, 45, 152, 233
Inose Naoki, 381, 398
Inoue Kaoru, about, 391
institutions of high-speed growth. See
    high-speed growth institutions
Intel, 173
intellectual property, 365
Interior Ministry (Naimusho), 112
International Finance Bureau, 194
International Monetary Fund (IMF), 193,
    357n13
International Trade and Industry, 112
Internet, 136n4, 181
iPhones/iPads, 206, 332
Iranian revolution of 1979, 172
Iraq, 305–6, 306n18, 334
Iron Curtain, 104
Ise Shrine, 7
Ishiba Shigeru, 399
Ishibashi Tanzan, 256, 399
Ishihara Shintaro, 272n2, 352–53, 353n11,
    362, 399
Ishikawa Ryo, 249
isolation, Tokugawa period, 35–38
Israel, 102, 323, 333
Itagaki Taisuke, 68, 80, 391
Italy, 90
Itami Juzo, 222n10
Ito Hirobumi, 379, 391
Ito Masatoshi, 208
Iwakuni, US Marine base at, 324
Iwakura Tomomi, 64, 65–67, 67, 391
Iwasaki Yataro, 62f, 65–67, 392
Iwate Prefecture, 292
Izumo no Okuni, 46

Jameson, Sam, 335n8
Japan Association of Corporate
    Executives, 140
Japan Defense Agency, 303
Japanese gardens, 23
Japanese government bonds (JGBs), 359
Japanese language, 5, 5n1, 12, 77, 134, 218,
    218n8
Japanese, written, 5, 5n2, 12–13, 134n3
Japan, Inc., 141, 142, 332, 363

Japan Restoration Party, 362
Japan Socialist Party (JSP)
    changes name to Social Democratic
        Party of Japan, 301
    DJP and, 344
    factions joining, 270
    LDP and the, 299–300
    as opposition party, 122
    Ozawa and the, 295
    scandals and the, 297
    US/Japan relationship and the, 277
Jesuits, 30, 36–37
Johnny's Jimusho, 245, 249, 250
Johnson, Chalmers, 97, 98, 372
Johnson, Lady Bird Taylor, 280
Johnson, Lyndon, 169, 279–81, 283n6,
    285, 317, 331, 383
JSP. *See* Japan Socialist Party
Judaism in Music (Wagner), 78
judiciary, 81

Kabuki
    beautiful boy archetype in, 17
    Kanadehon Chushingura, 308
    male prostitution and, 77
    Noh vs., 46
    origins of, 43, 45–46
Kabukicho Red-Light District, 176f
Kadena US Air Force base, 325–26, 344
Kagemusha, 28
Kagoshima, 58
Kaieda Banri, 344, 399
Kaifu Toshiki, 291, 399
Kaku Michio, 261
Kamakura, 18, 19
Kamakura period sculpture, 23
Kamakura shogunate, 19–21, 23, 24
Kamei Shizuka, 400
kamikaze (divine wind), 3, 20
kamikaze pilots, 17, 20, 307
Kamo River, 46
Kanadehon Chushingura, 308
Kanemaru Shin, 289–92, 292–93, 297,
    309, 400
Kan Naoto, 257–58, 262, 310, 340–45, 400
Katayama Tetsu, about, 400
Kato Koichi, about, 400
Katrina (hurricane), 257, 263, 334

Katsura Taro, about, 392
Kaus, Mickey, 252
Kawabata Yasunari, 279
Kawakubo Rei, 233
KBR, Inc., 280
Keenan, Joseph, 109
Keidanren, 140
Keizai Dōyūkai, 140
Kennedy, John F., 121, 279, 280
Kerry, John, 379
Keyence, 202f, 205
Keynesian policies, 95, 96, 358–59
Keynes, John Maynard, 121, 173, 188, 192, 195
Kido Koin, about, 392
Kim dynasty, 4
Kim Jong-Il, 338–39
kimonos, art of donning and wearing, 161
Kishi Nobusuke
    about, 88n11, 100, 400
    adoption of, 278n4
    good qualities of, 256
    the Left and, 270
    as mandarin, 278
    police powers and, 366
    resignation of, 121
    Tanaka and, 288, 361
    treaty signing, 314f
    ultra-right and, 286
    war criminal, 119
Kissinger, Henry, 283
Kitagawa Utamaro, 32f, 49, 162
Kobe earthquake of 1995, 262
Kobo Daishi, 13, 13n5
Koch brothers, 318n1
Kodama Yoshio, 286, 401
Koga Makoto, 401
Koizumi Junichiro
    Abe and, 355
    about, 303–10, 303n14, 304nn15–16,
        305n17, 306n18, 401
    Aso Taro and, 313
    Bush, G.W. and, 334
    Hosokawa and, 382
    Oda Nobunaga and, 36
    political capital of, 363
    Tanaka machine and, 287
    Treaty to move Futenma and, 326
Koizumi Shinjiro, about, 401

Kokoro (Natsume Soseki), 79–80
Komatsu, 173
Komei, Emperor, 58
Komeito, 274–75
Komeito Party, 122, 275*n*3
Komoto Toshio, about, 402
Konoe Fumimaro, 90
Kono Yohei, about, 402
Koo, Richard, 179, 180, 195–96, 358
Korea
    China and, 5
    comfort women, 378, 380, 380*n*22
    division of, 100
    East Sea, 380
    Hideyoshi and, 30, 370
    high-speed growth institutions, 98
    industrial organization in, 66
    iPhones and, 206
    Japanese alliance with, 378–79
    Japanese assurance regarding WW II
      and, 110
    Japanese engineers in, 212, 217
    Japanese vs. Korean corporations,
      225–27, 225*n*11
    Japan's economic methods and, 142
    Kublai Khan and, 20
    Nakasone and, 288
    navy vessel explosion, 338–39
    premodern Japan and, 3–4, 35
    reunification of, 377
    Senkaku Islands and, 346–47, 347*f*
    sex holidays in, 166, 379
    Sino-Japanese War of 1895, 69–70
    US defense of, 93
    See also North Korea
Korean War, 113, 324, 362*n*16
Koshien Giants/stadium, 155–56
Kotchian, A. Carl, 284, 285
Krugman, Paul, 358, 366
Kublai Khan, 19–20
Kurile island chain, 348
Kuroda Haruhiko, 357–59, 360
Kuroda, Hiroki, 157
Kuroda Kiyotaka, 392
Kurosawa Akira, 28
Kuwait, 293
Kwantung Army, 87–88, 91
Kyoto

based nobility, 63
companies in, 156–57, 156*n*1
daimyō and, 39
high growth years and defacing of, 151
premodern, 10
Shimabara, 45
Kyoto Tower Hotel, 148*f*, 151

labor/labor unions, 106, 118–19, 120–21, 133
laissez-faire policies, 96, 97
Last Samurai, The, 16–17, 66*n*2
LDP. *See* Liberal Democratic Party
leadership, decline of leadership class,
    256–63, 260*n*8
League of Nations, 88
Lee, Robert E., 17
Left, Japanese (political)
    Communism and the, 103
    goals and strategy, 383
    Komeito and, 275
    LDP and the, 118, 270, 272
    as opposition party, 122
    phase of the Occupation, 111–12
    policies of the, 270–71, 276–77
    power and the, 118–19
    re-emergence of the, 101
    Reverse Course and, 106
    Right, Japanese (political) and, 273
    Security treaty and the, 119–20
    sovereignty and the, 99, 100
    theories of the, 98
    See also Japan Socialist Party (JSP)
Lehman Brothers, 189
LeMay, Curtis, 109
Levin, Carl, 344
Levitt, Theodore, 206*n*2
Liaodong Peninsula, 70
Liberal Democratic Party (LDP)
    Abe and electoral victory for the, 360–63
    after Koizumi, 310–13
    business and the, 271, 275–76
    CIA and the, 113, 116
    Constitution and, 356
    creation of the, 118–19, 270, 270*n*1, 286
    election reforms and the, 301–3
    factionalism of the, 116–17, 272, 273–74
    formation of the, 113
    Fukuda Yasuo and the, 312

Liberal Democratic Party (*cont.*)
  Fukushima and the, 355
  JSP and the, 299–300
  Koizumi and the, 303, 309–10
  Korea and, 378
  New Japan Hands and the, 318
  nuclear power plants and the, 260
  Official Secrets Act, 367
  Okinawa US Marine Base and the,
    325, 326, 327–28, 331
  Ozawa and the, 295–96, 311
  rich persons in the, 252
  on sovereignty surrender to the US, 332
  US financial crisis and the, 312
  See also Right, Japanese (political)
Life magazine, 283n6
Liliuokalani, Queen, 71
Limbaugh, Rush, 252
limited-liability corporation, 128, 227–29
Lind, Michael, 252
literacy, during Tokugawa period, 45
literature, Heian, 11–15, 16–18
Lockheed scandal, 284–87
Lombard Street (Bagehot), 189
London, Japanese expatriates in, 215–16
Long Term Capital Management, 195
Long Term Credit Bank of Japan, 191
lords. *See* daimyō
*Lovers in the Upstairs Room of a
  Teahouse*, 32f, 49–50
loyalty, unquestioning, 222–23

Macao, 36
MacArthur, Douglas, 34, 101, 102, 103
McCain, John, 344
McCarthy, Joseph, 101
McGovern, George, 116
Mad Men, 238
Maehara Seiji, 341, 343, 402
Mailer, Norman, 272n2
Malacca, 36
Malay peninsula, 91
Malaysia, 98, 205, 350
management of reality, 142–47, 145n8,
  146n9, 235
Manchuria, 87–88, 88n11, 91, 112, 146, 380
Mandela, Nelson, 383
manga, 44, 233, 235, 236

manufacturing sector, 203–8
Mao Zedong, 90, 101, 370
March 2011 earthquake/tsunami, xii, 199,
  203–4, 229, 256–58, 340–45, 360, 390
Marco Polo Bridge, 89
marriage
  foreign company employment and,
    210–11
  Imperial succession and, 8
  lower-class women and, 253
  salaryman culture and, 153, 254–55
  social expectations for, 247
  women's role in, 158–60, 162, 167
Marubeni Corporation, 285
Maruyama Masao, xxv, 92
Marxism, 22, 54–55, 88, 95–96, 112, 123,
  211, 228
Masamune Shiro, 233
mass culture. *See* popular/mass culture
Masuzoe Yoichi, 381, 402
Matsuda Seiko, 166–67, 167n6
Matsukata Masayoshi, 67, 392
Matsushita, 129, 130, 187
Matsushita Institute of Government and
  Management (*Matsushita Seikei
  Juku*), 341, 344, 361
Matsushita Konosuke, 256, 341
May Day, 120–21
meat eating, 77, 77n6
media/press
  Abe and the, 311
  earthquake/tsunami of March 2011,
    260, 261, 262
  Hatoyama and, 328, 329
  Kanemaru and the, 298
  Koizumi and the, 304
  Komeito and the, 122n6
  NHK, 298, 380–81
  Noda and the, 354
  Ozawa and the, 361
  political/business order and the,
    106–7, 145–47, 298, 328, 355
  politics and, 266
  scandals and the, 297
  Tanaka and the, 283, 286, 298, 361
  US media in and on Japan, 320–21,
    334, 355n12
  Yomiuri, 154–55

Meiji, Emperor, 59
Meiji restoration to occupation
    baseball in the Meiji, 154
    bureaucracy beyond control, 81–82
    capital accumulation and constitutional
        government, 67–68, 68n3
    fascism roots, 82–88, 82n8, 84n9,
        87n10, 88n11
    Iwasaki and modern industrial
        organization, 65–67
    Marco Polo and Nomonhan incidents,
        89–90
    Meiji legacy, 79–81, 222, 227
    Meiji roots of Japan's modern tragedy,
        71–79, 76n5, 77n6, 78n7
    overview, 63–65
    Pearl Harbor, surrender, and legacy of
        war, 90–93
    Russo-Japanese War of 1904–1905, 70–71
    Sino-Japanese War of 1895, 69–70, 70n4
    State Shinto, 7
    Tokugawa rule replaced by Meiji, 34
men, Japanese
    arts and, 24
    conscription, 72–73
    dividing time between factory and
        farm, 72
    employment of, 131–33, 133n2, 136
    herbivore, 242–46, 243n2, 244n3, 251
    male group dynamics, 248–51, 248n6
    masculine identity, 246–48, 247nn4–5
    part time work, 167
    sex in the Tokugawa period, 46, 47–49
    See also salaryman culture
merchant class, 25, 38, 74
Mexico, 193
Michiko, Empress, 76n5
Microsoft, 173
Miki Takeo, 284, 402
Mikitani Hiroshi, 208, 209
military
    father of the modern Japanese, 81–82
    Heian, 15–17
    Meiji period daily life and, 73
    Self-Defense Forces, 105
    spending, 85, 114n3
    US military presence in East Asia, 150,
        170, 308, 319, 321, 365

Minami-Soma, 261
Minamoto (Genji) clan, 16–18, 19
Ministry of Agriculture, 272, 274
Ministry of Construction, 271–72, 274
Ministry of Finance (MOF)
    Asian Development Bank and the, 357,
        357n13
    bank failures and the, 190
    banking system and the, 136–37, 138
    Budget Bureau, 276
    debt levels and the, 197
    exchange rates and the, 173
    Ikeda and the, 121
    Kanemaru and the, 290
    leadership of the, 256
    on stronger yen, 170
    support for real estate and equity
        prices, 179
    Tanaka and the, 282
    taxation and the, 196, 197–98, 302
    yen/dollar rate and the, 194
Ministry of International Trade and
    Industry (MITI), 112, 140, 256, 278
Ministry of Labor, 143
Ministry of Posts and
    Telecommunications, 272, 291
Ministry of Transportation, 272, 274
Minsky, Hyman, 178, 181
Mishima Yukio, 78, 152
MITI and the Japanese Miracle
    (Johnson), 97
MITI. See Ministry of International
    Trade and Industry
Mito Komon (TV series), 56
Mito School, 76, 78
Mitsubishi, 62f, 112, 129
Mitsui, 65n1, 112, 120, 129
Mitterrand, François, 288
Miyamoto Kenji, about, 402–3
Miyazawa Kiichi, 291, 293, 295, 403
MOF. See Ministry of Finance (MOF)
monopolies, 40, 142n7, 205, 229
Monsanto, 365–66, 366n18
Moon, Sung Myung, 222n10
Mori Arinori, about, 392
Morita Akio, 219, 256
Mori Yoshiro, 302, 403
Morris, Ivan, 14, 17

movies and television serials, 145–46,
    233, 237–38, 243–44, 254, 292, 292*n*8
Mt. Hiei, 10
Mt. Koya temple, 13*n*5
Murakami, Haruki, 233, 371
Murayama Tomiichi, 300, 403
Muromachi period, 21, 23, 27, 299
Muromachi shogunates, 23

NAFTA, 193
Nagasaki, 38, 65–66, 84, 91, 109
Nagasaki harbor, 40
Nagashima Shigeo, 155
Nakasone Hirofumi, 335, 403
Nakasone Yasuhiro, 174, 260, 288, 403–4
Nakata Hidetoshi, 249
Namba, Osaka, 153, 249
Nanjing massacre, 84, 91, 381
Nara, 9–10, 9*nn*3–4, 10–11, 18
nationalism, 308
National Rifle Association, 306
Natsume Soseki, 79
Navy, Imperial Japanese, 71, 86, 112, 268
Naylor, Craig, 219, 220
Nazis, 87, 88, 89, 90, 110, 112, 308
NEC, 205
Nehru, Jawaharlal, 96
neo-Confucianism, 25, 35, 38, 52, 55–56
New Frontier Party, 301–2, 309
New Japan Hands, 318–22, 318*n*1, 327,
    334–36, 335*n*8, 336, 338, 363,
    363*n*17, 368
New Komeito, 276*n*3
newspapers. See media/press
Newsweek, 283
New York Times, 221
New Zealand, 365
NHK (public television network), 298,
    380–81
Nichiren school, 25, 25*n*8, 122
Nietzsche, Friedrich, 308
Niigata, 287
Nikon, 173
Nintendo, 204
Nintoku, Emperor, 2*f*
Nippon Foundation, 318*n*1
Nippon Sheet Glass, 219, 220
Nippon Steel, 173

Nishio Suehiro, about, 404
Nissan, 112, 129, 219, 220
Nitta Yoshisada, 21
Nitze School of Advanced International
    Studies at Johns Hopkins, 318
Nixon, Richard, 101, 116, 171, 172,
    281–84, 349
noble loser, 16–17
Noda Yoshihiko, 341, 345–46, 353, 354, 404
Nogi Maresuke, 79–80, 392
Noguchi Yukio, 115
Noh drama, 23, 24, 46*n*2
Nomo, Hideo, 157
Nomonhan, 89
Nomura, 43
Nonaka Hiromu, about, 404
Norman, E. H., 81
Northern Ireland, 333
North Korea, 4, 226, 289, 309, 319, 324,
    334, 338–40, 377
Nosaka Sanzo, about, 404
nuclear power, 229, 256–58, 259–62, 266
nuclear security, 315–18
Nye, Joseph, 320, 338
Nyerere, Julius, 96

obachan ("auntie"), 240–41
Obama, Barack, 180, 316–17, 321, 335, 337,
    338, 342
Obuchi Keizo, 302, 345, 404
occupation of Japan, 96, 99–114, 104*n*1,
    107*n*2, 133–34, 207, 308–9, 332
Oda Nobunaga, 10, 27–29, 36, 74
Odorokubeki Nihon (Amazing Japan)
    (*The Economist*), 97
Official Secrets Act of 2013, 107*n*2,
    366–68, 380
Ohga Norio, 219, 256
Ohira Masayoshi, 287, 288, 350, 404–5
Oh Sadaharu, 155
Okada Katsuya, 329, 405
Okinawa, 323, 349
    See also Futenma Marine Base
Okochi Masatoshi, 280
Okubo Toshimichi, about, 392
Okuma Shigenobu, about, 392
Old Japan Hands, 103, 319–20, 319*n*2
Olympics, 363, 389

Olympus, 219, 220–21, 222
Onin War of 1467–77, 23, 27
OPEC oil price hikes/embargo, 149, 172
Opium Wars, 52, 369
order and stability, Tokugawa period,
    38–40, 38n1
Ore wa Abare Hatchaku (TV series),
    243–44, 246
Organization for Economic
    Development, 140
Orwell, George, xxv, 147, 298
Osaka
    companies in, 156–57, 156n1
    daimyō and, 39
    Hanshin Tigers, 156
    puppet theater in, 46
    trading office in, 65–66
    urban craziness of, 297
Osaka castle, 31, 40
Osano Kenji, 280
Oshio Heihachiro, 52
Oswald, Lee Harvey, 380
otaku, 250
Oyama Iwao, about, 392
Oyoge, Taiyaki-kun! (popular song),
    235–36
Ozawa Ichiro
    about, 292–98, 294nn9–10,
        295nn11–12, 405
    China and, 309
    Clinton, Hillary and, 336, 352
    Hatoyama government destruction
        and, 328–31
    Ishihara and, 353
    Kan and, 340–41, 342
    LDP and, 295–96, 311
    Lower House elections and, 312
    New Frontier Party and, 301–2
    Oda Nobunaga and, 36
    resignation of, 340
    US and, 309, 336

Pacific Metals, 205
pacifism (Article 9), 100, 105
painting, *Namban-e* (pictures of the
    southern barbarians), 27
Pakistan, 317
Palestinians, 323

Panasonic, 173
paper-making and dyeing, 5
Parent Teacher Associations (PTAs),
    160–61, 276
parliament. *See* Diet
patriotism, 74
Patterson, Torkel, 318, 353
Paul V (pope), 27
Pearl Harbor, surrender, and legacy of
    war, 90–93, 386
peasants
    Christianity and, 37
    class order and, 38
    girls in Tokugawa period, 47–48
    Meiji period, 71–74
    universal education and
        indoctrination of, 73
    uprisings, 117
    wages and living standards of, 67–68
pederasty, 37, 46, 247
Peel, Robert, 121
Peloponnesian war, 369
Pendergast, Tom, 116, 274
Penghu islands, 70
People's Republic of China, US
    recognition of the, 171
People's Rights movement, 68, 72, 80, 117
Perón, Juan, 96
Perry, Matthew C., 51–54, 57
pharmaceutical companies, 205n1, 258,
    365, 366
Philippines, 36, 92, 109, 166, 325, 350
Pillow Book, The, 12, 13–15
*Plan for Remodeling the Japanese
    Archipelago* (Tanaka), 281
Plaza Accord, 184, 225, 289
Pokémon, 233, 234
Poland, 327
police, 142
police, military thought, 146
politics
    1955 system, 118–19, 270–77, 270n1,
        272n2, 275n3
    accountability, 82
    bureaucrats above, 337
    capo regimes (Kanemaru and
        Takeshita), 289–92, 291n7
    Chinese political institutions in Japan, 9

politics (*cont.*)
    divine right of kings, 56
    electoral reforms of 1994, 300–303,
        301*n*13
    foundations of high-speed growth,
        116–24, 117*n*4, 120*n*5, 122*n*6
    government run like business, 341–42
    guardians of political order, 298–300
    Heian period, 11
    Koizumi Junichiro, 303–10, 303*n*14,
        304*nn*15–16, 305*n*17, 306*n*18
    LDP after Koizumi, 310–13
    Lockheed scandal, 284–87
    marriage, 8
    national political identity, 6
    national use of force, 34
    neo-Confucianism and, 25
    Nixon shocks, 281–84, 283*n*6
    overview, 265–69
    Ozawa Ichiro, 292–98, 292*n*8,
        294*nn*9–10, 295*nn*11–12
    Shinto and, 75
    Tanaka Kakuei, 278–84, 278*n*4,
        283*n*6, 287–89
    US and Japanese, 182
    US anti-Japanese sentiment, 182
    Yasukuni Shrine and foreign relations,
        306–10
    See also elections; Japan Socialist Party
        (JSP); Left, Japanese (political);
        Liberal Democratic Party (LDP);
        Right, Japanese (political); *Specific*
        politicians
pollution, 150
Polo, Marco, 26, 26–27
popular/mass culture
    female archetype in, 232*f*
    high growth period, 152
    Tokugawa period, 45–50, 46*n*2
    in the two postwar decades, 152
    women and, 165–68, 167*n*6
pornography, 48–50, 233, 234, 236, 236*n*1
Porté, Thierry, 219
Portsmouth, Treaty of, 82*n*8
Portugal, 26, 36
Posen, Adam, 358
post office, privatization of the, 304–5,
    304*n*16, 338

postwar miracle
    exceptional circumstances of postwar
        decade, 99–114, 104*n*1, 107*n*2
    high-speed growth, 114–24, 117*n*4,
        120*n*5, 122*n*6
    overview, 95–99
Potsdam declaration, 89
poverty, 95
predictability, 115–16, 127
premodern Japan
    capital city of Nara, 9–10, 9*nn*3–4
    Europeans' arrival, 26–27
    feudalism, 21–27
    Fujiwara family, 8–9
    Heian order collapse, 15–18
    Heian period, 10–15
    Imperial Institution, 6–8
    influences on, 3–6, 5*nn*1–2
    literature in, 11–15, 16–18
    Mongol invasion, 19–20
    reunification of Japan, 27–31
    shoguns, 18–21
press. *See* media/press
Privy Council, 81, 82
profit, corporate, 130
prostitution, 47–48, 72, 77, 143, 153, 161,
    162–64, 163*n*3, 165
protests, 119, 120–21
public prosecutor
    Hatoyama government, 328–29
    Kanemaru and the, 298
    Ozawa and, 299, 336, 383
    political/business order and the, 107, 145,
        220, 266, 297, 298–300,
        305, 328–29
    Tanaka and the, 286, 298
puppet theater, 46
Pure Land sects, 25
Pu Yi, 88

Qing dynasty, disintegration of, 69, 370

race, 78–79
railroad bubble, 181, 181*n*1
Rakuten, 208, 210, 211*n*6
rape of Okinawan girl, 325, 362*n*16
Rattner, Steven, xix–xx
Rayburn, Sam, 280

Reagan, Ronald, 173, 183, 194, 288, 304, 317, 382
reality management, 142–47, 145n8, 146n9, 235
recession (1973–75), 149
recession, balance sheet, 179–88, 184n2, 185n3
Recruit, 187, 291
Red-Light District Kabukicho, 176f
Reform Bureaucrats, 112, 129, 272, 378
Reischauer, Edwin, 22, 121–22
religion
    aesthetics and, 24–26, 25n8
    in Heian literature, 14–15
    new, 122, 222n10, 273, 274–75
    Oda Nobunaga and, 28
    Shinto, 7, 20, 75, 77, 306–10
    Soka Gakkai, 122, 222n10, 274–75, 275n3
    See also Buddhism; Christianity
Renault, 219
Renesas Electronics, 229
Republican Party (US), 174, 187, 193
Return of the Living Dead, 240–41
return on equity (ROE), 130
return on investment (ROI), 130
Ricardo, David, 121
rice, as basis of economy, 15
Richie, Donald, xxii
Ricoh, 173, 229
Right, Japanese (political)
    makeup of the, 272–73
    neoliberalism and the, 304
    overreach of the, 311, 379–85
    phase of the Occupation, 111–12
    postwar settlement and the, 354, 356
    sovereignty and the, 99
    theories of the, 98
    Yasukuni Shrine and the, 306, 307, 308, 312
    See also Liberal Democratic Party (LDP)
Ripplewood Holdings, 219
rock gardens, 24
Roosevelt, Franklin D., 90, 121, 280, 382, 383
Roosevelt, Theodore, 82n8
Rosin, Hanna, 242
Rove, Karl, 355–56
Rubin, Robert, 190, 193, 194

Rumsfeld, Donald, 263, 326
Runaway Horses (Mishima), 78
rural areas, 117, 117n4, 271
Russia
    arms race and, 150
    default on debt, 195
    East Germany and, 327
    Liaodong Peninsula lease, 70
    Northern Territories (Southern Kuriles) and, 347–50, 347f
    Orthodox religious evangelizing in Japan, 75
    in Poland, 327
    WW I and, 84
    See also Soviet Union
Russo-Japanese War of 1904–1905, 70–71, 79, 82, 82n8, 348

Sagawa Kyubin, 291, 293, 297, 299
Saigo Takamori, 66, 66n2, 392–93
Saionji Kinmochi, about, 393
Saito Jiro, about, 405–6
Sakai, City of, 2f, 57
Sakakibara Eisuke, 194, 406
Sakamoto Han, 280
Sakamoto Ryoma, 58–59
Sakamoto Tsutsumi, 222n10
Sakoda, Robin, 353
salaryman culture
    baseball and the, 152–57, 156n1
    lower-middle class, 143
    negative portrayal of, 235
    young salarymen, 247–48
Samsung, 66, 142, 205, 216
samurai
    Buddist education of sons, 74
    during Tokugawa Shogunate, 43, 54, 58–60
    ethic, 44, 73
    fealty to daimyō, 39
    Heian period, formation of a distinct class during, 16
    Kamakura Shogunate and, 23–24
    Meiji government and, 65
    pederasty and, 37
    Sat-Cho clique, 81
    self-immolation, 44
    Tale of the 47 Rōnin, 50–51

samurai (cont.)
   Tokugawa Shogunate overthrow by, 39
   women and, 48
   Zen as the samurai religion, 25
samurai swords, 5
San Francisco Peace Treaty, 100, 113,
   270, 278
Sarkozy, Nicolas, 256, 341
Sasakawa Peace Foundation, 318*n*1
Sasakawa Ryoichi, 318*n*1
Sato Eisaku, 171, 278, 281, 406
Satsuma, 39, 59, 63, 66
savings, 137–38, 159, 179, 193, 199–200, 360
Scaife, Richard Mellon, 318*n*1
Sea of Japan, 380
Sega, 204
Seiko, 173
Sekigahara, battle of, 30, 37, 39
Self-Defense Forces, 105
Sendai, 27, 203, 343, 389
Senkaku/Diaoyu Islands, 345, 346–54,
   347*f*, 353*n*11
service sector, 208–9, 208*n*4
Sesshu, ink paintings by, 23
7-Eleven stores, 208
sex
   cuddling, xxiii, xxiii*n*1
   depictions of, 233, 236
   single women and, 166
   Tokugawa period, 45–50
sexual promiscuity/fidelity, Heian
   literature in, 14
Sharp, 173, 224
Shibusawa Eiichi, about, 393
Shimazu of Satsuma, 39
Shimomura Hakubun, 377
Shinjuku, Tokyo, 153, 176*f*, 249
Shinsei Bank, 219
Shinto, 7, 20, 75, 77, 306–10
Shirakawa, Emperor, 16
Shirakawa Masaaki, 356–57
Shogun (mini-series), 37
shoguns, 18–21
Shubun, ink paintings by, 23
Silicon Valley, 143, 213, 216, 219, 374
Simon, Hermann, 206*n*2
Sinawatra, Thaksin, 341
Singapore, 91, 92, 217, 365

Singer, Kurt, xxii
Sino-Japanese War of 1895, 69–70, 70*n*4,
   77, 349
Skyscrapers of Shinjuku in Tokyo, 176*f*
Smith, Adam, 253
Smithsonian Conference of December
   1971, 172–73
Snow Country (Kawabata), 279
social and cultural change
   class re-emergence, 251–56
   divorce, 241–42
   Gyaru (gal), 238–40, 255
   herbivore males, 242–46, 243*n*2, 244*n*3
   leadership class decline, 256–63,
     260*n*8
   male group dynamics, 248–51, 248*n*6
   masculine identity, 246–48, 247*nn*4–5
   obachan ("auntie"), 240–41
   overview, 233–38, 236*n*1
   sodai-gomi (big piece of junk i.e.,
     useless retired men), 241
   Tokugawa Shogunate, 40–45
Social Democratic Party of Japan, 301
Social Insurance Agency, 311
socialist economy, 141
society, 44–45, 115–16
sodai-gomi (big piece of junk i.e., useless
   retired men), 241
Softbank, 208, 210, 211*n*6
Sogo Department Store, 191
Soka Gakkai, 122, 222*n*10, 274–75, 275*n*3
Son Masayoshi, 208, 209
Sony, 130, 140, 141, 173, 187, 204, 205,
   219–20
Soseki, Natsume, 79
Southeast Asia assembly operations, 217
Southeast Asia colonies, 89–90, 90
South Korea. *See* Korea
Soviet Union
   arms race with the US, 150
   collapse of, 65
   Finland and the, 377
   in Hungary, 327
   Japan's surrender and the, 103–4
   Kurile islands and the, 348–49
   LDP and the, 272
   US ideological struggles with, 170
   See also Russia

speech, free, 95
Spencer, Herbert, 78
Spring Snow (Mishima), 78
Stalin, Joseph, 88, 89, 95, 101, 103
Stevenson, Adlai, 331
stock market crash, 185, 186
Straits of Shimonoseki, 58
strikes, 119, 120
Stringer, Howard, 219–20
subsidized housing, 132
Suga Yoshihide, about, 406
suicide
    Hojo and their retainers mass, 21
    Japanese soldiers' suicide missions, 44
    kamikaze pilots, 17, 20, 307
    in *Kokoro*, 79–80
    mutual, 45
    Okinawa mass, 323
    ritual, 17, 381
    spiritual, 308
    supposed by Sakamoto Tsutsumi,
        222n10
Sukiyaki Song, 236
Sumitomo, 43, 65n1, 112, 129
Summers, Larry, 194
sunk costs, writing off, 222–25
Sun Microsystems, 173
Sun Yat-sen, 370
Suzuki, Ichiro, 157, 249, 250
Suzuki Muneo, about, 406
Suzuki Zenko, 288, 406–7
Sweden, 64
Switzerland, 64, 206n2

Taika Reform, 8–9
Taira (*Heike*) clan, 16
Taisho Emperor, 81
Taiwan
    China and, 324, 351
    high-speed growth model and, 98
    iPhones and, 206
    Japanese workers and corporations in,
        212, 217
    LDP and, 283
    relations with Japan, 265
    Senkaku Islands and, 346, 347f,
        350, 353n11
    as Shogunate colony, 70

US defense perimeter and, 93
Takahashi Korekiyo, 84, 85
Takenaka Heizo, 304, 407
Takeshita Noboru, 184, 289–93, 299,
    303, 407
Tale of Genji, The, 12, 13–15, 16, 47
Tale of the 47 Rōnin, 50–51
Tale of the Heike, 16–18
Tamogami Toshio, 382, 382n24
Tanaka Kakuei
    Abe and, 361
    about, 278–81, 407
    bureaucracy and, 329–30
    China and, 342–43
    Fukuda Takeo and, 303
    Ikeda on, 279
    JSP and, 299
    Koizumi and, 304
    Lockheed scandal, 284–87
    MOF and, 302
    Nixon shocks and prime ministership
        of, 281–84
    North Korea and, 309
    Ozawa and, 292–93, 295, 296
    photograph of, 264f
    Senkaku Islands and, 350
    as *Yami Shogun*, 287–89
Tanaka Makiko, 407
Tanaka Yoshikazu, 208
Tanegashima, 26
Tang culture, 11
Tanzania, 96
TARP legislation, 190
taxation
    bureaucracy and, 340–41
    consumption, 196, 198, 302, 340–41,
        345–46
    debt and, 196
    farmers and, 197–98
    Heian period, 15
    inheritance, 151
    land, 72
    Noda and, 345–46
Taylor, Lady Bird, 280
tea ceremony, 23, 24, 162
Teacher's Union, 133, 273
television serials and movies, 145–46,
    233, 237–38, 243–44, 254, 292, 292n8

temples, 13, 13n5, 19
temporary workers, 212, 213–14
tempura, 27
Tenno Heika (heavenly sovereign), 7–8
TEPCO (Tokyo Electric Power), 229,
    257–58, 261–62, 343
Thailand, 33, 166, 203
    floods in, 203
    Japanese companies in, 205
    Japanese expatriates in the, 215–16
    Japanese investment in, 267
Thatcher, Margaret, 288, 317, 345, 383
Tiananmen massacres, 376
Tibet, 323, 352
Tōdai-ji, 13, 19
Togo Heihachiro, about, 393
Toji Temple, 148f
Tojo Hideki, 85, 91, 100, 109, 307
Tokugawa (Edo) period
    corporations and the, 128–29
    economic and social change during
        the, 40–45
    fall of the Shogunate, 57–60, 58n5
    isolation during the, 35–38
    order and stability, 38–40, 38n1
    overview, 33–35
    peasantry and taxes during the, 71–72
    pederasty, 37, 46, 247
    Perry and the fall of the, 51–54
    popular culture, 45–50, 46n2, 234
    revolution of 1868, 54–57, 55n3, 56n4
    senior harem women *otsubone*
        modern usage, 240
    Senkaku Islands, 346
    Tale of the 47 Rōnin, 50–51
Tokugawa Ieyasu, 30–31, 57
Tokyo
    American Embassy in, 318
    earthquake of 1923, 83, 84
    fire bombing, 84
    Olympics, 363
    radiation exposure in, 260
    Red-Light District Kabukicho, 176f
    rise of Edo, 24, 31
    Skyscrapers of Shinjuku in, 176f
    urban craziness of, 297
    Yomiuri Giants, 156
Tokyo stock market, 290

Tokyo War Crimes trials, 108–9, 307
tombs of emperors, 2f, 6
Tosa, 39
totalitarian states, 267
Toyota, 129, 130, 173, 205, 224
TPP (Trans Pacific Partnership), 364–66,
    366nn18–19
trade
    with China, 25, 35
    Dutch traders, 36, 40
    exports and economy driver, 182–83
    financing, 137
    global economic framework, 168–74,
        172n8
    with Korea, 35
    with Portugal, 26, 36
    premodern Japan, 25
    rice, 15
    tariff rates, 144
    Tokugawa period, 35, 36, 40, 57–58
    TPP, 364–66, 366nn18–19
    with US, 114, 168–74, 183, 184–85
    US/Japan conflicts, 320
Trans Pacific Partnership (TPP), 364–66,
    366nn18–19
treaties
    Anglo-Japanese Alliance of 1902, 70
    Portsmouth, 82n8
    San Francisco Peace, 100, 113, 270, 278
    Unequal, 57–58, 64, 67, 80
    US–Japan Security, 119–20, 308,
        314f, 332
    Versailles, 82
trees during the Tokugawa Shogunate, 43
Tripartite Pact, 90
Triple Intervention, 70, 82n8
Trollope, Anthony, 181n1
Twenty One Demands, 87

Ue o Muite Arukō, 236
unemployment, 149
Unequal Treaties, 57–58, 64, 67, 70, 80
Unification Church, 222n10
unions, 118–19, 120–21, 133
Union Tool, 205
United States
    agriculture and development, 64
    airline manufacturing and the, 206

Asia and, 351
baseball in, 155, 156, 157
black males in the, 249
bombing of Japan, 109
business practices, 225
China and the, 170, 319, 342–43, 350,
    351, 368–71
class division in the, 252–54
contradiction and the, 385n25
control of Japanese foreign relations,
    119–20
debt as percentage of GDP, 197
deficits, 150, 173
earthquake in Japan and the, 343–44
education, 64
emotional bonds between boys in
    pre-World War II, 247n4
empire, 373–74
employment rates, 180
FDI and the, 217
football bowl games, 155–56
foreign investment in, 24–25
global currency crisis, 193
Gulf War, 293–94, 294n9
Hatoyama Yukio and the, 315–18
Hawaii, 69, 71
hegemony, 98
Hidden Champions in the, 206n2
housing bubble, 177, 178, 180, 186
iPhones and, 206
Iraq invasion, 305–6, 306n18
IT companies in the, 204
Japan and financial crisis in, 312
Japanese bank bailout and the, 190
Japanese companies in, 205
Japanese expatriates in the, 215–16
Japanese politics and the, 266
Japanese Right and the, 309
Japan's agents of influence and the,
    332–40, 333n7, 335n8, 336n9, 339n10
Japan-US alliance, 371–74
Korea and the, 93
Lockheed scandal, 284–87
mass layoffs in the, 211
media, 334
men in the, 250–51
military bases in Japan, 262
military buildup, 150

military industrial complex, 372, 374
military protection of Japan, 150
National Rifle Association, 306
New Japan Hands in the, 318–22,
    318n1, 353–54
North Korea and, 39–40
occupation of Japan and the, 96,
    99–114, 104n1, 107n2, 133–34, 207,
    308–9, 332
Ozawa and the, 309
political order in the, 267
political power and money in the, 280
popular media in the, 146
presidential election of 1989, 186–87
Protestant religious evangelizing in
    Japan, 75
railways in, 67
responsibility for mistakes in the, 259
rich persons in the, 252
securities, government, 200
7th Fleet, 324, 335
stimulus package, 180
stock market crash, 185, 186
Taiwan and the, 93
Tanaka and Nixon shocks, 281–84, 283n6
territories of, 69
thermonuclear test, 119
TPP, 364–66, 366nn18–19
trade with Japan, 114, 168–74, 183,
    184–85, 187
unemployment, 211
Vietnam War, 108
world economy and the, 258
See also Futenma Marine Base
University of Tokyo, 135, 154, 157
Uno Sosuke, 291, 291nf, 408
untouchables, 38n1
US Congress
    blocking IMF funds for Mexico, 193
    Immigration Act of 1924, 82
    TARP legislation, 190
    TPP and, 366, 366n19
US Democratic Party, 116–17
US Federal Reserve, 172–73, 357–58, 358n14
US Immigration Act of 1924, 82
US–Japan Security Treaty, 119–20, 308,
    314f, 332
US military, 123

US Pentagon, 318, 319, 325, 334, 367–68
US Senate, 117n4
US State Department, 318, 320, 334
US Treasury, 173, 194
Utsunomiya Kenji, 382

van Wolferen, Karel
    Enigma of Japanese Power, 294–95
    Management of Reality, 143
    Ozawa and, 295n12
    on political accountability, 82
Versailles Treaty, 82
video games, 44
Vietnam, 5, 123, 205, 317, 350
Vietnam War, 108, 169, 170, 324, 332
Volker, Paul, 172–73

wage declines, 214, 214n7
Wagner, Richard, 78, 308
Wall Street
    commercial paper and, 189
    corruption of, 186
    headquarters economy, 374
    as an international financial center, 71
    ruined companies and, xxv
    TPP and, 365
    trading floors of, 255n7
    transformation of, 228
    working hours on, 143
Wall Street Journal, 221
Walsh School of Foreign Service at
    Georgetown, 318
Wang Yangming, 52
war criminals, xxv, 100, 109, 119, 307, 318n1
Watanabe Michio, about, 408
Watergate, 172, 283
water trade (*mizu shobai*), 161, 162–64,
    163n3, 165
Waugh, Evelyn, 251
Way We Live Now, The (Trollope), 181n1
Webb, Jim, 344
West
    early encounters with Japan, 26–27
    herbivore males and the press in the, 242
    heterosexuality in the, 246
    imperialism and the, 63–64
    Japanese culture in the, 233, 234–38
    Kamakura and Muromachi

    shogunates and, 23
    Meiji period and the, 64, 75–79, 76n5,
        77n6
    political order in the, 267
    powers during WW II, 91–92
    Sino-Japanese War of 1895 and the,
        69–70, 70n4
    Tokugawa Shogunate and the, 40
    understanding of Japan, 294–95, 294n10
Westphalian notions, 323
Westphalian system, 6
White, Edmund, 14
White, Harry Dexter, 382n24
Wikileaks, 366
Wilde, Oscar, xx
Wilson, Woodrow, 82, 323
Wolfowitz, Paul, 263
women, Japanese
    boyfriends, 242–43
    divorce and, 241–42
    during the Tokugawa period, 46–50
    employment of, 132, 162–66
    equality of, 106, 107
    factory workers, 72
    future for Japanese, 389
    gangurogyaru, 251
    Gyaru (gal), 232f, 238–40, 255
    Heian literature by, 11–15
    hereditary regency, 19
    in the high-growth era, 158–68, 162n2,
        163n3, 164n4, 165n5, 167n6
    Kabuki during the Tokugawa period
        and, 46
    obachan ("auntie"), 240–41
    prostitution, 47–48, 72, 77, 143, 153, 161,
        162–64, 163n3, 165
    rights advocates, 119
    sodai-gomi (big piece of junk,
        i.e., useless retired men), 241
    See also marriage
women, Korean comfort, 380, 380n22
    sexual exploitation of, 379
Woodford, Michael, 219, 220, 221
working hours, 143
World Bank, 357n13
World Economic Forum, 341
World of the Shining Prince, The
    (Morris), 14

World War I, 83–84, 258
World War II
    industrial groups after, 66
    internment of Japanese-Americans
      during, 333n7
    kamikaze pilots, 17, 20, 307
    newspaper coverage in Japan, 261
    Okinawa, during, 323–24
    Pearl Harbor, surrender, and legacy
      of, 90–93
    soldiers' actions in the, 362n16
    soldier's letters home, xv–xvi

Xi'an (Chang'An), 9, 10

yakuza, 142–43, 222n10, 254, 273,
    276, 286
Yamada Denki, 208
Yamada Noboru, 208
Yamagata Aritomo, 81–82, 106, 349, 393
Yamaguchi Momoe, 167n6
Yamaha, 130, 131, 173
Yamamoto Yōji, 233
Yamasaki Taku, 408
Yamashita Tomoyuki, 109
Yamazaki Takashi, 383–84
Yanai Tadashi, 208
Yasuda, 112, 129
Yasukuni Shrine, 306–10, 312, 354, 368,
    379, 379–80

yen
    confidence in the, 359–60
    dollar/yen rate, 169, 170, 172–73, 179,
      183–84, 193–94, 194–95
    gold standard and, 84
Yokohama, 34
Yokosuka, 324
Yomiuri Giants, 155, 156, 157
Yomiuri Group, 154–55
Yoritomo, 17–18, 19
Yoshida Hideo, 146, 262, 280
Yoshida Masao, 261
Yoshida Shigeru
    about, 408
    current leadership compared to, 256
    as mandarin, 278
    military spending and, 114n3
    old Japan hands and, 103
    on recovery from defeat, 99
    San Francisco Peace Treaty and,
      100, 312
    on success of occupation, 106
    US and, 102
Yoshino, 21
Yoshiwara, 153

Zelda game series, 233
Zhou Enlai, 92, 283, 289, 317, 350
Zhu Xi, 35
Zuckerberg, Mark, 208